ACADIA 2000:
Eternity, Infinity and Virtuality in Architecture

Edited by Mark J. Clayton and
Guillermo P. Vasquez de Velasco

Published by the Association for Computer-Aided Design in Architecture

Copyright 2002 by the Association for Computer-Aided Design in Architecture

All rights reserved by the authors of the individual papers and digital media projects who are solely responsible for their content.

No part of this work covered by the copyright hereon may be reproduced or used in any form or by any means, including graphic, electronic or mechanical, including photocopying, recording, taping or information storage and retrieval systems, without the prior permission of the copyright owner.

Book produced by Virtualbookworm.com Publishing Inc.
http://www.virtualbookworm.com

Library of Congress Control Number: 2002104384

ISBN 1-880250-09-8

ACADIA 2000:
Eternity, Infinity and Virtuality in Architecture

Preface vii

Technical Content Reviewers ix

Frameworks 1

Illusion, Frustration and Vision in Computer-Aided Project Planning: A Reflection and Outlook on the Use of Computing in Architecture 3
    Dirk Donath, Bauhaus Universität Weimar, Germany
    Thorsten Michael Loemker, Bauhaus Universität Weimar, Germany

Vision on ICT Developments for the Building Sector 11
    Sevil Sariyildiz, Delft University of Technology, Netherlands
    Rudi Stouffs, Delft University of Technology, Netherlands
    Bige Tunçer, Delft University of Technology, Netherlands

An Expandable Software Model for Collaborative Decision-Making During the Whole Building Life Cycle 19
    K. Papamichael, Lawrence Berkeley National Laboratory, USA
    V. Pal, Lawrence Berkeley National Laboratory, USA
    N. Bourassa, Lawrence Berkeley National Laboratory, USA
    J. Loffeld, Lawrence Berkeley National Laboratory, USA
    I. G. Capeluto, Technion - Israel Institute of Technology, Israel

Architecture, Speed, and Relativity: On the Ethics of Eternity, Infinity, and Virtuality 29
    Mahesh Senagala, University of Texas at San Antonio, USA

Collaboration 39

Between Friends: Support of Workgroup Communications 41
    Brian R. Johnson, University of Washington, USA

Testing the Space of the Virtual 51
    Brian Lonsway, Rensselaer Polytechnic Institute, USA

Exercising Collaborative Design in a Virtual Environment 63
    Christopher Peri, University of California, Berkeley, USA

Alternative Architecture 73

The Impact of E-Commerce on the Design and Construction Industry 75
Robert E. Johnson, CRS Center, Texas A&M University, USA
Ge Xia, CRS Center, Texas A&M University, USA

Places of Mind: Implications of Narrative Space for the Architecture of Information Environments 85
Peter Anders, CAiiA-STAR, MindSpace.net, USA

Data Representation Architecture: Visualization Design Methods, Theory and Technology Applied to Anesthesiology 91
Julio Bermudez, University of Utah, USA
Jim Agutter, University of Utah, USA
Dwayne Westenskow, University of Utah, USA
Stefano Foresti, University of Utah, USA
Yi Zhang, Wind River System Inc., USA
Debra Gondeck-Becker, Pine Technical College, USA
Noah Syroid, University of Utah, USA
Brent Lilly, University of Utah, USA
David Strayer, University of Utah, USA
Frank Drews, University of Utah, USA

Representing Virtual Places - A Design Model for Metaphorical Design . 103
Fei Li, University of Sydney, Australia
Mary Lou Maher, University of Sydney, Australia

Gizmos 113

Structural Gizmos 115
Samir Abdelmawla, Illinois Institute of Technology, USA
Mahjoub Elnimeiri, Illinois Institute of Technology, USA
Robert Krawczyk, Illinois Institute of Technology, USA

Intuitive and Effective Design of Periodic Symmetric Tiles 123
Ergun Akleman, Texas A&M University, USA
Jianer Chen, Texas A&M University, USA
Burak Meric, Knowledge Based Information Systems, Inc., USA

Introductory Computer Programming as a Means for Extending Spatial and Temporal Understanding 129
Mark Burry, Sambit Datta, Simon Anson, School of Architecture and Building, Deakin University, Australia

The Intelligent Sketch: Developing a Conceptual Model for a Digital Design Assistant 137
Rohan Bailey, Victoria University of Wellington, New Zealand

Off The Page: Object-Oriented Construction Drawings 147
Michael Kilkelly, Edificium, Inc., USA

Classroom 153

From Dreamtime to QuickTime: The Resurgence of the 360-Degree Panoramic View as a Form of Computer-Synthesised Architectural Representation 155
Robert D. Hotten, University of Auckland, New Zealand

Peter R. Diprose, Unitec, Auckland, New Zealand

Some Experimental Results in the Assessment of Architectural Media 163
    Osman Ataman, Temple University, USA

Evaluating the Complexity of CAD Models as a Measure for Student Assessment 173
    Scott Chase and Paul Murty, University of Sydney, Australia

Web 183

Immersive Redliner: Collaborative Design in Cyberspace 185
    Thomas Jung, University of Washington, USA
    Ellen Yi-Luen Do, University of Washington, USA

WebOutliner: A Web-Based Tool for Collaborative Space Programming and Design 195
    Wassim Jabi, University at Buffalo, The State University of New York, USA

A Virtual Reality Tool to Implement City Building Codes on Capitol View Preservation 203
    Chiu-Shui Chan, Iowa State University, USA

Work in Progress 211

Synagogue Neudeggergasse: A Virtual Reconstruction in Vienna 213
    Bob Martens, Vienna University of Technology, Austria
    Matthias Uhl, Mediatecture, Austria
    Wolf-Michael Tschuppik, Vienna University of Technology, Austria
    Andreas Voigt, Vienna University of Technology, Austria

Architectural Education: Students Creating a City Model 219
    Wolfgang Dokonal, Graz University of Technology, Austria
    Bob Martens, Vienna University of Technology, Austria
    Reinhard Plösch, Graz University of Technology, Austria

Use of Computers in Reconstruction of Ancient Buildings 223
    Ming Zhou, Wenzhou Institute of Architectural Design and Research, China

AGENCY GP: Genetic Programming for Architectural Design 227
    Peter Testa, Massachusetts Institute of Technology, USA
    Una-May O'Reilly, Massachusetts Institute of Technology, USA
    Simon Greenwold, Massachusetts Institute of Technology, USA

Computer-Simulated Growth Processes in Urban Planning and Architecture 233
    Bernd Streich, University of Kaiserslautern/University of Bonn, Germany
    Rivka Oxman, Technion, Israel
    Oliver Fritz, University of Kaiserslautern, Germany

Mass-Customization in Design Using Evolutionary and Parametric Methods 239
    Cristiano Ceccato, The Hong Kong Polytechnic University, China
    Alvise Simondetti, The Hong Kong Polytechnic University, China
    Mark C. Burry, Deakin University, Australia

Responsive Architecture: An Integrated Approach for the Future 245
    Stylianos C. Zerefos, Aristotle University of Thessaloniki, Greece

Anastasios M. Kotsiopoulos, Aristotle University of Thessaloniki, Greece
Andreas Pombortsis, Aristotle University of Thessaloniki, Greece

Digital Architectures 251
Branko Kolarevic, University of Pennsylvania, USA

Towards Real Time Interaction Visualization in NED 257
Thomas Fischer, Hong Kong Polytechnic University, China
Christiane M. Herr, University of Kassel, Germany
Cristiano Ceccato, Hong Kong Polytechnic University, China

Plank Lines of Ribbed Timber Shell Structures 261
Karen Kensek, University of Southern California, USA
Judith Leuppi, University of Southern California, USA
Douglas Noble, University of Southern California, USA

Computer Simulation and Visualization of Geometrically Changing Structures 267
Katherine A. Liapi, University of Texas at Austin, USA

The Composite Building Sketch 273
Anton C. Harfmann, University of Cincinnati, USA
Peter E. Akins, University of Cincinnati, USA

The Anthropometric Measurement and Modeling Project 281
John Jay Miller, Mississippi State University, USA
Weidong Wang, Mississippi State University, USA
Gavin R. Jenkins, Mississippi State University, USA

Digital Media Exhibit C-1
Darlene A. Brady, Archi-Textures, USA

Academic – Student Projects

CMC2000 - Internet Aided Design C-3
Rodrigo Paraizo, (Jose Ripper Kos, Faculty Advisor), PROURB-FAU-UFRJ, Brazil

Mega Sound Stage and Bungalow C-4
Keith Ireland (Douglas Noble and Karen M. Kensek, faculty advisors)
University of Southern California, USA

Millennium Cyberia C-5
Martin Adamec (Igor Kosco, Advisor), Slovak University of Technology, Slovakia

From Generative Design To Genetic Design C-6
Jorge Alberto Lopes Gil (Lesley Gavin, Faculty Advisor), The Bartlett School of Architecture - University College, London, UK

The Fine Art, the Scenical Design C-7
Marek Németh (Igor Kosco, Faculty Advisor), Slovak Technical University, Slovakia

The Skyscraper Gate C-8
Jozef Seman (Igor Kosco, faculty advisor), Slovak University of Technology, Slovakia

Academic – Digital Studio Project

Project Web Diary - Design of an Artist's Studio C-9
The PANDA Group: Sarah Jayne Patterson, Kieron Porter, Vajira Premadasa, Christina Goh (Alan Bridges and H. Grierson, Faculty Advisors) The University of Strathclyde, Scotland

Favela-Bairro Program C-10
    Adriana Barbosa, Andre Bianche, Benar Correia, Carlos Krykhtine, Concepcion Pedrosa, Erivelton Silva, Gil Louzano, Johanna Looye, Jose Kos, Luciano Souza, Marcel Pereira, Marcia Duarte, Marcia Furriel, Julia Guimaraes, Niuxa Drago, Renata Jardim, Roberto Segre and Rodrigo Paraizo (Jose Kos and Roberto Segre, Advisors)
    FAU-UFRJ - Predio da Arquitetura, Cidade Universitaria, Brazil

Professional – Individual

Mind's Eye C-11
    Darlene A. Brady, Archi-Textures, USA

Form Generation: Creating Hilbert's Building Blocks C-12
    Robert J. Krawczyk
    Illinois Institute of Technology, USA

Implicit Art C-13
    Ergun Akleman, Texas A&M University, USA

Professional – Team

The City That Doesn't Exist: Hypermedia Reconstruction of Latin American Cities C-14
    Jose Kos, Adriana Barbosa, Carlos Krykhtine, Erivelton Silva, and Rodrigo Paraizo, FAU-UFRJ - Predio da Arquitetura / Reitoria, Cidade Universitaria, Brazil

Camera Painting C-15
    Ergun Akleman, Scott Meadows and Jianer Chen, Texas A&M University, USA

Morphogenetic Surface Structure (MoSS) C-16
    Peter Testa, Una-May O'Reilly, Devyn Weiser, Markus Kangus, Axel Kilian, and Janet Fan, MIT Department of Architecture, Emergent Design Group, USA

Preface

Eternity, time without end, infinity, space without limits and virtuality, perception without constraints; provide the conceptual framework in which ACADIA 2000 is conceived. It is in human nature to fill what is empty and to empty what is full. Today, thanks to the power of computer processing we can also make small what is too big, make big what is too small, make fast what is too slow, make slow what is too fast, make real what does not exist, and make our reality omni-present at global scale. These are capabilities for which we have no precedents. What we make of them is our privilege and responsibility.

Information about a building flows past our keyboards and on to other people. Although we, as architects, add to the information, it originated before us and will go beyond our touch in time, space and understanding. A building description acquires a life of its own that may surpass our own lives as it is stored, transferred, transformed, and reused by unknown intellects, both human and artificial, and in unknown processes. Our actions right now have unforeseen effects. Digital media blurs the boundaries of space, time and our perception of reality. ACADIA 2000 explores the theme of time, space and perception in relation to the information and knowledge that describes architecture.

Our invitation to those who are finding ways to apply computer processing power in architecture received overwhelming response, generating paper submissions from five continents. A selected group of reviewers recommended the publication of 24 original full papers out of 42 submitted and 13 short papers out of 30 submitted. Forty-two projects were submitted to the Digital Media Exhibit and 12 were accepted for publication. The papers cover subjects in design knowledge, design process, design representation, design communication, and design education. Fundamental and applied research has been carefully articulated, resulting in developments that may have an important impact on the way we practice and teach architecture in the future.

Many people have contributed to the preparation of these proceedings. Hoonsik Seo served as Webmaster and provided the software support for the collection and review of abstracts and papers. We would like to thank Li Nan for the compelling image reproduced on the cover. Keith Malone, Antonieta H. Angulo Mendivil, Kathy Wascom, and Karthik Swaminathan assisted with proof-reading and layout. Bob Johnson and the CRS Center provided administrative support and mentorship. Thank you to all of the authors for their thoughtfulness and enthusiasm for this publication. Many others contributed in large and small ways and we thank you all.

      Mark J. Clayton and Guillermo Vasquez de Velasco
      Texas A&M University
      ACADIA 2000 Technical Chairs

Technical Content Reviewers

Ergun Akleman, Texas A&M University, USA
Jamal Al-Qawasmi, Jordan University of Science and Technology
Peter Anders, Mindspace, USA
Scott Arvin, Autodesk, Inc., USA
Osman Ataman, Temple University, USA
Michael Berk, Mississippi State University, USA
Julio Bermudez, University of Utah, USA
Jonti Bolles, Prairie View A&M University, USA
Carl Bovill, University of Maryland, USA
Mark Burry, Deakin University, Australia
Scott Chase, University of Sydney, Australia
Nancy Cheng, University of Oregon, USA
Ellen Yi-Luen Do, University of Washington, USA
Dirk Donath, Bauhaus University, Germany
Maia Engeli, ETH Zurich, Switzerland
John Gero, University of Sydney, Australia
Anat Geva, Texas A&M University, USA
Glenn Goldman, New Jersey Institute of Technology, USA
Mark D. Gross, University of Washington, USA
Anton Harfmann, University of Cincinnati, USA
Wassim Jabi, SUNY - University at Buffalo, USA
Shailesh Jain, University of Tennessee, USA
Brian Johnson, University of Washington, USA
Robert Johnson, Texas A&M University, USA
J. Peter Jordan, 3D/International, USA
Kevin Klinger, University of Cincinnati, USA
Branko Kolarevic, University of Pennsylvania, USA
Jose Kos, Universidade Federal do Rio de Janeiro, Brazil
Thomas Kvan, University of Hong Kong, China
Mary Lou Maher, University of Sydney, Australia
Bob Martens, Vienna University of Technology, Austria
Raymond McCall, University of Colorado, USA
Margot McDonald, Cal Poly State University, USA
Vallie Miranda, Texas A&M University, USA
Arturo Montagu, University of Buenos Aires, Argentina
Fred Morgan, University of Florida, USA
Volker Mueller, NBBJ, USA
Douglas Noble, University of Southern California, USA
Konstantinos Papamichael, Lawrence Berkeley National Laboratory, USA
Marcelo Paysse, Facultad de Arquitectura - Universidad de la Republica, Uruguay
Jelena Petric, University of Strathclyde, Scotland
Jens Pohl, Cal Poly State University, USA
Sevil Sariyildiz, Delft Technical University, The Netherlands
Thomas Seebohm, University of Waterloo, Canada
Mahesh Senagala, University of Texas, San Antonio, USA
Yunsik Song, Texas A&M University, USA

Keith Sylvester, Texas A&M University, USA
Milton Tan, University of Singapore, Singapore
John O. Tector, North Carolina State University, USA
Ken Tobin, Lessard Architectural Group, USA
Robert Woodbury, University of Adelaide, Australia

Digital Media Exhibit Reviewers

Anne-Louise Marquis, Smithsonian Institute, USA
G. Martin Moeller, Jr., National Building Museum, USA
B. J. Novitski, ArchitectureWeek, USA
Beverly Willis, FAIA, Architecture Research Institute, Inc., USA

Frameworks

Research in architectural computing has always included attempts to make sense of the complex processes of design and the complex industry of construction. Broad frameworks have often fervently been suggested with a claim that the major problems can be solved if only the profession would adopt the framework. The faith in frameworks and fundamental principles is probably inherent to the human psyche. The articles in this section are the most recent thoughtful contributions to this tradition of CAD research. The frameworks that the authors advocate differ from those of the past by acknowledging the successes and failures of the past and building upon them. Each article provides a critique of the past and suggests ways of understanding broad trends and phenomena to guide decisions in the future.

The article by Donath and Loemker provides an overview of the past, the present and the future with regard to using computer technology to integrate the practice of architecture. The vision of the future reflects a growing awareness that software systems cannot be conceived as a unit but instead are messy, growing, organic things. Sariyildiz, Stouffs and Tuncer offer a similar conclusion that future systems will provide a loose integration of diverse tools and support a facilities processes that are less sequential or hierarchical and more of a network.

Many past proposals have suggested frameworks that can integrate software around a common data structure. Papamichael, Pal, Bourassa, Loffeld, and Capeluto have devised a software framework that is based on a model of decision-making throughout the building life cycle. By using a thoroughly object-oriented approach and recognizing the conditionality of building parameters as a result of options and the passage of time they have achieved a plausible scheme for a universal solution to a digital representation of a building.

Senagala presents a thoughtful reflection upon changes in fundamental perceptions of the world, as people perceive it through technologies of different eras. His framework is a historical and epistemological one that can perhaps be used to understand where we are now and where we are going in this time of dramatic social and technological change.

Illusion, Frustration and Vision in Computer-Aided Project Planning: A Reflection and Outlook on the Use of Computing in Architecture

Dirk Donath, Bauhaus Universität Weimar, Germany

Thorsten Michael Loemker, Bauhaus Universität Weimar, Germany

Abstract

This paper examines the progressive and pragmatic use of computers and CAAD systems in the architectural practice. With the aid of three scenarios, this paper will illustrate gainful implementation of computer aided project planning in architecture. The first scenario describes an actual situation of implementation and describes conceptual abortive developments in office organization as well as in software technology. Scenario two outlines the essential features of an integrated building design system and the efforts involved in its implementation in the architectural practice. It clearly defines preconditions for implementation and focuses on feasible concepts for the integration of different database management systems. A glance at paradigms of conceptual work currently under development will be taken. The third scenario deals with the structure and integration of innovative concepts and the responsibility the architect will bear with regard to necessary alterations in office and workgroup organization. A future-oriented building design system will be described that distinguishes itself from existing programs because of its modular, net-based structure. With reference to today's situation in architectural offices and according to realizable improvements, this article will demonstrate courses for future IT-support on the basis of an ongoing research project. The presented project is part of the special research area 524 "Materials and Constructions for the Revitalization of Existing Buildings" which is funded by the Deutsche Forschungsgemeinschaft. It deals with the integration of various parties that are involved in the revitalization process of existing buildings as well as with the provision of adequate information within the planning process resting upon the survey of existing building substance.

Additional concepts that might change the way an architect's work is organized will also be presented. "Case-based-reasoning" methods will make informal knowledge available, leading to a digital memory of preservable solutions.

1 Introduction

Starting with an assessment of today's use of computers in architectural practice, we have to admit that architects use a great variety of software and hardware components that do not fit together well. Even if the software industry tries to make us believe that architects' demands find fulfillment in the newest release of their software packages, we should confess that unimpeded exchange of data for instance is still not possible. Who has not experienced a system crash in conjunction with loss of data while importing? Who has ever been able to perfectly import dxf-data from the structural engineer without having to cope with hatching or text that appears distorted, enlarged or incomplete?

Nonetheless, after the decision is made to use computers in architectural practice and after experiencing the advantages and disadvantages of stand-alone applications, the architect desires an integrated information basis to exchange data (product model). Interfaces exist and most CAAD-packages deliver functionalities to import / export files and to convert them into other formats - but have you ever tried to import dxf-data from the surveyor? Usually, the exchange of data involves heavy losses (Haas 1998). Do you use an integrated information system in your office that administers simple items like geometric information of the proposed building, details, building costs, load bearing behavior, type and degree of building and land use or addresses of the people involved in the building process? Common systems available on the market do not fulfill most of these general demands and demonstrate that they do not meet the requirements of the architect's duties. However, the development of integrated systems is making progress. In the text that follows, three scenarios will be given to describe an ordinary, a possible and a visionary – yet feasible - situation in computer aided project planning. Besides the exclusive use of a CAAD-system as a design and construction tool, Scenario Three will glance at the future use of CAAD-databases as being part of an overall spatial expression within architecture.

2 Scenario One – The Ordinary Situation

Most software and hardware used in building design begins with so called "stand-alone" applications. These programs serve a single specific task, are used in an isolated manner from other programs, and the generated data is stored individually. In general, the structure of these programs relates to the way the architect's work is organized. Conventionally the architect uses the CAD-system to draw 2-dimensional plans, elevations and sections, each of which will be stored separately. Site plans will be adapted manually, by redrawing them in the CAD-system. The architectural functionality of the system is more or less limited to the use of predefined symbols from CAD libraries. In Germany, drawings of the project will usually be sent by postal mail to the structural engineer. In some cases, more future-oriented offices use modem-connections to deliver the drawings. The "bill of quantities" (BOQ) and project documents are created manually, based on printed plans and sections. In most cases, spreadsheets and, sometimes, specific stand-alone applications are used to generate the BOQ but usually without making use of the digital CAD-data. Changes that occur during the building process are recorded in revised plans, sections and elevations that very often follow no filename-convention. In most cases, the files will be renamed into filename-old, filename-1, etc., leading to a variety of different planning stages, which are not catalogued or documented. After several changes to the building design, the architect is no longer able to reproduce which drawings represent which planning stage. In addition, data might be stored in arbitrary directories on a central server, the local hard disk or possibly on floppy disk, depending on the users' needs or conventions and preferences of the operating system the office uses. In specific cases, the software used by the architect mandates a specific filename convention and determines in which directories the user has to store his or her data, thus making it nearly impossible to archive the project or even worse - recover a specific planning stage of the project at a later point in time.

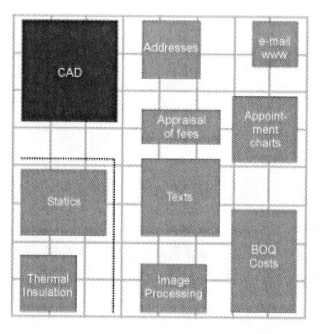

Figure 1. The ordinary situation

Nonetheless, this way of working has some advantages in comparison to a consistent data-model. If any one of the system components fails, the remaining components are unaffected and continue to work. The various programs can provide a quantity of features that justify expenditures of costs and training period. The demands made to the system performance are less than those made to a system with a consistent data-model. These applications provide the architect with the flexibility to equip his office with exactly the stand-alone tools and the staff that meet his demands. (Figure 1 – The ordinary situation).

3 Scenario Two – The Possible Situation

With today's software applications, processes in building design could be reformed and improved, reaching an effectiveness that is not possible to achieve with stand-alone applications and the methods described in Scenario One. To utilize these applications, the architect has to assume a certain risk and expenditure in training that should not be underestimated. Software specialists and system administrators are required to maintain an integrated information processing system in the architect's office. New and specialized systems expand the architect's capabilities and range of duties. An example of such a system would be a digital survey of an existing building that provides accurate CAD data directly from the survey on the building site (Donath and Maye 1996). In this and other cases, i.e. facility management, the architect can adopt new fields of activity, which provide him with increasing competence, improved sales potential on the market and in the end, new clients. Several processes depend on each other and were made consistent with each other by utilizing standardized data exchange formats. With this type of system, project documents could be generated automatically by the use of the 3-dimensional CAD model. An integrated information processing system could consist of specific building elements, providing the architect with the required data. Without doubt, the architect has to ensure that the masses generated and exchanged between the CAD and the BOQ system are appropriate and consistent. It is an essential precondition that both systems make use of the same data specification; otherwise the data-exchange could cause a surprise. STEP (Standard for the Exchange of Product Model Data), for instance, lays claim to map consistent information about a specific product, i.e. material characteristics or the expansion of a building. In the near future ProSTEP will be an interface with which data exchange will be further improved. However, in light of the diversity of existing systems in building planning, this step is comparable to the exchange of a single carburetor between various automobile manufacturers. (Figure 2 – The possible situation).

Single processes in building planning are better supported and more efficient and logical because information can be used in another module, transformed or further developed. Object-oriented database management systems (OODBMS) do not allow one to administer a consistent data model containing interwoven modules, whereas Scenario Two requires consistent models within each aspect of the planning to ensure unrestricted data exchange. A possible solution, such as active relationships or the adaptation of the "event-condition-action-paradigm," is not ideal either because they are often specified for particular cases only (Bergmann et al. 1994; Kolender 1997; Olbrich 1998). The main criteria and characteristics of Scenario Two that current systems are capable of meeting will be described in the following:

- Digital survey as a basis for planning with CAAD in the revitalization and conservation process of existing buildings:
- Beginning with digital building surveys, the architect faces an urgent need for the development of a software concept that delivers a structured way of collecting and organizing information about existing buildings.

Before the actual planning task begins, a comprehensive consideration of the existing built situation has to be undertaken. The results of this complicated process are a variety of individual aspects relating to the building. The building's geometry and structure express themselves in the form of single "drawings" - plans, sections, elevations, details, it's documentation in the form of analyses, log books, statistical information, project descriptions, photographs or expert reports. It is then up to the architect, not just to "read" the information, but also to find connections specific to the situation.

On the basis of an in-depth analysis of traditional methods and processes involved in architectural surveying, a system is required to allow structured surveying, preparation, organization and use of digital information about existing architectural objects. The information gathered has to be stored in an integrated building information system, which provides the basis for further development of the building project with the aid of CAAD-systems. Particular emphasis should be given to the systematic breakdown of a building into its component parts, information relevant to its use and planning, and to the integration of different methods of capture and presentation of this information.

- Availability of complex CAD-systems which provide specific architectural functionality (CAAD).
- Links between CAAD-data and databases (DBMS) providing information for room-books and administration of utilization.
- Links between CAAD-data and BOQ and tender-documents for the exchange of quantities and masses.
- Data exchange capabilities to deliver CAAD-data directly to other professionals.
- Architectural visualization, presentation and simulation derived directly from the CAAD-package.

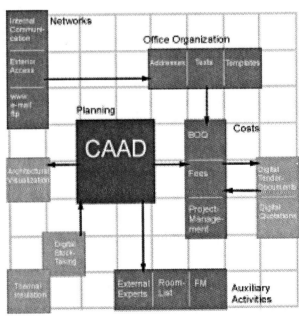

Figure 2. The possible situation

- Structured and classified office-organization, including a standardized filing and archive system.
  Well-defined, standardized office organization is still one of the most important factors in a viable architectural practice. The use of electronic data processing doesn't take away the staffs' responsibility to adopt specific rules and organizational structures within the office. On the contrary, the use of computers forces the architect to clearly organize the electronic work-environment. Management of user-access, software versions, document patterns, central databases and the use of standardized, up-to-date binding forms for correspondence and planning applications are indispensable.
- Integration of programs to create and exchange digital BOQ and project documents as well as price indices.
- Establishment of networked computing equipment, i.e. client-server architecture with appropriate input/output devices, power failure and backup systems, hierarchical control mechanisms observing user access and an intranet.
- An intranet with standardized access to global networks and net-services (www, e-mail, telnet, ftp, fax-server, etc.). Problems affiliated with these demands derive from incompatibilities between various input / output devices and the net-traffic that is to be expected to increase on the Internet. A peculiarity to German Internet users is the high fee charged by domain providers making it difficult to intensely use net-services.
- An intranet providing access for external temporary users, such as freelancers, partners or external specialists, who need to obtain data stored on the architects' server. Implementation of these structures requires tremendous security mechanisms, which the architect is usually not able to establish on his own. Therefore, external service providers must be engaged in providing the appropriate hardware and software solutions to ensure the highest security for the network. Always it is wise to employ a systems administrator who can fix bugs or problems that occur in everyday use of the network and its components.

4 Scenario Three – The Visionary Situation

It seems that today's situation in computer aided planning is unsatisfactory for the architectural profession. Various factors contribute to this situation. On the one hand, there is often a misunderstanding between the architect's demands and the actual ascendancy these demands have on software developers – thus onto the conversion of these demands into commercial software packages. On the other hand, the use of electronic data processing in architectural practice requires the architect to rethink and reorganize his or her work environment. Today's systems are not capable of providing a work environment that can adopt the methods and strategies used in older established work environments. And if they would, the intention to establish computer aided architectural design would demonstrate absurdity. However, to benefit from new ideas in CAAD, the architect has to be receptive to new ideas and he has to be able to clearly define his objectives, requirements and goals that he hopes to gain from the use of computers in his practice.

Will the increasing integration and complexity of CAD tools provide a detectable benefit? Yes, the benefit will exist, but not through the use of small, specialized products. These specialized applications separate themselves from each other, whereas the planning and realization process of a building inevitably requires loss-less and consistent exchange of data between numerous branches that are involved. At present time, data exchange works in principle only. Single pieces of information can be processed, but it is based on arbitrary standards. The planning process itself is characterized by high loss of information. For a long time, computer science tried to create a complete, yet classical mapping of our world, i.e. an object-oriented model. Sufficient research and theoretical foundations exist to map such complex issues. At first glance, these basic approaches are possible. But looking at them more closely, they are complex, but not hopeless. There has been noticeable progress in the development of complex, unified data interfaces. Great hope could be laid in the Industrial Foundation Classes (IFC), even if their implementation and development is slow and inflexible. With the IFC, the industry tries to provide unified data exchange and a consistent model for a variety of CAAD-systems. Therefore the IFC offers individually definable objects relating to specific branches, which contain information about building elements as well as about design, building and administration. (Industrie Allianz für Interoperabilität 1995, http://www.opb.de/iai/)

The central idea of innovative and future-oriented CAAD-systems will lay in a modular conception. The performance of the system will be controlled by the specific user, dependent on his current tasks and necessities. Centralized or de-centralized stored integrative building models will be standard (EDBMS – Engineering Database Management System), which will be accessed on request by individual tools the user defines on the basis of his specific needs. These queries will be realized through CAAD-functionality made available on the Internet, passing through continuous improvement by the developer. Instead of complex and isolated CAAD-programs provided by different suppliers, architects will make use of a variety of functions they could assemble arbitrarily. Thus the architect who has no need to draw 3-dimensionally could concentrate on the functions that allow him to draw, sketch and render 2-dimensionally. To provide experts from other fields, i.e. heating, ventilation, structural engineering, etc. with the functionality they need, the system is always ready to be expanded with the appropriate functions. Thus, troublesome conversion, data exchange as well as internal and external binding do not apply. The user models for instance the 3-dimensional external structure of the building and calculates the verification for heat insulation later on. New plans are no longer necessary for this project. If the user needs to work solely on the digital survey of complex data of the buildings surroundings in the next few weeks, then this function will be added. The user is able to lease this function for a specific time. There is no need to buy a specific product. If the architect uses specific functions more often (e.g. wall modules) he could subscribe to them for a longer period. The biggest advantage is that the architect always has access to the most up to date software, and he will be billed for it based on his usage. Today, applications in building planning exist that demonstrate this paradigm. BOQ-programs are stored on a central server and with the aid of software that works at close range to the operating system (e.g. ZITRIX), the content of the screen as well as mouse and keyboard entries will be transferred to the personal computer in the office. By this method, the amount of data sent through the Internet remains within the realms of acceptability. (Figure 3 – The expected situation). Building information systems will be established which support digital survey. All aspects related to the building project will be captured, evaluated and structured on the building site. As far as possible, mapping of planning conditions will correlate to our natural perception. (Bauhaus Universität Weimar 1999). This means that a downspout for example, will be mapped as a complex object with its origin and natural characteristics like material, delivery time, complexion and dimensions. Each object modeled in the CAAD-system enacts geometric properties and representation as well as a connection to an object management system. This modular system could be extended, depending on the diversity of the planning task. If the architect needs voluminous analysis of the objects, the administrative system would be extended by the requested items. Each specialist could access specific modules, which relate to his or her profession. To describe building objects, the various modules make use of the technical terms the professional is used to. The modules themselves belong to domains, characterized by a superordinated communication / information interface, that mediates between the domains (Huhnt and Grosche 2000). The system allows interpreting building data according to its technical terminology and pertinence. (Figure 4 – The visionary situation). The basis of our vision of an integrated planning model as mentioned above will be built by a digital building model. In terms of a "virtual building" this model represents an existing building to be revitalized or a building that has to be newly designed. It constitutes itself through abstraction of attributes and properties of a commemorated / real building.

Consequently it represents a system of ordering of the totality of belonging data. The main task and functionality of a building model alike is the administration of all information necessary and the exchange of data between the specialists involved. This information and data interchange takes place on the basis of universally valid, formalized data structures.

Accordingly planning actions are temporal and spatially distributed cooperative processes, whose coordinating platform is the modeled representation of the planned object. The domain models reflect a relevant dynamically modifiable clipping at a time, i.e. survey, the architectural model, the load bearing model of the disposable data of the building (SFB 524, 1999). Further information about the research project is available at the following address:

http://www.uni-weimar.de/architektur/InfAR/forschung/GebIS/index.html

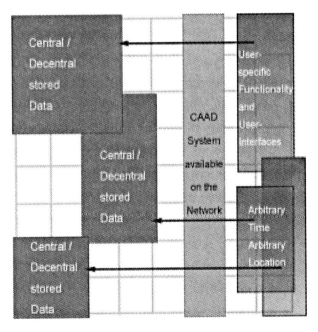

Figure 3. The expected situation

The intuitive and creative phases of architectural design work will also be supported. The architect could make use of functions like virtual reality or rapid prototyping – (possible today in well equipped universities and institutes) (Donath and Regenbrecht 1998, 1999; Streich and Weisgerber 1996). With the aid of these tools, the architect generates visualizations and appraisals that will further be edited in the net-based CAAD-system. Classic design techniques like sketching and model building will find their counterparts in new communication techniques like sketch recognition, gesture recognition and 3D scanning. The use of digital images and animations as "beautiful pictures only" will change. Complex product presentations, showing different aspects of the building, will become relevant, making good economic sense: the visual model of the building costs, the load bearing model, the model related to building physics – immersive, multi-sensorial, possible to be experienced, discussed and explored in its original size simultaneously with others.

Informal components will assist the architect in every occasion, at each planning stage. Your personal software agent informs you of the norms and standards your building has to comply with. It delivers information about a specific brick you'd like to use, it's common and fast-selling formats, delivery times, as well as addresses of potential manufacturers within the periphery of the building site. In accordance to the quantities derived from the digital CAAD-model, the agent contacts these manufacturers, asking them to submit an offer. Information about building regulations is stored on the system, or could be queried through the agent who automatically contacts online representatives of building authorities. The delivered appropriate standards or norms will find entry into the modules you hired for this dedicated architecture project. The norms will assist the architect in his design work by suggesting solutions and providing information he usually obtains from books or encyclopedia. Without depriving the architect of his creativity that is an essential and indispensable component of architectural design work, this will provide a specific set of rules the building has to adapt to. Imagine the massive amount of information dependent on primary and secondary grids and sub grids the architect has to co-ordinate when designing an office building. The general layout of the building, its load-bearing structure, its room structure, its network of pipes and conducts, the arrangement of the facade down to the layout of tiles in the restrooms – they all follow binding principles. Within future systems, these tasks could be performed by your personal agent, reminding you - while designing - that the grid of the facade you've chosen is disharmonious with the size of the parquet flooring, and possibly suggesting a better solution that is even cheaper.

Case-based-reasoning methods allow the architect to look up and examine proven solutions for design or construction severities and adjust and transfer them to his planning situation – leading to a digital memory of preservable solutions. (Steinmann 1997).

The place where the design-work was actually done or where it is stored is not a crucial factor anymore. To save the whole project in a central place, storage facilities will be leased, including services for maintenance, archival and conversion. Office networks are - apart from security mechanisms - no longer distinguishable from global networks. Wherever you are, security and access mechanisms occur and it is of no importance whether your workplace is still in the local office or anywhere else in the world. (Donath et al. 1999). Traditional data communication will become an item of the past. (Figure 4 – The visionary situation).

Accordingly, architecture will find new means of expression by the use of digital space. Not in the form of built objects, but by cultivating its digital representation in networked computer environments and virtual communities. Architecture will turn into an interface, a designed virtual communication space. Without making this thesis the focus of the discussion one could indicate that we have to face developments in the near future that might distort our traditional way of looking at things. The implications for architecture will be beyond our imagination and experiences (Anders 1998; Mitchell 1995)

5 Conclusion
The computer aided planning process will influence automated building processes as long as it takes human peculiarities and attributes into consideration. Highly effective, automated prefabrication exists and its usage will be increased in the future. But it seems that there will always be the sewerage gully located somewhere on the street, not known by any computer program, but by the caretaker.

The future of computing in architecture has to be invented before it becomes real. Therefore it is essential to reconsider existing technologies and to develop visions to become an indispensable component of the gainful use of IT in the architectural practice.

References

Anders, P. (1998) *Envisioning Cyberspace.* McGraw Hill, 1998

Bauhaus Universität Weimar. (1999) *Revitalisierung von Bauwerken.* Sonderforschungsbereich Nr. 524, DFG, 1999

Bergmann, A., Bode, Th., Cremers, A.B., Reddig, W. (1994) *Modelling Civil Engineering Constraints with Inter-Object Relationships.* Proceedings of the European Conference on Product and Process Modelling in the Building Industry, Dresden, 1994

Donath, D., Kruijff E., Regenbrecht H., Hirschberg U. (ETH), Johnson B. (Univ. of W. ,Seattle), Kolarevic B. (Univ. of Honkong). Wojtowicz J. (Univ. of BC, Vancouver). (1999) *Virtual Design Studio 1998 – a Place2Wait – using a VRAD system in a Virtual Design Studio.* eCAADe 99, International Conference, Liverpool, 9/99

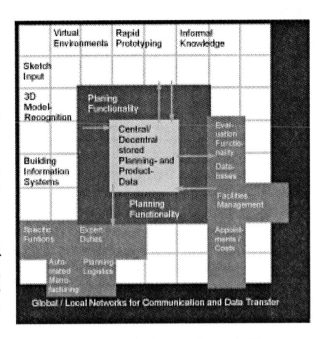

Figure 4. The visionary situation

Donath, D., Maye H.G. (1996). *Computergestützte Verfahren der Bestandaufnahme, Techniken, praktische Erfahrungen und Trends.* bausubstanz, Meininger Verlag Neustadt, 1996, Teil 1: pp. 49-54, 3/96, Teil 2: pp40-43, 4/96

Donath, D., Regenbrecht H. (1998). *Using an Immersive Virtual Reality System for Spatial Design.* First International Workshop on Usability Evaluation for Virtual Environments: Methods, Results and Future Directions. Leicester, UK, 17th December 1998

Donath, D., Regenbrecht H. (1999) *Der Bleistift im 21. Jahrhundert. Das architektonische Entwerfen in interaktiven VR Umgebungen.* IAO Forum Architektur im Informationszeitalter FhG Stuttgart, 1999, proceedings chap. 7, p 10

Haas, D. (1998) *Datenaustausch bei CAD-Anwendungen im Bauwesen – Wunsch und Wirklichkeit.* VDI-Bericht Nr.700.4 VDI-Verlag, Düsseldorf, 1998

Huhnt,W., Grosche,A. (2000) *Information models as a basis for communication in A/E/C projects.* Courses at Summer Academy 2000, Weimar, July 2000

Industrie Allianz für Interoperabilität. (1995). *Industry Foundation Classes.* Management Overview, November 1995, http://www.iai.org

Kolender, U. (1997) *Qualitätssteigernde Maßnahmen bei der Entwicklung von Software-Systemen im Bauwesen durch Objektrelationen.* Dissertation, Technisch wissenschaftliche Mitteilungen TWM, Mitteilung 97-4, Institut für Konstruktiven Ingenieurbau, Ruhr-Universität Bochum, 1997

Mitchell, W. (1995) *The city of bits.* MIT Press, 1995

Olbrich, M. (1998) *Relationenorientiertes Modellieren mit Objekten in der Bauinformatik.* Dissertation, VDI-Berichte Reihe 4 Nr. 150, Düsseldorf 1998

Steinmann F. (1997) *Modellbildung und computergestütztes Modellieren in frühen Phasen des architektonischen Entwurfs.* Dissertation, Bauhaus Universität Weimar, 1997

Streich B., Weisgerber W. (1996) *Computergestützter Architekturmodellbau.* Birkhäuser Verlag, Basel, 1996

Vision on ICT Developments for the Building Sector

Sevil Sariyildiz, Delft University of Technology, The Netherlands
Rudi Stouffs, Delft University of Technology, The Netherlands
Bige Tunçer, Delft University of Technology, The Netherlands

Abstract

The building sector is entering a new era. Developments in information and communication technology have an impact throughout the entire life cycle of a building, not only from a process and technical point of view but also from a creative design point of view. As a result of developments of advanced modeling software for architectural design, the gap between what the architect can envision and what the building technician or product architect can materialize is enlarging. Internet technology has already started to provide a closer link between the participants in the building process, their activities, knowledge, and information. Concurrent and collaborative engineering will be the future of building practice in respect to efficiency and quality improvement of this sector. The nature of the building process is complex, not only from a communication point of view, but also from the information of the number of participants, the spatial organization and the infrastructure etc. In the near future, soft computing techniques such as artificial neural networks, fuzzy logic, and genetic algorithms will make contributions to the problem solving aspects of the complex design process. This paper provides an overview of these and other future developments of information and communication technology (ICT) within the building sector.

1 Introduction

Looking back to historical developments in the building sector we conclude that the technological developments in general have always had an impact on how people designed, built, and lived in a built environment. If construction iron had not been found there would not have been an Eiffel tower, or if the car had not been invented we would still have the narrow streets of the middle ages. There are numerous examples that show the impact of the technological developments on the society itself, by changing habits and the way of living, hence the changes on the built environment.

As in any other science, ICT also has an influence on the building sector. We are entering a new era! This will bring innovations, improvements, and new challenges in this sector.

If we focus only on the design process as a part of the building process, we can generally say that there are four main domains of application of ICT in the design process.

1. Creative design oriented ICT (applied in the conceptual design or inception phase)
2. Materialization oriented ICT (building physics and building technology aspects such as calculating bearing structures and detailing)
3. Realization oriented ICT
4. Process and management oriented ICT (linking the first three categories or activities)

Within the ongoing developments of ICT, the role and the daily work of the people who are involved in the design process are changing. Until now this process was cut into few phases. When the architect has designed the concept, this then goes to the constructor who works out the step and, afterwards, to the contractor who builds it. There is also the supervisor, or manager, who leads this process. We are now entering into a new stage where this process is no longer sequential, but more of a network type, which we call information, communication and collaboration networking in the design process.

2 ICT in the Building Design Process

When we look at the developments of ICT in the building sector, we see that computers were first put into practice as a tool, as an instrument for achieving a specific result, whether to produce a final drawing, an animation, a simulation, or an interactive visualization. Nowadays, computers have taken on a slightly different role as a new medium besides the existing media within the architectural design process. Especially the widespread use of Internet and the developments of the Web have pushed the computer into the role of a medium.

In the very near future, we can expect another shift in the role of computers in the design and building processes, namely, as a partner (Schmitt 1999; Sariyildiz et al. 1998; McCullough 1996). We are now at a stage that ICT allows us to develop new techniques and methodologies to use the computer as a partner by means of knowledge integration, decision support, and artificial intelligence. Decision support systems allow the computer to support the user through knowledge provided by experts or by the user herself. The computer can also be a partner when we teach it things it can reason with. It can even be a valuable and reliable friend when we let it solve problems that are not clearly defined, fuzzy, or uncertain. It can also assist us in generating forms by processing information that influences the shape, supported by self-learning techniques. Here, artificial intelligence techniques such as fuzzy logic, genetic algorithms, and neural networks play an important role.

ICT as a tool, medium, and partner provides the following support in the entire design process:

- *Tool*
  3D modeling
  CAD (Computer Aided Drafting)
  Presentation (Animation, Simulation, Composition, Rendering, etc.)
  Analysis
- *Medium*
  Interactive visualizations (VR-Virtual Reality, Cyber Space)
  Information processing
  Communication (Internet Technology)
  Collaborative and Concurrent engineering, CSCW
  CAD-CAM, CAE, EEM (Enterprise Engineering Management), etc.
- *Partner*
  Knowledge Integration (ANN-Artificial Neural Networks, Fuzzy Logic, Intelligent Agents, etc.)
  Decision Support Systems-DSS
  Advanced Modeling (Genetic Algorithms, Grammars, etc.)
  Intelligent Management

Finally, ICT is meant to support the designer in the design process in order to achieve the intended goal. This goal can be very different from user to user. The flexibility and the efficiency of these ICT means are important factors in the future.

3 Complexity in the Design Process

Buildings are becoming more and more complex nowadays, not only in their form and functions, but also in their infrastructure: their techniques and communications. Naturally, the design process is also becoming more complex. It is complex in the sense that many, often conflicting, interests and criteria are involved, and that many different types of expertise are required to find an optimal solution. Additionally, there is the uncertainty of the future use of the building, requiring the meeting of new criteria that are not defined explicitly at the moment of design. That means that a designer must have the ability to meet a certain range of criteria in a flexible way so that future demands are also met to a certain degree. The outcome of the design process has to fulfill different requirements of functional, formal, and technical nature. These requirements concern aspects like usability, economics, quality of form and space, social aspects of architectural design, technical norms or laws, and technical and mechanical aspects of the design.

Building design is a multi-actor, multi-discipline, and multi-interest process. Design is teamwork among architects, designers, and consultants for various fields, e.g., building physics, construction, material science, electrical engineering, acoustics, geotechnics, building economy, and environmental engineering. The process of decision-making is often intuitive and based on experience. Tedious discussions may occur in committees where all or many of the criteria are presented. The resulting decision obviously is a compromise, but it is often unclear how the decision was reached and whether better solutions exist. In this respect, the ICT tools and their integration form an essential component in the *knowledge integration* process of the various disciplines. As such, they are increasingly becoming a valuable and, hopefully, reliable partner in the design process.

To reach better communication and information exchange during the building design, there have been some initiatives to try out concurrent engineering in Europe, but these were not successful for many reasons. In the first place because the building sector in Europe is very much fragmented and still a bit old-fashioned in thought concerning the innovations and technological developments. Concurrent engineering is now turning into collaborative engineering, especially through the influence of the Internet. There is no time and location dependence anymore. Work can be continued at any time and anywhere in the world. By means of Virtual Reality (VR), participants can communicate visually with each other. Therefore, it is worthwhile also in Europe to put an effort in the developments of broadband technology.

As it was mentioned earlier, in the building process we have to deal with complexity. There are many partners and knowledge disciplines involved in this process. This information must be ordered and the communication must be realized between various disciplines and people involved. Thus, the management of Information, Communication, and Collaboration between the partners in this process has to be done in a most efficient way. Therefore, the ICT means are inevitable tools in the future of the building sector. Collaborative engineering techniques can be a good start to reach this goal.

4 The Role of ICT in the Creative Design Process

When we look at the role of the designer in the building process, we see that as a professional she has to deal with three main categories of sciences, sometimes called alpha, beta, and gamma sciences. Alpha sciences deal with the subjective world of beauty and moral, as expressed by the artistic, intuitive soul. Beta sciences bring in the objective world of facts and logic, represented by the rational mind. Gamma sciences consider the interest of the society and culture. The integration of these sciences makes the task of the designer more complex, but also extraordinary and unique. This means that the designer must have the skills to integrate the various disciplines of knowledge, involving besides the artistic form expression of the building also the dimensioning of the structure, building physics, applied mechanics, the calculation of structures, building materials and techniques, etc. The most famous designers, such as Santiago Calatrava, are the ones who have the ability to combine these various disciplines in their designs as architect and building engineer at the same time.

It is known that when computers were first introduced in the building sector, the initial applications mainly concerned administrative tasks. Gradually their functionality has been extended to support repetitive tasks; nowadays, software applications are becoming essential tools for creative design, for materialization (building technical aspects), and also for the management of the entire building process. Already, for many architects, such as Peter Eisenman and Frank Gehry, the employment of computational programs is an instrumental, if indispensable, means, even if it holds no explanatory power over the results (Forster 1996).

With respect to creative design, we see that the spatial software developments for design during the last years have an influence on the form finding and the spatial design of the creative designer (figure 1). The designing architects are more and more using 3D modeling software such as Maya. During the International design workshop in the Dutch Architecture Institute (NAI), we experienced that the design tools that are offered to the designer have a considerable impact on how the designer is stimulated by the possibilities of the 3D modeling software. It is a fact that the designer dares to design more complex forms and has more flexibility to do so, than she needs. In order to see the influences of the new software in design, the NAI organized an experimental workshop last summer in Rotterdam. Dutch designing architect Lars Spuybroek guided the students within the design context in collaboration with the staff of the chair of Technical Design & Informatics. Our staff guided the students in the informatics aspects and, within a few days time, the students were able to learn to cope with various software, including Maya, in order to design a stadium. The design outcome was very extraordinary, even futuristic, concerning the form aspect (figure 2).

5 Advanced Modelling Software and its Impact on Practice

Figure 1. Student work using advanced modeling software.

As a result of developments in advanced modelling software, and its use for architectural design, the gap between what the architect or designer can envision, on the one hand, and what the building technician or product architect can materialize, on the other hand, is enlarging. The Guggenheim Museum (figure 3) in Bilbao, Spain, designed by Frank Gehry, is a prime example. Designed using Catia, a modeling software first developed for the aerospace industry, it is a fact that the form of this design would be much more difficult to establish using traditional tools and methods for designing than using this or other advanced modelling software. With such tools, the architect is provided with a richer form vocabulary and more flexibility to realise her spatial ideas on the computer. Design software has reached a point where it can stimulate the designer's creativity rather than impede it as has been argued in opposition to the use of CAD software. Also in Europe, we can see many architects who have adopted advanced modeling software for their creative design, such as Dutch architects Kas Oosterhuis and Lars Spuybroek (Schwartz 1997).

The developments in the field of building technology and building materials have not followed these advances in modeling software, such that they can no longer answer all the requirements and demands of the new architectural forms. ICT may play an important role in narrowing this gap. CAD/CAM already counts heavily in the realization of such buildings as the Guggenheim Museum. Electronic form information is transferred directly from the design model to computer-controlled manufacturing machines, as in the case of stone cutting for a curved wall. Unlike

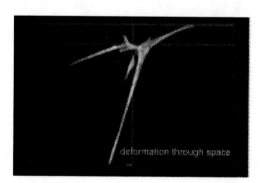
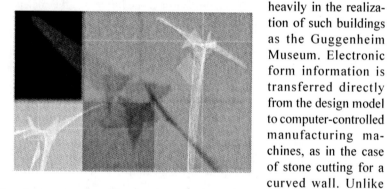

Figure 2. Results from the NAI international design workshop.

straight or even cylindrical surfaces, free-formed surfaces cannot be composed simply of standardised components; potentially each element may be of a different size. This strongly complicates the manufacturing process and causes astronomical costs. Numerically or computer-controlled equipment enables custom components to be produced at a lower cost. Connecting such equipment to the Internet such that these can be controlled directly from the design model further cuts cost. As custom manufacturing increasingly replaces standardised production, these costs will further decrease. Furthermore, as electronic catalogues are extended to include information on custom manufacturing techniques, possibly allowing designers to check manufacturability and price in the design phase, custom production will become more accessible and common.

6 Communication and Collaboration over the Internet

As the Web and Internet technologies are filtering into every aspect of society, so will they have an enormous impact on the building practice. Already, architectural offices are using the Internet in order to communicate with partners across the globe, discussing their designs using whiteboard software and teleconferencing. As distances become smaller, architects are empowered to take on a global role. Examples already abound, such as the world's highest skyscraper in Kuala Lumpur, Malaysia, designed by Cesar Pelli Associates in the US. The use of Islamic geometric patterns in the design nevertheless shows a strong influence from the local culture.

Such global access requires new ways of managing the design process. Building projects are increasingly becoming teamwork, where no one person is solely responsible for a design. Well-defined control hierarchies and relationships are making place for more intricate collaborative processes that are not as easily planned and controlled. This requires an increasingly networked thinking that brings partners to closer interaction but, without appropriate computational support, impedes the ease of overview and understanding (Lottaz et al. 2000). Web-based document management systems serve as media for the exchange of information between the collaborative partners and provide facilities for organizing, viewing, and redlining drawings and images (Roe 1999). These systems can also serve the development and dissemination of tools that support specific needs and processes (Lottaz et al. 2000), leading to integrated software environments as platforms for various applications to communicate with each other over the Internet (figure 4).

Figure 3. The Guggenheim Museum, Bilbao, Spain.

This evolution is founded on several universal Internet technologies, such as TCP/IP, HTML, Java, and XML. Using these technologies, it is pretty straightforward to create a Web application that runs on any platform. The role of XML is as a universal data interchange format among applications, freeing "Internet content from the browser in much the same way as Java frees program behavior from the platform" (Johnson 1999). XML also simplifies communication and improves agent technology (Tidwell 1999). When exchanging XML-structured data, the only thing the partners need to agree on is the XML tag set used to represent the data. No other information about each other's systems is required. This makes it simple for new organizations to join an existing structure of data exchange. Similarly, XML-structured data makes it much easier for an agent to understand exactly what the data means and how it relates to other pieces of data it may already know, thereby easing one of the challenges when writing an agent, that is, to interpret the incoming information intelligently and respond to it accordingly. Another advantage to the use of XML for structuring data is that it can easily be applied to existing data and information, for the purpose of archiving or indexing such information. Unlike product model representations, XML structured data is easy for a human to read and understand, is flexible in its application, and can easily be applied for specific purposes (Tunçer and Stouffs 2000).

Figure 4. Four types of functionalities to support information processing in an integrated environment. Image by David Kurmann.

Many disciplines are in the process of developing a framework for using the XML standard for electronic communication and data interchange in their domain (Cover 2000), including the building industry (aecXML 1999). Considering the complexity of building projects and the unstructured and interrelated nature of the project data, it is sure that the building community can benefit from a unifying strategy for data interchange. This will not only make the current data exchange and reuse practices more efficient, but will also result in great savings by streamlining the worldwide transactions in the Architecture, Engineering, and Construction (AEC) community.

7 ICT in Architectural Education

In the near future, as a result of the ongoing developments of ICT, we, as designers and professionals who educate the future designers in the field of computing, need to think thoroughly and adapt ourselves to these rapid developments. Up to now, in most CAD curricula at faculties of architecture, more attention is paid to the computer as a tool and partially as a medium for communication and information processing. We are now at a stage that the technological developments allow us to look forward and go a step further than the present use of those tools in education.

It is now necessary to introduce the existing ICT means and techniques into the education and develop the above mentioned subjects of ICT. In the future, the architects must be able to extend the existing tools and integrate them for their specific needs. As such, the level of education must be pushed up to a higher level, to a level where the computer is used not only as a tool or medium but also as a partner with respect to knowledge integration and advanced modeling techniques, and as a support environment during the design process.

If these developments will be left to others than architects, the architects will be faced with the danger that they will become the slave of the tools and not the boss. Partially, we face the same kind of problems at the moment with the commercial tools. None of the commercial CAD products support the designer, as it should be. Each program has its advantages and lesser advantages or disadvantages. The user must have to learn the basic principles in order to be able to use the software and to make use of the advantages of each in an efficient way. This basic knowledge should be given to the architecture students from the first year.

On the other hand, the student of the future will be a mobile student who will be able to work at any time and at any place. Therefore, distance-learning possibilities will gain an important role in the future for the academics that are involved in the education.

8 The Impact of Artificial Intelligence on ICT Enhanced Building Technology

Design requires more comprehensive attention than ever before. Building design involves multi-dimensional aspects, which need to be considered with respect to conflicting criteria, that themselves must be reconciled for optimal design solutions, and this in an industry where cost effectiveness and efficiency are becoming dominant requirements due to a hard competitive environment. In this respect, there is no doubt that the available building information must be used effectively, and ICT can play a role in eliciting this information in a timely and exhaustive manner. Several emerging technologies have important relevance to the use of ICT in the building process and, ensuing, important implications. Various implications of these advances in communication technology have already been pointed out in the preceding sections. In particular, due to these advances, design information is now communicated over the Internet and a start is being made of storing information and knowledge in databases and knowledge bases, respectively. At the same time, the volume of information to be processed is exponentially growing.

As information and knowledge are being stored at a continuously growing pace, buried in gigabytes of records, these are becoming far less comprehensible. Faced with difficulties of retrieving them and making them available in an easily comprehensible format at higher levels of summarization, this information becomes less and less useful. No human can use such data effectively and be able to understand the essential trends in order to make rational decisions. With reference to this phenomenon of overwhelming information, the emerging technologies of knowledge discovery and data mining offer a prospect of help. Knowledge discovery is inherently connected to databases: in an interaction with a database, a search for patterns or objects is performed, eliciting meaningful pieces of knowledge. Data mining provides the means or methods to attain this knowledge. Among the most promising methods for data mining are artificial neural networks, fuzzy logic, and heuristic search methods such as genetic algorithms. Collectively, these are referred to as soft computing methods; heuristic search methods are also referred to as evolutionary algorithms. Artificial neural networks are invoked toward processing numeric data and building non-linear relationships. Fuzzy sets concentrate on the representation of data at a nonnumeric level. The symbiotic cooperation of these two technologies results in an effect on the granularity of information.

These soft computing methods are receiving growing importance in almost every field, including building technology, though here at a relatively slower pace. Presumably, the basic reason for this is the difficulty of formulating building technological problems in a way that these become convenient for artificial neural treatment. However, these methods are especially important in the building sector, as they can handle information in various forms such as numerical specifications as well as linguistic qualifications, thus, information coming from all three alpha, beta, and gamma sciences. At present, a unified representation for artificial neural networks and fuzzy logic is already established (Jang et al. 1997). From this, it can be anticipated that the communication between building technology and soft computing technology will be much easier than before. This is due to the possibility of processing information at hand more human-like in the coming years than is achieved today. Currently, such information processing, in combination with knowledge based systems, is mostly introduced in the form of expert systems or decision support systems. So far, these are in most cases unsatisfactory. In the future, however, we can expect such computational intelligence systems to play an important role in decision making support.

Intelligent systems are increasingly replacing conventional systems, as exemplified by intelligent manufacturing and intelligent design technologies. Some basic Artificial Intelligence (AI) fields associated with the emerging technologies connected to the development of ICT are indicated in figure 5. In order to cope with the demands of information acquisition and information handling of these intelligent technologies, new methodologies and techniques are being developed. Besides knowledge discovery and data mining technology, agent technology is another example of such emerging software technologies. An agent is a software program designed for a specific purpose or functionality that acts autonomously to some extent, and may be intelligent too (Jennings and Wooldridge 1998). Agent technology is closely associated with ICT in the sense that agents are generally conceived for communication with other agents or software and for transmission to a distant computer if the task requires it. The Internet allows this distant computer to be any machine on the globe. Agents are especially promising for mining databases as they act autonomously. As an example, a fuzzy engineering agent can interact with a building design database in order to identify various trends of engineering or architectural nature. In connection with VR, agents can assist in design by providing sufficiently realistic feedback early in the design process. This should ease the early integration of design components, in particular, in collaborative design (Abarbanel et al. 1997). Especially for collaborative design, agents have an important role to play in order to assist participants in their task or communications, or to offer additional functionality in project-management applications (Stouffs et al. 1998).

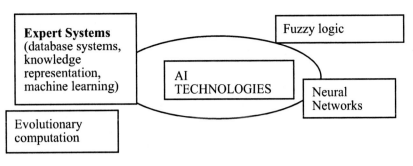

Figure 5. Some basic AI fields of importance to ICT developments with impact on building technology.

9 Future ICT tools for the building sector?

We are still dealing with the material world for which ICT is highly appropriate. But what will happen to the immaterial world? Can we 'teach' computers immaterial values?

Early developments of information technology in the field of architecture involved two-dimensional applications; subsequently, the significance of the third dimension became manifest. Nowadays, people are already speaking of a fourth dimension, interpreting it as time or dynamics. And what, for instance, would a fifth, sixth or X-th dimension represent?

We are now able to communicate verbally and with sign language with computers. In the future we will perhaps speak of the fifth dimension as comprising the tangible qualities of the building materials around us. And one day a sixth dimension might be created, when it will be possible to establish direct communication with computers, because direct exchange between the computer and the human brain will have been realized. The ideas of designers can then be processed directly by the computer, and we will no longer be hampered by the physicality of screen and keyboard.

This is mere speculation, and seems to be far-fetched, but even 50 years ago nobody could even imagine that today everybody could be walking the streets with a wireless telephone.

10 Conclusions

The ongoing developments in the field of ICT have an important impact on the design and building processes. Designers can allow ideas and intuitions to take physical shape in ways that have not been possible before (Forster 1996). At the same time, building technical developments are lagging behind and alternative, innovative solutions have to be adopted. In Eisenman's Aronoff Center at the University of Cincinnati, "all of the building trades (plumbing, tiling, painting) were carried out through a three-dimensional coordinate numerical control system implemented by an electronic laser transit on the site" (Zaera-Polo 1996). Future ICT developments for architecture and the building sector will be in the field of knowledge integration and decision support environments, leading finally, to ICT support in the entire building process, from initiative until demolition. Collaborative engineering will pervade the building design process. By means of these technologies, the various branches of scientific disciplines will come closer than ever before into an integration of their disciplines. In the future, each participant in the design process will need to be able to make her own computer model in order to build up her specific knowledge within this computer model and to use it for her own support as a partner in the design. Developments in the software industry already show that if software firms provide the software core, architects and building engineers will be able to develop their own application tools according to their specific requirements and needs. Independent of the existing tools, they will even be free to create their own language of activities. Ongoing developments of Internet technology require other ways of design management and communication (data and partners communication) in the building process.

References

Abarbanel, R., E. Brechner, and W. McNeely. (1997). FlyThru the Boeing 777. In *Formal Aspects of Collaborative CAD*, eds. M.L. Maher, J.S. Gero and F. Sudweeks, 3-10. Sydney: Key Centre of Design Computing, University of Sydney.

aecXML. (1999). *aecXML: A framework for electronic communications for the AEC industries*, IAI aecXML Domain Committee. http://www.aecxml.org/technical/

Cover, R. (2000). *The XML Cover Pages: Extensible Markup Language (XML)*, Billerica, Mass: Organization for the Advancement of Structured Information Standards (OASIS). http://www.oasis-open.org/cover/xml.html

Forster, K.W. (1996). Rising from the land, sinking into the ground. In *Eleven Authors in Search of a Building*, ed. C.C. Davidson, 114-119. New York: The Monacelli Press.

Jang, J-S.R, C-T. Sun, and E. Mizutani. (1997). *Neuro-fuzzy and Soft Computing; a computational approach to learning and machine intelligence*. Upper Saddle River, NJ: Prentice-Hall.

Jennings, N.R. and M.J. Wooldridge. (1998). *Agent technology: foundations, applications, and markets*, eds. N.R. Jennings and M.J. Wooldridge. Berlin: Springer.

Johnson, M. (1999). XML for the absolute beginner: A guided tour from HTML to processing XML with Java. In *JavaWorld*, April 1999. http://www.javaworld.com/javaworld/jw-04-1999/jw-04-xml.html

Lottaz, C., R. Stouffs, and I. Smith. (2000). Increasing understanding during collaboration through advanced representations. In *Electronic Journal for Information Technology in Construction* 5 (1), 1-24. http://www.itcon.org/2000/1/

McCullough, M. (1996). *Abstracting Craft: The Practised Digital Hand*. Cambridge, Mass: MIT Press.

Roe, A. (1999). New digital products boost collaborative design. In *CADENCE*, 14 (2), 26-29.

Sariyildiz, S., P. van der Veer, M. Schwenck, and Ö. Çiftçioglu. (1998). Computers as reliable and valuable partner. In *Cyber-real Design, 5th Conference on Computer In Architectural Design*. Poland: TU Bialystok.

Schmitt, G. (1999). *Information Architecture: Basics of CAAD and its future*. Basel: Birkhäuser.

Schwartz, I. (1997). A testing ground for interactivity. In *Archis*, September 1997. http://www.archis.org/archis_art_e_1997/archis_art_9709_ENG.html

Stouffs, R., D. Kurmann, B. Tunçer, K.H. Mieusset, and B. Stäger. (1998). An information architecture for the virtual AEC company. In *Product and Process Modelling in the Building Industry*, ed. R. Amor, 479-486. Watford, UK: Building Research Establishment.

Tidwell, D. (1999). *XML and how it will change the Web*, IBM. http://www-4.ibm.com/software/developer/library/xml-web/index.html

Tunçer B. and R. Stouffs. (2000). Modeling building project Information. In *Construction Information Technology 2000*, ed. G. Gudnason, 937-947. Reykjavik, Iceland: Icelandic Building Research Institute.

Zaera-Polo, A. (1996). The making of the machine: Powerless control as a critical strategy. In *Eleven Authors in Search of a Building*, ed. C.C. Davidson, 28-37. New York: The Monacelli Press.

An Expandable Software Model for Collaborative Decision-Making During the Whole Building Life Cycle

K. Papamichael, Lawrence Berkeley National Laboratory, USA

V. Pal, Lawrence Berkeley National Laboratory, USA

N. Bourassa, Lawrence Berkeley National Laboratory, USA

J. Loffeld, Lawrence Berkeley National Laboratory, USA

I. G. Capeluto, Technion - Israel Institute of Technology, Israel

Abstract

Decisions throughout the life cycle of a building, from design through construction and commissioning to operation and demolition, require the involvement of multiple interested parties (e.g., architects, engineers, owners, occupants and facility managers). The performance of alternative designs and courses of action must be assessed with respect to multiple performance criteria, such as comfort, aesthetics, energy, cost and environmental impact. Several stand-alone computer tools are currently available that address specific performance issues during various stages of a building's life cycle. Some of these tools support collaboration by providing means for synchronous and asynchronous communications, performance simulations, and monitoring of a variety of performance parameters involved in decisions about a building during building operation. However, these tools are not linked in any way, so significant work is required to maintain and distribute information to all parties.

In this paper we describe a software model that provides the data management and process control required for collaborative decision-making throughout a building's life cycle. The requirements for the model are delineated addressing data and process needs for decision making at different stages of a building's life cycle. The software model meets these requirements and allows addition of any number of processes and support databases over time. What makes the model infinitely expandable is that it is a very generic conceptualization (or abstraction) of processes as relations among data. The software model supports multiple concurrent users, and facilitates discussion and debate leading to decision-making. The software allows users to define rules and functions for automating tasks and alerting all participants to issues that need attention. It supports management of simulated as well as real data and continuously generates information useful for improving performance prediction and understanding of the effects of proposed technologies and strategies.

Keywords: Decision making, integration, collaboration, simulation, building life cycle, software.

1 Introduction
The phenomenal growth of information technologies has revolutionized the way we do business. These technologies now give us the ability to collect, manipulate, and disseminate massive amounts of data, offering decision makers the opportunity to access detailed information, often at the speed of thought. Current multimedia and networking technologies allow formatting and communication of information so that, using the Internet, anyone in the world can broadcast information that is instantly accessible to anyone else in the world!

The ability to quickly and inexpensively generate, store, and communicate vast quantities of information means that decision making can be based on access by many parties to extensive information. The building industry envisions using this technological capacity to make information available about all details of buildings' design, construction, and operation throughout their life cycle. The key question is how software can make this data management possible.

In this paper we identify key elements involved in decision making and then model them in ways that support the development of an expandable software model for collaborative decision making about buildings throughout their life cycles.

2 Background

Currently, many software applications can individually address partial needs of the building industry (e.g., visualization, lighting, energy, construction management, etc.). Digital drawings have become the norm, and are becoming increasingly "smarter" through links to object-oriented representations of building components and systems and their descriptive and performance characteristics. Computer-based simulations often allow very accurate performance prediction for a variety of criteria, such as comfort, aesthetics, energy, safety, environmental impact, and economics (Birdsall et al. 1990; Feustel 1992; Ward and Shakespeare 1998; http://www3.autodesk.com/adsk; http://www.lightscape.com/; http://www.lighting-technologies.com/Lumen_Micro.htm; http://www.primavera.com/). This information is critical to decision making during the entire life cycle of the building.

Various individual applications are now available, and more are on the way, to assist with tasks and decisions at different stages of the life cycle of the building, from schematic to detailed design, to construction, commissioning, operation, renovation, retrofit, and demolition (Cambell 1998; Clayton et al. 1998; Piette 1996). However, most available applications are stand-alone, without means of exchanging information with other related programs.

Several attempts are under way to integrate such applications or at least to allow them to exchange information. Although development is ongoing, significant potential has already been demonstrated for tremendous increases in efficiency and effectiveness of the decision making process (Mahdavi et al. 1996; Pohl et al. 1992; Papamichael et al. 1997; Jokela et al. 1997; http://iaiweb.lbl.gov/). Some efforts have been focusing on the development of applications that facilitate collaboration over networks (Kalay 1997; McCall et al. 1998). Some of these capabilities have already been integrated into commercial applications (http://www.bentley.com/products/projbank/dgn/index.htm).

In this paper, we describe an integrated approach that supports collaborative decision making throughout a building's life cycle. This approach involves the use of a very abstract decision-making model as the basis for the development of data and process models to address the specific needs of the various disciplines involved in building design, construction, and operation. The high degree of abstraction means that the model can, in theory, expand infinitely as the application-specific data and process information about a building grows.

3 Theoretical Conception of the Decision Making Process

In this section we present the theoretical considerations that are the foundation for the proposed model. These include our conceptualization of the decision making process and the required inputs to it.

3.1 Decisions

Decisions can be abstracted into *selections among options*, and thus require comparison. From this viewpoint, the main elements of decision making are options (at least two) and selection criteria. In other words, we make decisions by evaluating options with respect to various performance criteria and then choosing the option that best fits our preferences. For example, an architect may select from a number of glazing options based on aesthetics, view, and/or energy implications. Depending on the nature of the selection criteria, we use various processes to predict the performance of alternative options and then evaluate predicted performance by comparing among options.

Decisions become increasingly difficult as the options and trade-offs among selection criteria increase in number. Most building-related decisions involve multiple criteria and significant trade-offs among them. Moreover, they involve multiple players who have varying concerns and priorities and need to collaborate to predict and evaluate building performance. For example, a dynamic relationship is necessary among a building's architect, HVAC engineering consultant, and structural engineer.

3.2 Debate

The performance of alternative options can be abstracted into *advantages* and *disadvantages*, or *pros* and *cons*, which decision makers *weight* to form *preferences* among options. We cannot quantify how people go through the complex choosing process that entails both thinking and feeling (Papamichael and Protzen 1993). Decisions made by multiple collaborating parties often involve *conflicts* among preferences, i.e., different parties prefer different options. Person A may prefer glazing option 1 because of its aesthetic appeal while person B may prefer glazing option 2 because of its superior energy performance. The final decision is made by the most powerful player(s) in the decision making process who is generally influenced by the debate.

Decisions may also involve *factual* conflicts related to the predicted performance of options. These types of conflicts occur because of different *assumptions*, either inherent in different performance prediction methods or related to the information that is used as *input*, e.g., rule-of-thumb variations for HVAC design, or use of inappropriate weather data for computation of thermal loads.

All conflicts result from the availability of multiple values for a single parameter, or multiple *positions* on an *issue*. Issues are resolved through debate, i.e., formulation of arguments *for* and *against* positions, which is the equivalent of the *pros* and *cons* described above for the performance of alternative options (Kunz and Rittel 1970).

3.3 Parameter Types

The parameters that characterize the options considered in decision making for buildings are usually referred to as *design* parameters. The parameters considered when selecting among options are referred to as *performance* parameters. These depend not only on design parameters but on *context* parameters as well, i.e., parameters that characterize the conditions under which an option is considered.

Context parameters describe not only the *existing* conditions at the time of the decision but also the *assumed* conditions during the upcoming phases of the building's life cycle when *actual* performance will be realized. The values of design parameters are usually chosen with a goal of improving performance relative to one or more performance criteria. This relationship between design and performance parameters is referred to as *design intent*. The intent to improve performance with respect to certain criteria usually results in degrading performance with respect to other criteria, which introduces trade-offs among available options. For example, darkening the color of a wall finish to meet an aesthetic criterion will likely result in less reflected light and potentially greater demand for electric lighting.

Design intent is usually formed through combinations of several design parameters into a *strategy*. This is true at any level, from building components and systems, to the whole building itself, where the combination of the values of multiple design parameters is expected to produce the desired performance, rather than the value of any single parameter alone.

3.4 The Building Life Cycle

Although decisions are identical in nature throughout the building life cycle, they vary dramatically, not so much with respect to performance parameters but mostly with respect to the design and context parameters. During the design phases of the building life cycle, design parameters reflect mostly building characteristics and context parameters reflect mostly site characteristics. After construction, design parameters mostly reflect the operation of the building and relatively small changes in the details of the building, while the building itself becomes part of the context for these decisions. For example, the size of a window, which was a design parameter during the building design, becomes the context for decisions to control glare or temperature once the building is built. However, most of the parameters don't change, they simply switch from describing design to describing context.

The fact that the parameters involved in decisions throughout the building's life cycle are unchanging allows formulation of a model that can be used both during design and once a building is built. It also introduces the potential for a third type of conflict, which occurs when the actual value of a parameter is different from the one assumed during earlier phases. Such *expectation* conflicts can occur in any of the parameters involved in decision making. The major objective of commissioning a building is to identify such conflicts and make decisions based on the actual context.

Even though most parameters involved in decision making are unchanging during the entire life cycle of a building, the detail required for and the persons involved with each one may change. In most buildings, even today, a very large amount of information that is generated during the building design is not available to decision makers during construction, commissioning, and operation. Changes are often made without knowledge of the original design intent, which may have a significant negative effect on performance. This is especially true when the changes involve individual parameters that are part of a larger strategy. For example, darkening the color of a wall may interfere with a daylighting strategy that depended on the reflectance of the lighter-colored wall.

3.5 Formulating Options

The formulation of options is the creative part of design and a prerequisite to decision making. Although creativity can be defined as the invention of new approaches, there are strong arguments to suggest that many building-related decisions entail combinations of existing approaches and components. For example, the design of an HVAC system can be seen as the combination of readily available components. Even when custom-made components are used, they usually have similar characteristics to standard ones. This is less true for the form of the building and the arrangement of spaces.

Today, many building design decisions involve selection among readily available building components and systems, which have traditionally been available in the form of catalogs and are now becoming available in electronic form either through centralized efforts (http://www.sweets.com/; http://www.thomasregister.com/) or individual manufacturers. The Internet offers the opportunity for continuously updated information on building components. In some cases, the information is already in digital form that is compatible with available tools, such as CAD or simulation software, which can further automate consideration of options during design.

3.6 Model Requirements

A model that will address decision making during the entire life cycle of the building must include the design, context, and performance parameters used in all methods of performance prediction and evaluation of characteristics of a building at any time in the building's life cycle. Because most design and context parameters affect multiple performance aspects and remain the same during the life cycle of the building, the model must be *integrated*. It must address the data needed for predicting performance by multiple tools during the entire life cycle of the building.

Since the number of performance prediction methods is large and new methods and options are being developed continuously, the model needs to be *expandable*. This requires the development of a *meta-schema* (i.e., a structural framework for expansion of the model) that can incorporate data to allow the building schema (data and processes) to grow. The meta-schema must also include a *model of time* to support not only the dynamic parameters related to the building's operation (e.g., occupancy), but the static parameters of components (e.g., a window) that may be replaced during the life cycle of the building.

Because performance evaluation requires comparison, the model must support maintenance of multiple options. Moreover, it must support the integration of information about existing buildings, which forms the general context for evaluation of the predicted performance of proposed designs. Finally, the model must address opportunities for *automation*, not only for preparation of input and handling of the output of performance prediction methods, but also for assigning values to design and context parameters. For example, a designer may define aesthetic facade rules for a project and the model will then automatically assign properties, such as glazing color.

From a user's point of view, the model should answer questions, which means providing the values of design, context and performance parameters, along with the sources of these values and the arguments that support or negate them.

4 Proposed Implementation

In this section we describe the proposed implementation of the theoretical considerations described in the previous section for the development of an expandable model that will support collaborative decision making throughout a building's life cycle.

4.1 The Data Meta-Schema

The foundation of the proposed model is an integrated, object-oriented representation of both data and processes, in the form of a data meta-schema. The meta-schema is used to define and create data and process objects necessary for decision making during the entire life cycle of the building.

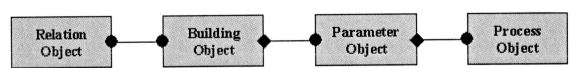

The building is modeled in terms of *building objects* that are related through *relation objects* and are characterized by *parameter objects*. Processes are also modeled as objects related to parameter objects through input/output relations. (Figures 1 and 2). A process may vary from a complex simulation engine that accepts a large number of input data and computes a large number of output data, to a simple if-then-else rule with minimal input and output. Data and processes can be added to this environment without restructuring the code of the meta-schema because the code operates on a model with a very generic conceptualization (or abstraction) of processes as relations among data rather than on the specific contents of data and processes.

Figure 1. A meta-schema where building objects are related to each other through relation objects, and process objects are related to parameter objects through input and output relations.

Modeling of Time

The issue of how to model the passage of time is especially critical for addressing the needs of the whole life cycle of a building. A building can go through multiple states during its lifetime. Each parameter can therefore take on multiple values according to the states of the building through time. In addition, each of these values may have resulted from different processes or measurement equipment, which may each use different representations of time. We need a model that is general enough to be mapped on variations of time models used by different software tools. In response to this, we include time in the data meta-schema.

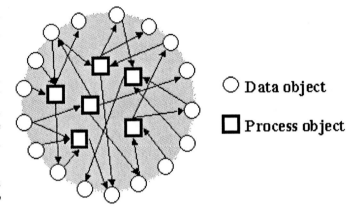

The proposed time model includes a *starting* point in time, an *ending* point in time, a *reference* point in time, and a *time step* (Figure 3). The reference point can be fixed in real time, e.g., 12 AM, January 1, 1973. The time step can be described in terms of a multiplier and a time unit, e.g., 0.001 seconds, or 20 years. Making the time step (i.e., the time resolution) into a variable is helpful for addressing multiple processes with varying time step requirements. Some processes, such as the DOE-2 building energy analysis tool, may need a time resolution on the order of hours. Other tools, such as the SPARK HVAC modeling tool, may need a time resolution on the order of seconds or milliseconds to model HVAC controls. The proposed model allows translation to and from any representation of time, handling even time periods such as seasons, weekdays, and weekends.

Figure 2. A data schema based on the meta-schema results in processes being modeled as links among data.

4.2 The Building Data Schema

In this section we describe how the data meta-schema is used to define and create the data schema that holds the data objects and processes to address the data needs for decision making during the building's life cycle. The data schema contains data and processes that address the specific need of the building industry. Process object instances (e.g., simulation tools, rules, data queries, etc.) serve as relations among data object instances (e.g., spaces, walls, windows, etc. and the parameters that characterize them).

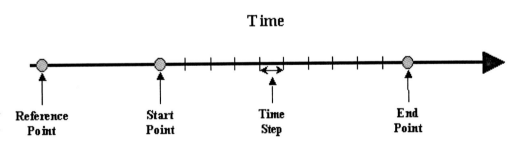

Figure 3. A general model for time that allows translation to and from any representation of time.

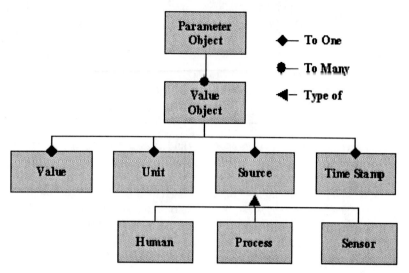

Figure 4. The data meta schema allows the creation of multiple values, each with its own source, for each parameter.

Modeling Data

The objects that will hold the building data are modeled in the form of interrelated objects. Building objects, such as spaces, walls, and windows are modeled as software objects that are linked to each other through relations (composed-of / part-of, has / owned-by, etc.). Building objects can then be created at any point and related to the rest of the building objects. The relations among objects are also modeled as software objects, so new relations can be defined as needed. The same is true for parameters that characterize building objects. Modeling parameters as software objects allows the creation of new parameter objects at any point, as required by the addition of new processes.

To support links to multiple processes and address the data needs of the whole life cycle of a building, even the values of parameters are modeled as software objects. Thus, each parameter can have multiple values, which may come from different sources at different times during the building's life cycle. The "value" data type includes data fields for the source of the value, the unit, a time stamp, the value of the parameter itself, and the time(s) for which the value is relevant. Value sources include humans, processes, and sensors (Figure 4).

Because evaluating predicted performance requires comparison among options, the whole building model is part of a "project" object, so that multiple options can be created and then compared for any of the parameters that characterize them. The creation of a new option for the whole project happens only when any user assigns different values to the same object or parameter. In that case, the system automatically alerts all interested parties, who may respond by "arguing" for and against options. If the new values for an object or parameter come from processes or sensors, these can be used to either create new project options, or value ranges (rather than single values as explained in Section 4.3).

External Databases

The definitions of building objects (e.g., space, wall and window) in the schema database are used to create alternative options and store them in external databases. *Composite* objects, i.e., objects composed of other objects, such as a "window" composed of a "frame" and "glazing", are stored in object-oriented databases. *Terminal* objects, i.e., building objects such as the "glazing" characterized only by parameter objects such as "transmittance", "reflectance" and "U-value" can be stored either in object-oriented or relational databases. These databases can be distributed and dynamic, that is, available on the Internet and continuously updated by manufacturers of building components and systems (for design information), or services and organizations (for context and performance information). External databases can be used to select options for building components and systems as well as to specify the values of context parameters during the development of the project database for a particular building, as illustrated in Figure 5.

Because external databases are closely tied to the building schema database, any expansion of the latter must be reflected in the external databases. An expansion of the building model is required when a new process is added to it and needs data (input or output) that are not available in the model. These data may be added to the building model, but the values for them will not be automatically available in the external libraries of building components and systems, or contextual databases. This is especially true for input parameters. For output parameters (e.g., heat flow through window glazing) the processes themselves provide the values. For example, if the schema includes glazing parameters for transmittance and reflectance and we add a process that requires the U-value of the glazing, the model will be expanded to include U-values. The external databases for glazing will also have to be updated to include U-values.

Modeling Processes

Processes are treated in the same way as data. A process is abstracted as an object that has one essential characteristic: when given values for a set of input parameters, it produces values for a set of output parameters. A process is created in the model in the same way that data objects are created, by defining relationships between it and the parameter objects of the data model. If a process needs data that are not already available in the building model, then the latter is expanded by adding the required data objects.

A process may be a complex simulation engine, such as DOE-2 or Radiance, or a low-level piece of procedural code such as the formula for computing surface area. Even simple rules can be modeled as processes: the input parameters to the rule are the parameters involved in the "if" block of the rule, and the output parameters are the ones involved in the "then" and "else" blocks of the rule (Figure 6). Even data queries can be modeled as processes. The search criteria are the input parameters, and the query results are the output. The output of a query may be a list of options to be considered as input to other processes.

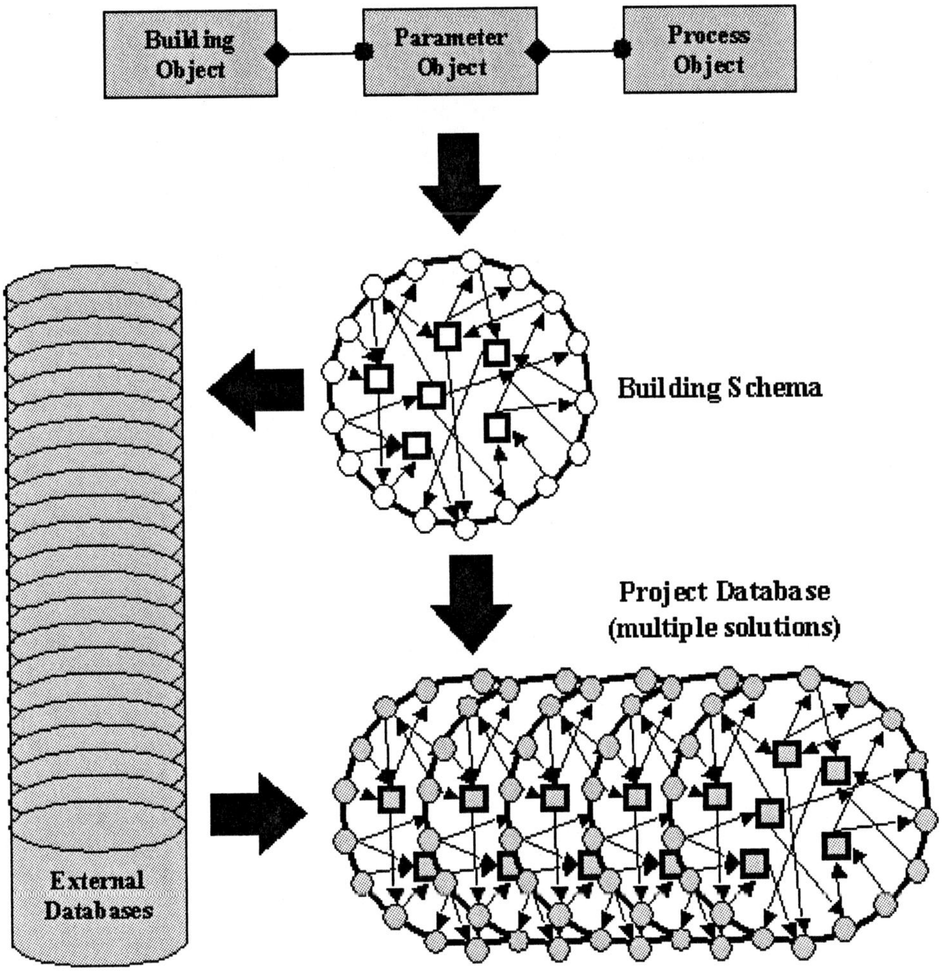

This very abstract model supports the automatic activation of processes and the use of the output of one process as input to others. Thus, the operation of the model can be managed by a relatively simple kernel that is independent of the contents of data and processes.

Figure 5. The relationships among the data meta-schema, the building data schema, the project database, and the external databases.

4.3 The Operation Kernel

The operation kernel manages the data and processes for the maintenance of the model. Two abstract types of user actions activate the kernel: the "assignment to" and "request for" values of data objects. Users, sensors, or processes assign values, and users or processes request them. When a value is assigned and/or requested, a chain of processes is activated to reflect the specified change in the design or to compute the requested value. This chain follows the input and output links among data and processes, as is explained in the following sections.

Assigning Values to Data Objects

Users and processes can either create new data objects within a project or change the values of existing data objects. When a new data object is created, the related objects and parameters required for that object are automatically generated following the definition of the data object in the data schema. When a new window is created, for example, the data schema is queried for the required objects and parameters, such as the frame and glazing, which are, in turn, created automatically.

The data objects that are created reflect the data needs (input and output) of the processes that have been already defined as part of the model. The values for these data objects are either entered by the users or specified by default through the use of *preference* rules. Preference rules assign values to data objects following design practices of users or design firms and can grow as users and firms gain experience based on feedback from the system, i.e., simulation results and actual measurements during building operation. Preference rules can also represent codes and standards, such as ASHRAE 90.1, and Title 24. Finally, preference rules can also be used to activate other rules or sets of rules.

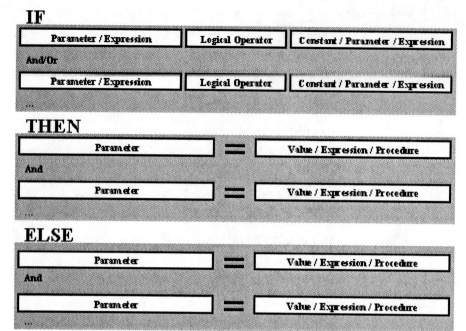

Figure 6. If-Then-Else Rule structure.

In addition to preference rules, *constraint* rules may be activated by the assignment of values to data objects. Constraint rules do not assign values to data objects. Instead, they check the validity of assigned values and notify users when discrepancies occur, e.g., when the window width is assigned a value that is greater than the width of the parent wall. When not used for the assignment of default values, preference rules can also play the role of constraint rules, notifying users when a preference is not met. This is further explained in Section 4.3.3., which describes the handling of conflicts and the assignment of values by sensors.

Preference and constraint rules may also activate simulation processes when the values of performance parameters are required as input. Processes are activated automatically when the value of an output parameter is needed. They can also be set for automatic activation when the value of one of their input parameters is changed. This triggers a forward chaining inference mechanism as illustrated in Figure 7.

Requesting Values Of Data Objects

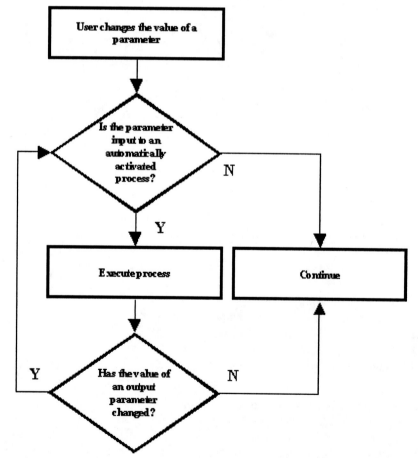

Figure 7. Activation of processes following the assignment of a value to a data object.

The value of a data object may be requested either by the user or by a process that needs it as input. In either case, the kernel first checks to see whether the value is already in the project database. If it is not, then the kernel looks for processes that compute the requested value as output. The processes can either be simulations (for values of performance parameters) or rules (for values of design and context parameters). If no process is available, the kernel prompts the user for a value. If one or more processes are available, the kernel recursively requests the values for all input parameters, stacking processes as necessary (Figure 8).

If there is more than one process that computes a requested value as output, the user is notified and can select the process or processes to be activated. If more than one process is selected, the kernel either generates *new project options* (when the output values are for design or context parameters) or *new values* (when the output values are for performance parameters) generating a value range for the expected performance.

Addressing Conflicts

A conflict occurs when a data object gets different values from different sources. Having multiple values is not in itself a problem because the system allows for multiple values. In many cases it is helpful to maintain multiple values that allow for model validation, parametric analyses, and systematic comparison of design solutions. However, users need collaborative control over the selection of multiple values and design options. The system allows each user to select which values to retain and which values to reject and to associate arguments in the form of comments with each value. The following four conflict scenarios are possible:

1. Different users and/or preference rules assign different values for the same design parameter.
2. Different users or processes, e.g., data queries or rules, assign different values to context parameters.
3. Different performance prediction simulations compute different values for performance parameters.
4. Measured values, e.g., those noted during construction and/or operation of the building, are different from the intended, assumed, or expected values of design, context, and performance parameters, respectively.

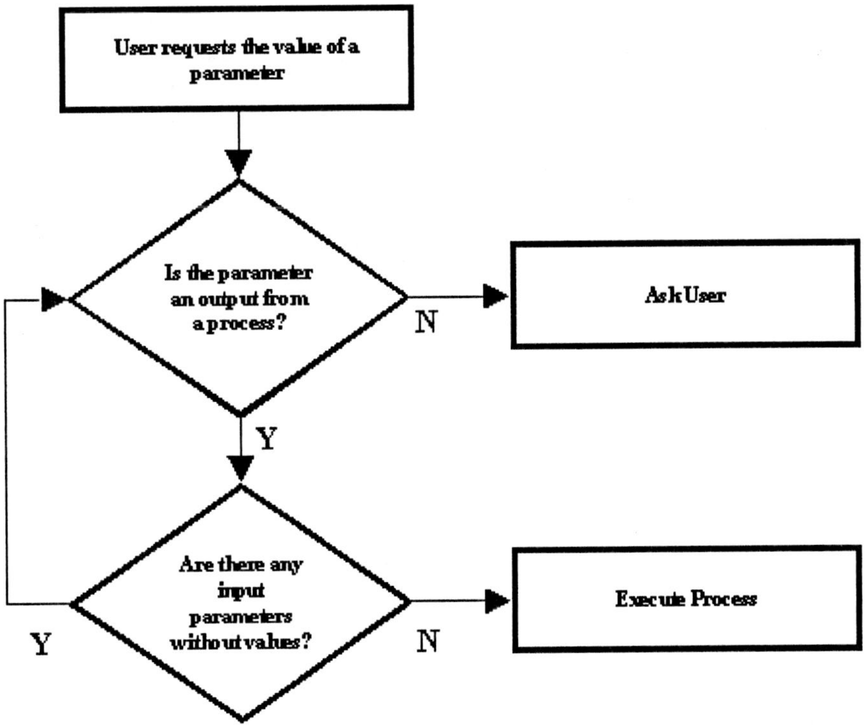

In the first case, the kernel alerts the users, who may agree on one of the assigned values or define different project options, i.e., alternative designs that can be further explored. Users are also given the opportunity to argue for and against the different options, referencing the values of performance parameters. In the second and third cases, the kernel alerts the users, who may select one of the available values as the most valid, or retain multiple values to create a confidence range in place of a single value (Figure 9).

Figure 8. Activation of processes following a request for the value of a data object.

In the fourth case, the kernel alerts the users, who have several options for resolving the issue, depending on the type of parameter under consideration. Conflicts in design parameters indicate discrepancies in the design and are resolved through reconsideration of specific decisions, which may involve requesting values for performance parameters and considering additional design options. Conflicts in context parameters once a building is constructed indicate discrepancies in assumptions about the context and can be used to improve context assumptions in future projects. Conflicts in performance parameters once a building is built indicate discrepancies in expected performance and can be used to reconsider and/or adjust the performance prediction methods for better accuracy in future projects.

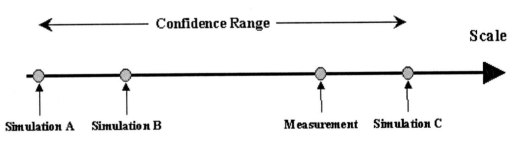

The number of values for a particular parameter can grow over time and be stored in the database as life cycle information. Storage of values facilitates systematic comparison among them at different stages of the building's life cycle. Being able to compare values from different sources and times can facilitate troubleshooting and validation/improvement of performance prediction methods. For example, a simulation tool may provide values that are consistently higher than the corresponding measured values, or trends may be observed for measured values over time and can be used to diagnose problems with the building's operation.

Figure 9. Multiple values for context and performance parameters are used to create confidence ranges.

5 Conclusion

The expanded use of computers and the communications revolution of the Internet offer unique opportunities to address the data needs of the whole building life cycle. In this paper we presented a software model for the integration of multiple processes and databases throughout the life cycle of a building, which will allow multiple participants to share information and make decisions. Significant work is needed for the implementation of the described model into a working tool and even more work for testing and validation. Successful implementation will eventually require development of standards for the electronic description of building components and systems, as well as building context parameters. Such efforts have already been underway (http://iaiweb.lbl.gov/). We hope that the thoughts and modelling approaches presented in this paper will contribute towards the realization of the overall vision.

Acknowledgements

This work was supported by the Assistant Secretary for Energy Efficiency and Renewable Energy, Office of Building Technology, State and Community Programs, Office of Building Systems and Office of Building Equipment of the U.S. Department of Energy, under Contract No. DE-AC03-76SF00098.

References

Birdsall, B.E., Buhl, W.F., Ellington, K.L., Erdem, A.E. and Winkelmann F.C. (1990). "Overview of the DOE-2 building energy analysis program, version 2.1D." Lawrence Berkeley Laboratory report LBL-19735, Rev. 1, Berkeley, CA.

Cambell, D.A. (1998). "Architectural construction documents on the Web: VRML as a case study," *Proceedings of ACADIA '98 Conference*, Quebec City, Canada, October 22-25, pp. 267-275.

Clayton, M.J., Johnson, R.E., Song, Y., and Al-Qawasmi, J. (1998). "Delivering facility documentation using intranet technology," *Proceedings of ACADIA '98 Conference*, Quebec City, Canada, October 22-25.

Feustel, H. E. (1992). "Annex 23 multizone airflow modeling – an international effort," Proceedings of the International Symposium on Air Flow in Multizone Structures, Budapest, Hungary.

Jokela, M., Keinänen, A., Lahtela, H., and Lassila K. (1997). "Integrated building simulation tool RIUSKA," *Building Simulation,* Prague, Czech Republic.

Kalay, Y.E. (1997). "P3: An integrated environment to support design collaboration," *Proceedings of ACADIA '97 Conference*, Cincinnati, Ohio, October 3-5.

Kunz, W. and Rittel, H. (1970). "Issues as elements of information systems (IBIS)," Working paper 131, Institute of Urban and Regional Development, CED, UC Berkeley.

Mahdavi, A., Mathew, P., Lee, S., Brahme, R., and Kumar, S. (1996). "On the structure and elements of SEMPER," *Proceedings of ACADIA '96 Conference*, Tucson, Arizona, October 31 – November 2, 1996.

McCall, R., Holmes, S., Voeller, J., and Johnson, E. (1998). "World Wide Presentation and Critique of Design Proposals with Web-PHIDIAS". *Proceedings of ACADIA '98 Conference*, Quebec City, Canada, October 22-25.

Papamichael, K., LaPorta, J., and Chauvet, H. (1997). "Building Design Advisor: automated integration of multiple simulation tools." *Automation in Construction*, Vol. 6, pp. 341-352.

Papamichael, K. and Protzen, J.P. (1993). "The Limits of Intelligence in Design," *Proceedings of the Focus Symposium on Computer-Assisted Building Design Systems*, Fourth International Symposium on System Research, Informatics and Cybernetics, Baden-Baden, Germany.

Piette, M.A. (1996). "Commissioning Tools for Building Life-Cycle Performance Assurance," LBNL Report-38979, presented at the *4th National Conference on Building Commissioning*.

Pohl, J., LaPorta, J., Pohl K.J., and Snyder J. (1992). "AEDOT Prototype (1.1): An Implementation of the ICADS Model." Technical Report CADRU-07-92, CAD Research Unit, Design Institute, School of Architecture and Environmental Design, Cal Poly, San Luis Obispo, CA.

Ward, G. and Shakespeare, R. (1998). *Rendering with Radiance: The Art and Science of Lighting Visualization.* Morgan Kaufman.

Architecture, Speed, and Relativity: On the Ethics of Eternity, Infinity, and Virtuality

Mahesh Senagala, University of Texas at San Antonio, USA

Abstract:

The main purpose of this essay is to provide a critical framework and raise a debate to understand the spatial and temporal impact of information technologies on architecture. As the world moves from geopolitics to chronopolitics, architecture with its traditional boundaries still vociferously guarded is becoming further marginalized into sectors of mere infrastructure. The essay begins by clarifying the notions of space, time, and speed through a phenomenological interpretation of Minkowskian/ Einsteinian notion of relativistic space-time. Drawing from the cultural critiques offered by Paul Virilio, Marshall McLuhan, and Jacques Ellul, the essay argues that we are at the end of the reign of space-based institutions and transitioning rapidly into a time-based culture.

Keywords: Space-time, virtuality, critical theory, and ethics

1   Introduction

To see the universe in a grain of sand

And heaven in a wildflower,

Hold infinity in the palm of your hand

And eternity in an hour.

—William Blake

Indeed Blake was prophetic in his vision of the universe in a grain of sand. Cultural critics dating back to Jacques Ellul have repeatedly pointed out the shift—in technological societies—from space-centered institutions to time-centered institutions, from material-based economies to information-based economies and from fixed, coherent belief systems to fluid, fragmented worldviews. The proposition put forth in this paper is that architecture, as it is traditionally defined and practiced as a space-based profession, is being increasingly marginalized. Time and speed have come to be the major realms of world action today. Architecture of space has become impotent, immaterial and marginal while architecture of time is becoming increasingly significant. This paper examines the impact of such transformations in the context of information technologies.

1.1   Architecture as (timeless) space

For millennia, architecture has been understood, practiced, and theorized as the discipline of space. Space is defined here as a 'domain of possibilities or activities'. Place maybe defined as a set of institutionalized spaces. The shift during Modernism from place to space indicates a breakdown of traditionally instituted space and the emergence of a radical, fluid and unformed conception of space. See Steven Peterson's article "Space, Anti-space" (Peterson 1980) for further discussion on these issues. Also see Edgar Casey's The Fate of Place for an in depth discussion of various issues of space and place from antiquity to the present times (Casey 1995).It is an eternally held notion that architecture fundamentally deals with the formation and configuration of space through the use of material. Traditionally, architecture has been employed to determine and fix social conditions through the use of materials and spatial patterns.

Various discourses of architecture have so far revolved around static formations of physical space.

Theoretician K. Michael Hays rightly pointed out that we have "moved from Sigfried Giedion's modernist notion of space-time to Henri Lefebvre's Marxian 'production of space' to a Foucaldian linking of space, knowledge, and power, to most recently, a concern shared by those interested in the construction of gender, sexuality, and difference with space and its physical internalization" (Hays 1998). Henri Lefebvre's seminal work Production of Space effectively sums up the discourses of production of space (social, physical, political, etc.) and how various disciplines—from mathematics to art—have tried to territorialize those discourses (Lefebvre 1991). The discourses of space have undergone major transformations from Aristotle to Descartes, from Leibniz to Kant and from Freud to Foucault.

1.2 From Space and Time to Space-time

Speed finally allows us to close the gap between physics and metaphysics. (Virilio 1991)

The physics and metaphysics of Theory of Relativity transformed our understanding of space, time and the inseparability of space, time, and movement. Back in 1939 Giedion wrote the famous book Space Time and Architecture (Giedion 1971). He was the first to bring the issues of interconnectedness of space and time albeit he does not explicitly discuss the impact on or applicability of Theory of Relativity to architecture.

In 1908, Minkowski remarked, following Einstein's formulation of the Theory of Relativity in 1905, that "from now onwards space and time are to degenerate to mere shadows and only a sort of union of both retain independent existence," there was a deep sense in which time and space are 'mixed up' or interlinked (Born 1962). This is evident from the Lorentz transformations of special relativity that connect the time t in one inertial frame with the time t' in another frame that is moving in the x direction at a constant speed v. The relationship is:

$$t' = [t - vx/c^2]/[\sqrt{1- v^2/c^2}]$$

In this equation, t' is dependent upon the space coordinate x and the *speed*. In the language of relativity, events are describable only as "*space-like*" or "*time-like*" or "*space-time-like*" (Born 1962). In this way, time is not independent of either space or speed.

While most people have assumed that the inseparability and interdependence of space and time are not a matter of common sense or day-to-day experience, the interdependence of space and time manifests itself in an intriguing if not baffling manner in large systems such as cities. The physics of space-time interdependence is directly connected to the metaphysics of the relationship between space, time and movement. This dynamic becomes very evident when we examine the impact of speed on the dematerialization of space and valorization of time.

Unlike many people (including architectural theoreticians) who have come to treat Theory of Relativity to be applicable and observable at only a cosmic scale, Paul Virilio has poignantly pointed out the metaphysical implications of space-time and speed: "If as suggested by relativity theory, speed expands time in the instant it contracts space, we arrive finally at the negation of the notion of physical dimension, and we must ask once more, 'what is a dimension'." (Virilio 1991)

1.3 From timeless to spaceless: the end of architecture?

For contextual contiguity of the ideas being presented here, and for reasons of brevity I am consciously avoiding a discussion of the role of automobile in the transformation of architecture.

2MPH-30MPH (10,000 BC to present): Somatic Space

At the beginning was the space of the body: the material space. Movement of knowledge was synonymous with the movement of the body. Being and knowing unfolded in the material world with human body at its center. Architecture, the first mass medium known to humankind was the chosen agency to organize, control, stipulate, and command the space structure of civilizations. Architecture was the construction of reality. Therefore, politics was firmly rooted in the architecture of the material space. *Architecture was the central realm of communion and communication.* Architecture was conceptually "timeless." Public buildings were built to last forever —for eternity, if you will.

2MPH-1000MPH (1400 AD to present): Textual Space

Not until the advent of printed text did the grip of somatic space loosen on the human civilizations. As Victor Hugo exclaimed, word killed stone. Knowledge could now move by itself through the virtual medium of printed text with the human messenger being only an infrastructural carrier—relegated to a marginal status. Knowledge was, for the first time in human history, liberated from being "embodied" in architecture and human body. Soon, societal institutions began finding legitimacy in printed text, the 'document'. Consequently, architecture was stripped of its central political and cultural role and pushed aside. However, architecture was still a place to "commune" while communication was relegated to print medium.

186,000MPH (1900 AD to present): Broadcast Space

The next wave of virtual media—radio, telephone, telegraph, cinema, photography, and television—transformed the composition and ethos of how societies built themselves. While text was still rooted in the physicality of paper, with the electronic media one did not have to move a thing in order to communicate. While print media undercut the epistemological contiguity of the built world, *electronic media undercut the ontological contiguity of experience and context*. Political debates and propaganda could "take place" and reach millions of people without moving a thing — all happening in simultaneous time. As Marshall McLuhan noted, there would have been no Hitler without radio. While books could be banned and locked up in buildings, electromagnetic waves could not be. Walls, windows, and doors of traditional architecture lost their meaning as knowledge and communication could not be organized, controlled, or prohibited through conventional architectural means. The traditional notions of wall, enclosure, perspective, horizon, etc., which were based upon somatic space, became meaningless in the light of televisionic space. Solar day held little meaning in the televisionic day, which came to structure new rhythms of the cities in technological societies. Architecture was further marginalized. Hence, architects had to ask such a seemingly basic question as "what does a brick want to be" ten thousand years after we first built with a brick. This turn to legitimacy in the use and truth of material was symptomatic of the *im*materialization of architecture, as we have known it so far.

186,000MPH (1946 AD to present): Cyberspacetime

Cyberspace and virtuality are two of the many notions popularized by the advent of general-purpose computers. No other medium has received so much hype and attention (with an obsessive fascination for William Gibson's portrayal of cyberspace) albeit some of it is well needed. Unlike the previous media, electronic or not, we now have a medium and technological environment that holds the prospect of rivaling human intelligence or at least a few aspects of it. The new medium is truly cybernetic and digital with its interactivity. In my explorations to follow, I will stay away from Gibsonian narratives of cyberspace.

2 The Messages of the new Medium-environment

...the "message" of any medium or technology is the change of scale or pace or pattern that it introduces into human affairs. (McLuhan 1964)

Let us now discuss a number of significant characteristics of the new medium-environment by tracing various symptomatic techno-cultural trends.

Figure 1. U.S. Army Photo A51244. Bell Relay Computer, *showing racks in which the computing, storing and controlling relays are mounted.*

2.1 Trend #1: Miniaturization: Honey, I Shrunk the World!
Now all you need to do is create a vacuum in a rectilinear tube so as to allow one ray of light to pass through. No more roads to be laid, no more surfaces to be leveled. Now one produces vacuum out of volume. (Virilio 1991)

Cyberspace is non-spatial. The suffix *space* in the word *cyberspace* is a misnomer and a metaphor at best. In sharp contrast to the material space of the pre-print civilizations, space is now a simulation, a representation, and a metaphor for our bodily experience of four-dimensional space. The logic of cyberspace is non-spatial in its propagation, generation, manifestation, and production. What then is

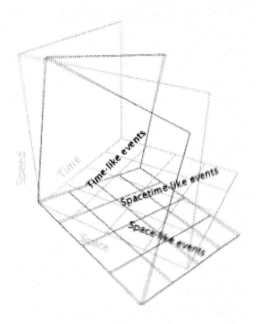

Figure 2. Lorentz transformations

the true logic of cyberspace? The true logic of cyberspace is in its reliance on time. 600MHZ, 10MB/Sec, 56K BAUD, real-time (1/10th of a second), nanosecond, refresh-rate ... do you hear anything related to space in this list? The measure of cyberspace is time— the digital, technological time of the pulsating electrons. An email sent to you is measured in terms of size and time taken to reach you, but not in terms of the space that it traveled to reach you. Interestingly, printed media and electronic analogous media both contain within them traces of space they travel. A letter from your friend in Finland will contain the traces of its trajectory. A radio reception fades away as you move away from the transmitter. However, with digital environment, space and distance bear no effect on its content. Here, it would be apt to recall Marshall McLuhan's discussion about light bulb as a medium. He shows how its content and message are inseparable. He says "the electric light is pure information . . . For electric light and power are separate from their uses, yet they eliminate time and space factors in human association exactly as do radio, telegraph, telephone, and TV creating involvement in depth." (McLuhan 1964, pp. 23-25).

Miniaturization, which is at the heart of de-spatialization of our world is, according to Daniel Bell, one of the major transformative trends of technological development (Bell, 1973). In 1946, world's first general-purpose computer, ENIAC (Electronic Numeric Integrator and Computer) was unveiled in Philadelphia. It occupied a room of nearly 23,000 square feet. It consisted of 18,000 vacuum tubes, 70,000 resistors, and 10,000 capacitors, arranged in 40 panels in an 80-foot "U." It weighed about 30 tons. It performed 5,000 additions in one second or 2.50 multiplications in one second. Given below is an original lay out of the various machinic components.

In 1996, all the original capabilities of "ENIAC" were built on a microchip of size 7.44 by 5.29.mm (0.004237 square feet) using a 0.5 micrometer CMOS technology: a 5,429,138 fold shrinkage in space!

Figure 3. ENIAC at University of Pennsylvania. 1945 AD. U.S. Army Photo.

First, architecture was robbed of its communicational significance by printed word. This was followed by the electronic media stripping architecture of its material significance and communal role. Till the advent of microchips, architecture was at least performing an infrastructural role, which was very different compared to the politically central role it played in antiquity. Finally, the slaughter of architecture — the most conservative profession by any account — is complete with the arrival of the computer-mediated and networked virtual worlds. Architecture has paid its price for its inflexibility of methods, materials, techniques, and boundaries by being robbed of its fundamental roles. All the powerful technological nations have moved into a time-centered system of economy and politics. The world has migrated from geopolitics to chronopolitics. What is left behind? Architecture, definitely.

Paul Virilio comments:

A strange topology is hidden in the obviousness of televised images. Architectural plans are displaced by the sequence plans of an invisible montage Where geographical space once was arranged according to the geometry of an apparatus of rural or urban boundary setting, time is now organized according to imperceptible fragmentations of the technical time space, in which the cutting, as of a momentary interruption, replaces the lasting disappearance, the "program guide" replaces the chain link fence, just as the railroads' timetables once replaced the almanacs. (Virilio 1991)

He goes on to observe that "The new produced and projected space has less to do with lines, surfaces and volumes than with the minutiae of view-point, the dynamite of tenths-of-seconds. These viewpoints are simultaneously time-points in the tele-topological continuum of long-distance projection and reception." (Virilio 1991)

Going back to Minkowski's notion of interconnectedness of time, space and speed, we could conclude that the human quest for speed, the quest to conquer space, the quest to save time, translate to the end of space or at least the end of its centrality. Speed, pursued through the internal combustion engine (the automobile) had transformed the structure of our cities. Automobile-centered city development had led to movement-based (infra)structure of the cities. Speed pursued through instantaneous communication of electronic and digital media is now leading us to a total subversion of four dimensional space-time into fractured and discontinuous melange of artificial horizons, perspectives, juxtapositions, connections, light and knowledge flowing through non-spatial infrastructure. The quasi-optics of electronic remote projection have eliminated such a spatial requirement in its entirety.

The metaphysical transformation initiated by non-spatial technologies, simply put, is that speed transforms space into time. Alternatively, we could say that acceleration transforms space-like events to time-like events. All the powerful institutions of socio-political transformation have now moved into the non-spatial and non-material domains. Less than 2% of the US economy is paper-based; the rest is electronic and digital. Where money is, is where action is. As architects, we certainly know that there is no money in architecture. That is simply a consequence of having no money in space-based ventures. Virilio exclaims how the last bastions of space have been taken away from architects: "So it makes perfect sense that when we discuss space technologies today, we are not referring to architecture but rather to the engineering that launches us into outer space." (Virilio 1991)

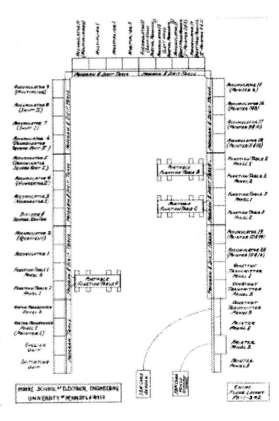

Figure 4. U.S. Army drawing. A layout sketch of ENIAC. 1945 AD.

There is really no use grieving over the marginalization of architecture. However, we must be aware of, if not understand, the shifts and inversions in the today's technology-dominated world.

2.2 Trend #2: Ubiquity: Being Everywhere and Being Nowhere

With acceleration there is no more here and there, only the mental confusion of near and far, present and future, real and unreal—a mix of history, stories and the hallucinatory utopia of communication technologies. (Virilio 1995, p.35)

Another bastion of spatial primacy is being breached through technology's pursuit of ubiquity. To be everywhere negates the spatial notion of being here or there. Being everywhere also negates the notion of center and periphery. Whole world becomes a homogeneous field of unvarying value. Marshall McLuhan noticed this phenomenon already a few decades ago: "Electric speeds create centers everywhere. Margins cease to exist on the planet." (McLuhan, 1964) Architecture has traditionally worked with configuring body's position in space in relation to another body or activity. This configuration created the notions of here, there, orientation, direction, juxtaposition, adjacency, distance etc. These notions are now being replaced with the arrival of ubiquity. You carry your cell phone and your computer around, as one advertisement of a dot-com company makes it amply clear, the place, and orientation of your body and its relationship to the built world simply does not "matter" anymore. The advertisement by mySAP.com shows how easy, quick, and advantageous it is to book your tickets "on line" irrespective of your physical position as opposed to standing "in the line" in an airport terminal. That advertisement at once avouches the death of architecture, at least as we had known it till yesterday.

2.3 Trend # 3: Communing in Time: Real-time, simultaneity, and instantaneity

For telecommunications, coming together in time means, inversely, distancing oneself in space . . . it is as if telecommunication's 'populating of time'—such as vacations, interruptions, and so forth suddenly replaced all the ancient cohabitations, the populating of space, the actual urban proximity. (Virilio 1991)

Real-time is defined as the simultaneity of events occurring within $1/10^{th}$ of a second. In a large auditorium, it may take up to $1/3^{rd}$ of a second for you to hear a speaker if you are seated at the other end of the room. In the meantime, its broadcast or cybercast would have already reached a person thousands of miles away! If one of the fundamental laws of space dictates that no two objects can occupy the same place at the same time, it meant that no two people could experience exactly the same event. However, that phenomenon is circumvented through electronic broadcasts where millions of people could occupy the "same seat" in the auditorium and experience the same image and sound even when they are thousands of miles apart! The existence of electronic real-time necessarily precludes possibility of material space. The mantra of real estate industry used to be "location, location, location." The new slogan for the virtual real estate is "time, time, time."

Theory of Relativity makes it clear that there is time dilation between one frame and another. For example, the faster a clock moves (say, in a space ship), the slower it runs, relative to stationary clocks. Time dilation shows itself when a speeding twin returns to find that his (or her) Earth-bound twin has aged more rapidly. Interestingly, we have been experiencing a time dilation in architecture and culture today. Speed exposes the finest nuances of time to human experience. Each nanosecond expands to become eternity. The impatience of a driver experiencing time dilation at a traffic light, the rush of people speeding to escape the time dilation of the expressway, the impatience of a person in front of a slow computer which takes an extra second to perform a complex calculation are things that each of us have experienced. In architecture, we once used to build for eternity. We now design buildings that are made to last for 10-20 years. For we cannot visualize a future beyond such a time frame anymore.

2.4   Trend #4: The Omega Point: The Formation of Noosphere

Nearly five decades ago, much before the computer became a popular machine, Teilhard deChardin prophetically proclaimed that the human evolution is heading toward a global coalition of an interconnected world. He called such a world "Noosphere" (the sphere of interconnected human beings). He predicted that such a coalition would happen at a point in time called "Omega Point." Not in a too distant future, we can easily envision people being connected with the invisible threads of digital communication where material space will not have much meaning. As of today, there are an estimated 56,000,000 hosts the Internet. The Internet is growing at a rate faster than television, radio, and telephone combined. What does this mean to architecture? It means one of these two possibilities: architecture will remain a space-centered, marginalized and conservative profession; or architecture redefines its boundaries to address the contemporary developments and jumps up to the center stage.

Fluidity is one of the conditions experienced everywhere in this global economy. In economics, one of the problems faced is the fluidity of money and transactions. According to some analysts 98% of US economy is electronic. The condition of fluidity coupled with motion at the speed of light leads to volatile local conditions and intensified global conditions. Fluidity positions any human activity to be handled temporally.

The problem with the education and practice of architecture today is that, in general it ignores or even denies the transformations occurring everywhere in the technologically advanced parts of the world. We revel in the glory of the past because that is all we have left. Or we sell ourselves as a service-oriented industry bending over backwards to respond to the "needs" of the clientele at the expense of larger ethical issues. Recognition of a phenomenon does not automatically mandate an acceptance of a condition. Nevertheless, it does mandate a response. Ignorance and denial or a reliance on past glory is certainly not a very intelligent response.

2.5   Trend # 5: Virtuality: All that is sold literally melts into air

Greg Lynn raised a valid question when he said that "The term virtual has recently been so debased that it often simply refers to the digital space of computer aided design. Virtuality is also a term used to describe the possession of force or power." (Lynn 1999) If by virtuality we mean the force and potential or quality and essence of being without material existence, then we are reminded of Daniel Bell's notion that our economies have begun to do more and more with less and less material agencies (Bell 1973). Economies are becoming increasingly based on mental labor and movement of information, rather than physical labor and the movement of matter. Nicholas Negroponte has made a similar observation when he noted that the world is being increasingly concerned with the movement of bits than the movement of atoms (Negroponte 1995).

However, contrary to a widely-held belief that virtuality is somehow a direct offspring of the computer, we need to recognize that the notion of virtuality, at least as far as architects are concerned, dates back to the day when we as a profession started drawing instead of building. Once again, as Greg Lynn critically noted, "Architecture is the profession concerned with the production of virtual descriptions as opposed to real buildings". We have been designing the buildings virtually. Legally speaking, we do not even "oversee" or supervise the construction process; rather, we "observe" it distantly. Surely, a virtual medium, an intermediate agency to try, visualize and evaluate various conditions "virtually" on paper or through a model or in a computer helps one thing: control over failure. Truly speaking the built work becomes a representation of the virtual drawings than the other way round. The drawings become the master bodies of knowledge from which to build the "result". It now takes less than 9 months for Chrysler to begin a new model car, design it, test it and put it on the assembly line. It used to take them 3 years before the use of the computers.

2.6   Trend #6: Anamnesia: Persistence of (a different kind of) Memory
There is no political power without control of the archive, if not of memory ... in the past, psycho-analysis would not have been what is was (any more than so many other things) if E-mail, for example, had existed . . . electronic mail today, even more than the fax, is on the way to transforming the entire public and private space of humanity, and first of all the limit between the private, the secret (private or public), and the public of the phenomenal. (Derrida 1995)

In his book Archive Fever, Jacques Derrida traces the relationship between technologies of inscription and psychic processes. He argues that with the advent of instantaneity and anamnesis (lack of forgetfulness) the notion of memory undergoes a phenomenal transformation in cyberspace-time. The distinction between memory and live experience is eliminated. In the Derridan analysis of the notion of archive, it becomes clear that archive is a "place" set apart by law and institutionalization of the documents. In the computer world, such a distinction ceases to be.

In the physical world, there are things and then there are files in their file cabinets. In the computer world, there are virtual files in virtual file cabinets, which in turn contain virtual things. In physical world the epistemic is housed in the ontic. In the physical world files are material things. In the computer world, things are virtual files. In the computer-mediated cyberspace-time, everything is an archive and everything is a live experience. Just as architecture once held the privileged role of being the "archive" of the society, just as printed/written word was once held and still being held as the archive, now the stored patterns of zeros and ones have become the archive with one distinction: it is a space-time where everything is remembered and where everything is an archive. *There is no cyberspace-time without memory.* Being, remembering and knowing coalesce into one flow.

Let us look at one instance where memory behaves differently in the material space: In architecture, a monument is rooted in physical space usually through the use of heavy materials and 'monumental' scale. A physical monument gathers spatial events. In cyberspace-time a monument gathers memory by *moving around* and gathering 'time and connection stamps'. The reader maybe familiar with the TWA Flight 800 electronic monument, which is essentially an email message sent around the world gathering the traces of its trajectory. In 'times to come', cyberspace-time will transform the way we think, represent and relate to the notion of memory.

3 Strategies for a Resurrection of Architecture:
[Human being] has been liberated little by little from physical constraints, but he is all the more the slave of abstract ones. He acts through intermediaries and consequently has lost contact with [material] reality . . . Man as worker has lost contact with the primary element of life and environment, the basic material out of which he makes what he makes. He no longer knows wood or iron or wool. He is acquainted only with the machine. His capacity to become a mechanic has replaced his knowledge of his materials. (Ellul 1964)

One might pose the question "does the discussion thus far mean the end of architecture?" Far from and worse than that, architecture is (going to be) alive but, in general, it will continue to lead a life of insignificance. Instead of being the bone or muscle of the society, it is being reduced to the fat of the society and relegated to remain in the societal margins. When the economy is doing well it swells. Otherwise it flinches. The field of architecture is surely at a point of its existential crisis. What then are the strategies that may restore the vitality and centrality to the field of architecture? To begin with, here are a few strategies:

1. Reassert the basic prerogatives of architecture, as discussed below.
2. Redefine and redraw the boundaries of what we call architecture. To embrace virtual worlds on one end and entrepreneurial initiatives on the other maybe a good place to start. This strategy would also entail intensification and expansion of the discourse of architecture. Architecture needs to overcome its reputation of being a conservative profession that used to thrive only on

the strategy of resistance.

3. Architecture, in any event, must become a critical practice as opposed to being a merely technical service provider who produces infrastructure in response to the so-called clients' needs. While most of the societal institutions find their centers of action transferred to virtual worlds, until we can say "Scotty beam me up!" we are bound by the laws and limitations of being embodied in a corporeal body. Toyo Ito calls it the primitive body. Disease, pain, death, pleasure, sexuality, and the primacy of having to interact "face-to-face" (as opposed to "interface-to-interface") in the material world, still govern our existence. Liberation from the constraints of material space and bodily existence does not mean marginalization and neglect. Human body has lost its centrality. Nevertheless it is still the center of existence.

One reason that people turn to architecture is that it mediates how humans dwell (in a Heideggeran sense of dwelling as an ethical prerogative of human beings) in this world. Architecture has the potential to mediate between the tangible and the virtual, between the material and the ethereal. Such mediation definitely invokes a critical role for architecture. Instead of merely "housing" and "accommodating" things and flows, instead of degenerating to a status of infrastructure, architecture could, through a critical response to its "times", provide the much needed connection and mediation between various realms of existence and experience.

Traditionally a majority of the architectural professionals have vociferously maintained the narrow boundaries of architecture as that which is physically built. Evolution often involves a transformation of a species into a whole other kind of species. Perhaps a greater tolerance, if not an enthusiastic promotion of expanding the boundaries of architecture to embrace a number of adjacent territories may lead to a revitalization of the field of architecture.

4 New Critical Directions: Time-like Architecture

The cultural expectation that buildings must be permanent infers that building's physical and symbolic form should persist. Rather than designing for permanence techniques for obsolescence, dismantling, ruination, recycling and abandonment through time can be studied. (Lynn 1999)

A number of architects have directly or indirectly addressed the notion of time-like architecture: Greg Lynn, Peter Eisenman, Toyo Ito, Bernard Tschumi, Rem Koolhaas, Zaha Hadid, Richard Rogers, Neil Denari, Wes Jones et al. have developed work that takes into account the time-like events that dominate our world today. Although it is not possible to go into the details of their works to exemplify the ideas discussed in this essay, a brief survey of some of their ideas might help.

Greg Lynn discusses the role of digital technologies in enabling ways to deal with time-like events in architecture:

The introduction of time and motion techniques into architecture is not simply a visual phenomenon .... Another obvious aesthetic fallout of these spatial models is the predominance of deformation and transformation techniques available in a time based system of flexible topological surfaces. These are not aesthetic choices but technical statements of the structure of the topological medium. (Lynn 1999)

While Lynn stays away from any discussion of the ethical and socio-political issues and repercussions of time-like architecture, his work does open doors to further thought in this direction.

5 Conclusions

In the age of telepresence and networked virtual worlds, the notions of space, time and materiality have undergone dramatic shifts. The metaphysics of Theory of Relativity explicate the interdependence of space, time, and speed in a discontinuous field of forces. Where movement is relatively little, events become "space-like." Where movement takes precedence over stillness, events become "time-like." Speed is the distinguishing factor between these two kinds of event readings. Through various communication and transportation technologies, we have moved far beyond the 2MPH speed of a walking human being to 186,000MPH speed of radio waves. We have moved from populating space to populating time. In the process, architecture has lost most of its social, political, cultural and existential significance. This was partly due to the conservative nature of the profession and its allegiance to "timelessness" and static tectonics even in the age of Noosphere.

The latest information technologies possess dramatic new potential. They allow ubiquity, simultaneity, instantaneity, virtuality, remote-interactivity and capable of real-time computation. These phenomena are anti-spatial and pro-temporal in nature. Thus, architecture is faced with the most daunting prospects of all time, contrary to the proclamations of some cyberspace proponents.

New technologies raise new ethical questions and open up new possibilities. Architecture needs to address the time-like environment in which it finds itself today. The tasks for architecture and design computing are many. Architecture could mediate between the tangible and the intangible, between the material and the virtual, and between space and time. Architecture could become the point of contact of the realms that are worlds apart. To reduce the universe to a grain of sand, to hold infinity in the palm of your hand, and to experience eternity in an hour may not be quite an appropriate architectural strategy, although it may be a sound technocratic vision. If, as Heidegger proclaimed, dwelling is the primary ethical imperative of human beings, then architecture needs to be brought into the world with a critical mission of connecting, re-spatializing and temporalizing a world that is fast disintegrating into bits of sand.

References:

Bell, Daniel. (1973). *The Coming of Post-Industrial Society*. New York: Basic books, Inc., Publishers

Benedikt, Michael. (1991). *Cyberspace: First Steps*. Cambridge, Massachusetts: MIT Press.

Born, Max. (1962). *Einstein's Theory of Relativity*. New York: Dover Publications, Inc.

Casey, Edgar (1995). *Fate of Place: A Philosophical History*. University of California Press.

Derrida, Jacques. (1996). *Archive Fever*. Chicago: University of Chicago Press.

Ellul, Jacques. (1964). *The Technological Society*. New York: Vintage Books.

Giedion, Sigfried. (1971). *Space, Time and Architecture*. Cambridge, Massachusetts: Harvard University Press.

Hays, K. Michael. (1998) ed. *Architecture Theory Since 1968*. Cambridge, Massachusetts: MIT Press.

Lefebvre, Henri. (1995). *The Production of Space*. Cambridge: Blackwell Publishers.

Lynn, Greg. (1999). *Animate Form*. New York: Princeton Architectural Press.

McLuhan, Marshall. (1964). *Understanding Media: The Extensions of Man*. New York: The Signet Book.

Peterson, Steven. (1980) *Space and Anti-Space*. Cambridge, Massachussets: Harvard Architectural Review number 01.

Virilio, Paul. (1991). *Lost Dimension*. New York: Semiotext(e).

Virilio, Paul. (1995). *The Art of the Motor*. Minneapolis: University of Minnesota Press.

Collaboration

Computer-Aided Design is often restricted in people's minds to graphics, particularly vector graphics. Some commenters constrain CAD even further to merely drafting or construction documentation. However, ACADIA has long embraced a much broader view of the CAD in its name. Computer-Aided Design is any use of computers, or devices that contain microprocessors, by architects or in the pursuit of creating architecture.

The convergence of computing with telecommunications has legitimized what has long been an area of research among ACADIA members. Digital telecommunications as a design collaboration medium is the subject of the papers in this section.

Johnson describes experiments that attempt to strengthen "tele-presence" or the sense of being present while interacting with someone else using he Internet. He demonstrates that additional features in communications software can allow participants to monitor each other and engage in low-grade communication that may build familiarity and fill in the blanks of a relationship beyond direct conversation.

New hardware and software that can extend telecommunications to collaborative interaction in a virtual space is presented in the article by Lonsway. The discussion pushes the boundaries of existing tools to envision a medium that exploits very broad bandwidth communication to make being here or being there irrelevant to the discussion.

A more prosaic application nevertheless is equaling tantalizing. Peri presents a design studio exercise in which students build a virtual city, interacting together with the Web, databases and VRML to address the universal challenges of urban design.

In these papers, there is much to emulate for not only educators, but also software developers and those who are charged with inventing technologies.

Between Friends: Support of Workgroup Communications

Brian R. Johnson, Design Machine Group, University of Washington, USA

Abstract

The web offers both business and academic users potential benefits from on-line collaboration. On-line education presents universities with a means of handling the "baby boom echo" without expanding physical campuses (Carnevale 2000). Business "extranets" allow greater coordination amongst team members on projects where the cast of players involves experts in different locations. Both involve substituting computer-mediated communications (CMC) for traditionally face-to-face communications.

Over the past several years, the author has deployed several of the available CMC technologies in support of small group interaction in academic and administrative settings. These technologies include email, video conferencing, web publication, web bulletin boards, web databases, mailing lists, and hybrid web BBS/email combinations.

This paper reflects on aspects of embodied human interaction and the affordances of current CMC technology, identifying opportunities for both exploitation and additional development. One important but under-supported aspect of work group behavior is workspace awareness, or peripheral monitoring. The *Compadres* web-based system, which was developed to support workspace awareness among distributed workgroup members, is described.

These findings are relevant to those seeking to create online communities: virtual design studios, community groups, distributed governance organizations, and workgroups formed as parts of virtual offices.

1 Introduction

1.1 A Workgroup Scenario

Members of a design team are at work in their downtown office space. Mary is editing the draft specifications for the latest project using her computer, looking up information in a reference text. John enters and begins working at his desk. Sam enters, moves to John's desk and begins talking. Mary overhears the word "entry" as they speak, at which she approaches John's desk.

Earlier, before John came in, she had looked at the floor plan on his drawing board and was curious about his handling of the entry. Sam turns slightly to include Mary in the conversation as she approaches. John glances up and smiles. The three discuss the entry for some time.

Finally, Mary says, "Ok. We'll do it that way. Now, a while back you said ..." and the conversation veers onto a new topic. Eventually the three decide to go to lunch together. Mary returns to her desk, scribbles "Back at 2" on a Post-It, and sticks it to the front of her monitor. The three go to a nearby pub where they continue the conversation, but at a much higher volume because of the background noise.

1.2 Deconstructing the Scenario

The scenario describes a minor but common type of interaction within an office or design studio work-group. Members, working in proximity to each other, are passively aware, through audio and visual cues, of changes in the workspace without explicit communication attempts. In response to information gathered from this sense of place, they may initiate active communications. They utilize a complex repertoire of task and interpersonal communications skills involving privacy, social distance, topic threading, and body language, skills that are context sensitive.

Can these behaviors be found in a computer-mediated communications (CMC) situation such as a distributed work group, distance education situation, or virtual design studio? Are they supported by the tools available, or hindered?

It is a common observation that distributed workgroups (indeed, all workgroups?) perform better when pre-bonded through face-to-face (f2f) interaction prior to beginning their task. It takes time to associate a "voice" with the way in which an individual writes their email.

What are the fundamental ingredients of this scenario and how are or can they be managed in a computer mediated interaction?

2 Background

It is important to review the common terminology used when discussing interpersonal and group communications in order to fully understand the following discussion. Much of this terminology predates the emergence of CMC, so some nuances relevant to the current discussion are also identified.

An **individual**, a single human being, may join with a knowable set of other individuals to form a **group** (Bass 1974). At any given time an individual may be a member of several groups. Similarly, the membership of a specific group changes from time to time. If they share a common task we might call it a **workgroup**. In order to satisfy the common interest or accomplish the task, they need to communicate with each other.

Interpersonal communication is often described in terms of the "conduit metaphor" (Bogen 1999). When an individual wishes to communicate, they produce an **utterance**. While utterances may take one or more of several forms—verbal, textual, body language, or graphical—this paper will refer to all utterances as *speaking*. If another individual responds to the utterance with an utterance of their own, which the first speaker understands as being related to their utterance, a **conversation** can be said to take place. Face to face conversations follow fairly complex rules or **protocols** for **turn taking,** backtracking and **repair** of the conversational thread (Knapp 1978). It is also possible that more than one **topic thread,** or sequence of related utterances, will be pursued during a single conversation.

The form and content of an utterance on the Internet is influenced by the temporal character of the communication. Face to face communication, with topically focused conversation, provides the model for **synchronous** (at the same time) communication. Written correspondence, with it's greater reliance on formality and context setting, provides the **asynchronous** (at different times) model. The final category found in the scenario above is the expository, or **achronic** (outside time) mode. Books, speeches, and web sites that include no mechanism for engaging the author in conversation, fall into this category.

The form and content of an utterance is also influenced by an awareness of the **social context** of the utterance (Barnlund 1973). This term is used here to refer to the character of the audience who will hear the utterance, ranging from *personal* (shared only with self), to *friend* (shared with one), to *group* (shared with a finite, knowable several), to *public* (shared with an unknowable, possibly infinite multitude).

The social context of an utterance is partly informed by the form and content of the utterance (shouts in a library are almost always of public scope) and partly informed by **workspace awareness,** an awareness of the presence and activities of others (Dourish, 1999; McGrath and Munro 1999), drawn from a mixture of direct observation and environmental cues (after closing, a pair of janitors might well shout to one another in a library while carrying on a personal conversation).

Workspace awareness, what Goffman calls "unfocused interaction" (Goffman 1963), is the mechanism through which individuals maintain an understanding of their surroundings, often without explicit thought. By monitoring disturbances caused by persons in our local environment, such as voices, shuffling feet, chair squeaks, keyboard and mouse clicks, and so on, we maintain a map of who is near us. Coupled with other considerations, the workspace awareness allows us to shift our active attention to events of importance, such as the arrival of a particular colleague, flirtation partner, etc.

Workspace awareness includes a variably detailed sense of the activities of others in the group. This may be gathered from knowledge of formal group responsibilities, and by overheard conversations (eavesdropping), desktop overview (looking at documents left open on a colleague's desktop), circulation of draft documents, meeting reports, etc.

The importance assigned to eavesdropping in the educational setting can be seen in policies such as that used in the first design studio course at University of Washington. Personal sound systems, even with headphones, are not permitted during studio hours and students are encouraged to listen-in on the desk crits of their peers, and even join in if appropriate (Ching et al. 1999).

Significant effort has been invested in research concerning face-to-face interaction, interpersonal communication in groups, and so on. Research into CMC social organizations, communications, and social mores is more limited and has tended to focus on casual associations such as those found in MUDs (multi-user dungeons) (Turkle 1995). Recent research in the field of Computer Supported Co-operative Work (CSCW) has demonstrated the value of workspace awareness in terms of enhanced task performance and worker attitude (Gutwin and Greenberg 1999).

Individuals do not always speak out the moment they establish a need to communicate. They may **queue** the utterance for a time when the social context better matches the content ("I'll tell you when we get home") or the form ("I wanted to tell you face to face."). They may also queue it for **refinement**, wishing to make the utterance more communicative in some way. Examples of refinement include polishing a poem for a heartthrob or a paper for publication.

2.1   The Scenario Reconsidered

Mary is working in semi-privacy, available to her group but not to the larger public. The document she is working on (the specifications) is private to her work-area at the moment and undergoing change, though she will accept and seek input from others within the workgroup. When the scene opens she is utilizing a reference document, which is assumed to change infrequently. She is able to observe the work on John's desk without violating social norms, though it remains a "read only" document, and she is able to passively monitor the conversation between John and Sam. That conversation is being conducted within the group's social context, though there are only two group members participating initially. Mary deduces this from the subject, and conversational volume. She approaches. Their awareness of her proximity, and their acceptance is signaled by their body language. The three participants continue on the same topic thread, and then backtrack to an earlier branch at Mary's request. The work task is suspended while they discuss lunch. When the lunch decision is made, Mary takes a moment to post a note in case someone comes looking for her at her desk (a group-context and group-maintenance communication). When the three arrive at the public domain of the pub, they find that they must employ much louder voices in order to carry on their conversation, but though they are almost shouting, they can still be said to be carrying on a group-scope discussion due to the background noise levels of the pub and the minimal likelihood of an eavesdropper caring about their subject.

There are several benefits that Mary's workspace awareness is able to provide. Mary is able to monitor the group's presence while working, probably without looking up from her work. By lightly eavesdropping on the conversation between John and Sam, she is able to identify an appropriate time in which to engage both of them in a discussion of a topic relevant to her task. Without workspace awareness she would have to invest more time in active monitoring (perhaps calling John and Sam every 10 minutes or so in order to set up a meeting), postpone or forego the desired communication (possibly requiring a more extensive rewrite later), or implement it through an alternative strategy (perhaps a "call me" Post-It on John's drawing).

3 Mapping CMC Tools to the Scenario

Computer Mediated Communication (CMC) technologies are many and varied and actually include many overlapping paradigms. Those shown in Table 1 have been organized according to the primary temporal domain and social scope within which their use makes sense. The table includes contact managers, calendars, electronic mail, web pages, videoconferences, chat rooms, bulletin boards, and web cams. Some (e.g., email and video conferencing) primarily support point to point communications linking two individuals, while others (e.g., chat rooms) support small groups, and some (web pages) are essentially public broadcast mechanisms rather than two-way communications.

These technologies are designed to enhance communication between individuals, where communication is the primary goal. Information access and data sharing while running programs where the primary goal is data editing, such as CAD and word processing, are other important areas of workgroup function. However, network file systems, ftp servers and clients, and http file uploads, are not addressed in this paper.

4 CMC Technologies and Small Groups

Table 1 categorizes technologies according to the social context and temporal conditions in which they are deployed. Clearly there are tools available for practically any combination of social context and interaction condition. Unfortunately, the number of separate applications and interfaces, as well as the weak penetration of standards in some areas, means that few users move fluidly among these many applications, or keep applications open against the modest chance that a colleague or co-worker will need to make a connection. Instead, one mode of communication, often email, is used to orchestrate use of the others. That is, users derive their workspace awareness from their inbox.

	Social Context			
	Self, 1:0	Friend, 1:1	Group, 1:N	Public: 1:infinity
Achronous	Local file system	Sent-mail archives	Archives (email and Web BBS)	Web publications
Asynchronous	Calendars, to-do lists	Email	Email list Web BBS	Web BBs
Synchronous	Contact management, bookmarks, text editors	Email, chat, videoconference, whiteboard	Chat, whiteboard, Web BBS	WebCam

Table 1. CMC Tools Mapped to Temporal Domain and Social Context

The hypothesis, which this paper presents, is that one of the important requirements as yet unaddressed by the tools available in workgroup CMC is passive workspace awareness. In preparation for describing the prototype system developed to test this theory, let us consider some of the existing tools in terms of the workgroup communications issues discussed above.

4.1 Chat and Email

Face to face communications, by their very nature, involve participants in a synchronous process. When a CMC system is inserted into a communication situation the technology may require perceptible time to pass utterances between the participants. In spite of this, if all parties to an exchange are willing to maintain focus on the exchange for its duration, we may still call it synchronous, or *conversational* communications.

Communications that involve an appreciable delay between individual utterances, such that attention wanders or is directed elsewhere while waiting for the response, fall into the category of asynchronous exchange, or *correspondence*. This category includes both traditional letter writing and email. In such situations the topic thread is more readily lost, so email users frequently include copies of the mail to which they are replying.

Achronic, or *expository* communications are one-sided utterances not intended to be part of a conversation, such as books, static web pages, and archival data. As such, issues of response time, awareness, and so on are of much less importance, though the information accessed might still be important.

While physical reality is truly synchronous, few CMC systems are. Chat systems usually distribute your utterances only *after* you hit the enter key. We characterize such systems as synchronous in part because participants generally must be connected at the same time in order to follow the conversation. By that measure, two people on a fast network connection can carry out a fairly synchronous conversation via standard email software and careful turn taking. On the other hand, email becomes completely chaotic as a means of synchronous exchange for a group of people because there is no good turn-taking protocol and conversational continuity (threading) breaks down because separate simultaneous replies to a single email cannot be readily quoted in a subsequent reply, and the vagaries of email distribution sometimes deliver a reply before the mail that sparked it.

This had led the author and others to the conclusion that discussions carried out via email, must be expected to operate on *slow time* (Tu 2000). That is, you must allocate extra clock time in order to conduct the same discussion, even when participants are actively engaged.

4.2 Web Bulletin Boards

The author, and others, have deployed bulletin board systems in support of various projects, often to find them wholly or largely ignored by the intended beneficiaries. One reason for this is that it is almost impossible to passively monitor a "conversation" on a web board. Users must actively call up the relevant URLs in order to detect activity. On a low-volume board, this will not often be rewarding. Further, because of the perceived permanence of web BBS utterances, and confusion or ambiguity regarding the social context of the board, utterances are often queued for refinement, and finally abandoned.

Hybrid systems, employing a web bulletin board to maintain the conversational thread(s) and email to distribute new utterances (postings), has remedied some of these problems. Required utilization of the system can break down barriers relative to social context and permanence through familiarity.

4.3 CMC Dangers

Some writers are generally concerned about 'disembodied' communications technologies (Lakaff 1995). Certainly, when we employ voice, body language and written words to communicate with our self or with others, we select communication content and adjust the form depending on who is "in range" of the communication. That is, we tag content according to its appropriate social context and are constantly aware of the anticipated *social context* of the communication, and favor certain forms over others.

When we employ CMC the communication process is divided into stages, creation of the communication message (or "utterance"), and reception. We continue to use a model of the social context, based on our understanding of the intervening technology, but the technology often introduces opportunities for a mismatch to arise between the anticipated and realized scope.

Our understanding of the CMC technology influences the content and form of the utterance. For example, we may be quite comfortable with the use of a video camera to record a family gathering in our home for viewing by a distant family member, but be revolted at the idea of someone mounting a web cam in his or her home. While a camera is present in both cases, the social context of the utterance is entirely different.

Changes in the context, form or content of an utterance can have a large impact on its meaning. While we might object to having our activities filmed by an unknown videographer, actors and actresses perform for the camera with the intention of public viewing. Elevated environmental noise causes us to raise our voices, even when conducting a "whispered" conversation. It is embarrassing when the noise level drops suddenly and the "private" utterance becomes public. Most email users have witnessed, if not experienced, the difference between "reply-all" and "reply" when participating on an email list.

In addition, while we may sit in privacy to compose and read our email, we recognize that it has a different legal status than handwritten correspondence and that it may reside in someone else's email system for years, subject to accidental or malicious disclosure.

For these reasons even individuals with access to CMC often conduct sensitive communications via telephone, or face-to-face, where the chance of a surprise change in social context is unlikely (though not impossible, as Monica Lewinski discovered after talking to Linda Tripp!).

4.4 *Web cams, Anonymity, and Voyeurism*

Email and chat, those CMC systems that most directly support group communications, both provide some persistent sense of presence. Email systems display not only the name of the message source, but also who else received it. MUDs and chat systems often require users to log in, registering their screen name, and displaying a list of those "present" for all participants to use. Web BBS systems often permit the user to attach any name they wish to a posting. This has lead to rampant identity experimentation, and study of the same (Turkle 1995).

Physical environments offer fewer opportunities to masquerade, and fewer opportunities to present illusory personae. The lack of persistent, verifiable identity, while certainly a problem in public environments, should not be a challenge in workgroup environments, where access can be controlled and identity verified reasonably carefully.

Technologies that offer their users no workspace awareness can actively interfere with their use. I have an occasional web cam mounted on my monitor, a window at my side, and a glass panel in my office door. Each offers the potential for public intrusion into my office, but because it is impossible to tell when the web cam is being monitored, and by whom, that technology is the most uncertain. Even if I become aware of an observer, the medium lacks the symmetry of the glass door, where I can look out and see who is looking in.

5 The Compadres Workgroup System

As indicated in the "Group" column of Table 1, there is support available for basic asynchronous communication through mailing list software, and support for synchronous communications through chat applications. However, neither of these supports such aspects of workspace awareness as passive display/review, or peripheral monitoring of group "lurkers" (group members who are present, but not communicating). Neither do they present a single interface for both asynchronous and synchronous communications.

Obviously, none of the widely available CMC tools are truly passive. After all, they are programs that you run when you want to communicate! The most passive component of computing *per se* is probably the operating system, but few of us have access to developing applications at this level. The next most common application, and one which includes significant communications capabilities, might well be the web browser.

The **Compadres** workgroup system, illustrated in Figure 1, was developed to address the need for a shared group workspace, with individually customizable personal work areas, or desktops. These features provide a passive presence monitor, opportunity to display and review work-in-progress, and a unified interface to a variety of traditional CMC tools. Individuals, called *compadres* join a workgroup, or *cadre,* of co-workers.

Built on http tools, the Compadres console takes up minimal screen space, but provides both a group presence monitor and individually customizable personal data pages through which users may observe and communicate.

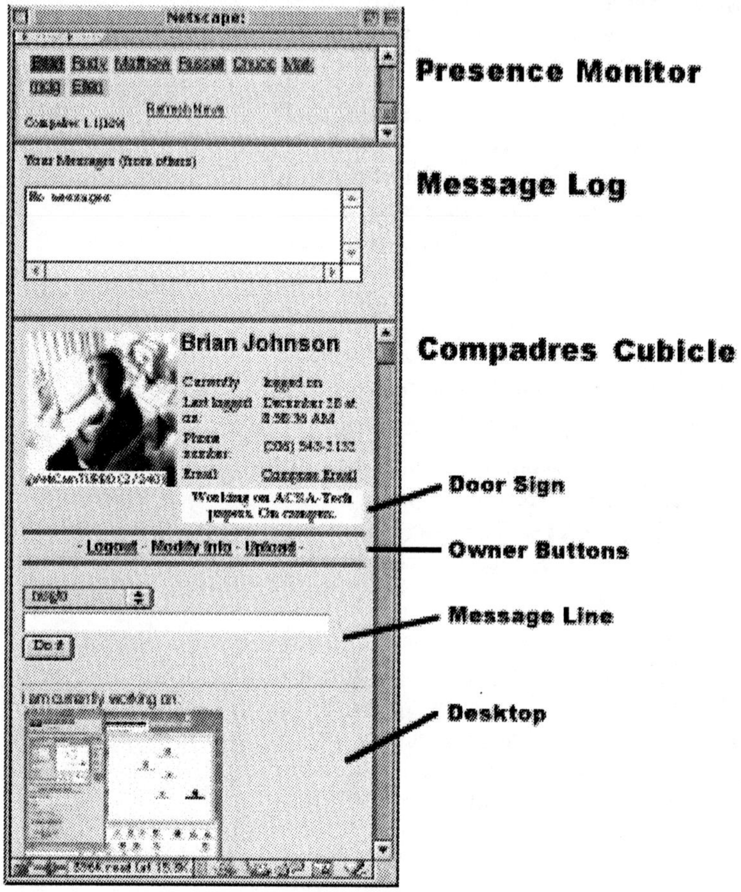

Figure 1. The Compadres workgroup console, showing the presence monitor (top) and a member's cubicle (bottom).

5.1 Presence Monitor: Cadre Membership and Connection Status Buttons

After a compadre (user) logs on, the console is displayed. It consists of three frames. The top frame of the console provides the workspace monitor for their cadre (group). It presents the names of each member of the cadre, with colored backgrounds indicating whether they are connected or not (red for no, green for yes). This frame is automatically refreshed at regular intervals using an HTML META refresh tag, so the user need take no action to become aware of a co-worker's "arrival".

5.2 Message Log and Communications Console

The middle frame of the console displays messages, provides access to the group level communications, and owner (personal) actions such as desktop modification, a file upload option, and logging out.

5.3 Compadres Cubicles: Personal Data Pages

Each user has a personal data page, or cubicle. These are displayed in the bottom frame of the console when the user clicks on the related name button in the presence monitor. The cubicle displays certain standard information, and provides the owner with options for the display of other information. It is also the channel through which others in the work group contact the individual.

Fixed data includes: time and date of last log-on, and a one-line messaging form for jotting quick notes to the owner. Variable data can only be modified by the page owner. Fields include an HTML <IMG> link to a personal graphic (usually a portrait), editable first and last name fields (separate from the permanent logon ID/PW), phone number, and email address. An easily modified "Door

Sign" provides the equivalent of Mary's quick Post-It note. Finally, an <IMG> link, coupled to an HREF link, provides a means of passive overview, by linking the visitor to the owner's most recent work.

The "Message Line" is not meant to replace email, chat, or face-to-face communications (when available), but it does provide a quick, means of asking simple questions, arranging for face-to-face discussion, etc. Messages to the individual are queued in the Compadres database until the next time their presence monitor is updated (which might be only a matter of seconds). At that time the message is embedded in a JavaScript ALERT and included in the cadre monitor page. This brings it to the active attention of the user, even if the browser window has been buried by other application windows.

6 Implementation

Compadres is currently implemented as an Applescript Common Gateway Interface (CGI) application running on a Macintosh web server with a FileMaker Pro database for compadres and cadre data.

6.1 Database Schema

Figure 2 shows the Compadres database schema in a schematic form and illustrates the connection between the cadre and compadres data. A database calculation field collects the individual "logged-in/logged-out" status button fields, which are calculated from the status field, and passes a complete HTML table to the CGI with just a single database access. By caching this table between changes in the numbers of connected users, the CGI makes updating the presence monitor a relatively quick process.

Access to the system is gained through a standard HTML form, with the username and password data being submitted to the Compadres CGI for verification. During login, the Compadres CGI sets the user's status in the database as well as recording the user's IP number and starting a countdown timer in a run-time database.

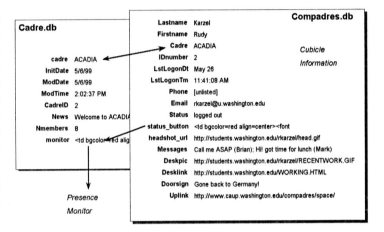

Figure 2. The Compadres database schema.

System functions, including the presence monitor, happen through varying invocations of the CGI. Each query is tested to make sure it originates from a known (trusted) IP number, giving the cadre it's privacy, and refresh queries from trusted IP numbers renew the user's countdown timer in the CGI's database. If the timer expires, the CGI automatically logs them out. Thus, while not immediate, closing the console window is equivalent to logging out.

6.2 The use of Live Feeds

Two interesting pieces of supplemental software, WebCamToo and WebCamTurbo, are currently available for the Macintosh platform and offer some particular insights into how a more mature version of this system may operate (Paperjet 2000). Both are HTTP servers in their own rights. Both stream images. One uses a camera such as the Logitech QuickCam as the data source. The other uses the computer's screen buffer as the source, streaming a full or reduced-size image of the host computer's desktop (including open application windows, etc.).

By running these applications in the background on a Compadre's desktop computer, and properly adjusting the "portrait" and "desktop" URLs in the Compadres database, other members of the workgroup can literally monitor, in real time, the activities of the group member running the software, both by looking *at* their screen and by (in a sense) looking *from* their screen. The existence and use of such tools radically transforms the nature of your "personal" computer. Fortunately, in the interest of privacy, it is possible to adjust the size of the streamed image, so that a somewhat abstract representation is broadcast. Still additional controls and feedback mechanisms are desirable (knowing who is watching, etc.)

7 Discussion of Results

7.1 User Feedback

Compadres has been used experimentally as part of two traditional courses in web content development. Students were encouraged to use the system, but were not required to, and had ready access to face-to-face communications as a fallback. After using the system for a few days, they were asked to provide feedback. Table 2 shows some of the comments received.

Informal verbal suggestions for improvement included a more chat-like messaging service, and multiple-recipient messaging options. While some of these would require a different (non http) support base, others represent fairly minor modifications and are being explored for the next generation.

7.2 Opportunities for further development

Within the Compadres system, further development is focusing on enhancing message management, group message broadcasts, logging of messages, and configurable forwarding of messages via email. We are also looking at the use of non-screen cues (sound, environmental lighting, etc) as a means of presenting the presence data.

Provision of personal workspaces is probably not necessary. The degree of privacy and separation of work that is provided by the typical personal computer file system seems adequate. As with individual communications mechanisms, the development of shared group workspace's, with managed circulation of files, so you know who has which file, would be a vast improvement over sharing of networked virtual disks, shared ftp server access, and so on. Existing tools, such as source-code management systems may be suitable for this task.

Student #1	"Works as well as any other instant messaging service." "A great feature is having the person's picture and bio on the page" "It would have been nice to have a place to archive messages, " "I [found] it annoying that any messages that [were] sent to you offline pop up instantly as you log in"
Student #2	"I think compadres works very well "
Student #3	"compadres ... is a wonderfull communication tool. I believe the two things i most appreciated were including the picture of the person you are talking to and the 'connected/disconnected' green buttons." "You could enable a 'history of messages received'"

Table 2. Comments from student users of Compadres.

It would be interesting to explore the potential of interfaces in which increasing social proximity was explicitly displayed, monitored, and possibly rebuffed and where it might be possible to monitor the form, but not the content of a workgroup communication (e.g., where a user might detect that Mary is talking to John, but not what they are saying unless invited to join the conversation). Similarly automated eavesdropping through interest matching or communications monitoring ("Who is working on the entry?" or "Mary is talking to John about the entry") might offer opportunities for development.

7.3 Conclusions

Application of results from research on human-to-human interaction in small groups is useful in understanding the observed behaviors of users in computer mediated communications situations. While there are many CMC tools available, they generally lack adequate feedback to maintain workspace awareness, and do not support passive overview or informal monitoring of group activity. Initial response to the Compadres system, which blends different web-based communications systems, suggests that use of a communications console that offers workspace awareness can significantly enhance the group members' sense of participation. Issues related to management of privacy, social proximity, and automated eavesdropping remain.

8 Summary

There are numerous applications that support communication between individuals and within small and large groups in both the synchronous and asynchronous temporal domains. However, few of these presently support both synchronous and asynchronous workgroup presence monitoring and messaging in a unified interface. The Compadres system developed at the University of Washington represents one approach to such a system, providing a consistent group "workspace" with passive group presence monitoring, personalized "desks", support for different levels of intragroup communications, and simple messaging.

References

Barnlund, D. C. (1973). Introduction: Interpersonal Communication. In *Communicating Interpersonally: a reader*, eds. R. Pace, B. Peterson and T. Radcliffe. Columbus: Charles E. Merrill Publishing Co., pp 4-11.

Bass, B. (1974). The Definition of "Group". In *Small Group Communication: a reader*, eds. R. Cathcart and L. Samovar. Dubuque, Iowa: Wm. C. Brown Company, pp 19-27.

Bogen, D. (1999). *Order Without Rules: critical theory and the logic of conversation.* Albany: State University of New York Press.

Carnevale, D. (2000). "New Master Plan in Washington State Calls for More Online Instruction" in *The Chronicle of Higher Education*, vol XLVI, #22, February, 2000, p A50.

Ching, F., S. Hampden, B. Johnson, P. Maulden, J. Swain, D. Zuberbuhler (1999) Course Syllabus, University of Washington, Architecture 300, Autumn 1999, p 7.

Dourish, P. (1999). Where the Footprints Lead: Tracking down other roles for social navigation. In *Social Navigation of Information Space*, eds. A. Munro, K. Höök and D Benyon. London: Springer-Verlag, pp 15-34.

Goffman, E. *Behavior in Public Places*, The Free Press of Glencoe, 1963.

Gutwin, C. and S. Greenberg. (1999). The Effects of Workgroup Awareness Support on the Usability of Real-Time Distributed Groupware. In *ACM Transactions on Computer-Human Interaction*, v 6, # 3, pp 243-281.

Knapp, M L. (1978). *Nonverbal Communication in Human Interaction.* New York: Holt, Rinehart and Winston, p 353.

Lakoff, G. (interviewed by I.A. Boal) (1995). Body Brain and Communication. In *Resisting the Virtual Life: the culture and politics of information*, eds. J Brook and I.A. Boal, City Lights Books, pp 115-130.

McGrath, A, & A Munro. (1999). Footsteps from the Garden - Arcadian Knowledge Spaces. In *Social Navigation of Information Space*, eds. A. Munro, K. Höök and D Benyon. London: Springer-Verlag, pp 253-278.

Paperjet. WebCamToo & WebCamTurbo web site. <http://webcam.paperjet.com/>

Tu, C.H. (1999). Critical examination of factors affecting interaction on CMC. In *Journal of Network and Computer Applications*, **23**, 39-58.

Turkle, S. (1995). *Life on the Screen: identity in the age of the Internet.* New York: Simon & Shuster.

Testing the Space of the Virtual

Brian Lonsway, Informatics and Architecture, Rensselaer Polytechnic Institute, USA

Abstract

Various modes of electronically mediated communication, perception, and immersive bodily engagement, generally categorized as "virtual experiences," have offered the designer of space a new array of spatial conditions to address. Each of these modes of virtual experience, from text-based discussion forums to immersive virtual reality environments, presents challenges to traditional assumptions about space and its inhabitation. These challenges require design theorization which extends beyond the notions of design within the electronic space (the textual description of the chat forum, the appearance of the computer generated imagery, etc.), and require a reconsideration of the entire electronic and physical apparatus of the mediating devices (the physical spaces which facilitate the interaction, the manner of their connection to the virtual spaces, etc.). In light of the lack of spatial theorization in this area, this paper presents both an experimental framework for understanding this complete space of the virtual and outlines a current research project addressing these theoretical challenges through the spatial implementation of a synthetic environment.

1 Proposition

Like most binary oppositions, that formulated between virtual reality (VR) and real life (RL) does little to advance our understanding of the complex spatial and cultural implications of new immersive technologies. If we, as designers, are to competently address the systemic shifts that may or may not be induced by these technologies, it is imperative that we have the capacity to understand their explicit and implicit modes of operation. And in particular, as designers generally concerned with the manipulation of space, we should have the capacity to understand the way in which they operate *spatially*. The commonly accepted but reductive framework, which categorically separates the space of the virtual experience from our larger spatial context, privileges technological apparatus over socio-spatial context, perception, and inhabitation. This attitude is echoed in most cultural representations of VR: product advertising promotes the ability of users to leave their real environments and enter fantastic ones with the aid of certain devices, developmental research of VR systems focuses almost entirely on technical implementation and discusses social or psychological issues only where these are a result of technological development, and popular fiction invents myriad mechanisms and devices which provide novel ways to travel *from* "RL" *into* cyberspace. Not all research in VR technologies, of course, so naively fails to recognize the significant amount of interconnectedness between the "virtual" part of the experience and that part not conceptualized as such (the existence of the body, the physical manifestation of the technological apparatus, etc.).[1] However, even a perfunctory analysis of VR research concerned with spatial implications reveals that the opposition between the *real* and the *virtual* has become quite instrumentalized. The commonly accepted space of VR is that representation of space, which is presented perceptually *to* the user. This conceptualization of space privileges, through technological capability, the representational aspects of space – the conception of space as a geometric (and due to dominant representational systems, Cartesian) realm accommodating placement, movement, and proximity. This geometrically instrumentalized conception of space fails to recognize space's material or social aspects, and therefore excludes the space of immersive operation (i.e., that space within which the VR experience takes place). I would like to argue for an expansion of this narrow spatial conceptualization as a way of transcending the merely technological manner in which VR technologies are currently being developed. This expanded notion positions the space of the VR experience as a mediated (specifically, "informed") realm, which includes not only the domain of representation, but the physical domain of the apparatus and the physical and psychological domain of those who interact with it. Through this reformulation, the domain of VR design and implementation must become productively engaged with the domain of human social experience.

I would like to borrow a term that has been used to conceptualize the realm of human interactions with technology as a socially engaged phenomenon: virtuality. Margaret Morse, in particular, has embraced this notion in her book of the same name to examine a wide range of technological and spatial constructs, which are highly relevant to the discussion at hand (Morse, 1998). Morse explains virtualities by tracing elements of Heideggerian phenomenology through the viewpoint of a contemporary cultural anthropologist: "cultural forms from television graphics and shopping malls to the apparatus of virtual reality, as well as practices from driving to conducting war to making art employ various forms of engagement to construct a *virtual relationship* between subjects in a here-and-now." She later suggests "monitor-human relations are thus bubbles or pockets of virtuality in the midst of the material world." By generalizing the notion of a virtuality to include all conditions of *in-effect-but-not-in-fact*, Morse is able to contextualize the concept of VR and virtual experiences within a social framework. Morse begins her argument with an analysis of the subjectivity-constructing effects of television. The television, she argues, continually positions its viewers as a "you" through the single-sided dissemination of information. The act of broadcasting, most apparently in news and advertising, although equally at play in all configurations of market-directed programming, is an act of subjectivity construction through the emphasis of the "you," the receiver of televisual utterances. Advertisements speak to a valued consumer and are placed during programs that have been proven to be popular with specific demographic groups. Their transmissions are directed to "you" as "you" are supposed to be. Viewers form subjective representations of their selves through the identification of themselves as this "you," even if, as Morse suggests, the "you may not actually be in that position," having flipped channels, left the room, or otherwise broken the dissemination. This temporal "you" as a subject of televisual utterance exists as a kind of virtuality: a realm that appears in effect, although not in actual fact. On one hand, you are still the you you were before the utterance, but you are also now the "you" who should buy detergent, tune in later, wear particular clothing, etc.; effectively, your subjectivity has multiplied. Furthermore, with regard to interactive experiences, Morse argues that there has been a shift from the subjectivity discourse of the "you" to the subjectivity discourse of the "I," where technological interaction is used to construct an "I" which, similar to the "you" of television, is located in a particular space and time. With the special case of the immersive VR experience, the user is (in actual fact) located in physical space within the apparatus of the technology. The computer-mediated environment suggests (in effect) a trans-location outside of this domain, but only through the construction of a subject centered on the self ("I"), controlling an abstract position in a graphic database of spatial coordinates. The individual, of which this newly positioned subject is but one component, is participant in a virtuality: a spatio-temporal moment of immersion, virtualized travel, physical fixity, and perhaps, depending on the technologies employed, electro-magnetic frequency exposure, lag-time nausea, etc.

This is hardly a new concept; similar notions of subjectivity formation that have evolved from Lacanian psychoanalysis proliferate in late 20th century cultural theory. What is potent about Morse's observation, however, is the way in which she commodifies the term virtuality to refer to this moment of subjective multiplicity as a moment of technological engagement.[2] If the notion of virtuality is expanded to include any moment of such multiplied identification or subjectivity formation, then the virtuality becomes a way of conceptualizing these mediated moments of subjectivity identification. There is, by this argument, no substantial distinction between the mediation of our perception by VR apparatuses and by our genetic, cultural, physical, or other technological mediations. All such mediations, technologically manifest or not, form our senses of reality and subjective positions within it. VR, therein, is merely another one of these moments, taking place in the space of our lives. It's space is not, therefore, the instrumentalized space of its presentation devices, but the subjectivity-forming space of its physical, cultural, and social manifestation. The understanding of so-called VR experiences as virtualities rather than technologized events in which a virtual experience takes place suggests that the latter fails to recognize the larger context of such interactions or events, and places complete faith in a technological system to address the complexities of human social experience. These technologically determinate models, I argue, are unable to account for complex social and human behavioral conditions not because of technological limitations, but because of the restrictive means of conceptualizing the very nature of such environments

Primary among the existing models of understanding the design and development of virtual systems is that of *presence*. (Barfield, Zeltzer, Sheridan, Slater, 1995; Schloerb, 1995; Darken, Allard, Achille, 1998) This metric evaluates the success of a virtual environment system as a measure of an individual user's sense of feeling present in the simulated environment. While clearly rooted in the proprioceptive reactions of the user, this means of measure is biased toward the matter of technological facilitation rather than spatial or social engagement with the facilitated environment. The evaluative question basically asks "does the technology of the virtual system interfere in any way with your ability to believe that you are located in a space different than the one your body is in?" The technical literature concerning presence enumerates those things which obstruct or hinder its perception, including obstructive aspects of gear, lag time in image updating, lack of realism in visual, aural, or tactile presentation, or lack of a complete multi-sensory environment. Philosophically, I find it somewhat untenable to evaluate the concept of presence without first establishing a measure of the socio-spatial context within which presence is measured. In particular, I see three significant problems inherent in this assumption. First, the measure of presence in a virtual environment above all assumes that the sensation of presence is a natural means of human interaction with and perception of our social and physical environments. This privileges the already-present or assumed present within a given cultural context. N. Katherine Hayles and Alluquere Stone among others have written extensively on the cultured associations of such assumptions, arguing that the privileging of that which is present merely privileges predominant cultural types: the male, the "normal," etc. (Hayles 1999; Stone 1995). Successful presence, of course, privileges certain abilities: the ability to afford (financially or temporally) to interact with a VR environment, the knowledge of how to navigate, the level of comfort with the cultural environments represented (often warlike or gender-biased), the lack of fear of technology (in particular when it has to be worn or applied to the body). Those without these abilities are, by the VR industry's measure of presence, already absent. Second, aside from these social and psychological problems, it has not yet been established that those of us who are considered present by this measure exist capably in the world by measuring our successful interaction with our surroundings via the question "do I feel present here?". An empirical assumption derived from early existentialist thought, this belief fails to address a myriad of other possible models for spatial interaction that extend beyond the primarily visceral and psychological concept of spatial interaction and into the socio-cultural. And finally, there is an irony in even conceptualizing the need to have such a measure as presence. If we take a less technologically mediated condition of virtual existence – immersion in the plot of a printed book – it is impossible to conceive of one's immersion in the book and one's spatial immersion in a physical environment independently. With the imperative to sensorially immerse a participant completely in another realm with advanced technologies, however, the problem of the electronic replacement of the physical comes to the fore. The technology draws a distinction between the technologically mediated and the non-technological. The immersive technology of virtual environments, a direct manifestation of the philosophical underpinning of VR research, itself raises the problem of presence.

In addressing these limitations of the presence model for evaluating virtual environments, I find Morse's notion of the virtuality to be most instructive.[3] If the moment of interaction with the virtual environment is conceived to be akin to the moment of interaction with a television or a telephone, then we can more easily see how this immersion is no different than any technological engagement. The engagement is an event of mediated socialization (socially and spatially *immersive*) rather than technologized escape from the everyday (socially and spatially *divisive*). The space of this engagement is multi-scalar, encompassing the space of computer-assisted vision as well as the space of subjectivity inducement and the space of cultural association. But what is, in fact, the space of the virtuality, and how specifically is the theorization of this space different than that within existing conceptualizations of virtual space or cyberspace?

To best answer this, in particular as theorization in this specific area of exploration is limited, I would like to offer three independent digressions which collude in a revealing way with respect to this line of thought: one each into phenomenology, cultural geography, and post-structuralism. I offer these as observations towards an experimental theorization of virtuality, as I have only begun to explore the practical implications of this theoretical framing. The entry of these digressions into my own work was via radically distinct paths, but the network of ideas they represent is highly provocative to the exploration at hand. Most importantly, they have proven essential as foundations for our applied work in the implementation of the Synthetic Space Environment (SSE) at Rensselaer's

Informatics and Architecture program. After these digressions, I will provide an introduction to our current development of this spatial environment, which is an attempt to reexamine "VR" as a virtuality. This will also serve to elucidate the more arcane notions of space, subjectivity, and virtuality, which have just been, or are about to be, presented.

2 Digression 1: Being

Martin Heidegger bases his phenomenology on a philosophical inquiry into a set of concepts considered essential to human existence, and which he argues lie underneath our more readily understandable social concepts like body, space, and time. These essential or primordial concepts are rooted specifically in the notion of our being. It seems irresistible to link the technical exploration of presence in VR environments with Heidegger's *being*, as the act of being present is one of his own philosophical foundations for his notion of *being-in-the-world*. Heidegger classifies these essential concepts as what we would now call second-order classifications via terms like "embodiment" and "spatiality." Hierarchical relationships are set up between these concepts and their primary referents (spatiality is an essential concept for the recognizance of space, embodiment for body, etc.) I find it difficult not to see *virtuality* within this system of fundamental concepts, even though Heidegger's hierarchical and essentializing theorization is quite remote from Margaret Morse's (and my own) theoretical positions. Nevertheless, by framing the virtuality as a kind of essential concept which precedes the virtual, and which constitutes the level of engagement of the phenomenal being-in-the-world (presence), we find support for the understanding of presence not as a measure of virtuality; but as a result of it. Rather than postulate the examination of presence within a context of technological facilitation, as do current writers on virtual systems, we can make the argument that presence has as its core the entire, experienced spatial system (spatiality) within which this technology is situated, the entire construct of the physical body (embodiment) which is used to engage the technology, and the entire system of technologically mediated subjectivity (virtuality). In order to measure presence, in other words, it is not acceptable to merely inquire of VR experiment participants how present they might have felt. What is required is that these participants be given the opportunity creatively, subjectively, and personally to establish their own sense of embodiment, to understand their spatiality, and to conceptualize their virtuality.

3 Digression 2: Space

The understanding of space is part of a long philosophical tradition, and my brief analysis here is no attempt to categorize this history or even to succinctly address its significant moments. This is not even an attempt to offer any kind of totalizing conception of space. It is an attempt, nevertheless, to position a multiscalar reading of the modes of spatial operation, which we seem to most regularly encounter implicitly or explicitly in our contemporary actions and discourses. Much of this outline is grounded in the post-Marxist tradition of writing on space in the last three decades, notably that of Henri Lefebvre, Michel Foucault, Manuel Castells, and Edward Soja (Lefebvre, 1974; Foucault, 1970; Castells, 1989; Soja, 1989). Fundamentally, actions and discourses form an array of operations that constitute three scales of spatial practices: the Cartesian, the landscaped, and the organizational. Cartesian spatial practices are formed from essentially geometric readings of space; consisting entirely of quantitative spatial relationships, spatial activity is limited to location, extension, and proximity. Movement is implicitly addressed but not facilitated (i.e., vectors and curves can be constructed within a Cartesian system, but the rules of Cartesian ordering do not provide the tools to construct them). The landscaped (or landscopic) mode of spatial practice introduces a social arena that is produced or constructed in certain arrangements to facilitate cultural sustenance or human desire. Where the Cartesian framing of space introduces location, distance, and direction as spatial operatives, the landscopic introduces inhabitation, navigation, and movement (Zukin, 1991). One can speak of a landscape of power, or an urban or suburban landscape, or a landscape of thoughts. Spatially, the landscape is a framing device, collecting diverse and discrete phenomena into a collective realm of social interaction. And finally, the organizational practice of space extends the spatial into the tropic realm of conceptualization. Here, the metaphors of Cartesian and landscopic spatial practices are used to form spatial domains for any phenomena that could benefit from the vocabulary of spatial relationships. When we speak of navigating the World Wide Web, or refer to the proximity of one piece of information to another, we are spatializing these phenomena through our rhetorical modes of operation.

It is the entire complex of these three modes of spatial operation that I take as the foundation for exploring the virtuality. Typical models of virtual systems base any notions of spatiality (via measures of presence) on only a Cartesian definition, limiting social and metaphorical applications of the broader framework of space to quantifiable phenomena: the establishment of *wayfinding*, the determination of participant location, the tracking of user orientation, etc.[4] Socially, however, we always operate in all three spatial modes (and perhaps others) in the spatial engagement of our everyday lives. The fluidity of space allows us or even requires us to shift modes of occupation invisibly, to engage multiple models at once, or even form our own transitory models to contend with particularities. And likewise, as our interactions with the machinery of the virtual are participant in our common lived space, we must fluidly engage these spatial modes of operation when interacting or performing within the virtuality.

Edward Soja, in his highly influential *Postmodern Geographies*, explores the role of space within Marxist and post-Marxist critical social theory, and attempts to engender a critical investigation of spatial practices as fundamental to contemporary processes of capitalist development (Soja, 1989). Explicit in his work is a critique of the failure of much contemporary social theory to recognize the spatial practices at work in socio-economic development. Soja recognizes the need to couple this critique with certain ontological investigations of *spatiality* as a component of his reassertion of space as a political project. Briefly examining Marxist and Giddensian economics, and Sartre's and Heidegger's phenomenology, Soja presents two moments of "misplaced spatiality:" the illusion of opacity present in materialist thought failing to recognize the social aspects of space because of obsessions with objects-in-space, and the illusion of transparency present in existential phenomenology which fails to recognize space as a physical and material phenomenon. The illusion of opacity is fundamentally a restatement of my critique of the technologically determinist model; the illusion of transparency is a critique of the essentializing problem of Heidegger's theorization of spatiality. Spatiality for Soja operates fluidly across material and mental realms, serving as much as a result of material processes as an intangible conceptualization of social processes. If we insert this notion of spatiality into Heidegger's model of presence, we more clearly see how popular measures of presence (the understanding of presence as a measure rather than a result) fail to address the spatial complexity inherent in a virtual experience. But in what manner is this failure realized, and why do these myopic investigations of a representational spatiality dominate technical explorations of virtual reality?

4 Digression 3: Myth

I have suggested earlier how the rhetoric embedded within technological implementation privileges the popularly divisive manner of understanding the space of the virtuality as an opposition of the virtual to the real. To more clearly understand the principles at work in this rhetorical system, I would like to turn to Roland Barthes' articulation of a cultural construction he calls *myth*.[5] This notion of myth is devised to explain a new cultural form of communication that, for Barthes, has replaced the traditional forms of ideological discourse. Unlike the manifestations of the latter, which form clear statements of unmasked intentionality, mythological articulations are constructed from careful manipulations of semiotic structure so as to defer their ideological intentionality and to present instead their distortions as truth. For the ideological, what is said is important; for the mythological, how one says what is said is important. This latter fashion of communication dominates our cultural landscape, where substitutions of significance replace meanings through associative presentation. When we see an advertisement for toothpaste which shows images of happy couples in love, the myth is operating to equate happiness in life with oral hygiene; the ideological intention is to support the pharmaceutical industry through toothpaste purchases, but this message is deferred through its carefully manipulated representation. This mythical practice extends through all areas of communication, including that of technological validation. In the same way that Soja feels a need to reassert the importance of space in the critical practices of cultural production, I feel that there is a need to reassert its presence in the domain of technological production. The cultural myth of high technology operates to sustain its self-importance at all costs. Practices that engage such technology are frequently absorbed into its mythical self-sustenance, becoming a proponent of the technology itself. This is certainly true in the development of virtual reality technologies, where their rhetorical and practiced fetishization subsumes critical discourse positioned outside of the technological system. It doesn't even make such sense at first, for example, to speak of the non-technological components of virtual reality: the very way that we understand VR is grounded in the technology that facilitates it. Thus, the myth stipulates that the virtual is *only* that which exists inside of, or because of the VR gear; the spatial is *only* that representation of space that exists on screen; the *present* is only (ironically) a state of escape, etc. Only technological research is validated as VR research; critical analyses are (merely) cultural theory.

5 Implementation

Addressing this technological obsession returns me once again to the virtuality, and to a need to creatively explore the implications of these digressions and the theoretical framework in which I have placed them. Understanding the virtuality – a socio-spatial construct that includes, but does not privilege the technologically mediated experience of engagement with a specific set of interactive devices – requires that its tenants be tested in practice. I have, within the Informatics and Architecture program at Rensselaer Polytechnic Institute, begun this testing through the implementation of a unique type of computer-mediated spatial environment, the Synthetic Space Environment. This environment has been framed from its conceptualization as a spatial enterprise that accounts for the theoretical complexity I have introduced in this paper. Our research specifically attempts to engage the development and implementation of a synthetic reality environment[6] on socio-spatial terms (i.e., as a virtuality), and argues that this means of conceptualizing the domain of virtual reality environments may more substantially address current limitations of VR research than typical technology-focused means. Through this broader spatial framework, problems which are typically seen as purely technical (rendering speed, tracking accuracy, ergonomic design of worn equipment, etc.) become problems which may be addressed through a variety of spatial mechanisms.

Our current work has involved the creation of a real-time network-based synthetic environment, which has addressed the spatial complexities called for above through the simultaneous pursuit of technical development, design, and evaluation. The project calls for a multi-sited venue for the collaborative teaching of architectural design based on existing studio-based models of design teaching. For this reason, it is important that user obstruction by head-mounted displays, tracking devices, etc. be eliminated, and that the spatial mode of user interaction be highly intuitive, and at as close to full-scale as is possible. From our theoretical interests, we also wanted to avoid any qualitative predeterminations about what is and is not virtual, and to put into question the fundamental separation of real and virtual spaces which existing technologies reify. For these reasons, we chose to work with a derivation of virtual set or virtual studio technologies, which use chroma-key technologies to visually and aurally compose participants into computer-generated or video-based environments. Interactions among users in the space and between users and the computer-generated environment occur in the physical space of the user at full scale. By using this kind of technology, therefore, we were immediately able to both eliminate the need for head-mounted displays and to work at the full scale of the users' physical surroundings. Again because we did not categorize any spatial condition as either *real* or *virtual*, we were able to opportune ourselves of a technological artifact of virtual set systems to expand the space of user interaction. A typical virtual reality system is concerned primarily with the eradication of the physical environment so that its user may have a greater sense of presence in the virtual environment. Even augmented reality systems, which superimpose computer-generated overlays onto a user's physical environment via transparent head-mounted displays, limit the augmented spatial interaction of a user to objects that have been previously coded into the system. Each of these systems relies on the spatial division of the real and the virtual, as they require an active insertion of one into the other in order to operate. Virtual set systems, on the other hand, expand space in their technical operation, composing the environment of the user's bodies with the computer-generated environment, and presenting this final composition as an augmentation of the original space (figure 1). Our physical configuration proposes to present this resultant composition at full scale as a mirror-like complement to the space of the users (figure 2)[7]. In this way, the user's doubling is also a spatial doubling, as the newly expanded space includes both the original space of the physical user and the image-based space of the double. The spatial construction of the synthetic environment is a physical manifestation of Morse's virtuality: a spatio-temporal multiplication of self through social mediation.

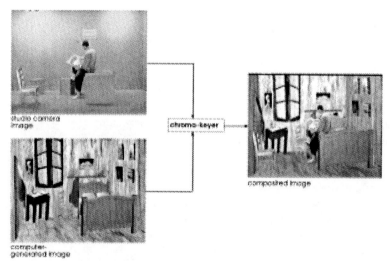

Figure 1. Example of the chroma-keying process, taken from an early prototype of the synthetic environment. Note the second-pass chroma-keying employed to composite the foot of the bed in front of the participant.

Figure 3 presents a diagram of the complete collaborative environment, which multiplies yet again the complete space of its operation. Each of the scenarios described above exists at one of two sites, and spatial and image data from each location is sent to the other. In this way, the space of the doubled user is also inhabited by remote participants. Interaction between participants at each site is facilitated in this part of the synthetic space. With this as the complete diagram for the synthetic environment, not only are the studio configuration and videographic design important components of the overall spatial configuration, but the imaging, tracking, collaboration enabling, and networking implementations become productively spatialized. Typical virtual set, virtual reality, or even augmented reality systems implement each of these systems through specialized technologies: image rendering and calibration software for imaging, optical or magneto-electrical hardware systems for tracking, sharing software and communication protocols for collaboration, and network-optimized video codecs for communication. The SSE, however, integrates these essential technical requirements into a single (spatial) problem. There are still specific technical specialties within this spatial development, but they are not seen as autonomous technical problems but rather as a single complex implementation. Through our consideration of the problem of the SSE within the domain of the *space of the virtuality* rather than the *technical requirements of a collaborative virtual set system*, we have shifted the primary focus from isolated techniques (manifested in particular technological products) into a complex socio-spatial system.

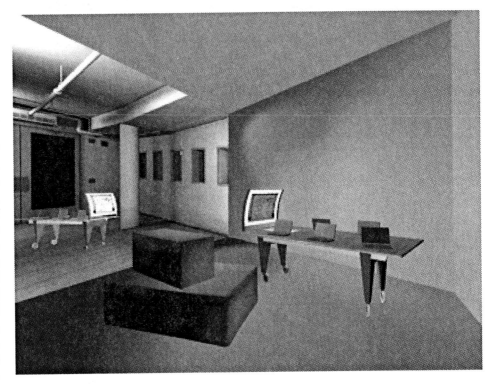

Figure 2. Representation of the mirror-like configuration for the presentation of the composited image to the SSE participants.

6 Implementation Detail

As the spatiality of the VSE relies upon many design variables that are interconnected, it is important that these be pursued in a parallel fashion. We can divide these variables into two general categories for the purpose of explanation: there are the traditionally spatial design variables, and the computation-based design variables. The first category includes both architectural and videographic variables like studio layout, lighting and acoustics, and camera direction; the second includes specific concerns of CGI implementation that affect the presentation and perception of space in the VSE like image fidelity, tracking accuracy and compression loss. While admittedly there is some autonomy of these two categories of variables from each other, our requirement is that the physical spatial arrangement and design of the shared VSE have a symbiotic relationship with the computational techniques employed. To date, we have implemented a Virtual Set system that offers the opportunity to examine the impact of the first category of variables on the space of the virtuality; before concluding, I will introduce our next phase, focusing on the spatial framing of the computational processes. We are at the beginning research phase of this work that will facilitate untethered camera and participant tracking, spatial consistency between multiple sites, and proper spatial composition of participants from any location

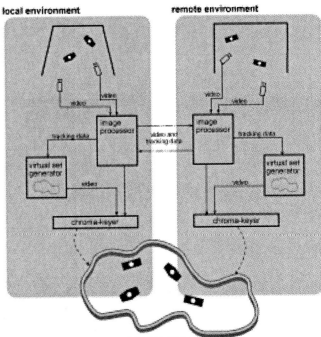

Figure 3. The overall diagram of the shared synthetic environment.

within the multiple sites. Within this framework, our main challenge is combining the images from the local site, the remote site, and the virtual model into a seamless image that appears consistent with a single viewpoint (which may be different at each site). This consistency must be maintained to present to all users a coherent and understandable representation of the spatial environment. Essentially, there are three problems related to the SSE, which we have framed as problems of camera-based tracking. First, the position and orientation of the studio cameras must be determined as they are moved around the local and remote sites in order to coordinate the movement of the camera in the CGI environment with the studio cameras. This coordination is required to properly position the SSE users in the CGI image. Second, the position of the users must be determined relative to the cameras and, using the camera's position and orientation information, relative to the local or remote site. This is required to properly position users from the local site in the proper spatial relationship to users in the remote site. And third, the two images of the users from the local and remote sites must be combined and transformed relative to the virtual camera within the virtual set to create the composite image. All of this must be done at or near the frame rate of the camera, and no slower than the lowest frame rate which is acceptable for avoiding time-based visual artifacts (generally accepted to be ten frames per second). This is all accomplished in the "image processor" areas indicated in figure 3.

Each of these problems has been studied extensively, with many results appearing in the research literature (Dhond and Aggarwal, 1989; Hartley, 1998; Kanade and Okutomi, 1994; McMillan and Bishop, 1995; Okutomi and Kanade, 1993; Seitz and Dyer, 1996; Stewart, Flatland, and Bubna, 1996). Our goal is not to invent new theory in addressing the problems, but rather it is to use spatial constraints that can naturally be imposed within the SSE to solve the problems reliably and efficiently. The resulting techniques, in particular, will not depend on the particular configurations of the cameras and the site; as components of a spatial system, they are transferable to a wide variety of environments and applications. The fundamental insight facilitating the diverse accomplishment of a single computational algorithm is the assertion of the primacy of space within the SSE. Specifically, this is due to three implementations: the use of chroma-keying to simplify the camera's image sources, the full-scale nature of the installation which requires only one point of view to be displayed to all participants at a site, and the use of the actual bodies of the participants rather than digital avatars to represent existence in the SSE. Each of these implementations is based on standard modes of spatial occupation: situating the place of interaction in a room rather than on a desktop, use of an architectural element (metaphorically, a mirrored wall) rather than an HMD to display output, and deployment of actual bodies rather than iconographic representations to situate participants in the virtuality.

7 Future Work

Our current implementation of the project is primarily concerned with the way in which we construct an appropriate spatial vocabulary in a complex mediated spatial condition. We have completed the development of a system which includes immersive three-dimensional computer-generated environments with static single-camera viewpoints, interactive computer-generated sets controlled by technicians and participants, and foreground matting which allows computer-generated objects to appear in front of participants as well as behind them based on a limited implementation of their z-depth tracking. Of the proposed model, we have yet to implement camera and participant position tracking or network communications of the shared site. Even at this stage, however, we have creatively engaged our spatial concerns through the development of live performances that address the complex nature of the proposed environment. These performances are a part of our preliminary design phase, and are surrogates for the type of spatial practices that we will need to understand when we finally engage participants at multiple sites. Even at this preliminary level, however, we have found the conceptual device of the virtuality to be quite instrumental in breaking through the continuous technical constraints that we have encountered. It will only be through the continued parallel development of such operative theoretical devices and iterative spatial implementations that this project will be able to challenge the assumptions embedded in VR technologies. For example, what is most significantly perceived as a limitation on immersive perception of the SSE is its mirror-like display. On one hand, we argue that, on the terms of human spatial perception, this is a more natural mode of spatial interaction and immersive presentation than those offered by HMD's, which require the portage of physically obstructive equipment, or of CAVE's, which even at best limit social interaction and present, across the well-defined edges of a cube, an ostensibly seamless image. On the other hand, we see a number of impending technologies that could be absorbed into the space of the virtuality. Real-time filtering of background images could eliminate the need to be in a chroma-key studio, remote participants could be projected into the physical space (beyond the mirror) with three-dimensional holographic projection, or multiple-viewpoint enabled 3-D projection could replace our proposed 2-D projection.

While we are by no means uninterested in including such new technologies in the model of the SSE, it is not essential to our theoretical project. Above all, we are concerned with the meaningful socio-spatial development of new forms of intensely mediated environments. As technologies become available, they will be incorporated into the SSE only so long as they can be adopted within – and in close conjunction with – a spatial framework. Our process is one of a forced ambiguity between space and technology, a conjunction that is not exactly simple to maintain when working so closely with systems that prefer expected, enumerated, and consistent input. However, we believe it to be a process worth maintaining, lest we return again to uncritical oppositions. If the real is inseparable from the virtual, then so is the theoretical, from the applied.

Acknowledgements

I would like to acknowledge four individuals who have contributed greatly to this work. Most importantly, Kathleen Brandt, professor of video and installation art at Rensselaer, co-directed the performances that formed our first major public presentation of the SSE and has been a major influence on the creative and theoretical direction of our work. Karel Dudesek and Martin Schmitz, from the University of Applied Arts in Vienna, and members of Van-Gogh TV, have helped develop the shared model for the SSE and are our remote collaborators for our upcoming online-shared SSE experimentation. And Charles Stewart, professor of computer science at Rensselaer, has contributed substantially to the conceptual model for the computer imaging system that forms the core of the SSE. Without the dedicated support of these individuals, our work on the subject would have scarcely evolved.

References

American Heritage Dictionary. (1985). Boston: Houghton Mifflin Company.

Barfield, W., Zeltzer, D., Sheridan, T., and Slater, M. (1995). Presence and Performance Within Virtual Environments. In *Virtual Environments and Advanced Environment Design*, eds. W. Barfield and T. A. Furness. New York: Oxford University Press.

Castells, M. (1989). *The Informational City: information technology, economic restructuring, and the urban-regional process.* Oxford: Blackwell.

Cambridge Dictionary of American English (2000). Available from: http://www.cup.cam.ac.uk/esl/dictionary. Accessed April 15, 2000.

Darken, R. P., Allard, T., and Achille, L. B. (1998). Spatial Orientation and Wayfinding in Large-Scale Virtual Spaces: An Introduction. *Presence*, 7(2), 101-107. Cambridge: MIT Press.

Dhond, U., and Aggarwal, J. K. "Structure from stereo — a review." *1999 IEEE Transactions on Systems, Man, and Cybernetics* #19, 1489-1510.

Foucault, M. (1970). *The Order of Things.* New York: Vintage Books.

Hartley, R. "Minimizing Algebraic Error in Geometric Estimation Problems." *1998 IEEE International Conference on Computer Vision*, 469-476.

Hayles, N. K. (1999). *How We Became Posthuman : Virtual Bodies in Cybernetics, Literature, and Informatics.* Chicago, University of Chicago Press.

Heim, M. (1993). *The Metaphysics of Virtual Reality.* New York: Oxford University Press.

Kanade, T., and Okutomi, M. "A Stereo Matching Algorithm with an Adaptive Window: Theory and Experiment." *1994 IEEE Transactions on Pattern Analysis and Machine Intelligence*, 920-932.

Lefebvre, H. (1974). *The Production of Space.* Trans., Donald Nicholson-Smith. Oxford: Blackwell.

Lynch, Kevin. (1960). *The Image of the City.* Cambridge: Harvard University Press.

McMillan, L., and G., B. "Plenoptic Modeling: An Image-based Rendering System." *SIGGRAPH '95*, 39-46.

Mirriam-Webster's Collegiate Dictionary. (2000). Available from http://www.m-w.com/cgi-bin/dictionary. Accessed April 15, 2000.

Morse, M. (1998), *Virtualities: Television, Media Art, and Cyberculture.* Bloomington, Indiana University Press.

National Research Council (1995). *Virtual Reality: Scientific and Technological Challenges.* Washington D.C.: National Academy Press.

Okutomi, M., and Kanade, T. (1993). "A Multiple-baseline Stereo." *IEEE Transactions on Pattern Analysis and Machine Intelligence,* #15, 353-363.

Ronell, A. (1989). *The Telephone Book.* Lincoln, University of Nebraska Press.

Schloerb, D. (1995). A Quantitative Measure of Telepresence. *Presence,* 4(2), 64-80.

Seitz, S. M., and Dyer, C. R. "View Morphing." *SIGGRAPH '96,* 21-30.

Soja, E. (1989). *Postmodern Geographies: the reassertion of space in critical social theory.* London: Verso.

Stewart, C. V., Flatland, R. Y., and Bubna, K. (1996). "Geometric Constraints and Stereo Disparity Computation." *International Journal of Computer Vision,* 20(3), 143-168.

Stone, A. (1995). *The War of Desire and Technology at the Close of the Mechanical Age.* Cambridge: MIT Press.

Strong, J. and Woodbury, R. (1998). "Psyberdesign: Designing the Cognitive Spaces of Virtual Environments." *Digital Design Studios: Do Computers Make a Difference?, Proceedings of 1998 ACADIA conference.* Quebec City, Association for Computer Aided Design in Architecture.

Tolman, E.C. (1948). "Cognitive Maps in Rats and Men," *Psychological Review* 55: 189-208

Vasquez De Velasco, G. and Hutchison, D. (1999). "An Immersive Environment for Virtual Design Studios." *media and design process, Proceedings of 1999 ACADIA conference.* Salt Lake City: Association for Computer Aided Design in Architecture.

Zeltzer, D. (1992). Autonomy, Interaction, and Presence. *Presence,* 1(1), 127-132. Cambridge: MIT Press.

Zukin, S. (1991). *Landscapes of Power: from Detroit to Disney World.* Berkeley: University of California Press.

---

[1] From the online Mirriam-Webster Collegiate Dictionary, virtual is defined as "being such in essence or effect though not formally recognized or admitted" (Mirriam-Webster, 2000). The online Cambridge Dictionary of American English defines it to be "almost, but not exactly or in every way" (Cambridge Dictionary, 2000). And finally, a 1985 American Heritage defines it to be "existing or resulting in essence or effect, though not in actual fact, form, or name" (American Heritage, 1985).

[2] A possible weakness of her suggestion is that it privileges the self – the self before the transmission-imposed "you" or the interactivity-imposed "I" – as a self without subjectivity, where the self is somehow seen as actual fact; the subject as in-effect-but-not-in-fact. I accept this as a rhetorical weakness of the text, however, as Morse is clear to articulate that, within the complex realm of subjectivity formation, notions of original have little significance.

[3] I use Margaret Morse's explicit concept of virtuality because of its clarity and relevance to my arguments herein. However, it is important to note that this notion, whether in name or not, has formed the basis of many writings on the virtual realm. In particular, I would like to acknowledge the writings of Michael Heim in *The Metaphysics of Cyberspace*, N. Katherine Hayles in *How We Became Posthuman : Virtual Bodies in Cybernetics, Literature, and Informatics* and Avital Ronell in *The Telephone Book* in influencing my work on the subject (Heim, 1993; Hayles,

1999; Ronell, 1989).

[4] An interesting exception to this can be found in "Psyberdesign: Designing the Cognitive Spaces of Virutal Environments" by Strong and Woodbury, where the authors explore the implications of using Kevin Lynch's (originally E.C. Tolman's) notion of a cognitive map to design virtual environments (Lynch, 1960; Tolman 1948). Nevertheless, my critique of the congnitive map model is that it fails to address the significant variable of social behavior and interaction in space. Meaningful spatial models for collaborative virtual environments should certainly take these social variables into effect.

[5] My exploration into myth is intentionally restricted to Barthes' formulation, which is quite distinct from the larger concept of social, historical, or cultural myths.

[6] Synthetic reality is defined as a general term by the National Research Council which includes virtual reality, augmented reality, and telepresence environments. I prefer the generic nature of this term and use it perhaps most importantly in our research to avoid problematic associations with the adjective "virtual" (National Research Council, 1995).

[7] This form of presentation is similar spatially to the work presented by Guillermo Vasquez De Velasco and David Hutchison from Texas A&M University at ACADIA 99. (Vasquez De Velasco and Hutchison, 1999)

Exercising Collaborative Design in a Virtual Environment

Christopher Peri, University of California, Berkeley, USA

Abstract

In the last few years remote collaborative design has been attracting interest, and with good reason: Almost everything we use today, whether it is the structure we inhabit, the vehicle we travel in, or the computer we work on, is the result of a number of participants' contributions to a single design. At the same time, more and more design teams are working in remote locations from one another. In a distributed design situation with remote players, communication is key for successful and effective collaboration.

Archville is a distributed, Web-based VR system that allows multiple users to interact with multiple models at the same time. We use it as a platform to exercise collaborative design by requiring students to build individual buildings as part of a city, or village and must share some common formal convention with their neighbors.

The Archville exercise demonstrates to students how we can use computing and the Internet to design collaboratively. It also points out the need to have correct up-to-date information when working on collaborative projects because of the dynamic nature of the design process.

In addition to architectural design and computer modeling, the exercise immerses students in the political and social aspects of designing within a community, where many of the design constraints must be negotiated, and where group work is often required. The paper describes both the pedagogical and the technical attributes of the Archville project.

Keywords: Collaboration, Virtual Reality, Design Studio, Real-time, VRML

1 Introduction

When Alberti started managing building construction from afar, the workers were forced to rely on drawings and written instructions (Jestaz 1995). Today's buildings have become far more complex and need to be completed in far less time, but we are still relying on drawings and written instructions to communicate. In addition, the amount and complexity of information have grown as well as the number of people who need information and have information to share.

Due to these changes, the potential for error is increasing accordingly. A large contributor to these errors is professionals who must rely on incomplete or incorrect information. We can reduce the potential of these errors significantly if we provide complete, up-to-date information for all those involved in the project. By accessing the information from the source instead of from a paper copy, viewers will always be assured that they are using the latest information.

The need to move design communication from static 2D pieces of paper is not a new idea. Researchers from the early 1970s have been trying to come up with a system that can improve communication and reduce the number of errors in design. What has changed is the power of computing and the explosion of access to the internet. We can see evidence of that change occurring already. There are now services that can provide document tracking for a project, but we are still bound to the limitations of the 2D media, i.e, multiple documents that refer to the same entity. Making sure that all documents reflect the same information is a difficult task and requires a large number of labor hours to maintain. Many companies offer services that will store and track documents for production companies. They also support virtual meetings, virtual whiteboards and video conferencing. The next logical step would be to have the information to be displayed, whether 2D or 3D, created from a single reference and only by storing this information in a 3D format can this be accomplished. Although the tools to create 2D drawings from 3D are still in their infancy, we have already seen some of them make their way into professional CAD packages. Consider this review from *CADENCE* AEC Tech News # 22 (March 17, 2000) by Geoffrey Moore Langdon:

> For years, architects with AutoCAD have been wishing they could make that leap from 2D CADD drafting to the 3D CADD architecturally smart building model approach (where plans, sections, elevations, and details get generated automatically) without disrupting their whole office (by switching to software other than AutoCAD) and now here with Bricsnet Architecturals there is a very good way of making that transition.
>
> The software uses a system of organization called Styles, which automatically keeps track of how the building is presented on screen and on paper, showing different floor stories, showing proper sections, rendering perspectives, and displaying construction documents as well as presentation drawings. Built into the software is even an ability to automatically post the drawings, if desired, on an architect-controlled project web site on the Bricsnet Project Center extranet service.

With the addition of animations and virtual environments, we could interact with the spatial information. By moving through an environment, animating objects, or even hiding and un-hiding different design alternatives, we can begin to think of the information display as an ever-changing dynamic medium instead of the static medium of paper (Pagels 1988).

When we are able to view this information informally from various sources, we begin to perceive the information as a Gestalt; that is, design information is seen as one large document instead of a series of documents that need to be resolved against each other. [Gestalt theory is a broadly interdisciplinary general theory which provides a framework for a wide variety of psychological phenomena, processes, and applications. Human beings are viewed as open systems in active interaction with their environment. It is especially suited for the understanding of order and structure in psychological events, ... (as) opposed (to) the elementistic approach to psychological events, associationism, behaviorism, and to psychoanalysis. SOCIETY FOR GESTALT THEORY AND ITS APPLICATIONS (1998) http://www.psycho.uni-osnabrueck.de/fach/gta/]. For example; imagine someone creates a Web page. Displayed on this page are a title and three articles. The person who created the page wrote the title. The articles, however, are actually pulled automatically from other documents. Once viewed in conjunction, each article influences the other articles meaning and impact. When a reader goes to the web page, the reader may or may not be aware that the page is a collection of separate articles; instead, the page is viewed as a single document. When we can make this example work within 3D communication, as it already does for web pages, the same results will occur. We will begin to think of a design document as a Gestalt instead of a collection of documents, and it is then that we will see the beginning of a new paradigm in design communication, which may lead to changes in the design process itself.

The ability to navigate a space at one's own volition can substantially accelerate cognitive understanding. As information about the environment is no longer abstracted into a static 2-dimensional image, the viewer does not have to make a cognitive leap to understand the environment that is being presented. Using VRML, Java and HTML, we can now create an environment that will allow information from various specialists to be viewed simultaneously by anyone at anytime. (The Virtual Reality Modeling Language (VRML) is a language for describing multi-user interactive simulations — virtual worlds networked via the global Internet and hyperlinked within the World Wide Web. VRML is to 3D what HTML is to 2D. Rather than describing the location of 2D text and images on a page, VRML files describe the location of objects in a 3D space. As with HTML, VRML objects may be links to other objects, URLs, inline images, movies and sounds. In addition to the properties of HTML, VRML objects may be animated and interact with other objects and the user.) We can also expand the nature of that information by allowing animations, as well as allow the user to choose what information is to be viewed. This paper describes such an environment, called Archville. Currently it is being used as an example in the instruction of collaboration of design and the use of the Internet to exchange information.

2 Cardboard City

The inspiration and guide to the work reported here was a design studio, called 'The Cardboard City Exercise,'[1] which was intended to teach students about the collaborative aspects of architectural design. Its premise was that Architecture is a collaborative enterprise, where virtually all building projects are the product of the contributions of many professionals, as well as public agencies and users. Traditional design studios in most schools, however, ignore the social, political, and other collaborative dimensions of the problem, and instead promote the individual experience of each student. This abstraction is intended to equip students with the basic proficiencies needed for their professional careers. Having been sheltered from the social, collaborative dimensions of the problem, graduates are often shocked to discover that the 'real' world of architectural design is very different from their academic experience; it is much 'messier,' in terms of the number of individuals who are involved in the decision-making process, and in terms of the constraints their 'creations' must meet.

Figure 1. View of Cardboard City.

The Cardboard City exercise was given to third-year architecture students from the late seventies until nineteen eighty-seven. It was intended to teach them, among other things, how to deal with the creation of spaces as a collaborative form-making effort, rather than as an individualized effort. The exercise involved the design and physical construction of a cardboard 'city,' on 3'x 3' plots in a pre-designed 'urban landscape' (Figure 1). Students were assigned 'city' plots through a lottery system, and instructed to design a 'defined place for sitting.' Although the project was assigned as an individual design task, students were given the option to join with other students and build a larger structure collectively. Many students opted to work in groups, thus maximizing resources. As in real life, group work often entailed endless discussions and political power plays, which offset the time and resources saved.

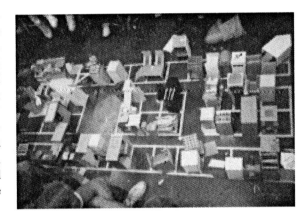

Figure 2. Design phase of Cardboard City.

Students were also required to make an effort to conform their designs to the designs of their neighbors, or come to some common agreement on the vocabulary of form. This last requirement, together with group work effort, turned the Cardboard City project into an exercise in collaboration, as much as it was an exercise in physical design (Figure 2). Students learned the importance of politics in design, the destructive force of separatists, and the impact of decisions made by others on their own designs. It became the 'right of passage' exercise to upper-level studios, and a source of pride to the students who participated in it. But the creation of Cardboard City by 75 students also inflicted so much damage on the design studio facilities, in terms of cardboard mess, gouged tables, floor tiles, and any other surface the students could use for cutting, that the exercise had to be discontinued.

2.1 Resurrecting the City

The advent of computing technology, in particular the Internet, allows us now to resurrect the Cardboard City exercise, using computer visualization in lieu of cardboard. Archville, as the new exercise is called, is pedagogically similar to the Cardboard City exercise (Figure 3). As with the Cardboard City exercise, each student is given a plot in an urban landscape and must design their houses for each plot in agreement (or disagreement) with their neighbors. Specifically, they are required to establish some common design elements with their closest neighbors.

Archville allows students to walk through the 'city' at anytime to experience their design as well as those done by others in the class. Students can interact with the model and query information from it. They can also see each other walking though the environment, in the form of avatars, and communicate with fellow students. Finally, work that has been done in previous semesters need not

Figure 3. View of Archville in a VRML player.

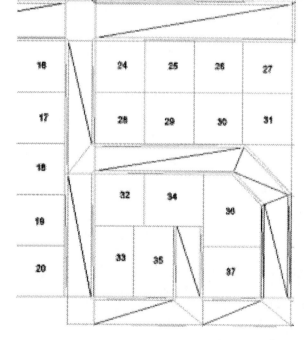

Figure 4. Plots used in Archville.

be 'taken down' at the end of the exercise. Rather, buildings can be left where they are, creating a sense of history and a city that can grow and evolve over the semesters. If more space is needed, the instructor can simply create more landscaping within the computer model. Since we are working within a virtual environment, there is no limit to the size of Archville.

3 The Archville System

Archville is a distributed, Web-based VR system that allows multiple users to interact with multiple models at the same time. Using a combination of HTML, Java and VRML, the system can display information, such as text, images and geometry, in a single dynamic environment. (The idea behind distributed VR is very simple; a simulated world is stored not on one computer system, but on several. The computers are connected over a network (typically the global Internet) and people using those computers are able to interact in real time, sharing the same data in the same virtual world.) It does so by calling files from distributed sources, integrating those files, and then displaying the information.

The heart of the Archville system is a small set of files referred to as the 'Address Book.' These files contain, in a structured manner, the URL address of each student that is involved in the project. As each file is read from the Address Book it is loaded from the Internet, the VRML viewer integrates the file's content into the scene. This continues until all the files have been loaded. If a file cannot be found, the visitor is alerted and the program then goes on to the next file.

A model of the urban layout is placed on the Web in the format of the 3D tool employed that semester (Figure 4). Students then download the model to their computers. Students locate each site they are assigned; and design their own buildings within it. When the students are finished with their designs, they 'post' them by saving the files in a public directory that are accessible by the Archville program through the Internet. The URL of each file is entered in the Address Book, so the files can be loaded into the combined scene. When the student accesses the Archville Web site, his or her model is displayed on the plot they were assigned, along with all the other students' buildings.

Although currently implemented in 3D Studio Max (3dsMax), the Archville system will work just as well using AutoCad, MicroCad, FormZ, or any other 3D-modeling program that supports the VRML format. There are also many translator programs that can convert most 2D and 3D vector formats into VRML. 3dsMax was chosen because it supports some VRML nodes (programming) within the modeling program itself. Many of these nodes support attaching hyperlinks to 3D objects, for starting animations based on the viewer's location or the clicking on an object. For example, the elevators in the office buildings are programmed to take the viewer to the floor selected on the elevator control panel. Once there, the VRML scene is reloaded with the interior of the selected floor. Another example is the sculpture in Archville's central park. One student programmed the rings to move when the user presses a button at the base of the sculpture. The other button takes the viewer to that student's Web page. This student had no idea about VRML programming; this was all done in 3dsMax (Figure 6). Recently, students have been asked to place 'mail boxes' in front of their building such that anyone can email the author or download a copy of their model.

A Java applet can control the content of the displayed scene. When Archville is launched, only the landscape (streets and sidewalks) appears in the 3D scene. Using a set of buttons located at the bottom of the browser window, the user can load selected files. Once loaded, that same button controls the visibility of those files. For example, the students can load only those files that were created by their classmates. Alternatively, they can load files created in former semesters. This facility helps avoid information overload, and the problems associated with displaying a large model on a relatively slow machine. If they use a powerful enough machine, all the files can be loaded. With over 90+ students using Archville each semester, and with 1000+ polygons per student, the VRML scene quickly exceeds 100,000 polygons every semester, not including structures that were left behind from previous semesters.

Also available to the viewer is a 'chat box.' Using a Java program created by Stephen White called Vnet, this program displays a window below the VRML viewer that allows users to talk to other users who are logged onto the system. When Vnet first appears, the users are asked to choose a name to login as, and then choose an avatar to represent them in the VRML scene. When encountering other users in Archville, they can see each other and talk to each other. Conversations can be logged for future examination to track the evolution of the design.

Figure 5. View of the Central Park and sculpture.

3.1 How Does Archville Work?

The students create all the 3D files, with exception to the landscaping and the urban layout, which is created by the instructors. A model of the urban layout, known as the 'master reference model,' is placed on the Web in the format of the 3D tool employed that semester.

The file that links the works of individual students with the site is a simple HTML file that loads a VRML file and any Java applets that are to be used in the scene. The HTML file (Archville.html) looks like this:

```
<HTML>
....
<BODY>
<embed src="Root.wrl" width="600" height="400"
<APPLET CODE="visabilityControl.class" WIDTH=600 HEIGHT=100 maytag></APPLET>
.... </BODY> </HTML>
```

The third line loads the VRML viewer and the VRML file called Root. The next line brings up a Java program used to load/hide/unhide groups of geometry within Archville.

The VRML file (Root.wrl) that is loaded looks like this:

```
#VRML V2.0 utf8
DEF Start Viewpoint {
        description "one"
        position 40 5 10
        orientation 0 1 0 0
}
Background {
        skyColor [0.62353 0.62353 1, ]
        groundColor [.3 .4 1, ]
}
DirectionalLight {
  ambientIntensity  1
  color             1 1 1
  direction         -0.612 -0.4598 -0.6435
  intensity         .7
  on                TRUE
}
Inline { url "streets.wrl" }
Inline { url "treasureIsland.wrl" }
Inline { url "groupA.wrl" }
Inline { url "groupB.wrl" }
Inline { url "groupC.wrl" }
...
```

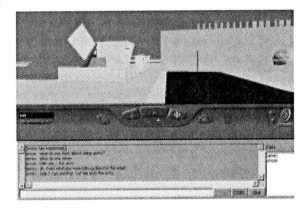

Figure 6. Vnet chat box within Archville. Avatar in center.

Figure 7. A group of houses using color and shape to resolve collaboration effort.

This code sets up the basic environment of an initial viewpoint, lights, and background. The Inline statements load the street geometry and the surrounding landscape. The other Inline statements call the Address Books of the different groups contributing to Archville.

The URL address of each student is placed into a file based on the student's subgroup. This file is known as the Address Book. A typical group file (groupA.wrl) looks like this:

```
#VRML V2.0 utf8
# Group A, Spring Semester
Inline { url "http://...berkeley.edu/~studenta/plot12.wrl" }
Inline { url "http://...berkeley.edu/~studentb/myhouse.wrl" }
Inline { url "http://...berkeley.edu/~studentc/assignment4.wrl" }
...
```

When the student accesses the Archville program (Archville.html), his or her model is displayed on the assigned plot, along with all the other students' buildings. As each file loads, that geometry appears in the scene, so as time goes on, more and more objects 'pop' into the scene. Each time the viewer goes to the site, or when the viewer clicks on the 'refresh' button on his or her browser, he or she will always see the latest files.

3.2 Pedagogy

Archville is not a computer program as much as it is a teaching tool. In most design schools, students tend to work in a vacuum, unaffected by what is done by other students. By going through the Archville exercise, students are exposed to the idea that design is derived from

Figure 8. View of paths that do not completely match up.

more than a grand concept from one person, but from the cooperation of many people.

Although Archville is used in two courses, the collaborative aspect of the exercise is only explored in the Introduction to 3D Modeling course. This is a 7-week course that meets once a week, given twice each semester with an average enrollment of 17 students per half-semester. Here the students spend three weeks on the exercise and although the amount of time the students are exposed to the environment is far too short, the students still get hands-on experience with posting files, loading files and collaborating with others in a design environment.

The exercise begins with a quick explanation of collaborative design as well as an explanation of the Archville system. Students are assigned a plot in the landscape that they are to build on and then shown how to place an external reference of that landscape into their computers. This is an example of referencing library objects. The 3D model for the urban landscape resides on the server, and any changes made to the streets are automatically updated in the students' models.

Typically the students are allowed to build anything they wish and encouraged to let their imaginations run free as long as the model does not exceed 2000 polygons. Typically, a wide range of designs are created by the students, from common-looking houses to interesting sculptures, to a tree house designed by one student. The first part of the assignment is due the same day the assignment is given to encourage quick and highly abstract designs. Students are then shown how to post their VRML models to a web site and then look for their model when they open Archville. The end result is an urban setting that is populated almost overnight with 17 unique buildings. Surprisingly, the most common question I get from students is: 'How does my model show up in the correct place in the urban landscape?' Since the landscape model is the same model of which the VRML landscape was created, the coordinates will have the same points of reference. For example, if the student's plot was 154' from the center of Archville, when that student starts building his or her model, she or he is building it 154' from center. When it is exported and then viewed in Archville, it will appear 154' from center.

After one week, students are told that they must adapt their design, and/or convince their neighbors to change theirs, such that there is an agreed-upon design element in common with each of their local neighbors. Local neighbors are those students whose properties are directly across from, and adjacent to, the student. This keeps the number of collaborators in check. Normally color is used to accomplish this but scale and language is acceptable also. The idea is for students to experience the challenge and frustration of a moving target when designing. As a student makes a change to work with one neighbor, that element may no longer be valid because that neighbor changed to meet the task criteria for some other neighbor. Surprisingly, by the end of the week, most issues have been resolved. Students begin to realize the importance of up-to-date information that is easy to access. In the Cardboard City exercise, students would not know what their neighbors' design changes would be until a week or more after the changes took place.

The third week of the exercise asks the students to make a path that connects from one neighbor to another. This forces the students to rely on files from other people. To accomplish this, students must now share their models with each other instead of just viewing them. Using 3dsMax, the students are shown how to make links in their VRML models to allow others to download the VRML file to their computers. This is a difficult task in such a short amount of time for beginning students. Typically less then half of the class is able to complete this phase.

4 Conclusions

The Archville exercise demonstrates to students how we can use computing and the Internet to design collaboratively. It also points out the need to have correct up-to-date information when working on collaborative projects because of the dynamic nature of the design process. Archville also allows the students to think about their designs more dynamically since 3dsMax supports animation and simple interactive programming for VRML.

Over the many semesters Archville has been used, there have been certain problems that have been difficult to resolve. First, there is never enough time. This course is an introduction to 3D modeling. Students are just learning how to create objects much less learning how to deal with the difficulties of collaborative design. To mediate this problem we underplay the design aspect of the exercise as much as possible. This allows the students to do what they like without worrying about "good" design. Second, the students who already have some 3D experience, or are quick studies, tend to have a greater influence on design conflict resolution than more beginning students. To reduce the influence of the more experienced students, we try to cluster students with like skills as much as possible. Finally, learning how to use a 3D modeling program is difficult enough, but to also understand the principles of low-polygon modeling is an extra learning step. This skill is also important for the teaching assistants, most of whom only have a functional understanding of the software, much less are trained in low-polygon modeling and VRML environments.

Despite these problems, student feedback on the exercise has been positive. For many students these classes are the first exposure they have had to 3D modeling, or being able to walk through a model on the computer in real time. By providing an alternative view to drawings and scale models, the students begin to deal with issues of multiple views, of movement within an urban context, and issues of how other students interact with their designs. Many students are amazed at the ease they can create virtual environments and some go beyond the scope of the assignment to create wonderful models with interesting animations and VRML programming. Students are also surprised at the difficulty of working with others on a project, especially one that progresses as fast as Archville does. And it is just this understanding, as well as the benefits that having a collaborative digital environment, that Archville is meant to demonstrate. Creating a large virtual environment takes quite a bit of work. By sharing the task, a virtual world can be created in a short amount of time. This is an example of different professionals working together to create something that is too large and diverse for one person to create alone. Although in our case each student is creating the same thing (a building), this idea is not hard to expand into different specialties (Engineers, HVAC, etc.) working on the same building.

It is quite clear that Archville needs to be more than a three-week exercise. We are currently exploring the possibility of extending it into a semester-long design studio. In this studio, students will not only create VR models, but also create the data behind those models. We will also look at issues like construction costs. For example, we can give students a certain budget that they can spend on 'purchasing' the property they want. The more they spend on the property, the less money they will have left over for their building. Each building will be priced based on the number of polygons they use. The students may then have to form associations with other students to combine their resources. We have also discussed the possibility of students working in teams, in which one student will be responsible for the circulation of the building, another for the façade and landscaping, and another for the layout of the rooms or offices.

References

Barrea, Deborah, Cheryl Eslinger, Kim McGoff, Cynthia Tonnesen, "GROUP COLLABORATION IN THE VIRTUAL CLASSROOM: an Evaluation of Collaborative Learning in the Virtual Classroom of CMSC 828S and the Technology that Supports It" Unpublished evaluation of "Virtual Reality, Telepresence, and Beyond." University of Maryland in the fall of 1993.

Chastain, Thomas, Yehuda E. Kalay, Christopher Peri, (1998) "Square Peg in a Round Hole or Horseless Carriage? Reflections on the Use of Computing in Architecture " pp. 4 - 15 Media and Design process, ACADIA 1999, ed. Ataman and J. Bermudez

Davis, Stephen Boyd (1996) Contributors Avon Huxor, John Lansdown. "The DESIGN of Virtual Environments with particular reference to VRML" Centre for Electronic Arts Middlesex University

Downs, Roger M. and Stea, David. (1973). Image and Environment: Cognitive Mapping and Spatial Behavior. Chicago: Aldine Pub. Co.

Fraser, Glen and Scott S.Fisher, "REAL-TIME INTERACTIVE GRAPHICS Intelligent Virtual Worlds Continue to Develop." Telepresence Research Inc. Vol.32 No.3 August 1998 ACM SIGGRAPH

Hughes, Kevin. (1995). From Webspace to cyberspace. Enterprise Integration Technologies. Menlo Park, CA.

Leigh, Jason, Andrew E. Johnson, Christina A. Vasilakis, Thomas A. DeFanti "Multi-perspective Collaborative Design in Persistent Networked Virtual Environments." VRAIS'96, http://www.evl.uic.edu/spiff/calvin/calvin.vrais/index.HTML Electronic Visualization Laboratory (EVL), University of Illinois at Chicago

Laiserin, Jerry (January 1999) "The Future of AEC Technology," CADENCE magazine (jan) pp. 20-26

Jestaz, Bertrand (1995). Architecture of the Renaissance: From Brunelleschi to Palladio. Discoveries, Harry N. Abrams, Ltd., New York.

Stanney, Kay M., Ronald R. Mourant, Robert S. Kennedy "Human Factors Issues in Virtual Environments: A Review of the Literature " Presence, Vol. 7, No.4, August 98, 327-351, MIT

Lansdown, John. (1994). Visualizing design ideas. In Lindsay MacDonald and John Vince (Eds.), Interacting With Virtual Environments. New York: Chichester.

Lasko-Harvill, Ann. (1993). Interface devices. In Teresa Middleton (Ed.), Virtual Worlds : Real Challenges. Papers from SRI's 1991 Conference on Virtual Reality. Westport, CT: Meckler.

MacDonald, Lindsay, and Vince, John (Eds). (1994). Interacting with Virtual Environments. New York: J. Wiley & Sons.

Nasar, Jack L. (winter 1990). The evaluative image of the city. Journal of the American Planning Association, 56, no. 1.

Neisser, Ulric. (1976). Cognition and Reality : Principles and Implications of Cognitive Psychology. San Francisco: W. H. Freeman.

Pagels, Hienz R. (1988). The Dreams of Reason: The Computer and the Rise of the Sciences of Complexity. Simon and Schuster, New York.

Passini, Romedi. (1984). Wayfinding In Architecture. New York: Van Nostrand Reinhold Company.

Proffit, Dennis R., and Kaiser, Mary K. (1993). Perceiving environmental properties from motion, information: minimal conditions. In Stephen R. Ellis (Ed.), Pictorial Communication In Virtual and Real Environments, (2nd ed.). Bristol, PA: Taylor & Francis.

Rapoport, Amos. (1990). The Meaning of the Built Environment: A Nonverbal Communication Approach. Beverly Hills: Sage Publications.

Rheingold, Howard. (1990). What's the big deal about cyberspace? In Brenda Lauren (Ed.), The Art of Human-Computer Interface Design. Reading, Mass: Addison-Wesley Publishing Company.

Trieb, Marc. (1983) The Cardboard City Exercise, the Journal of Architectural Education

White, Stephen. Vnet. http://nvrcad.coventry.ac.uk/Vnet/

Alternative Architecture

"Is it architecture?" is a question that the authors in this section have probably faced. In the narrow sense of the considered participation in design, construction or criticism of buildings of a certain type and pretentiousness, thee papers may not fit into the classification of architecture. However, if one understands architecture as a discipline and pattern of thought, these papers are clearly well within the tradition.

The paper by Johnson and Xia is closely an extrapolation beyond narrow architectural concerns to address the concerns also of owners of buildings. The examples that they describe show how those who have learned from the recent boom in e-commerce and e-business can define new an unique value opportunities within the broad field of facilities and habitable environment.

Literature, art and expression are topics addressed by both Anders and Li and Maher in their respective papers. New media and multimedia art are examined as to their spatial implications. They each make strong theoretical cases that the spatial talents of architects are important to successful design of places on the web. The print metaphor is inadequate, or merely a missed opportunity, for Webzines, chat rooms, and other communication media that are emerging on the Internet.

The final paper, with a long author list led by Bermudez, applies principles that are widely accepted and understood by architects in a field that previously has been largely unaware of them. Visual thinking and visual design are so widely accepted in architecture that they are often taken for granted. However, the medical professions have often suffered from visual illiteracy that, when expressed in the display of vital signs, can be dangerous or even fatal.

These papers exhibit vital and far-ranging intellects that are inseparably architectural in characteristics. They are examples that, if more widely perused, can bring hybrid vigor into the architecture discipline and profession.

The Impact of E-Commerce on the Design and Construction Industry

Robert E. Johnson, CRS Center, Texas A&M University, USA

Ge Xia, CRS Center, Texas A&M University, USA

Abstract

Historically, the design and construction industry has been slow to innovate. As a result, productivity in the construction industry has declined substantially compared to other industries. Inefficiencies in this industry are well documented. However, the potential for cost savings and increased efficiency through the use of the Internet and e-commerce may not only increase the efficiency of the design and construction industry, but it may also significantly change the structure and composition of the industry. This is suggested because effective implementations of e-commerce technologies are not limited to one aspect of one industry. E-commerce may be most effective when it is thought of and applied to multi-industry enterprises and in a global context.

This paper continues the exploration of a concept that we have been working on for several years, namely that "…information technology is evolving from a tool that incrementally improves 'back-office' productivity to an essential component of strategic positioning that may alter the basic economics, organizational structure and operational practices of facility management organizations and their interactions with service providers (architects, engineers and constructors)." (Johnson and Clayton 1998) This paper will utilize the case study methodology to explore these issues as they are affecting the AEC/FM industry.

1 The Problem

As figure 1 shows, construction productivity seriously lags behind other industries. It is not hard to see why. According to one article, "inefficiencies, mistakes and delays account for $200 billion of the $650 billion spend on construction in America every year." (The Economist 2000). This article goes on to say that the typical $100 million building project requires 150,000 separate documents such as working drawings, contracts, change orders, and requests for information.

Other industries have improved productivity through investing in information technology. The advent of the Internet and business-to-business e-commerce promises a continued increase in this trend. The definition of e-commerce has evolved as the use of the Internet has evolved. We use e-commerce in this proposal to mean all aspects of business and market processes enabled by the Internet and web technologies, including supporting issues such as data standards for interoperability. However, we also interpret e-commerce as something that is more than a collection of computer technologies. As in our previous study, we view e-commerce as the strategic deployment of technologies. The US Department of Commerce has estimated 1) that high technology has driven more

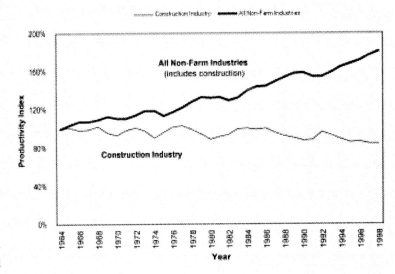

Figure 1. Construction Productivity Index, 1964-1998 (Constant $ of contracts / workhours of hourly workers). This table was developed by Paul Teicholz, Professor Emeritus, Stanford, from data published by the US Bureau of Labor Statistics, Department of Commerce.

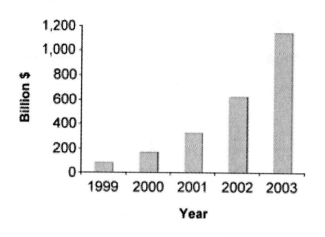

Figure 2. Business to Business E-commerce Revenue Estimates (www.idc.com 2000).

than a quarter of all economic growth since 1993 and 2) information technology sectors are growing at double the rate of the overall economy. The International Data Corporation (IDC) has reported (see Figure 2) that business-to-business e-commerce in the US is expected to grow from $80 billion in 1999 to almost $1,140 billion in 2003 (www.idc.com 2000).

The Internet and related applications associated with e-commerce have grown much more rapidly than anyone guessed even five years ago, spawning often radically new ways of communication, collaboration and coordination among consumers, businesses and trading partners. At the time of our 1996 survey, the web was being used primarily as a reporting mechanism. By late 1997 it had already become clear that the Internet would have an important impact on group decision processes and that database connectivity would transform the web into a dynamic decision support system. Still, the advent of business-to-business e-commerce ventures such as business-to-business procurement and "cybermediaries" (who bring together previously unknown buyers and sellers) is an even more recent phenomenon with significant implications for design, construction and facility management. The purpose of this paper is to try to outline some of these implications.

Since innovations in the design and construction industry tend to lag behind others, an example from another industry might be instructive. Ford Motor Company recently announced their intention to become a New Economy, e-business company. Buy 2010, Ford expects to look more like Cisco, a company that manufactures very little (Akasie, 2000). The new Ford vision is to enable customers to purchase cars the way computers are bought at Dell. Business-to-Business e-commerce processes will facilitate the substitution of outside companies for manufacturing that is currently company-owned (outsourcing). The idea is to connect the car buyer directly with the "supply chain." Substantial cost reduction is anticipated from improved efficiencies in transactions to lower inventories. In addition, Ford will have the ability to, for the first time, track consumer preferences after the sale through the life cycle of the automobile.

2 Conceptual Framework

In order to conduct this study we developed a conceptual framework (see Figure 3). The conceptual framework adopted by this research is an outgrowth of our earlier research that explored the role of information technology in facility management. This research began with a survey of how information technology is being used in Fortune 500 companies. We continued this research with studies on intranets, "best practice" site visits, and a series of studies with USAA that focused on as-built drawings and the use of information in a specific corporate environment. This research resulted in a number of findings that may be summarized in the conceptual model below (Figure 3).

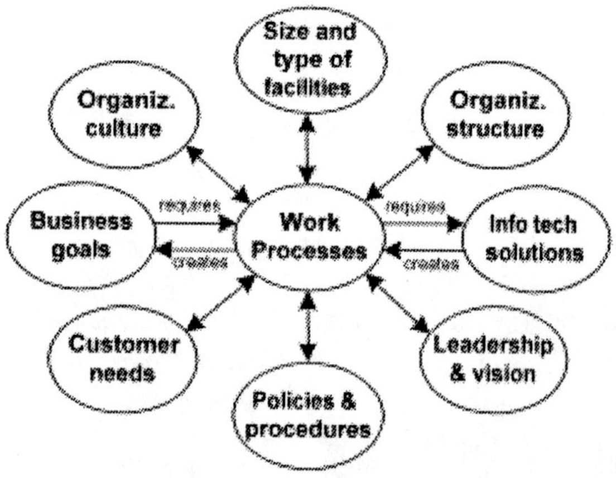

Figure 3. Summary of Recent Research on IT and Facility Management.

Through our research we found that the role of information technology was significantly influenced by a variety of factors that appeared to be unique to a given organization. The type of information technology solution adopted to improve work processes in a facility management organization was strongly influenced by the characteristics and goals of the parent corporation. For example, facility management departments that were managing multiple sites in different countries were likely to plan and implement information technology solutions in a manner that is entirely different from departments that manage space within a single building. Companies that had adopted charge-back policies used different information to drive decisions than companies that did not have such policies.

The adoption of information technology was also influenced by the type of industry. Different industry groups tended to adopt technology in different rates and in different ways. We concluded that a number of organizational characteristics may be important factors that will influence how information technology was adopted within a given organization.

More recently, we have extended this model as indicated in Figure 4, below. This revised model hypothesizes that business goals are linked to investments in e-commerce because of the desire to improve efficiency and effectiveness. However, it also suggests that e-commerce is not only causing companies to rethink business processes, but is also creating the possibility for entirely new forms of business processes and organizations (see also Huang 1999 and Malone 1993). The purpose of this paper, therefore, is to explore the impact that e-commerce is having on the design, construction industry and facility management industry.

3 E-Commerce Definition

E-commerce is most commonly referred to as Internet-based buying and selling of goods and services. Another way to think of e-commerce is simply as conducting business on-line. This includes, for example, buying and selling products with digital cash but it may also include trading products, goods and services. Using this definition, e-commerce has many similarities with catalog shopping and home shopping using cable TV. But e-commerce is not limited to this definition of on-line buying and selling. It also leads to fundamental changes in the way products and services are distributed and exchanged, involving all aspects of a business. The real revolutionary potential of e-commerce is in its effects on three different kinds of business processes: a) within-business processes, b) business-to-business processes (e.g., supply-chain management) and business-to-consumer processes. Improvements in all three of these areas will impact the AEC/FM industry.

Figure 4. E-Commerce Research Framework.

4 Research Questions

The framework we presented above has suggested two fundamental questions that we sought to explore as part of this research:

1. What is the affect of e-commerce on the ability of AEC organizations to achieve their business goals? How might e-commerce significantly alter those business goals?

Business-to-business e-commerce is used for coordinating the purchasing operations of a company and its suppliers. It also is being used to improve customer service and maintenance operations. Companies of all sizes can communicate with each other without the need for traditional intermediaries. We will discuss developments in supply-side management in the AEC/FM industry and provide some examples of how this is changing the thinking of the role of real property design, construction and facility management.

2. What is the effect of e-commerce on business work processes? Does the effective design and implementation of e-commerce solutions vary among organizations?

E-commerce technologies are emerging in the AEC/FM industry and may significantly change the way business is done. Through our case studies we will explore several examples of within-business processes, business-to-business processes, and business-to-consumer processes in order to learn how different types of organizations in the design and construction industry are using e-commerce.

5 E-Commerce Case Studies

The following case studies help to illustrate how various organizations in the AEC/FM business are thinking about and using e-commerce today. As this is an exploratory study, these cases are not intended to be comprehensive.

5.1 E-Commerce Solutions for Project Management (3D/International)

The use of information technology and the Internet to manage projects was identified early on as a very good way to improve value. Sites such as BidCom, Cephren and BuildPoint are attempting to create globally recognized web portals for design and construction. Because of the extensive publicity surrounding these web sites, these sites will not be covered in this paper. These sites have proven to be effective for typical project management tasks such as document and RFI management and are vying for positions as major portals for business-to-business online purchasing in the construction industry. However, some of the largest architecture/engineering firms are pursuing a different strategy in attempting to improve their competitive position by providing customized e-commerce tools to clients. One of those firms is 3D/International.

3D/International (3D/I) was founded in 1953 as an architectural practice. Today it is a multidisciplinary architecture/engineering firm with its headquarters in Houston, Texas and multi-project offices in 12 locations. What makes 3D/I unusual in the industry is the fact that they invest about $1 million per year on research and maintain a staff of about 15 people who are dedicated to developing program management information systems to support their design and construction management services (Thomsen 2001).

Description of Software Solution

3D/I's software has been created to support what is now their core business: the management of large design and construction programs. The programs they have developed include three major software tools (COMET, IMPACT and COSMOS) as well as a number of project-specific web sites and web-based project manuals (see Figure 5). This software is typically customized to the needs of individual clients. 3D/I typically gives the software (code plus data) to clients for their use after the project is completed at no charge. Custom-developed modules are written in standard languages such as Visual Basic so that they may be maintained by the client.

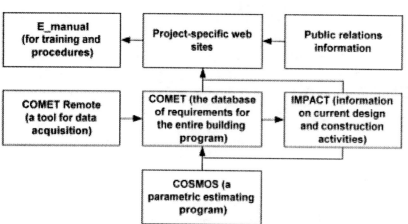

Figure 5. 3D/I Project Information Systems.

COMET (Condition Management Estimation Technology) was developed to help assess and evaluate facilities. COMET provides a method for inventorying, estimating and tracking facility deficiencies as well as projecting future facility renewal costs. It includes *COMET Remote*, which runs on a hand-held Pentium Windows-based PC, and *COMET PC*, which is used to facilitate uploading data from COMET Remote. This software system is used to record building deficiencies, project repair costs, and bundle deficiencies into projects.

IMPACT (Integrated Management, Project Accounting & Controls Technology) operates on a LAN, a WAN, and the Internet but keeps cost, schedule and quality information in one central database. It tracks details on each project, and can produce reports on total program management. Information, activities and agreements are organized by categories of cost, schedule and scope (quality). Report formats can be tailored to meet the unique needs of project managers or clients.

COSMOS (Cost Model System) is conceptual estimating software that is integrated with the RS Means cost database as well as 3D/I's historical construction estimate database. The system creates cost models from its historical data that are modified to fit different projects and conditions. The software allows the user to test the cost implications of changes in any building system or component.

3D/I also develops and maintains project and program websites to publish information about construction management projects and programs. This enables team members to communicate with each other, clients, contractors, and with the public. They are similar to other project management web site systems in that they are used to share cost and scope information, schedules, meeting minutes, web-based procedure manuals and drawings and other project information.

3D/I is an example of how one company has used e-commerce applications to differentiate itself from other service providers in an industry where design and construction management services are increasingly seen as commodities. Instead of using one of the increasingly popular web-based project management approaches it uses software to not only leverage its abilities and skills, but more importantly to customize its products in such a way that it's services become unique and different from those sold by its competitors. It is an approach that is only available to the largest companies in the industry. The remaining question is whether or not even the large companies have the resources to keep up with the emerging "dot-coms" in the design and construction industry.

5.2 Operational Effectiveness (Conoco)

A major benefit for introducing concepts of e-commerce into an organization is to improve operational effectiveness. Common operational improvement objectives include improving productivity, decreasing costs or avoiding costs. One organization that exemplifies this approach is the facility management department at Conoco.

Conoco Inc., is a global energy company with 17,000 employees in 40 countries and is involved in various aspects of the oil and gas industry. Its revenues in 1998 were $23.2 billion. Previously a subsidiary of DuPont, Conoco Inc. completed its separation in August 1999. The headquarters of Conoco is located in Houston, Texas and occupies 16 buildings of 1.25 million square foot on a site of 64 acres. The on-site population is about 2,570 employees and the churn rate is 60-70%.

The structure of the facility management (FM) group reflects the company's "small and smart" strategy. The FM group was downsized and reengineered and since 1992 the staff decreased from more than 100 to only 9. The majority of the maintenance and operation work orders are outsourced to about 40-50 contract workers who reside on site. Every effort is made to maintain a small in-house staff that is both competent and efficient. As a result of downsizing it became essential to adopt e-commerce approaches.

In their attempt to automate facilities management, many companies acquire comprehensive CAFM packages that end up sitting on their shelves gathering dust (Teicholz & Ikeda 1995). The best strategy to prevent the "shelfware" phenomenon is to "put first thing first" – clearly state your key objectives and aim at them. In Conoco's case, their highest priorities were project management, operations and maintenance, and customer services. After carefully evaluating their needs, Conoco decided on a two-part strategy for improving operational efficiency:

1. Use of a non-graphical system. Many computer-aided facility management systems utilize spatial management functions, such as CAD and space management. In Conoco's case, however, the configuration of the physical facilities did not change very much and therefore a graphic-based system was not necessary. Therefore, they selected a computerized maintenance management system (MAXIMO Advantage) that did not incorporate a graphical space management component.
2. Use of standard, off-the-shelf software. Instead of purchasing specialized FM software, Conoco facilities managers exploited the fact that the company had standardized on Microsoft Office throughout the corporation. Although other software may provide more functionality, the fact that virtually every employee in Conoco had the identical Microsoft Office configuration was identified as a significant advantage. Applications were developed using Microsoft Outlook, Access, and Microsoft Exchange Server to handle many scheduling, communication, and space allocation functions.

The standardized and extensive use of the off-the-shelf software enhanced productivity, allowed the facility management group to easily connect with all employees in Conoco, and substantially reduced the cost of both implementation and training. Using this approach, issues such as interoperability and CAFM integration with the larger enterprise were non-existent. It is an example of how the implementation of e-commerce technology can be used to significantly improve within-business processes with minimal expense.

5.3 Web Portals (HomeWrite)

Among the recent "dot-com" start-ups in the AEC/FM industry is HomeWrite (www.homewrite.com). HomeWrite has positioned itself as an interactive Web-Portal for homeowners, builders, remodelers, contractors and anyone else whose business or interest is homes. Its mission is to provide web-based services and tools that are tailored to the needs of various providers and customers in the homebuilding industry.

To achieve its goals, HomeWrite has forged alliances with other web sites such as www.repairnow.com (a web site designed to help home owners keep their homes in good repair and find qualified service providers), www.thehomevine.com (a web-community for experts and amateurs to exchange information about homes), www.homepreservation.com (a web site for home preventative maintenance and repair services), www.homeportfolio.com (a site that lets users choose favorite home products and organize them in an online scrapbook for communication spouse, builder, architect, or designer), and others. In addition, they have created a permanent, web-based online home record and owner's manual for homeowners. Think of it as the homeowner's equivalent of Quicken. All information about a home (floor plans, construction pictures, warranty information, etc) is accessible from the Internet. The idea is that contractors will input information as a value added for homebuyers. It is available when homeowners need it for repairs, remodeling, resale, etc.

The HomeWrite case study demonstrates the use of e-commerce for both business-to-business as well as business-to-consumer process improvement. It is an example of how one company is trying to position itself to be "the" electronic information broker for the home building industry.

5.4 Integrated E-Business Strategies (Luminant Worldwide)

A trend in the AEC/FM industry is the increased competition from non-traditional service providers such as Arthur Anderson Consulting. This trend was identified in last year's AIA convention by presenter Mike Brandon, "S56-Business Management Trends Affecting the A/E Industry", Friday, May 7, 1999. Consulting firms are getting involved in providing design services because their clients are demanding a single integrated strategy and solution for their business problems. Often, this strategy involves the design of buildings.

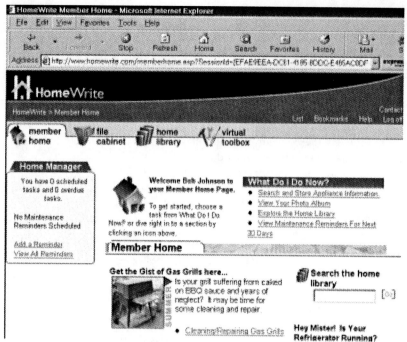

Figure 6. Screen image of a HomeWrite home page.

A related trend in the industry is the outsourcing of AEC/FM services to contract workers. Companies often do this to decrease costs, but another incentive is the ability to identify and organize "best in class" service providers so that they can focus on their "core business" and create more value for the corporation. This has resulted in the definition of a new term, "Infrastructure Management", which is defined as "the integrated management of non-core functions." (Wales 2000).

Luminant Worldwide (www.luminant.com) is a relatively new company whose mission is to provide a single integrated business strategy to those companies who have a special focus on e-business. Part of their service portfolio is developing strategies for the management of a company's infrastructure and facilities. They provide strategic planning services to Global 1000 and Internet-centric companies that specialize in creating Internet value. Of particular interest to this paper is the dual focus on corporate infrastructure management and e-commerce.

As described by Luminant (Wales 2000), "point" solutions that address specific operational needs have led to the proliferation of incompatible solutions and are no longer acceptable. The new goal of many clients requires managing all assets as a strategic component of overall business strategy. This can only be accomplished by creating truly corporate-wide infrastructure solutions using e-commerce principles and technologies.

One example of the impact of this strategy on the AEC industry is provided by Nortel. Material in this section is taken largely from a presentation by Mr. Juan Cano of Nortel at an IDRC Chapter Meeting, Houston, Texas, June 6, 2000. Not very long ago, Nortel was a manufacturer of telephone switch equipment; they have since reinvented themselves to be an eBusiness "virtual" enterprise providing support through both hardware and services. Nortel has embarked on a program code-named the Mercury Principle. Prior to this program, Nortel had a large, internal facilities department similar to that shown in Figure 7. In this traditional organization, Nortel had a large facilities staff with 10 separate departments and hundreds of employees. Each department had a manager and their own staff. Their role was to control all the service providers to achieve what Nortel wanted — high quality at a low price. Each department had separate contracts with service providers (e.g., architects and contractors as well as others) that had to be run through their legal department. Nortel decided that the cost of this way of doing business was prohibitive.

Their goal became to evolve to a new environment where, instead of stressing control of service providers, they stressed collaboration and interdependence among service providers. This included sharing knowledge, talent and resources among service providers who frequently compete with each other for clients. (Hence, the title "Mercury Principle", that derives its name from the propensity of mercury drops to attract each other and become one.)

In this new environment Nortel has a small number of facility employees called "client primes."

These people facilitate communication between Nortel and their service providers. Instead of separate contracts with each service provider for each project, Nortel has a limited number of "Tier 1" providers (Strategic Associates) with which they have sole-source contracts.

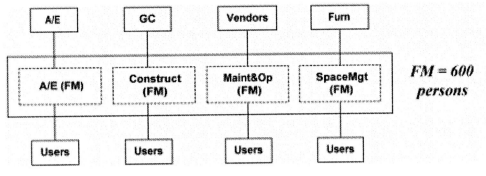

Figure 7. Traditional, in-house facilities organization.

Tier 1 providers are Grubb and Ellis (FM), CB Richard Ellis (FM), HOK (Architecture) and Herman Miller (furniture systems and services). Tier 1 providers are expected to work cooperatively ("co-opetition") to solve Nortel's facility problems. In turn, Tier 1 providers will have sole-source contracts with Tier 2 providers (Service Associates) and Tier 2 with Tier 3 providers (Supply Associates). Nortel, however, only has sole-source contracts with Tier 1 providers. In effect, the idea is that Tier 1 providers are a virtual facility management group for Nortel. For example, senior vice presidents from the Tier 1 providers participate in Nortel cabinet meetings.

Traditional roles in this arrangement tend to change in direct response to client needs. For example, Herman Miller is a manufacturer of Herman Miller workplace furniture. In this model, Nortel is less interested in workplace furniture than they are in servicing the needs of users. This means that Herman Miller becomes more of a service provider to meet user needs and, if necessary, will specify and deliver furniture from other manufacturers.

Last year Nortel saved $15 million while at the same time growing about 25% through this new arrangement. Their goal is to eventually have only 1 person in the whole of Nortel who is responsible for facilities (Figure 8). All other employees will be focused on their core business. As Nortel evolves to this organization, the way providers do business dramatically changes. E-commerce will be necessary to facilitate communication within this organization.

5.5 Web Auctions (FreeMarkets)

Web auctions are an intriguing example of how the Internet has approximated the essence of a "pure" free market economy where a typical assumption is that consumers and buyers have perfect information. FreeMarkets (www.FreeMarkets.com) is an Internet company that conducts online auctions for industrial parts, raw materials, commodities and services. In these "downward price" auctions, suppliers compete in real time for the purchase orders of large buying organizations by lowering their prices until the auction is closed.

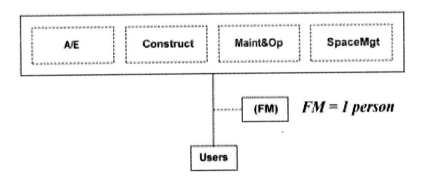

Figure 8. Nortel's facility organizational goal.

In one examples, a company that paid $745,000 for its last batch of plastic auto parts before using auctions was rewarded by paying only $518,000 for the same parts using a FreeMarkets.com "reverse" auction (Colvin 2000). Closer to home, the construction industry's "first" reverse auction was reported in an article by Paul Doherty (Doherty 2000), who gave a graphic description of how this auction worked even though the identities of the buyer and sellers were with held. Although both of these examples deal with products, FreeMarkets is also auctioning "tax preparation services, relocation services, temporary help, and other services." (Colvin, May 1, 2000, p. 74). It is entirely conceivable that design and construction services might also find themselves in bidding for someone to buy their services on the Internet.

6 Conclusions

The case studies in this paper illustrate how the Internet and e-commerce are causing many companies to redefine how value is provided to the end user.

A typical value chain (indicated in Figure 9) is the traditional way of thinking about how firms and their activities are organized. In this model, "value" refers to customer value, which is the ultimate source of profitability and survivability for firms. The construction industry is famous for the

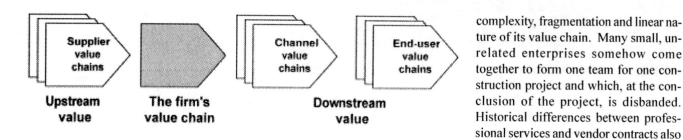

Figure 9. Value chain (after Porter, 1985).

complexity, fragmentation and linear nature of its value chain. Many small, unrelated enterprises somehow come together to form one team for one construction project and which, at the conclusion of the project, is disbanded. Historical differences between professional services and vendor contracts also impede integration. Within this approach working relationships may be difficult to maintain and it may be difficult to optimize customer value across the entire value chain. Nevertheless, it has been argued that this condition persists because of the inherent benefits of "small and flexible" production systems. For an interesting discussion of these two perspectives, see Tombesi, Paolo, "Travels from Flatland: The Walt Disney Concert Hall and the Specialization of Design Knowledge in the Building Sector," unpublished Ph.D. dissertation, UCLA, 1997.

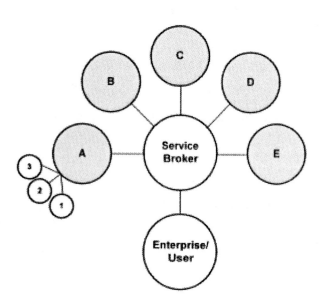

Figure 10. Networks and Service/Information Brokers.

Although the advantages of flexible production systems are significant, there is a tendency to sub-optimize on localized value chain production issues and to be relatively insensitive to upstream or downstream information needs. As one example of this problem, we have found that although facility management organizations have a great need for design intent, this upstream information is lost because it is not required for the construction of a building. Sharing information across value chain activities has been difficult to achieve in the AEC/FM industry. However, the trend towards outsourcing and the increased use of e-commerce technology to coordinate among various service providers may be changing the AEC/FM model from one of a linear value chain to more of a network model (see Figure 10). HomeWrite and Nortel both provide examples of this network model, where a "cyberintermediary" or service/information broker is responsible for organizing and supplying the needs of the end user.

E-commerce seems to have a dual effect on intermediaries. On the one hand, owners and owner's agents may be able to eliminate intermediaries in value chain transactions ranging from bidding to procurement. With the Internet, transactions will be able to occur on line directly among those individuals or firms that desire the transaction. Exchanges will be direct, instantaneous and efficient. Internet companies such as Cephren.com believe that the elimination of intermediaries will allow them to revolutionize inefficiencies in the $250 billion market for building materials. These web sites, not only share documents, but also provide a mechanism for construction materials to be purchased online. With the growth of web auctions it will not be long before these web sites organize online bidding for construction business.

On the other hand, examples such as Nortel suggest that, because every industry has specialized needs, intermediaries will become more necessary as more information becomes available and more connections are possible. Successful solutions will require comprehensive consulting, service and support. Intermediaries may become the electronic brokers in the chaotic information space. In any case, the cases reviewed in this paper suggest that e-commerce technologies may result in a significant restructuring of the AEC/FM industry.

References

Akasie, Jay. (July 17, 2000) "Ford's Model E," *Forbes*. p. 30.

Blackmon, D. (April 12, 2000) "eBricks, Gen-X Brainchild, Faces Off with Construction-Industry Barrons," *Wall Street Journal*.

Colvin, G. (May 1, 2000) "Value Driven." *Fortune*. p. 74.

Doherty, P. (March 27, 2000). "AEC Nightmare: Anatomy of a Web Auction." In the Archives section of "News and Views", www.buzzsaw.com.

Huang, J. (1999) "How do Distributed Design Organizations Act Together to Create Meaningful Design?" in Augenbroe, G. and C. Eastman (eds), *Computers in Building*. Boston: Kluwer Academic Publishers.

Johnson, R. E. and M. J. Clayton, (1998) "The Impact of Information Technology in Design and Construction: The Owner's Perspective," *Automation in Construction*, Vol 8, p. 3

Malone, T.W., Crowston, K., Lee, J., and Pentland, B. (1993) "Tools for Inventing Organizations: Towards a Handbook of Organizational Processes," Working Paper, Cambridge, MA: MIT Center for Coordination Science.

Orr, J. (January 3, 2000) "Change coming to CADD, and other thoughts at the start of the year," January 3, 2000, <www.joelorr.com>.

Teicholz, E., and Ikeda, T. (1995). *Facility Management Technology: Lessons from the U.S. and Japan*. New York: John Wiley & Sons, Inc.

Teicholz, E. (March 2000) "The Internet and New Software Make Room for Architects in Facility Management", *Architectural Record*, p. 176-180.

Thomsen, C. B. Personal conversation Charles B. Thomsen, CEO, 3D/International, March 27, 2001.

The Economist. Construction and the Internet, *The Economist* (January 15, 2000).

Wales, P. (2000) "Corporate Trends in Infrastructure Management Technology," White Paper, Luminant Worldwide, 2000.

Places of Mind: Implications of Narrative Space for the Architecture of Information Environments

Peter Anders, CAiiA-STAR, MindSpace.net, USA

Abstract

Virtual reality and cyberspace are extended spaces of the mind different from, yet related to, the spaces of fiction and ancient myth. These earlier spaces reveal how electronic media, too, may come to define our selves and our culture. Indeed, a better understanding of how we use space to think can lead to the design of better information environments. This paper will describe a range of traditional narrative spaces, revealing their varied relationships with the physical world. It will demonstrate the purposes of such spaces and how their function changes with their level of abstraction. A concluding review of current technologies will show how electronic environments carry on the traditions of these spaces in serving our cultural and psychological needs.

Keywords: cyberspace, narrative, space, Anthropic Cyberspace, cybrids

1 Narrative Space: Methodology for evaluation

In analyzing traditional narrative spaces I will use a methodology employed in my book *Envisioning Cyberspace*, Anders (1999), which presents artifacts and spaces in terms of a scale of abstraction (Table 1). This scale ranges from the most concrete to the most abstract, appealing to our senses and intellect respectively. Our scale also ranges from perception to cognition, our ways of appreciating the concrete and abstract. We use this in the knowledge that the categories discussed are provisional, and that current or future examples may conflict with their definition. However the risk is worth taking. The methodology helps us distinguish important features of traditional narrative space and gives us a framework for evaluating electronic spatial simulation.

I will compare spaces evoked by electronic media to those in traditional narrative to set a context for understanding hybrids of physical and electronic space – here called *cybrids*. *Narrative space* is here used to denote the spatial and social environment evoked in texts and narrative in various media. The term is used to describe the content of traditional narratives – *not* the media used to convey them. This helps us to categorize narrative types (history, folktale, myth, etc.) according to their relationship to the concrete world. We will find this useful in describing the interrelationship between "space" of electronic media and that of our physical environment.

2 The Space of History

Of all the extended spaces of history – the systematic, verifiable account of events – is most concrete. Events in historical space refer to specific people, places and times, all parts of our everyday experience. History is relayed dynamically; events are described in sequence of occurrence. Accepted as nonfiction, it is valued by empirical cultures and is the foundation for Western societies.

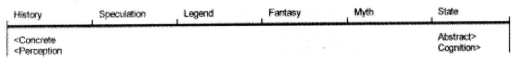

Table 1. Scale of abstraction for narrative space.

2.1 Speculation Space

Speculation ranges from rumor to plans of action. Such projections, while beholden to the world of experience, are hybrids of fact and fiction. The plan for a building addition relies on historical, current facts, although it is a hypothetical space. While speculation is not entirely factual its fiction is grounded and believable. The building addition cannot float on air, for instance.

2.2 Legend Space

Legend describes historical people in fictional places or, conversely, fictional characters in actual settings. It keeps at least one foot on the ground. Like speculation, legend may be hard to distinguish from history, for it is shared by the average citizen, its authorship unknown. But unlike speculation the fictional component of a legend may be fantastic. This magical component distinguishes legend from the more concrete categories of narrative space.

2.3 Fantasy Space

As we rise above legend to the levels of fantasy and fairy tales we increasingly encounter magic and the uncanny. These stories rely less upon material actuality than on symbols for cognitive and psychological states. Changes brought about by symbols are described in a magical way though the symbols themselves refer to the concrete world.

Fairy tales and folktales, in addition to defining a culture may also be didactic. They use fiction to relay psychological and cultural truths to children in fairy tales, and to adults through folk tales and parables (Bettelheim 1977). Magic often draws attention to important moments in a story, marking it in the reader's mind.

Authorship of the original fairy tales is often hard to determine because, like legends, they are a part of popular culture. But unlike legend the space of fairy tales and fable is stylized and general – a forest, a castle, the sea – as opposed to places of legend that may be cited by name. Likewise the characters populating fairy tales are stylized, often drawn as types rather than defined as individuals.

2.4 Mythic Space

Myth can be used didactically, like the folk tale and fable, but its primary purpose is to provide spiritual guidance. Its characters are archetypal ideals – deities, heroes and monsters. They reflect their surroundings, which symbolize aspiration (the heavens) or death (the underworld) more than actual, physical, locations. Actions there take place in no-time – eternity – or, in origin myths, at a time so far removed that conventional reality does not prevail.

Myths situate us in the world of man and nature. While fictitious, they are psychologically true (Campbell 1959). The entities and actions presented may be magical but their emotional structure is rooted in our everyday experience. Lust, jealousy, and anger among the gods engage the reader, however magical their actions may appear. Myth promulgates faith, provides spiritual guidance and assures the longevity of cultural institutions. While legend and folk tales are a part of common culture, myth is used by spiritual leaders to convey tradition and cultural values.

2.5 State Space

At the highest level of our scale we find the conceptual spaces of religious and philosophical tradition. These are metaphors for states of mind. Heaven and Hell belong to this category, as does the void of Nirvana. Such spaces are absolutes – resting places of the soul. Tellingly, they are rarely scenes of action in myth, for nothing really happens there. They are terminals to the road of life - beyond them lies nothing.

Even in this brief summary we can see trends that follow the ascent to abstraction. As we rise, we note a change of audience from the commoner to a select, sometimes religious elite. Use changes from conveying facts to values. And the subject itself changes: the concrete extreme is specific to time and place while idealized beings populate eternity at the other end. Heroes and gods occupy our minds more so than places on earth.

3 Cyberspace: The space of electronic media

In the ensuing discussion we will review the fictional spaces implicit in electronic media with respect to the present scale. Electronic media space is distinct from its precursors. Unlike text or painting electronic media is active and so resembles more the oral traditions of narration and theater. Also, unlike the traditional spaces of narrative, cyberspace is *inhabited* by users through their interaction within it.

Electronic media conveys spaces that appear incidental to the content. A telephone call gives the illusion of intimacy even though the topic of discussion may be impersonal. The story told by a talk-show guest occurs in a space distinct from the television studio seen by the viewers. The space influences, but is not dependent upon, the content. This media space differs from the conventional text or image as traditional media artifacts are confronted directly. Choices for engagement are limited to the illusion offered vs. the physical artifact, painting or book. There is no tacit intermediate space as with electronic media. It is this space that we will now relate to the illusory spaces of fiction. I will present the spaces by comparing them to the categories discussed earlier: history, speculation, legend, fantasy, myth, and state (Table 2).

3.1 Analog Media

History, the category that relies most upon perception of the world is already well-documented by conventional broadcast media, radio and television. Electronic, analog media can be used for immediate, live coverage of events. The space between events and viewer collapses. Returning to our earlier example, the studio space of the talk-show is directly apparent to us. The space of analog media warps our own, collapsing remoteness into immediacy. These media are nearly ideal for uses served by history, journalism, and direct narrative.

Analog media	Digital media	Cybrid	Domain	VR	Digital state
History	Speculation	Legend	Fantasy	Myth	State
<Concrete					Abstract>
<Perception					Cognition>

Table 2. Scale of abstraction for electronic media space (top) compared with narrative space (below).

3.2 Digital Space

Analog media have little separating events from the viewer. The processing of digital media, however, involves translational steps to turn input into digital information, then reverse the process to generate output. Two translations more than analog media, two more chances for error and manipulation to slip in. Digital media for this reason is attended by doubt. Doubt makes everything a potential fiction.

Digital media, particularly digital text and graphics used "realistically", hold a position similar to that of speculation. We see this in the gossip of BBS chat rooms, and plans generated using computer-aided design. Both contain fictional elements but even these fictions are grounded in reality, differing only in medium from their mundane equivalents.

3.3 Domain Space

It's no coincidence that fairy tale and fantasy themes are already popular in multi-user domains and digital Worlds. These online, role-playing environments require users to assume an identity – or avatar – for participation. Many users capitalize on the masking effect of the avatar to hide their real identities (Turkle 1984). These digital environments – while referring to the concrete world – are not subject to its laws. Magical actions are as common in these spaces as they are in fairy tales (Anders 1996). For this reason the space of online domains may be considered at a level of abstraction comparable to folk and fairytales. They share many attributes, 1) they are used to foster communities 2) their authorship is often unclear since many participate in their creation 3) they serve a dual purpose for entertaining users and serving as a learning environment for role-playing, 4) they contain fact-based characters (avatar) and fanciful beings (agents and bots), 5) they are popular and accessible to the average use.

3.4 VR Space

While the domains just discussed are technically virtual realities they emphasize user representation and social interaction often at the expense of experiential quality. However, virtual reality (VR) changes character once this quality is improved – the user and use change as well. Owing to expense and accessibility this level of VR is limited to those who can work with its technology. Recent work by artists in this medium contain features that recall, sometimes deliberately, the spaces of mythology. Like mythology the space of VR is often autonomous, free from geographical locale. Some of its authors, like Char Davies, use it to convey meaning and values, which, while not necessarily religious, are often philosophical.

As in mythic space the actions within VR are sometimes magical despite the ground planes, fixed light sources, recognizable objects and behaviors that relate to the material world. Unlike experience in domain space the user is unlikely to encounter someone else in VR. This changes the nature of VR space from being social to theatrical. The user is conscious of artifice despite the apparent freedom of interaction within it. This, too, recalls the space of myth as theater where players enact the ancient tales of culture.

3.5 Digital state space

At the extreme of abstract space – that occupied by metaphysical poles like Heaven and Hell – are electronic spaces that present states of being. Unlike VR and mythic space these are free of overt physical reference. Instead, they often manifest processes innate to computing.

As a result the space of artists working at this level is often disorienting as it makes few concessions to anthropic parameters of display. Without orientation, down and up do not matter. Coordinates, scales and dimensions are arbitrary. Each user's experience is unique, the spaces self-sufficient, closed to outside reference. Changes in such states are meaningless to the user. Effectively, as in the State Space of narrative, nothing changes. Curiously, the lack of reference in state space means its contents are not referential symbols. Instead they are traces as concrete as natural markings on stone. At this level abstract and concrete begin to merge.

3.6 Cybrid space

Suspended between these ideal states and mundane, historical space – midway down our scale – is legend, the unique blend of fiction and verifiable fact. Cybrids – the products of Augmented Reality and Ambient Computing (Anders 1999)– occupy this position on our scale and comprise integral yet distinct physical and cyberspaces. Augmented reality allows objects that only exist within the computer to be grafted onto the physical environment. Ambient – or distributed – computing makes the physical environment responsive to changes brought about through users or other agencies. Taken to its extreme the environment appears animate, equivalent to the magic, responsive world of our childhood. Similarly, Augmented Reality recalls tales of the paranormal, of mysterious places annexed to our world.

Like myth, legend is used to define a group of people with common customs. But unlike myth legend has a greater fidelity to actual details people and places. Objects, buildings, and features of the landscape offer a mnemonic structure lacing together cultural narratives. Seeing a mountain or an abandoned house triggers memories, tales otherwise forgotten. The physical recalls the invisible. In turn, the invisible holds truths latent in our perceived world.

The model that legend offers cybrids' technologies, augmented reality and ambient computing, is that of a communal memory palace (Yates 1966), the structures of which are seen in the features of mundane reality. Legend acknowledges that consciousness is only partly empirical, that psychology and culture play an equal or greater role. Legend's comparable technologies, may become media by which values, meaning, and solidarity are transmitted from one generation to the next.

3.7 Conclusions

Comparison of the fictional spaces of current technology with those of traditional narrative reveals many similarities and explains their success in the popular mind. This paper has shown how narrative, fictional space serves to maintain a culture's identity and preserve its values. These purposes were explained in light of the spaces' dependency upon the perceived and cognitive worlds. Cyberspace – in its many forms – extends this tradition into the electronic realm.

A crucial difference between the spaces of conventional narrative and that of cyberspace is that with the latter, users engage and interact with their surroundings. Multi-user domains and digital worlds – for all their fantasy – foster the interaction of real people. Their spaces form an architecture – a designed social setting.

Yet the connection with architecture is not literal, for as we ascend the scale of abstraction we lose many ties to materiality. The spaces are metaphors and no longer serve utilitarian purposes of buildings and other structures. Only at the scale's midrange, occupied by augmented reality and ambient computing, do we still have an integral link with the physical world. Here we find the rich blend of material fact and the magic of symbols – of places haunted by the structures of memory.

References

Anders, Peter. 1996. "Envisioning cyberspace: The design of on-line communities," in *Design computation: Collaboration, reasoning, pedagogy*. McIntosh, P. and F, Ozel, eds. Proceedings of

ACADIA 1996 Conference, Tucson, Arizona. pp.55-67.

Anders, Peter. 1999. *Envisioning Cyberspace.* New York: McGraw-Hill, pp. 47-50.

Bettelheim, Bruno. 1977. *The uses of enchantment: The meaning and importance of fairy tales.* New York: Vintage Books, pp. 111-116.

Campbell, Joseph. 1959. *The masks of God: Primitive mythology.* New York: Viking Penguin Inc. p. 48.

Turkle, Sherry. 1984. *The second self: Computers and the human spirit.* New York: Simon and Shuster, p. 82.

Yates, Frances. 1966. *The art of memory.* Chicago: The University of Chicago Press, pp. 27-49.

Data Representation Architecture: Visualization Design Methods, Theory and Technology Applied to Anesthesiology

Julio Bermudez, University of Utah, USA

Jim Agutter, University of Utah, USA

Dwayne Westenskow, University of Utah, USA

Stefano Foresti, University of Utah, USA

Yi Zhang, Wind River System Inc., USA

Debra Gondeck-Becker, Pine Technical College, USA

Noah Syroid, University of Utah, USA

Brent Lilly, University of Utah, USA

David Strayer, University of Utah, USA

Frank Drews, University of Utah, USA

Abstract

The explosive growth of scientific visualization in the past 10 years demonstrate a consistent and tacit agreement among scientists that visualization offers a better representation system for displaying complex data than traditional charting methods.

However, most visualization works have not been unable to exploit the full potential of visualization techniques. The reason may be that these attempts have been largely executed by scientists. While they have the technical skills for conducting research, they do not have the design background that would allow them to display data in easy to understand formats.

This paper presents the architectural methodology, theory, technology and products that are being employed in an ongoing multidisciplinary research in anesthesiology. The project's main goal is to develop a *new data representation technology to visualize physiologic information in real time.* Using physiologic data, 3-D objects are generated in digital space that represent physiologic changes within the body and show functional relationships that aid in the detection, diagnosis, and treatment of critical events.

Preliminary testing results show statistically significant reduction in detection times. The research outcome, potential, and recently received NIH grant supporting the team's scientific methods all point to the contributions that architecture may offer to the growing field of data visualization.

1 Background and Significance

In 1993, a report to the National Science Foundation (McConathy and Doyle 1993) stated that there was so much information being produced that all scientists could do was to find a place to warehouse it. The report concluded recommending visualization as the way to respond to this major challenge facing the sciences. The explosive growth of scientific visualization in the past 10 years has been a de-facto and clear validation of that report. There is now a consistent and tacit agreement among scientists that visualization offers a better representation system for organizing, studying (i.e., simulating, testing), using and communicating complex data. Case studies, Human Factors and Cognitive Sciences have shown that the human mind deals better with information complexity when data is displayed in graphic, real-world analog representations rather than in text-based or numerical representations (Adams et al 1995; Goettl et al 1991; Klima 1985; P1000 1996; Tufte 1997, 1990, 1983; Wurman 1996). Additional research in thinking, imagination, ideation, and learning has repeatedly shown that visualization plays a sophisticated and essential yet intuitive role in helping us associate, manipulate and infer information (Arnheim 1969, Egan and Nadaner 1988, Gardner 1983, Grinstein and Levkowitz 1995, McKim 1980).

These works suggest that effective data representation requires the presentation of information in a manner that is consistent with the perceptual, cognitive, and response-based mental representations of the user. When there is compatibility between the information presented to the user and the user's cognitive representations, performance is often more rapid, accurate and consistent. Conversely, a failure to use perceptual principles in the appropriate ways can lead to erroneous analysis of information. In other words, the way data is represented is of paramount importance as a means of augmenting human ability to make decisions while reducing stress and cognitive effort associated with them.

These findings lend strong support to the adoption of more qualitative methodologies in the design of data visualization systems. This, however, has not proved easy to implement. The reason is simple: most of the work on scientific visualization has been done by those who develop the data themselves: the scientists. Scientists have been largely trained in quantitative and not qualitative methods, in analytical and not integrative processes, in obtaining and not communicating knowledge. And yet, scientists find themselves with the growing pressure of communicating or just making sense out of increasingly more abstract data in ever larger amounts collected by ever more complex instruments.

The problem significantly escalates when dealing with *processes* as their study demand the monitoring of large data sets changing *in real time*. In addition to ordinary visualization requirements, representations depicting processes in real time call for difficult data management and display design techniques to assure the rapid discrimination of relevant information. The fact that the parameters normally used to monitor processes (e.g., temperature, pressure, rhythms, radiation, electromagnetism, etc.) are non-spatial does not make things any easier. Non-spatial numeric data create an apparent block in people's ability to represent them in any way other than in obvious mathematical space (i.e., function graphics such as 2D plots, pie charts, wave-form, etc.). Hence, despite some advances in Aviation and Process Control, disciplines such as the Physical Sciences, Finance, and Engineering are still using data visualization techniques of the pre-digital era to display data in real time.

This situation is evident in Medicine. Most of the work in medical visualization falls into three camps: (1) still imaging (e.g., X-rays, CAT scans, etc.), (2) interactive, but *not* real time, modeling of the body (MacLeod and Johnson 1993), and lately (3) interactive and real time dynamic representation of anatomic parts (for instance see Metaxas 1996). Little or no work has hitherto focused in visualizing *processes and states* (i.e., body function or physiology) instead of *organic structures* (i.e., body's forms —anatomy). This is remarkable given the relevance and power of *real time visualization of metabolic data in medical diagnosis*.

Recent research conducted in *anesthesiology* give clear evidence that visualization of physiological conditions offers faster and more accurate interpretations of medical data than the current numerical or wave-form representations, implying greater safety, decreased professional stress, and increased performance in patient monitoring (Cole and Stewart 1993, Deneault et al 1991, Gurushanthaiah et al 1995, Michels and Westenskow 1996, Michels et al 1997).

This paper reports on an interdisciplinary research project dealing with this undeveloped area of medical imaging: *the visualization of physiologic data*. The goal is to create a new visualization model and technology for physiologic change based on:

- a new *formal semiotics* using basic principles, elements and systems of graphic depiction. This implies the development of graphic conventions to make possible the translation and understanding between numerical parameters and images or shapes.
- *data integration*; the design of a multimodal virtual environment that expresses relationships among separate sets of measured data may not only reveal critical states more effi-

ciently and quickly than isolated representations, but also point at conditions that may not be apparent in separate displays of data.
- *interactivity*; the new model needs to allow the user to dynamically work with the data through diverse hierarchical layers, hyper-representations, and various multimodal formats. Easy and natural interface with data supports better understanding of the ongoing situation and improves performance.

Developing a visualization model that incorporates these three design premises would revolutionize the way the medical field detects, diagnoses and treats physiologic conditions. Traditional displays are characterized by numerical-waveform (as opposed to geometrically graphic), discrete (as opposed to integrated), and non-interactive data representations (see Figure 1).

Designing a visualization system for displaying physiologic data in real time implies significant computing challenges. The problem of visually displaying multiple data sets —which turn out to be of large size because of the evolution in time at high frequency— demand fast computations to guarantee the complete full cycle of data input, computation, visualization and interactivity within instants. Research in real time integrated 3-D visualization for representing multiple non-spatial time dependent data is still at primitive stages or unpublished (Farley et al 1993, Fuchs et al 1989, Gobel 1996, Gunther et al 1995, Jablonowski et al 1993, McCormick et al 1987, Mihalisin et al 1991, Rosenblum 1994, Sillion et al 1997). Studies of integrated information systems are being actively pursued in fields such as Process Control, Aviation, Telecommunication, and Defense. For obvious reasons of security or protection from competition, research in this area is not disseminated. Hence, an important goal of our visualization design research was not only to significantly enhance medical decision-making but also advance public knowledge and discussion in the field of real time process visualization.

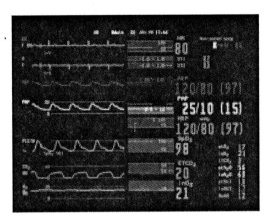

Figure 1. Current display of physiologic data (Hewlett Packard, Rockville, MD)

2 Relevance of Architectural Design in Medical Visualization

The importance of Architecture in the design of a data visualization system for Medicine cannot be overstated. Main stream medical visualization basically means to **enhance** a given set of anatomic images or behaviors so that they become more readable or act more accurately. In this type of work there is minimal need for design considerations because organic structures already possess their own characteristic shapes and movements. In contrast, physiologic data have no particular form and therefore demand the creation of representations. Numerical parameters (e.g., a blood pressure reading of 120/80, a heart rate of 70/minute, etc.) have no spatial or graphic imperative except in plots or charts constructed in mathematical space. This research work therefore deals with the **invention** *(not just the enhancement) of visualizations*. It clearly requires expertise in the area of visual design.

The importance of architectural design in the representation of physiologic data is also manifested by considerations such as

- the malleability of the digital canvas. Electronic space is neutral, in the sense that it may support any kind of representation design and format. This dimension refers to *formal aspects* of data representation design.
- communication demands. The data has particular meaning that needs communication (i.e., message) while the audience has particular ways to read and react to representations. This dimension refers to *functional and contextual aspects* of data representation design
- instrumental constraints. Hardware and software have inherent limitations to process complex dynamic databases that demand careful considerations at the time of visualization design. This dimension refers to the *economic aspects* of data representation design.

In other words, designing a new visualization system requires decisions about what information should be left out, highlighted or contextualized and how it should be represented. It is this essentially *qualitative filtering and visual depiction of information towards achieving a clear end that constitutes data visualization design.*

It is the design expertise in formal semiotics that makes architecture so relevant to this visualization research effort. Architects ordinarily deal with the syntax, semantics, and pragmatics of abstract 2D and 3D geometry. As a result the discipline has collected a comprehensive knowledge base of the nature, methods, and value of basic (i.e., abstract, geometrical) 2D and 3D design and its relationship to human collective and individual psychology and behavior (Albers 1975, Arheim 1977, Bloomer 1976, Broadbent et al 1980, Ciocier 1993, De Sausmarez 1964, Osgood et al 1957, Porter 1979, Wong 1977, 1972, Zettl 1973). This specialty area has been appropriately termed "Basic Design" and its theories, understandings, and methodologies are shared among all design disciplines (i.e., industrial design, graphic design, interior design, media design) and have a strong relationship with cognitive and environmental psychology. This knowledge base consisting of basic principles (e.g., scale, shape, rhythm, balance, color, tectonics, structure, etc.), elements (e.g., line, figures, objects, space, etc.) and organizational rules (e.g., hierarchy, layering, typology, symmetry, etc.) of formal design are used to create the representation model organizing physiologic data

The relevance of *architectural research* focused on the design, construction and communication of data representations is supported by the leading minds in the architectural field as a natural extension of designing and building functional forms and spaces (Anders 1999, Benedikt 1991, Mitchell 1995, Negroponte 1995). Until recently, most of the architectural work in the area had been restricted to cases involving simple and non-dynamic data sets with elementary functional and interface requirements. This is beginning to change as few and promising works show (Asymptote 1999, Chu 1998, Davis 1996, Möller 1996, Novak 1998, 1995). However, none of the ongoing data representation design activity addresses the type of theoretical and practical issues of this research proposal.

3 Application Area: Anesthesiology

Unexpected incidents are common in critical care medicine (Cook et al 1991, Cook and Woods 1994, Gaba 1994). Anesthesiologists face them during 20 percent of all anesthetics. One quarter of these incidents represent critical events posing significant danger to patients (Allnutt 1987, Forrest et al 1990, Emergency Care Research Institute (1985, Pierce 1985). Looking back at the patients who suffered injury over the past 13 years, 72% of the adverse outcomes could have been prevented if the patient had been better monitored (Webb 1993). "Critical incident studies", which originated in the mid-1950s in military aviation safety research, were introduced into anesthesia by Cooper et al in 1978 and 1980. The studies recognize that adverse outcomes frequently are catastrophic endpoints of an "evolving" chain of often subtle incidents, which alone might not have progressed into disasters (Gaba 1987). Therefore, quick and accurate decisions are a major concern in anesthesia.

The research team confronted the visualization design problem of having to represent 32 interrelated, non-spatial physiologic variables in real time *and* in a way that improved detection, diagnosis and treatment accuracy and speed over the existing data representation system. Presently, anesthesiologists watch all 32 parameters plotted separately as 2D waveform charts and numbers to determine if a patient is stable and in the desired physiologic state (see Figure 1).

4 Methodology and Procedures

The research has been conducted by an interdisciplinary team consisting of experts and graduate students in Architecture, Bioengineering, Computer Science, Medicine, and Psychology. If, on one hand, the importance of multidisciplinary work cannot be understated —the nature and complexity of the visualization problem could have never been addressed by any one discipline alone—, on the other hand there are great logistic, methodological and 'cultural' challenges in making people from different fields and locations work together.

During the first 2 years, the team interactions naturally evolved toward the operational framework of the design process. We found that the design process was the most effective and efficient collaborative methodology to get the members of the group talking and working with one another. Despite the fact that the validity of this type of inquiry has been amply demonstrated (Cross 1986, 1882, Lawson 1980, Rittel 1986, Rowe 1987, Schön 1983) (and to the surprise of those in architecture) this was a real finding for our colleagues in other disciplines. After some initial doubt, they have now come to accept the design process as a systematic and experimental procedure for advancing, developing, testing, selecting and communicating hypotheses. Design inquiry is thus our team's normal methodology for developing both basic and applied types of knowledge.

Each PI has primary responsibility in their field of expertise and is expected to communicate and collaborate with the rest of the team. Group meetings are held weekly (within a discipline) and monthly (of the whole group). Other meetings (e.g., between two disciplines) are often informally held through the interactions of graduate students and often overseen by at least one PI. All meetings are expected to include members from the other disciplines (often graduate students if PI may not attend). A protected web site with state-of-the-art features allowing collaboration is used to keep everyone updated of ongoing developments and allow feedback. The site also serves to maintain a record of the decision making and design process. External consultants have been often invited to evaluate and/or participate at various phases of the process. Web technology has enabled us to make most use of our out-of-town consultants input. A public accessible web site may be found at: http://infoviz.chpc.utah.edu/anes1.htm. Figure 2 shows a diagram of the overall design process circle we use in conducting our research.

More specifically, creating the visualization model involved the following steps:

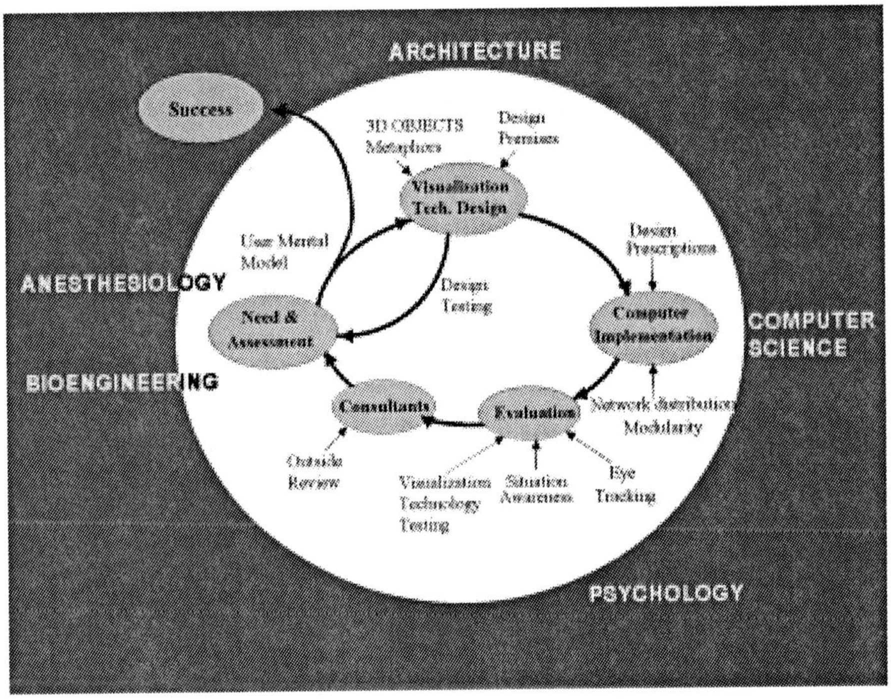

- analyzing known physiologic phenomena to be monitored, including desirable (i.e., normal) and undesirable states;
- analyzing the anesthesiologist's decision making process, including acquired behaviors and group influence;
- analyzing all available variables and relations or functional dependencies among them, and prioritizing their inclusion into the application;
- developing a conceptual model representing the critical functions to be monitored, including the relationships among their variables (user's mental model);
- analyzing and defining essential semiotics of 2D and 3D design based on existing research on human factors, cognitive psychology and architectural and design theory;
- formulating a visual design whereby 3D objects, attributes, spaces and frameworks follow the conceptual model;
- designing software, with principles of modularity and distribution over networks;
- testing the design and software with users;
- iterate the process, as described in Figure 2.

Figure 2. Team Operation Methodology. Design Process as Inquiry

During the initial part of the project, design ideas were developed and modeled using the non-real time programming environment of SGI Explorer or IBM Data Explorer. Still images of these visualization models were used to conduct direct interviews with anesthesiologists. Several iterations of these meetings took place until we arrived to a model in which clinicians could recognize variables and functions quickly and easily. At that point, we moved to encode the model's design prescriptions into a software running on both Unix and Windows operating systems. The software was also written to allow real time transmissions over networks with moderate bandwidth. During software development and testing we used the body simulator METI to generate the necessary physiologic data related to diverse clinical scenarios (see Figure 4 and "Evaluation" section below). Further evolution of the visualization software version took place in the past year based on continuous interactions with anesthesiologists and bio-engineering and medicine graduate students. The visualization model presented in this paper is the last version of this iteration (see Figure 3 below).

5 Premises

The research team agreed to apply the following seven design premises to guide its data visualization design process (the first three already introduced earlier):

- *inventing a formal semiotics* to link graphics and physiologic meaning;
- *integrating data* so that representations reveal data's relationships and interactions;

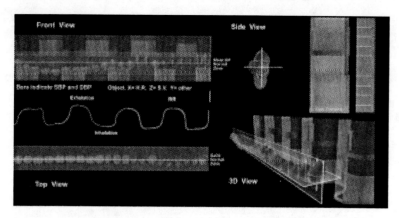

Figure 3. New visualization system for displaying physiologic data in real time.

- *providing interactivity* to facilitate user's access to the information;
- mapping information into a *3D data representation architecture* in order to improve recognition while supporting data integration and significant increases in the number of variables to be displayed;
- *using an ordinary PC platform* to insure universal adaptability and adoption in medical settings;
- *allowing network distribution* to support data visualization as well as raw data access at any distance (at moderate bandwidth);
- aiming at formal, functional, and technical *simplicity*.

Simplicity has been the key design premise that helped us to respond to all the rest of premises. It was evident from the outset and later proven correct that data integration, 3-D graphics, interactivity, successful graphic semiotics, real time computer processing on a PC platform as well as network distribution would only work if we kept a high level of design simplicity. This has been achieved by working with geometric primitives and abstractions related to fundamental laws of human perception. We used the following simple yet powerful design principles to encode perceptual clues:

(1) Choice of geometry
(2) Geometric deformation
(3) Overlapping/separation/intersection
(4) Figure-ground/layers
(5) Movement/Trajectory (up-down, front-back) (focus)
(6) Size and Location
(7) Scale and Proportion
(8) Attributes (color, texture, opacity, etc.)
(9) Spatial relationship between elements
(10) Composition and pattern recognition
(11) Interactive viewpoints of same data
(12) Reference frames

The project being presented in this paper shows the visualization modeling of 13 physiologic variables. The reason for reducing the number of parameters from 32 to 13 was based on the lack of enough resources at the start of this research project. This reduction made the task manageable while still presenting visualization design and computing challenges that were qualitatively identical (and thus any design solution transferable to) a fully-fledged 32 variable data representation architecture. In addition, having 13 parameters also allowed the testing and implementation of the seven design premises the team had established. For example, 13 variables changing in real time creates a multiple dimension representation problem that favors 3D over 2D graphics, as 3D visualizations tend to better express the range of variabilities and subtleties of multi-variable defined physiologic states.

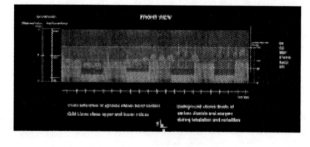

Figure 4. Front view of the visualization system

The choice of which 13 variables to depict was based on two reasons. First, the heart and the lungs are the two *"critical functions"* that require most medical monitoring and management during anesthesia. Second, cardiac activity and respiration are naturally interdependent, thus facilitating data integration design considerations. The 13 physiologic variables modeled correspond to:

- *Cardiac Function* (updated each heart beat) includes Stroke Volume, Cardiac Output, Heart Rate, Blood Pressures, and Arterial Oxygen Saturation.
- *Respiratory Function* (updated each breath) includes Tidal Volumes, Respiratory Rate, Nitrous Oxide, Oxygen, Carbon Dioxide, and Airway Pressure.

6 Result

Figure 3 shows our 3-D visualization system for displaying physiologic data in real time. The same data is displayed in four interactive windows; each one designed to show certain information in detail and complementarily. Departure from "normal" reference grids, shapes, spacing, and colors helps the clinician **discover change**. The display structure maps each variable to a clinician's mental model, to help **diagnose problems**. Functional relationships link the elements of the display to help the clinicians **treat problems**.

Data modeling follows specified configurations in X-Y-Z coordinates, in real time. A 3D data architecture first organizes the 13 measured variables into data sets or "critical functions" that are then mapped to 3D objects. These objects work as metaphors of cardiac and respiratory functions. The foreground red spheres represent cardiac activity. The background plane communicates respiratory activities. The objects' location and movement in space as well as their attributes (e.g., shape, texture, opacity, color, etc.) map further data. Specially designed lines and points establish referential datum to detect abnormality. Time moves from right to left (in X), with present conditions at the "front" or right edge of each view. Past states remain to permit a 'historical view' of the data.

More specifically, the "cardiac" object grows and shrinks with each heartbeat as data is updated. Its height is proportional to the heart's Stroke Volume and its width is proportional to Heart Rate. Its total volume is proportional to the heart's total Cardiac Output. The position of this spherical object in Y and Z space is proportional to the patient's (a) Mean Blood Pressure (moving up is higher, moving down is lower) and (b) the Oxygen Saturation in the blood (moving backward is lower, moving forward is higher) respectively. The object's color indicates the patient's overall oxygenation level. The graphic icon offers an useful similarity to a working heart, thus facilitating intuitive and quick recognition. A perfectly round object reflects normalcy whereas an oblong or squash one reflects abnormalcy. If the object is centered on the horizontal and vertical grid frame, the patient is normal. If it is above or below the reference line, the patient's blood pressure is abnormal. The front view shows a trend plot where the Blood Pressure fell and then returned to normal (Figures 3 and 4). In addition, the same view shows that the drop in the Blood Pressure was due to an inadequate Stroke Volume and decreased Heart Rate.

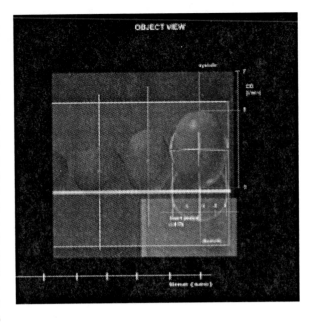

Figure 5. Detail of the Front View depicting present conditions.

Critical respiratory function data are mapped to a bluish 'curtain' plane in the background. This object's undulation back and forth in Z space plots Inhalation, Exhalation and Respiratory Rate information (Top View in Figure 3). Data relative to gas types and volumes are mapped in Y space. Variance of gray and green colors shows inspired and expired gases and their concentrations (Oxygen and Carbon Dioxide). Quantitative measurements of Gas Concentrations and Airway Pressure are best seen in the side view (Figure 6). The height of the "curtain" is proportional to Respiratory Tidal Volume.

A series of frameworks establishing normal values are offered to help detect departure from normalcy. The spherical grid frame that continuously appears with the 'cardiac' object in the present moment shows the expected normal values for Stroke Volume, Heart Rate and Cardiac Output. The horizontal reference lines correspond to a patient's normal values of Mean Blood Pressure (Front View) and Oxygen Saturation (Top View). Figure 5 shows a zoomed-in Front View of the present physiologic conditions. The spherical grid frame partially hidden by the cardiac object shows a normal Heart Rate and a slightly larger than ideal Stroke Volume. The position of the cardiac object within the band of normal Mean Blood Pressure assures normalcy. The display also permits to set the normalized reference grids so that they match a patient's normal condition. Similarly, referential planes are utilized to define normal respiratory rate and gas volumes for the "respiratory" object.

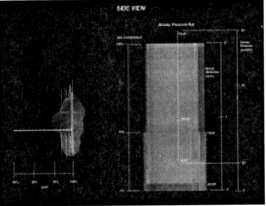

Figure 6. Side View of the visualization system

The data were purposely mapped into the objects and spaces so that the Front, Side and Top Views (or windows) presented users with specific physiologic information. For example, the Front View focuses on continuous and discrete depictions of a particular relationship among particular variables, i.e., the interactions among Blood Pressure, Heart Rate, Stroke Volume in relation to Gas Concentrations (O2, CO2, etc.).

Of the four views, the Side View (Figure 6 below) is critical in establishing the present physiologic state of the patient. It has been designed to work and look like a physiologic 'target' for the anesthesiologist to aim at. Attention is continuously drawn to this view. Only when conditions depart from

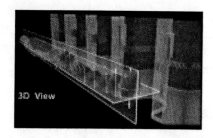

Figure 7. Interactive window displaying a 3D expression of the data. Note referential frame

normalcy, the clinician moves to the other views to detect and establish some pattern and trend in the data. Top and Front Views show the "life space" or physiologic history of the patient. These two views allow for analysis and comparison. The 3-D View provides a uniquely comprehensive, integrated and interactive view of all physiological data at once (Figure 7 below).

The combination of all 4 windows provides the anesthesiologist a hitherto unavailable depiction of the working relationship among 13 discreet variables in human physiology. Although this window system is very familiar to architects and designers in general given its reference to architectural views and CAD software, it constitutes a completely new way of looking at data for people in Medicine, Bioengineering, Computer Science and Psychology. This is a good example of how something quite ordinary and obvious in one discipline gets successfully exported to and praised as novel and useful by other disciplines.

7 Evaluation of the Visualization Model

Our research hypothesis had been that a 3D data representation architecture conveys the health status of a patient at a glance, thereby reducing the cognitive workload and speeding up the detection of problems when they occur. We tested this claim by comparing the traditional display and our visualization prototype (Figures 1 and 3 respectively). We used the body simulator METI to generate the necessary physiologic scenarios for the test (Figure 8). METI consists of a mannequin placed on an operating room table that simulates human physiologic functions and responses to anesthesia. METI generates all the physiologic data necessary to run both the traditional and new visualization display in real time.

METI was preprogrammed with 3 critical events in isolation and "situation awareness" tests conducted on two groups, one using the traditional display and the other one with ours. Subjects included bioengineering graduate students. The results show gains in recognition times that are statistically significant. See Table 1 below.

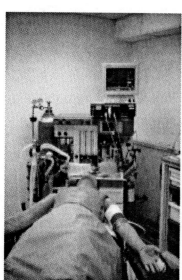

Figure 8. The METI body simulator

Another important finding was that experts were overtaken by being able to witness physiologic interactions between cardiac and respiratory activities that, although well known, have never been "seen" before. In fact, several new insights have been attained when analyzing their interactions during abnormal physiologic states. These insights have avoided anesthesiologists simply because of the way data has been presented to them until now. This points to a real advantage of visualization models that integrate variables: not only do they support ordinary decision making but also permit new ways of looking at the data that may lead to new detection, diagnosing and treatment methods.

After-test interviews, direct observations of how users interact with the new system vis-a-vis the traditional display, and informal conversations with anesthesiologists suggest that the visualization system developed tends to work very successfully at the qualitative level, as it provides a comprehensive understanding of physiologic states. However, it is less successful when detailed and quantitative types of information are necessary. It appears that our visualization model works best for rapidly detecting and diagnosing problems but that needs improvements when dealing with treatment and certain diagnosis as more detailed and quantitative information is often necessary. This perhaps suggests the necessity to incorporate some key quantitative indicators into our visualization model.

During informal testing and presentations, we also found that the integrated 3D data visualization design allows reasonable levels of operability even in people with little or no knowledge in human physiology. This may prove very important for applying the visualization method to medical areas in which lower levels of expertise may be available (e.g., nurse stations in critical care units and hospital bed monitoring, casualty care in theaters of war). Further work in this direction is clearly needed.

8 Conclusion

The interdisciplinary collaboration among Architecture, Bioengineering, Computer Science, Medicine and Psychology have produced novel methodologies and models to access, organize, represent, and interact with non-spatial databases in real time. Preliminary test results of our work, the development of a patent-pending visualization technology, and the legitimization of our premises and methodology by a recently received $2.2M NIH grant to support five more years of visualization research acknowledge the concrete contribution made by Architecture to the monitoring of physiologic states in Anesthesiology.

Based on this positive feedback, the research team is now working to enhance and extend the capabilities of the developed visualization system. Within the next 2 year we plan to pursue the following goals:

CRITICAL EVENTS	HYPOVOLEMIA		ISCHEMIA		BRONCHOSPASM	
	TRADITIONAL	CROMDI	TRADITIONAL	CROMDI	TRADITIONAL	CROMDI
Detection (# of correct answers)	1.8	2.4	1.8	2.2	2.8	2.8
Diagnosis (# of correct answers)	1.4	2.2	2.8	2.2	2.8	3.4
Recognition Time (seconds)	96	48	138	126	180	120

Table 1. Testing of visualization system for Anesthesiology Comparison testing between Traditional and the new Visualization System (CROMDI) was done using 12 Bioengineering graduate students. Situation awareness questions were asked every 2.5 minutes and recognition time was measured when critical changes were seen. (Zhang et al 2000)

- include the remaining 19 physiologic variables to allow the full monitoring of physiologic states during anesthesia;
- incorporate quantitative data representations to accommodate the need for specific numerical information;
- supplement our visualization design with sounds to significantly enhance the display of information;
- develop the software interface to allow more customization of visualization parameters, number and type of windows displayed, normal value definition, and data visualization formats.

Several tests with experts are scheduled for the next two years. The incorporation of a recently acquired eye-tracking device for some of these tests, the use of larger populations and more refined testing protocols will surely produce results that will improve our understanding of the mechanism behind data visualization. These results will in turn lead to improvement in the design and computation aspects of the visualization model.

We are hopeful that by addressing the largely forgotten visualization needs of physiologic monitoring in Medicine, we will be produce important improvements in the understanding of and response to critical medical conditions. Designing, building, and computing 3D data architectures may thus prove to not only serve the social welfare of people but also respond to functional, technological and indeed aesthetic needs not unlike those addressed by traditional physical architecture. Hence, we would like to conclude proposing that the architectural discipline must expand its too often narrowly defined area of expertise to acknowledge and include the exciting new areas of architectural practice opened up by the digital revolution.

Acknowledgements

This research has been made possible by two University of Utah Technology Innovation Grants (1998, 1999) and a National Institutes of Health grant (1-R01 HL64590-01). Support was also provided by the State of Utah funding of the Center for the Representation of Multi-Dimensional Information (CROMDI).

References

Adams, M.J., Tenney Y.J., and R.W. Pew (1995). Situation awareness and the cognitive management of complex systems. *Human Factors* 37:85-104.

Albers, J. (1975) *Interaction of Color*. New Haven: Yale University Press

Allnutt M.F. (1987) Human factors in accidents. *Br J Anaesth* 59: 856-64

Anders, P. (1999). *Envisioning Cyberspace*. New York: McGraw-Hill

Arheim, R. (1977). *The Dynamics of Architectural Form*. Berkeley: University of California Press.

Arnheim, R. (1969). *Visual Thinking*. Berkeley, CA: University of California Press.

Asymptote (1999). Ride the Dow, *Wired* 7:6 (June), pp.176-179

Benedikt, M. (1991). *Cyberspace, First Steps*. Cambridge, MA: The MIT Press.

Bloomer, C. (1976). *Principles of Visual Perception*. New York: Van Nostrand Reinhold.

Broadbent, G., Bunt, R. and C.Jenks (1980). *Sign, Symbol and Architecture*. Chichester, UK: John Willey & Sons.

Chu, K. (1998). Genetic Space, *A.D.: Architects in Cyberspace II*, vol.68, no.11-12, pp.68-73

Ciocier, R. (1993) *Manufactured Pleasures, Psychological Responses to Design.* Manchester, UK: Manchester University Press.

Cole, W.G. and J.G. Stewart (1993). Metaphor graphics to support integrated decision making with respiratory data. *Intl J Clin Monit Comput* 10:91-100.

Cook, R. and Woods D. (1994) Operating at the sharp end, *Human Error in Medicine* 13: 255-310

Cook, R, Potter S, and D.Woods (1991) Evaluating the human engineering of microprocessor controlled operating room devices. *J Clin Medicine* 7: 217-26

Cooper, J.B., Newbower, R.S., and C.D. Long (1980) Human error in anesthesia management. In *The Quality Of Care In Anesthesia*, eds. J.S. Gravenstein and B.L. Grundy, pp 114-30. Springfield, Illinois, Thomas Books,

Cooper, J.B., Newbower, R.S., Long, C.D., and B. McPeek (1978) Preventable anesthesia mishaps: a study of human factors. *Anesthesiology* 49: 399-406

Cross, N. (1986). Understanding Design: The Lessons of Design Methology. *Design Methods and Theories* 20:2, pp.409-438.

Cross, N. (1982). Designerly Ways of Knowing. *Design Studies* 3:4, pp.221-227.

Davis, E. (1996) Osmose; *Wired*, Vol. 4.08 (August) pp. 137-140, 190-192

De Sausmarez, M. (1964). *Basic Design: the Dynamics of Visual Form.* New York: Van Nostrand Reinhold.

Deneault, L.G., Stein, K.L., Lewis, C.M., Debbons, A., and A. Dewolf (1991). Comparing geometric objects and conventional displays in patient monitoring. *J Clin Monit* 7:111-113.

Egan, K. and D. Nadaner (1988). *Imagination and Education.* New York: Teacher College Press.

Ellis, S. (1993). *Pictorial Communication in Virtual and Real Environments*, Washington, DC: Taylor and Francis.

Emergency Care Research Institute (1985) Deaths during general anesthesia. *J Health Care Technol* 1: 155-75

Farley, J. F. and P. D. Varhol (1993). Visualizing Data in Real Time, *Dr. Dobb's Journal of Software Tools*, 18(13).

Forrest, J.B., Cahalan, M.K., Rehder, K., Goldsmith, C.H., Levy, W.J., Strunin L., Bota W., Boucek, C.D., Cucchiara, R.F., Dhamee S., et al. (1990) Multicenter study of general anesthesia. II. Results [see comments]. *Anesthesiology* 72: 262-8

Fuchs, H., Levoy M. and S. M. Pizer (1989). Interactive Visualization of 3-D Medical Data", *Computer*, 22(8).

Gaba D. (1994). Human error in dynamic medical domains, *Human Error in Medicine* 11: 197-224

Gaba, D.M., Maxwell, M., and A. DeAnda, (1987) Anesthetic mishaps: breaking the chain of accident evolution. *Anesthesiology* 66: 670-6

Gardner, H. (1983). *Frames of Mind: The Theory of Multiple Intelligence.* New York: Basic Books.

Gobel, M. (1996) Virtual environments and scientific visualization. *Selected Papers of the Eurographics Workshops in Monte Carlo*, Monaco, February 19-20, 1996, Springer Computer Science Series, Springer-Verlag Inc.

Goettl, B.P., Wickens, C.D., and A.F. Kramer (1991). Integrated displays and the perception of graphical data. *Ergonomics* 34:1047-1063.

Grinstein, G. G. and H. Levkowitz (1995). *Perceptual Issues In Visualization*, Springer-Verlag Inc.

Gunther, T., C. Poliwoda, C. Reinhart, J. Hesser, R. Manner, H-P Meinzer and H-J Baur (1995). VIRIM: A massively parallel processor for real-time volume visualization in medicine, *Computers and Graphics*, 19(5).

Gurushanthaiah, K., Weinger, M.B. and C.E. Englund (1995). Visual display format affects the ability of anesthesiologists to detect acute physiologic changes. *Anesthesiology* 83:1184-1193.

Jablonowski, D.J., Bruner, J.D., Bliss, B. and Haber, R.B. (1993). VASE: The Visualization and Application Steering Environment. *Proceedings of Supercomputing '93*, IEEE Computer Society Press, pp. 560-569.

Klima, G. (1985). *Multi-Media and Human Perception.* Elnora, NY: Meridian Press.

Lawson, B. (1980). *How Designers Think.* London: Architectural Press.

MacLeod, R.S. and C.R. Johnson (1993), Map3d: Interactive scientific visualization for bioengineering data. *IEEE Computer Society*, pp.30-31

McKim, R. (1980). *Experiences in Visual Thinking.* Boston, MA: PWS Publishers.

McConathy, D.A. and M.Doyle (1993). Interactive Displays in Medical Art. In *Pictorial Communication in Virtual and Real Environments*, ed. S. Ellis Washington, DC: Taylor and Francis, pp. 97-110

McCormick, B.H., T.A. DeFanti and M.D. Brown (1987). Visualization in Scientific Computing, *Computer Graphics*. 21(6).

Metaxas, D. (1996) *NSF 1996 Grant: Interactive Virtual Environment for Modeling Anatomy and Physiology*. Award number 9624604

Michels, P., Gravenstein, D., and D.Westenskow (1997). An Integrated Graphic Data Display Improves Detection And Identification of Critical Events During Anesthesia. *J Clin Monit* 13:249-259

Michels P. and D Westenskow. (1996) A graphic date display reduces the detection time for critical events. *Int'l J. Clin Monit* 13(2):137

Mihalisin, T. , J. Timlin and J. Schwegler (1991). Visualizing multivariate functions, data, and distributions. *IEEE Computer Graphics and Applications*, 11(3).

Mitchell, W. (1995). *City of Bits. Space, Place and the Infobahn.* Cambridge, MA: The MIT Press.

Möller, C. (1996). Interactive Architecture. *World Architecture* Vol.39, pp. 146-151.

Negroponte, N. (1995). *Being Digital.* New York: Alfred A. Knopf.

Novak, M. (1998) Next Babylon,Soft Babylon. *A.D.: Architects in Cyberspace II*, vol.68, no.11-12, pp.20-29

Novak, M. (1995) TransTerraFirma ; *Sites*, Vol. 26, pp. 34-53

Osgood, C., Suci, G. and P Tannemaum (1957). *The Measurement of Meaning.* Urbana, Il: University of Illinois Press.

P1000 Science and Technology Information Visualization. A roadmap to provide information visualization technology broadly within the intelligence community, 16 September 1996, Version 2.

Pierce, E. (1985) Reducing preventable anesthetic mishaps: A need for greater risk management initiatives, *ASA* 1985

Porter, T. (1979). *How Architects Visualize.* New York: Van Nostrand Reinhold Company.

Rittel H.; (1986) Principles for the Design of an Educational System for Design. *Design Method and Theories*, vol.20, #1.

Rosenblum, L. (1994). *Scientific Visualization: Advances and Challenges.* London: Academic

Rowe, P. (1987). *Design Thinking.* Cambridge, MA: the MIT Press

Schön, D. (1983). *The Reflective Practitioner.* New York: Basic Books

Sillion, F., G. Drettakis and B. Bodelet (1997). Efficient Impostor Manipulation for Real-Time Visualization of Urban Scenery. *Computer Graphics Forum*, 16(3).

Tufte, E. (1997). *Visual Explanations*. Cheshire, Conn: Graphics Press.

Tufte, E. (1990). *Envisioning Information*. Cheshire, Conn: Graphics Press.

Tufte, E. (1983). *The Visual Display of Quantitative Information*. Cheshire, Conn: Graphics Press

Webb, R.K., Currie, M., Morgan, C.A., Williamson, J.A., Mackay, P., Russell, W.J. and W.B Runciman. (1993) The Australian Incident Monitoring Study: an analysis of 2000 incident reports. *Anaesth Intensive Care* 21: 520-8

Wong, W. (1977). *Principles of 3-D Design*. New York: Van Nostrand Reynolds.

Wong, W. (1972). *Principles of 2-D Design*. New York: Van Nostrand Reynolds.

Wurman. S (1996). *Information Architects*. New York: Palace Press International

Zhang, Y., Westenskow, D., Agutter, J., Lilly, B., Bermudez, J. and S. Foresti (2000) Design And Evaluation of a 3D Integrated Display. *J Clin Mon* (forthcoming)

Zettl, H. (1973). *Sight, Sound, Motion. Applied Media Aesthetics*. Belmont, CA: Wadsworth Publishing Company

Representing Virtual Places - A Design Model for Metaphorical Design

Fei Li, University of Sydney, Australia

Mary Lou Maher, University of Sydney, Australia

Abstract

The design of virtual places is metaphorical because it relies on references to the physical world. The use of a consistent metaphor provides a sense of place that combines functionality, familiarity, richness and an awareness of the presence of others. In this paper we consider such designs from a representational perspective. We discuss the characteristics and distinctions of a model of metaphorical design representation and propose a framework for the development of the representation of metaphorical design. We illustrate this framework with examples of designs of virtual places.

Keywords: virtual worlds, architectural design, design representation, design model, metaphorical design

1 Virtual Worlds and Design

Virtual worlds are online environments for people to access information and have experiences with the added feature of an awareness of others. This awareness of others distinguishes a web page presentation of information from a virtual world. Most virtual worlds create a sense of place through metaphorical reference to physical places. In this paper we are concerned with the representation and design of virtual worlds that both create a sense of place and also include an awareness of others in the place.

The literature on virtual worlds addresses one or more of three aspects of their design and implementation (Maher, 1999a):

- Implementation level. The technology associated with the implementation of the virtual world, such as the use of a distributed or central database, the use of client-server technology, etc.
- Representation level. A consideration of the representation of the virtual world as a metaphorical reference to some aspect of the physical world.
- Interface level. The type of interface provided to people in the virtual world, such as interactive 3D models, command driven text, iconic images.

Many studies focus on the implementation level, presenting advantages and disadvantages of the use of databases that host the virtual world and its implementation in the design of the virtual worlds. For example, Rowley (1997) studies the implementation issues in lambdaMOO, an object-oriented text-based virtual world. Das (1997) presents a revised version of an object-oriented database that resolves some of the inefficiencies in the lambdaMOO approach.

Other studies focus on interface level and how they are used, for example, Curtis (1993) looks at non-recreational use of virtual worlds, Toomey et al (1998) consider the phenomena of meeting in virtual space, and Chen (1999) discuss the role of virtual worlds in information visualization. Some studies examine the social behavior of the participants in the environments, for example:

- Social navigation (Diegerger, A. 1997)
- Turn-taking in virtual meeting (Bowers, J. et al. 1997)
- Social position (Jeffrey, P. et al. 1998)

- Social activity in game (Muramastsu, J. et al. 1993)
- Patterns of social interaction (Schiano, D. J. et al. 1998)

A representation level study of virtual worlds design considers the concepts behind the design. There is little research on the representation of virtual worlds. However, there are studies that emphasize the role of design in virtual worlds. Cicognani (1998) studied a linguistic characterization of the design of virtual worlds. These examples of research in virtual worlds design reveal many ideas of how virtual places can be designed and the way they can be represented.

2 A Representation Study of Virtual Places

Many online virtual worlds have used a metaphor of physical place design. More generally, virtual worlds adopt a spatial metaphor and can be classified into two categories: non object-oriented systems like simple online chat systems and object-oriented systems like MOO based systems. Our representation study is based on the object-oriented VW system. An object-oriented system has many advantages over a non object-oriented system. In technological terms, the object-oriented system has a more robust and dynamic software core, which is easier to modify and expand. The merits of the object-oriented system in terms of design and representation are:

- When representing a virtual place (VP), we can represent the design as classes of objects in accordance with the object-oriented characteristics of the system. Thus the representation of the VP, which is based on the definition of objects and their relationship, can also be conceptually depicted as an object-based representation framework.
- Design in the sense of a sequential refinement process can be better handled with this object-based representation. The representation of a design model as class objects not only passes the common identifying design properties of the class to the descendants, but also provides a framework from which the refinement process starts. As such, the design itself can be more efficient and manipulable.
- Conceptual objects described by design can correspond to the objects in the object-oriented database. This makes possible the use, as an analogy, of the research in design of physical places that use the prototype formalism (Gero, 1990). For example, we can consider the function, behavior, and structure of objects in each case.

In most object-oriented VW systems, for example MOO systems, everything that exists in them is represented as objects. The fundamental class structure of these systems is shown in Figure 1. The root class has the basic properties of all objects. The next level of classes, Generic room, Generic thing, Generic player, and Generic exit, define the major types of objects in the world. The generic room is the basic representation of place. The generic thing is a representation of the objects that can be placed in a room. The generic player is an object representation of the people in the world. The generic exit is the basis for navigating and taking things and people from one room to another. In a VW based on a spatial metaphor, the "geographical locations" and 'buildings" distributed as places are actually composed by the arrangement of the objects created from the Generic room object.

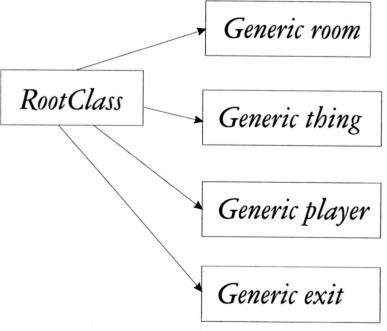

Figure 1. Basic class structure of the MOO based representation

2.1 Tappedin

Tappedin is an educational environment for teacher development (Schlager, Fusco and Schank, 1998). Tappedin is based on the lambdaMOO database (Rowley, 1997). The place resembles a conference center to evoke a professional atmosphere and encourage the kinds of discourse one would find at a conference institute.

As shown in Figure 2, Tappedin reinforces its spatial metaphor by 2D graphical layouts. The metaphor of a newly built office building is used, with the upper part of the building empty waiting for new users to occupy. There is an elevator to move people "vertically" to different levels in the building, and on each level and a person moves by clicking on a word or icon. Figure 3 summarizes the metaphorical structure of the whole environment: named objects and buildings, floors, and rooms.

The objects in Tappedin that compose the virtual place are referred to by their name. In a room of Tappedin, there are names on the floor plan images that are active links. A typical office is shown in the Figure 4. Most of these names stand for the exits (e.g. "ED's Oasis Library") and links (e.g. "out", "Elevator") to other areas. There are also names that stand for often used objects (e.g. "Whiteboard") and names that link to a web site (e.g. "ED's Website" in the "ED's oasis library"). In Tappedin there are also some things that don't have any substantial use but create ambience. For example, "Red Table" and "Blue Table" in the "ED oasis library" and the table, chairs and plant.

Figure 5 shows the object-oriented structure of the rooms in Tappedin. All rooms are derived from the Generic room. From the Generic Room to the specific rooms in Tappedin, there are several intermediate classes. Each inherits its predecessor class's "functions", and meanwhile has its own added "functions" which are special to this class and all of its descendants. This layered object-oriented structure of place representation is useful beause it simplifies the process of maintaining, designing and redesigning the VP.

2.2 The Virtual Campus

Another example of a non-recreational virtual world is the Virtual Campus (VC) in the Faculty of Architecture at the University of Sydney (http://www.arch.usyd.edu.au:7778; Maher, 1999). The VC uses the MOO object structure to create an inheritance hierarchy similar to Tappedin. Navigation in the VC is also hierarchical according to the function of the room, as shown in Figure 6. The VC is divided into several functional areas. It orients users to "go" layer by layer to a specific place or "out" all the way back to the "Main Hall".

In a VC room, there are several aspects determining the function of the room. There are icons or words that give access to the things in the room, for example the projector and recorder, and functions of the room, for example asking who is in the room and talking to someone in the room. An example of class structure of objects is the list of parents of the meeting room shown in Figure 6:

Generic Room(#3), Generic Improved Room(#184), Generic Improved Room with Cleaning and Scripts(#206), Meeting Room Prototype(#211)

The rooms then are created using a design verb "@sketch". @sketch combines the process of creating a room object from the class object and creating things and putting them into the room. The design prototypes and design verbs like "@sketch" were studied as part the linguistic design study of VWs (Cicogonani, 1998). This study presents a view of the design of VWs as a design representation interpretation and refinement process.

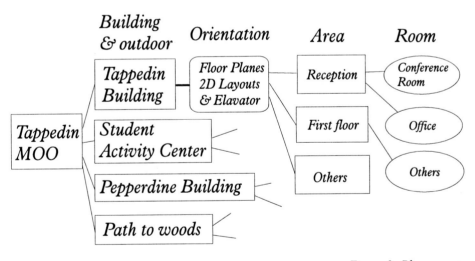

Figure 2. Visual representation of place in Tappedin

Figure 3. Place representation as an object hierarchy in Tappedin

Figure 4. ED's oasis li-

2.3 Active Worlds

Active Worlds (http://www.activeworlds.com/) is a collaborative 3D modeling world in which each object can have active links to behaviors and web pages. The basic representation outline is as shown in Figure 7. The Active Worlds environment is a universe with many worlds, for example, alpha world in Figure 8.

A world is a virtual geographical territory of a specified size measured by kilometers. This "land" is surrounded by a panoramic skyline picture, which gives the world a scene. The system provides users with modeling tools and object building blocks. Users can clone these building blocks to construct their own buildings. Figure 8 (left) is a "satellite view" of the Alpha world. It shows the construction distributed in the world is just as in the physical world. Apart from building models

brary and an office room in Tappedin

and land scenes, there are also avatars and events. Events are programs attached to a model in the world that provides interactions. For example, the most used events are those that change the position or orientation of an avatar or a model. In Active Worlds, despite the richness of a 3D enhanced place, the function of the place is restricted to talking and building.

From the representation point of view, we see that there is no place object existing in Active Worlds. A building is just the stacking of building blocks. Building blocks are objects with properties that can be modified. However, the buildings themselves are not objects. A building does not have a separate identification in the world. It doesn't have any properties and functional attachment; hence it does not have a dedicated representation.

3 A Representation Model for Metaphorical Design in Virtual Worlds

In this paper we focus on introducing and describing a model for representing the design of virtual places, drawing on developments in representing the design of physical objects and conceptual metaphor as a cognitive structure (Lakoff and Johnson, 1999). First we explore the use of the Function-Behavior-Structure framework (Gero, 1990) in designing physical objects and show how

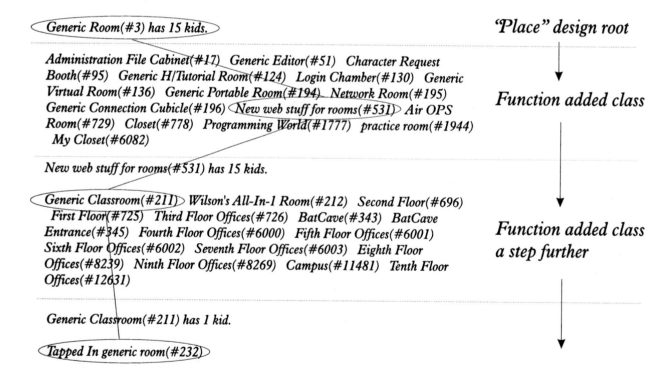

Figure 5. Inheritance hierarchy of rooms in Tappedin

this framework applies to the design of virtual places that have a metaphorical reference to physical buildings. Then we present the basis for conceptual metaphor as a representational framework for metaphorical design. We conclude with the benefit of using this framework when designing virtual places.

3.1   The FBS framework

The FBS framework characterises design objects and is the basis for a representation of designs. Here we consider the FBS framework for physical and virtual place design:

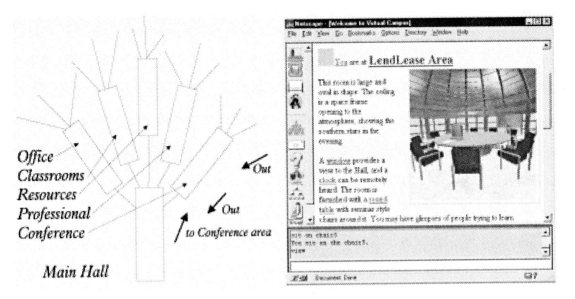

Figure 6. Place representation in Virtual Campus

- F (function) is related to the purpose of the design. It is not directly related to any substantial design structural component. A finished design as a product can serve many purposes. However, only the one that the designer intended is defined as the direct function of the design. The function of place design in physical worlds (PW) and virtual worlds (VW) are the same in the sense that in both cases the place is intended for similar purposes.
- B (behavior) reflects the performance of the design artifact or the design components. It is closely related to design structure. Behavior includes expected behavior (Be) and actual behavior (Ba). When Ba equals Be, we infer that the design satisfies the intended design function. In the designs in the physical world, it is generally known how B is derived from F and how B is linked to S. These relationships are defined by the long formed design convention and protocol. This is not the case in design in VW. A meeting room in the VW is not a room in a building even if we call it a "room". In metaphorical design, we name

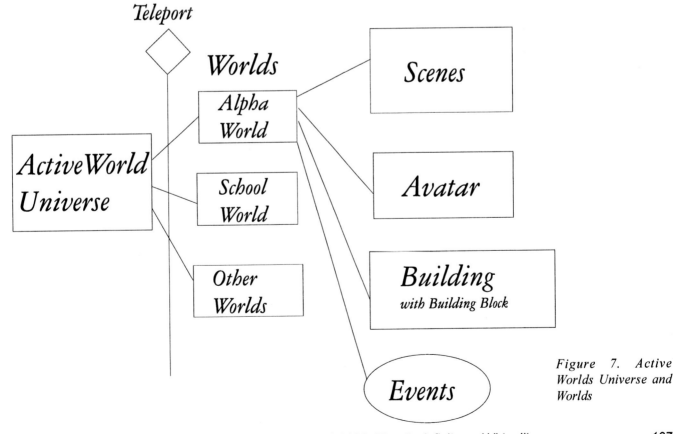

Figure 7. Active Worlds Universe and Worlds

ACADIA 2000: Eternity, Infinity and Virtuality

the design behaviors after those in physical place design. However, they aren't derived from either the function or the metaphorical structure of the object. Behaviors in a VW are defined by the code that implements the VW.

- S (structure) is the basic condition of existence, and it is the carrier of the design behaviors. In a VW, verbs and properties in the object permit the existence of virtual entities.

Figure 8. An example of a world in Active Worlds

What makes the design artifact a room and a room for meeting is totally different for the PW and VW. One of the differences of the (FBS framework) model for VW representation is in the identification of the design structure. In the physical world design representation, for example in the case of a wall design, the design structure is the wall itself, and the design structural elements are the components that make up the wall. The structure of the wall is the mechanism that produces the behaviors and together they are responsible for the fulfillment of the design function. However, in VP design, the metaphorical structure is not the mechanism that produces the behavior.

"Direct" design (in contrast to metaphorical design) is designing the design artifact as what it is; metaphorical design is to design something as if it is something else. The design artifacts of metaphorical design have two parts:

1. The design artifact in the form of what it is in the design environment. In metaphorical design, if the representation addresses the design artifact as only what it is, the design FBS can be too unfamiliar and too abstract to grasp. For example, to treat the design object as what it is in the computer, our understanding of the object and its performance may not be much higher than the "bit" level. If we use the metaphoric structure to help us understand the design, we can design behaviors and functions consistent with the metaphor.
2. A shell outside the design artifact that makes it seem to be something else. The shell is something added and unique to metaphorical design, which is not part of the FBS framework model.

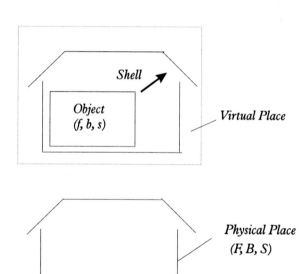

Figure 9. The use of a shell in representing the virtual place design

Figure 9 illustrates the analogy of object design representation based on the FBS framework model of the physical world design and the virtual world design. We use (F, B, S) to refer to a physical design object and (f, b, s) to refer to its metaphorical equivalent in a virtual world. In the metaphorical design of the virtual object, we take F as the design function of the virtual object. However, F only bestows f with meanings that are relevant to the physical world. F cannot replace f. B is introduced partly into the virtual design to name b, yet B and b are actually different because b is programmed and B is a physical phenomenon. s is only a metaphorical reference to S.

3.2 A model for metaphoric design

Lakoff and Johnson (Lakoff and Johnson, 1980, 1999) present four structures of the cognitive unconscious that provide the basis for understanding how metaphor influences our ability to make sense of subjective experience:

1) Basic level concepts
2) Semantic frames
3) Spatial-relation concepts
4) Conceptual metaphor

According to Lakoff and Johnson, the cognitive unconscious is all unconscious mental operations concerned with conceptual systems, meaning, inference, and language. Appealing to the cognitive unconscious in the design of virtual worlds allows us to conceive of and develop a virtual world that can be used by people with a more "natural" response. Since we are born and learn to act in a physical world, much of our unconscious thinking is based on our learned responses to the physical world. Lakoff and Johnson have argued that much of our thinking is also based on conjunctions of physical experiences with subjective experiences. In designing and understanding virtual worlds, creating a place that is consistent with our understanding of the physical world will allow us to consistently apply the primary metaphors we used.

Basic level concepts are a result of our innate ability to categorize the world. We categorize all the time to distinguish the things in the world in order to survive, but also in order to comprehend the world around us. Establishing the basic level of categories as the model for designing a virtual world allows people to use their intuition in interacting with the components of the world.

A semantic frame defines relationships among whole fields of related concepts and words that express them. Using a consistent metaphor allowing a person to draw on their semantic frames can be the basis for designing in a virtual world. For example, when designing a virtual classroom, appealing to the semantic frame, a person would be able to develop a relationship between the classroom, a lecture, a blackboard, a desk, etc. The use of these words as the design extends the metaphor to draw on the physical classroom to provide more functionality in the virtual world.

Spatial-relation concepts allow the designer to define consistent actions on the virtual object, as the person would expect to do with the physical object. A person would put things "on" the desk, go "out" of a room, and write "on" the blackboard. The world is a metaphor; the programmed virtual world does not exist spatially. The use of these words provides a consistent experience in the virtual world when compared to the physical world.

Conceptual metaphor allows us to conceptualize the virtual world in terms of time and motion in the physical world of architecture. Based on the analysis of virtual design in VW using the FBS framework model and Lakoff and Johnson's theory of metaphor concerning the four cognitive structures affecting the human's understanding of experience, we present a representation model for VP design in the VW. It consists of the following three elements:

1) conceptual basis,
2) semantic frame, and
3) realization shell.

Conceptual Basis (CB) is developed from the "Basic level Concept" of Lakoff and Johnson's theory about metaphor. It is the part of VP design corresponding to people's ability to categorize. In metaphorical design, CB defines the basic concepts and conditions of the existence of a design object. For example, in designing a VP, the CB assigns "Lend Lease room" to the room representation category; "Wilkinson Building" to the building category; "Slide projector" to the tool category. In metaphorical design, the CB not only clarifies the basic concepts for design, but also provides knowledge about the common characteristics and properties of this concept and the knowledge about common actions and the possible methods of interaction of the users with this concept.

In the VW, CB is the object in the system's object-oriented software environment. The object is the basic condition of existence. In the VW, the object is the basis for the use of the world. In a programming sense the object is made of groups of properties and verbs. Our task is not to study the verbs and properties or how they make the existence possible. These are the technological issues related to the software core of the VW system. Our task is to characterize and classify the design concepts using a building or room metaphor. For example, a room is a "container". A user can "go" in and out of it. It belongs to a building. It contains the characters of "exclusiveness" and "security", etc. In the design of VP, CB is in the set of class objects in a VW. A class object carries mechanisms that are responsible for the object's existence and use.

Semantic Frame (SF) corresponds to the "semantic frames" in Lakoff and Johnson's theory. A person understands the virtual environment he/she is experiencing through what can be done in the environment. And this is manifested as mechanisms that represent the technological possibilities of the virtual environment. In virtual place design, these mechanisms can either be in the design object that stands for the place, or they can be in the objects in the place, for example "recorder", "projector". In a VW, there are many mechanisms responsible for the "actions" in the design object. These mechanisms serve roughly the following general purposes:

- Communication (saying, whispering, paging, mailing other users)
- Activities (such as recording a conversation, showing slides on the projector)
- Information Access (links)
- Navigation (moving from one place to another)

Realization Shell (RS) is a shell that realizes the meaning the designer wants to put into the metaphorical design. It is those things that make the existence and action meaningful in the VW, for example, naming and defining the action of a kind of synchronized communication as "speak". For the place design in VW, RS creates spatiality for the design object. According to the methods RS uses, RS consists of the following:

> Names and a naming system for objects, properties and verbs
>
> 2D and 3D visual representation

Many forms of RS have been used in VWs, such as text, images and 3D. A 3D realization shell conveys more explicitly the spatial representation of the virtual place. We have developed 3 kinds of 3D realization shells in our Virtual Campus:

1) Ambience: With this kind of RS, the functions of the place are implied by the visualization of the place. The 3D models present the character of a certain kind of purposeful place. These characterized 3D models, like functional icons, remind users of the functions of its physical place counterpart or link the user's visual impression to their physical experience of a physical place. This "imply" type of RS can be created as part of the place object. In the place object, they are built into the object's properties that are related to the 3D description. For example, a 3D visualization of a table may only be creating ambience and does not provide any of the functions of a table.

2) Function: These are 3D models that have independent, functional objects behind them. Unlike the ambience type of RS, the functions related to this kind of RS are programmed as part of the objects behind these 3D models. For example, a door object can be opened, closed, locked, etc.

3) Action: The 3D models themselves, due to the description language they use, can carry a special kind of behavior. In VRML2.0, for example, it is called Event. However this kind of RS is not programmed as part of an object. They are embedded in the 3D description files of the 3D model. This kind of RS normally is used as an enrichment of the other two kinds of RS. For example, a part of a VRML object can be a hyperlink to a web page.

These three kinds of 3D RS are similar because they each provide the visualization of virtual place. They differ in how the visualization is related to the underlying object representation of the place and therefore the intended purpose of the visualized objects.

4 Summary

Computer models provide the freedom and flexibility to explore the "impossible" of physical design (Sakamura, and Suzuki, 1997). The design of virtual worlds can be begin with an analogy of place design – the design of virtual places. Therefore the design of virtual places is metaphorical. The design of VP as metaphorical design has characteristics that are different to that of a physical design. We proposed a (CB, SF, RS) model for the VP design. This model views the VP in a unique way so that when representing design, we recognize and make explicit the metaphorical nature of the design.

The benefit of using the (CB, SF, RS) model for designing a metaphorical place lies in the development of a consistent and comprehensive representation of the place from which the implementation can be derived. Rather than start and finish with a visual representation of the virtual world, this model starts with the definition of a set of categories of objects that will be part of the place and these categories establish the metaphor. For example, defining the categories of building as office building, house, or museum establishes the type of metaphorical design. Once the conceptual basis is established, the semantic frame elaborates on the design by filling out the intended use and the behavior of the place with a consistent set of properties and actions. The realization shell provides the visualization of the place and is constructed on a structured representation of the virtual place, providing consistency and ease of use. The realization shell, through the use of form as color and shape, can be developed into a particular design style. The visual representation of the virtual place need not look as if it were physical but can suggest the reference to the physical.

As more virtual places are designed, we are developing experience with their visualization and potential use. The development of a model for metaphorical design can provide the theoretical basis for new designs and new metaphors.

References:

Bowers, J., Pycock, J. and O'Brien, J. (1997). Talk and embodiment in collaborative virtual environments, *Proceedings of Computer-Human Interaction Conference*, ACM Press, New York, pp. 58-65

Chaomei, C., Thomas, L., Cole, J. and Chennawasin, C. (1999). Representing the semantics of virtual spaces, *IEEE MultiMedia*. **6**, (2):54-63

Cicognani, A. (1998) *A Linguistic Characterization of Design in Text-based VWs*, Ph.D. thesis, p 95

Curtis, P. and Nichols, D. A. (1993). MUDs *Grow Up: Social Virtual Reality in the Real World*, Technical Report, Xerox PARC, Palo Alto, Calif., 1993; ftp://ftp.lambda.moo.mud.org/pub/MOO/papers/MUDsGrowUp.ps

Das, T. K., Garminder, S., Mitchell, A., Kumar, P. S. and McGee, K.. (1997). *Developing Social Virtual Worlds using NetEffect*, Institute of System Science, National University of Singapore, http://www.iss.nus.sg/RND/cs

Dieberger, A. (1997). Supporting social navigation on the world-wide web, *International Journal of Human-Computer Studies*, **46**, (6): 805-825

Fuellen, G. (1996). *Biocomputing For Everyone*, http://www.techfak.uni-bielefeld.de/bcd/ForAll/welcome.html

Gero, J. S. (1990), Design Prototype: A knowledge representation schema for design, *AI Magazine*, **11** (4): 26-36

Jeffrey, P. and Mark, G. (1998). Constructing social spaces in virtual environments: A study of navigation and interaction, *Proceedings Workshop on Personalized and Social Navigation in Information Space*, pp. 24-38

Lakoff, G. and Johnson, M. (1980) *Metaphors We Live By*, Chicago: University of Chicago Press

Lakoff, G. and Johnson, M. (1999) *Philosophy in the Flesh : The Embodied Mind and its Challenge to Western Thought*, Chicago: University of Chicago Press

Maher, M. L. (1999). *Design the Virtual Campus as a Virtual World*, Proceedings of CSCL 99, Stanford University, pp 376-382. http://kn.cilt.org/cscl99/A47/A47.HTM

Mynatt E. D., Adler, A., Ito, M. and O'Day, V. L. (1997). Design for network communities, *Proceedings of CHI*, ACM Press, New York, pp.210-217.

Muramastsu, J. (1993). Computing, social activity, and entertainment: a field study of a game MUD, *CSCW Journal*, **7**(1/2):.87-122

Rowley, M. N. (1997). *Distributing MOO-Based Shared Worlds, Intermetrics*, Inc. IEEE 1997

Sakamura, K. and Suzuki, H. (1997) *The Virtual Architecture*, Tokyo: Tokyo Daigaku Sogo Kenchiku Hakubutsuka, p1

Schiana, D. J. (1998). The first noble truth of CyberSpace: People are people (Even when they MOO) *Proceedings of CHI*, ACM Press, New York, pp.352-359.

Schlager, M., Fusco, J. and Schank, P. (1998). Cornerstones for an online community of education professional, *IEEE Technology and Society*, **17**(4):15-21.

Toomey, L., Adoms, L. and Churchill, E. (1998). Meetings in a virtual space: Creating a digital document, *Proceedings 31st Anniversary Havaii International Conference of System Sciences*, IEEE CS Press, Los Alamitos, Califonia, pp.236-244.

Gizmos

Although much CAD research has focused upon broad conceptual systems and theories of design, other efforts have constrained the scope to something small and manageable. When successful, these constrained projects have often produces "neat hacks" or clever programs that implement limited tools that address some aspect of the architectural design process. One might terms these programs "gizmos", as have Abdelwawla, Elnimeiri and Krawczyk in their article. Gizmos advance architectural knowledge by thoroughly and definitively solving these constrained problems.

Abdelwawla, Elnimeiri and Krawczyk have applied the concept in its most precise form by building many very small application to solve and illustrate structural issues. Their medium for constructing these tools is Java and the medium for distribution is theWeb, an ideal combination for developing gizmos.

The article by Akleman, Chen and Meric is similarly about a gizmo. They have addressed the narrow yet fundamental concept of symmetrical design by inventing a clever algorithm and sharing it as a working tool on the Web.

The article by Burry, Datta and Anson is less clearly about gizmos, but the small programs that his students construct can be thought of as gizmos for generating form. These gizmos are "finger exercises" in software development that teach a budding software engineer the principles of implementation and project management. The creation of gizmos gives architects a glimpse into the world of professional software engineering and teach principles of procedural coding, object-oriented programming or rule-based programming. The interaction of gizmos created by loosely cooperating authors leads to effects and results that are not always predictable and thus can spur the imagination regarding spatial and formal options.

Future gizmos may result from the research described by Bailey. The experiment that he has devised also is a clever hack, although not a software one.

Kilkelly describes a "super-gizmo" or elegant hack that solves the broader problem of construction documentation.

The contributions to ACADIA 2000 have amply continued this tradition of CAD research in ways that are startling and admirable.

Structural Gizmos

Samir Abdelmawla, Illinois Institute of Technology, USA

Mahjoub Elnimeiri, Illinois Institute of Technology, USA

Robert Krawczyk, Illinois Institute of Technology, USA

Abstract

Architects are visual learners. The Internet has enabled interactive learning tools that can be used to assist in visual thinking of structural concepts, especially at the introductory levels. Here, we propose a visual approach for understanding structures through a series of interactive learning modules, or 'gizmos'. These gizmos, are the tools that the student may use to examine one structural concept at a time. Being interactive, they offer many more possibilities beyond what one static problem can show. The approach aims to enhance students' visual intuition, and hence understanding of structural concepts and the parameters affecting design. This paper will present selected structural gizmos, how they work, and how they can enhance structural education for architects.

> Precise computation is no more certain than a belief or a dream, but we must try by means of more exact analyses to prevent the harmful effects of human error.
>
> *Louis I. Khan*

1 Introduction: Structure for Architects

A major portion of an architect's education is structures. The study of structures includes engineering concepts presented in mathematical terms and architectural design presented in non-mathematical terms. The simulation and physical testing of structural concepts are considered the best approach to understand engineering and design. With the evolution of multimedia and animation, as computer-aided instruction techniques, an interactive learning environment can be developed to meet most of the needs of architectural students, who are best suited for such a visual approach.

1.1 Visual Intuition of Structures

A visual approach should enhance *visual intuition.* We need to enhance such intuition so students can *feel* when a system is not quite correct or when a structure member is not efficient. Through visual intuition, principles of structures become an unconscious part of student's way of thinking. We all possess a purely visual intuition of structural behavior through our daily experience. We understand why columns at the bottom of a building must be larger than those at its top, since they must support the accumulated weights of all the floors of the building. Without any theoretical knowledge, we are ready to say that a cantilever beam is right if shaped with a decreasing depth towards its tip, Figure 1a. The same concept applies to light poles or high rise buildings, Figure 1b. We may even have aesthetic feelings about this matter and say that the form is in the first case >*lovely*= and >*ugly*= in the second. We are trying to enable the student to understand the underlying reasoning for judging.

A *quantitative* interpretation of these examples should explain *why*. At the same time, a visual approach may introduce a *qualitative* presentation of structural concepts as the basis for *quantitative* analysis and selection of parameters that affect the ultimate design.

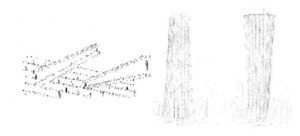

Figure 1. Intuitive judgment of correct and incorrect (a) cantilever beams, (b) high rise buildings.

1.2 The Beginning of Visual Approach

Although it is not necessary to make every architect an engineer, architects still need to understand the structural system and the structural performance of the design. Structural education has been addressed by some masters in the field, such as *Mario Salvadori, P. Corkill* and *Jafar Vossoughi,* who have written valuable books in the 1960s and early 1970s (Abdelmawla 2000). Salvadori had the talent of explaining. He wrote many books that simplify not only structures but math as well. He wrote *Math Games for Middle Schools, The Art of Construction, Why Buildings Stands Up, Structural Design in Architecture* and *Structure in Architecture.* Yet, the manual he put together for 70 lessons of *Architecture and Engineering* in 1963 is the first to use the concept of a visual approach, Figure 2a.

In 1998, W. Zalewski and E. Allen published *Shaping Structures: Statics* revives late nineteenth- and early twentieth-century graphical methods in which the relationship between structural forms and forces is explored geometrically through the manipulation of scaled vectors. This book, with a supplementary CD-ROM, invites students to analyze structures through the generation of simple structural forms of their own design.

Understanding Structures, published in 1999, by Fuller Moore is a survey style compilation of several classic non-quantitative approaches to structures education presented through analogies drawn from everyday life, diagrams of analytical concepts, and images of physical demonstration models. This book and the previous present a departure from the use of mathematical expressions and calculations as the primary vehicle for introducing structural concepts. Neither addresses the potential for using computer-based analytical methods to introduce students of architecture to struc-

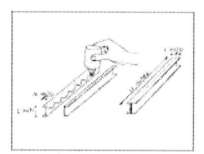

Figure 2. (a) Visual Approach through Building Models – M. Salvadori, 1963.

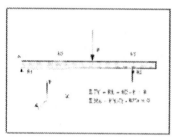

Figure 2. (b) Structure Programs in BASIC – Kern International 1983.

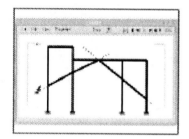

Figure 2. (c) CASDET – Piccolotto & Rio 1995.

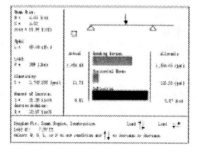

Figure 2. (d) Interactive Beam / Structural Workbench – Elnimeiri & Krawczyk 1996.

Figure 2. (e) Architectonics on the Web – C. Luebkeman, 1997.

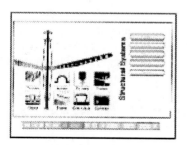

Figure 2. (f) Structures E-Book -- S. Vassigh, 1999.

tures (Theodoropulos 2000).

1.3 Computer-Aided Instruction and Visual Approach

At the same time as the introduction of personal computers in 1983, Justin Cole published a review for the role of computers in structural education at the School of the Built Environment, South Australian Institute of Technology. He also described the development of SSADS; a computer based Structural Selection Analysis and Design System.

In 1985 Kern International produced a set of simple structural programs. These programs were to be used as educational tools at the college level or engineers who may find them useful as a self-study course. They were also intended to be used as a supplement to a standard course in mechanics, Figure 2b.

In 1993 a team at the Illinois Institute of Technology built the first prototype of an interactive simple beam program. The Interactive Beam allowed the user to move or increase the load or move support location; at each change shear, moment and deflection diagrams are refreshed. The work was further developed in the "Structural Workbench" research project. The project was completed in 1996 and constructed a hierarchy of structural concepts as a prototype for a learning multimedia package (Elnimeiri 1996), Figure 2c.

In the annual conference of ACADIA in 1995 Piccolotto and Rio presented a paper entitled "Structural Design Education with Computers." The paper presented a program for the simulation of structures called CASDET (Piccolotto 1995). The program was quite advanced in the methods used for the composition and analysis of planer structures. The program as well displayed the results of user interaction and kept the analysis process behind the scenes, Figure 2d.

In 1996 Chris Luebkeman put to the Web a series of lectures for a structural course to be accessed online at University of Oregon. In 1997, he presented a paper about web-based interactive visualization tools to enhance the effectiveness of teaching/learning of Architectonics, at the ACSA National Conference. He also developed at University of Hong Kong interactive programs for simple beam behavior and pencil tower loading, Figure 2e.

At State University of New York at Buffalo, Shabin Vassigh developed another prototype for a multimedia instructional software package that utilizes a wide range of graphics, animation and sound to demonstrate the principles and application of structural analysis and building technology (Vassigh 1999), Figure 2f.

2 What is the Visual Approach?

Visual analysis relies on the ability to develop abstracted model and to get the sense of structure and how it works. Consider the simple truss shown in Figure 3, the questions below are to arouse student interest and create attention.

The student is asked to answer this group of questions before hand, i.e. (a) which member carries more load? (b) The lower chord of the truss is in tension or compression. (c) If we decrease the depth of the truss, the forces in members are going to (increase – decrease – stay the same)?

Through visual analysis we could answer these questions if the diagrams could 'talk' back to us. For the question in Figure 3a, as an example, as we move the load left, over the support, the vertical member would carry 100% of the load (as shown in Figure 3c). By the movement of the load moves towards the right, we can anticipate an increase of the force in the right member. This means the members will carry more load as they become vertical.

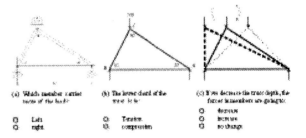

2.1 The Use of Visual Approach in a Structural Class

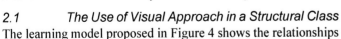

The learning model proposed in Figure 4 shows the relationships between the on-line supporting material and the direct instruction class at three level of: (a) offer information through lecturing, handouts, and web pages, (b) reinforce the concept through examples and the interactive gizmos, and (c) test students' knowledge through quizzes and exams.

Figure 3. Visual Analysis as Problem Solving Method.

Figure 5 delineates the hierarchy of basic knowledge of structures for architects. The flow starts with an introduction to structure; i.e. to define what is structure, structure development and its boundaries. The comprehension of "Basic Concepts" is considered as a prerequisite before getting into the analysis modules. Of course, these analysis modules could expand to cover other compo-

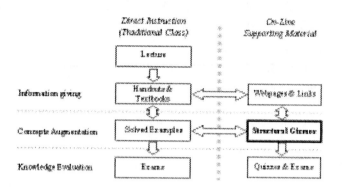

Figure 4. Structural Gizmos as Concept Support within a Class.

nents, e.g. frames and arches, cable structures, shells, etc. Evaluation can help students to identify points that need revision and test misconceptions. Series of quizzes and exams can take place after the completion of the prerequisites, as well after the completion of each module. Upon the understanding of the structural analysis process the student can proceed to the design phase.

3 What is a gizmo?

giz·mo also *gis·mo* (gzm). n., pl. *giz·mos*.
[20th c.: origin unknown.]
"any small and usu. ingenious mechanical device or tool. sl. a gadget" (Oxford Dictionary)
"a usually small and often novel mechanical or electronic device or contrivance" (Merriam-Webster Dictionary)

The gizmos as constructed here are interactive Java programs designed to simulate the behavior of structural components. They are mechanisms that are able to simulate a seemly mechanical property by having moving parts. As these parts move, forces can be applied and responses can be shown. In all aspects we consider these to be digital machines with the same qualities of real gizmos.

3.1 Visual Qualities of Gizmos

Visual analysis is supported with the gizmos through certain visual cues. These cues manage the visual representation of the concepts we are trying to convey which are based on calculated values. Some typical visual controls are shown in Figure 6. Testing of different values and/or geometric configurations is handled visually by dragging object grips, hot spots, or moving the object itself.

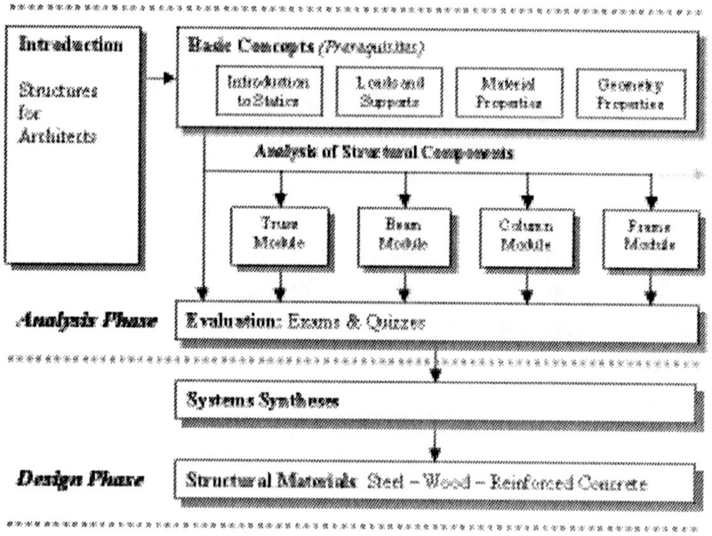

The student as well has the ability to plug in specific numerical values for testing components. Through the use of multiple text-fields, he/she can change force magnitude, application point, member angle, span, or locations for supports. Check-boxes are used as well to control the visibility of certain visual cues. By turning these check-boxes on or off, they are able to change the number of forces applied, control the visibility of reactions, or visual representation of force magnitudes, Figure 7.

Figure 5. Hierarchy of Basic Knowledge for Structures for Architects.

The response of the structural components and the magnitude of the forces induced in members or reactions is represented visually based on changes made by the student, Figure 8. These visual cues designate members subjected to higher strength and flow of forces within the structure. Reactions at supports are represented visually, as well as, by percentage values. These responses give the visual feedback of the behavior of the component under certain loading condition. Through the changes the student makes for different load and geometry conditions, he/she can begin to understand the parameters that affect the component performance and/or efficiency.

Visual representation of values is also supported by the display of values of forces induced in members or reactions at supports. The changes the student makes using visual aids such as grips are reflected at the same time as numeric values in the text-fields area, Figure 9.

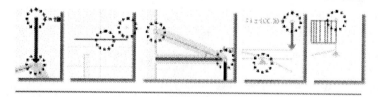

Figure 6. Visual Controls of Values and/or Geometry.

Critical values as well are shown in some modules, i.e. maximum bending moment and its location. At the same time, some values have been omitted from display for more clarity of the display area. Information, such as, forces in truss members are not shown but could be sent through email or displayed in another window.

Colors add another dimension to visual information representation. Colors are be used to differentiate between different types of forces, e.g. tension, compression, or zero-force members, as shown in Figure 10.

The gizmos, through interactivity, help in the comparison of different geometrical configurations and loading conditions. Figure 11 shows some of visual comparison possibilities. Through the changes of the cable angle shown in Figure 11a, we can see how cable angle affects the amount of tension induced in the cable as well as the compression in the horizontal rod. In the Section Properties gizmo, Figure 11b, the student can modify the selected section and compare its efficiency to other sections. Section efficiency is obtained in this case as a ratio of "Moment of Inertia" to "Cross Section Area."

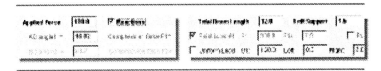

Figure 7. Numerical Input of Values and Visibility Options.

In the Truss gizmo, as to be discussed later in the following section, we would be able to see the forces flow and the pattern of tension/compression members in different trusses, Figure 11c. We also can compare the effect of changing the number of bays for the same truss and same span. High stressed members as well are represented wider than low stressed one. Through this designation we can see the effect of changing truss depth for the same truss and same span.

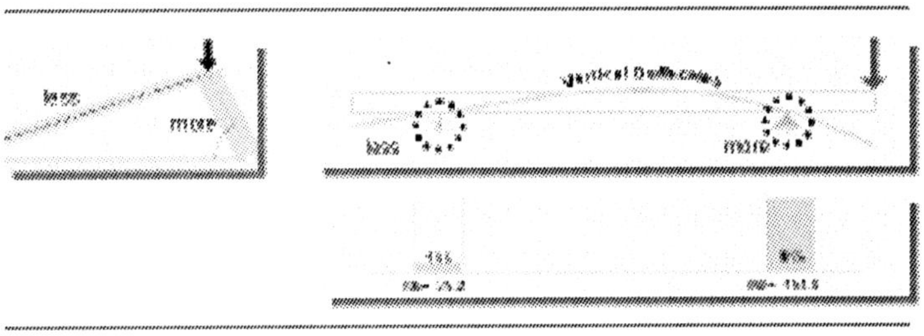

Figure 8. Visual Representation of Values and Structure Response.

3.2 Gizmos within Learning Modules

The following series of figures, Figures 12 through 18, outlines the complete set of modules that will be part of the course material. An attempt was made to have at least one gizmo in each module. In each module, the gizmo is accessed through accompanying web pages. A close examination of these gizmos demonstrates the variety of visual cues that can be implemented for each single structural concept.

Module A: Introduction to Statics - Resolution of Forces

Module B: Loads and Loading - Loads, Supports and Reactions

Module C: Members in Bending & Bending Moment Diagrams — Beams Shear force

Module D: Material properties - Stress, Strain and Modulus of Elasticity

Module E: Section properties - Centroid, Moment of Inertia

Module F: Members in Bending - Beam stresses

Module G: Axial Loading Members - Trusses

Figure 9. Display of Numerical Values.

4 Conclusions

Better understanding of structures leads to better architecture. Efforts have been made to make learning and teaching structures as easy as possible. But, there is no such thing as easy learning, or teaching; only methods or devices can make them distinguishable. The paper introduces visual representation of structural concepts as a natural approach for students of architecture to promote structural intuition. Meanwhile, intuition by itself cannot be expected to lead to quantitative knowledge in a field as complex as structures. For this, the visual approach considers both visual examination and numerical analysis of the structural component. The critical issues addressed in this part of this study are the visual cues that can be developed to enable greater understanding of structural concepts and what material can be applied which enhances, not replaces, classroom instruction.

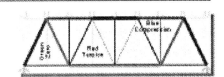

Figure 10. Usage of Colors.

The advantage of web-based learning aids is obvious. Anytime, anywhere learning reinforces the instruction in the classroom. The ability to introduce additional material and examples allows the instructor to concentrate on core concepts and detailed explanations knowing that the student will have the ability to examine them at great length on their own. The gizmos also allow the instructor to

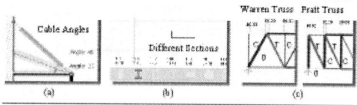

Figure 11. Visual Comparison.

show in class structural concepts that may be difficult with traditional means.

Future research will attempt to quantify the actual benefits of this approach. Using testing of structural knowledge before and after the use of the gizmos may begin to tell us better how this method can increase learning. The gizmo concept can also applied to other areas of architectural education. Most engineering related areas that rely on computations that can be visually demonstrated are good candidates. The greater challenge is to develop visual methods that could be used in teaching architectural form and spatial organization.

References

Abdelmawla, S. (2000), A Visual Approach of Structural Analysis for Architects. Unpublished Ph.D. Arch. Thesis, Chicago: Illinois Institute of Technology.

Elnimeiri, M. and R. Krawczyk. (1996). *Structural Workbench*, Unpublished, Final Report. Educational and Research Initiative Funds (ERIF), Illinois Institute of Technology.

Piccolotto M., and R. Olga. (1995). *Structural Design Education with Computers*. ACADIA' 95 Proceedings: 285-298. Association for Computer Aided Design in Architecture.

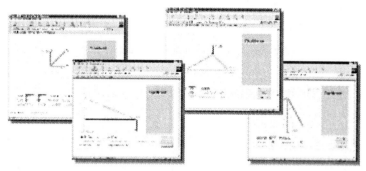

Figure 12. Group of Gizmos Designed for the Resolution of Forces Concept.

Theodoropoulos, C. (2000). Book Reviews, *Journal of Architectural Education*: Volume 53, Number 3, February 2000: 186-187. Washington, D.C.: Association of Collegiate Schools of Architecture.

Vassigh, S. (1999). *Structures E-Book*. ACADIA Quarterly. Volume 18, Number 3, 1999: 14-15. Association for Computer Aided Design in Architecture.

Figure 13. A Gizmo Showing Distribution of Reactions from a Simple Truss.

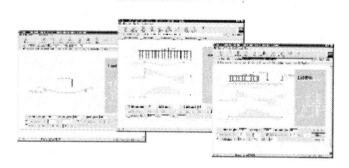

Figure 14. A Series of Beam Gizmos with Pointed and Distributed Loads.

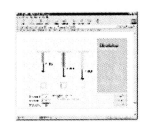

Figure 15. Modulus of Elasticity for Different Materials.

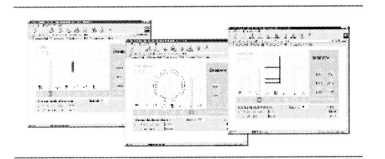

Figure 16. Comparison of Moment of Inertia for Different Sections.

Figure 17. Beam Shear / Moment Stresses and Critical Range.

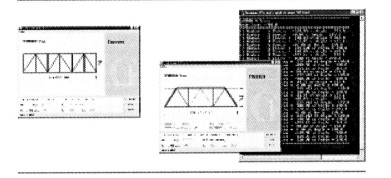

Figure 18 (a). The Truss Gizmo - Warren Truss Analysis with and without Forces Display and the Forces. Magnitude in Members as to be Emailed.

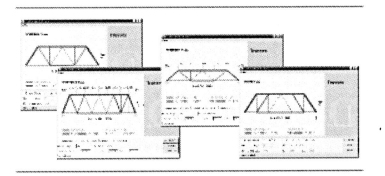

Figure 18 (b). The Truss Gizmo - Comparison for Different Truss Solutions by Different: Number of Bays, Truss Depth, and/or geometry.

Intuitive and Effective Design of Periodic Symmetric Tiles

Ergun Akleman, Texas A&M University, USA

Jianer Chen, Texas A&M University, USA

Burak Meric, Knowledge Based Information Systems, Inc., USA

Abstract

This paper presents a new approach for intuitive and effective design of periodic symmetric tiles. We observe that planar graphs can effectively represent symmetric tiles and graph drawing provides an intuitive paradigm for designing symmetric tiles. Moreover, based on our theoretical work to represent hexagonal symmetry by rectangular symmetry, we are able to present all symmetric tiles as graphs embedded on a torus and based on simple modulo operations. This approach enables us to develop a simple and efficient algorithm, which has been implemented in Java. By using this software, designers, architects and artists can create interesting symmetric tiles directly on the web. We also have designed a few examples of symmetric tiles to show the effectiveness of the approach.

1 Introduction

The symmetric patterns in Alhambra, Granada are probably the most well known architectural usage of symmetric patterns. In fact, symmetric patterns have been a part of the architectural world throughout the history and frequently used by almost every civilization in wallpapers and wall decorations, ceilings, floor tiles, street pavements and even facades of the buildings as shown in Figures 1.

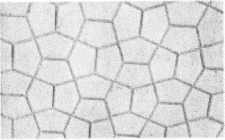

Figure 1. Examples of architectural usage of symmetric tile (Hargittai and Hargittai 1994).

Although, there has been a great interest in art and architecture, the theoretical classification of periodic symmetric patterns did not began until the early twentieth century when Russian crystallographer E. S. Fedorov enumerated the seventeen two-dimensional periodic symmetry groups. These groups today are also known as wallpaper groups, periodic groups or *(plane) crystallographic groups* (Grunbaum and Shephard 1987). Fedorov's result shows that, mathematically, there are only seventeen distinct types of patterns that have different symmetries. Since the paper of Fedorov was written in Russian the classification of the 17 symmetry groups were not known until the work of Niggli and Polya in 1924.

From the designer's perspective, the most important implication of Fedorov, Niggli and Polya's work is the identification of the symmetry groups as a set of distinct symmetry operations. This identification of symmetry operations encouraged artists such as M. C. Escher, F. Briss and K. Mehmedov to discover new and interesting patterns. The most famous drawings of symmetric patterns were created by M. C. Escher [1] and his works are still extremely popular.

Although, the knowledge of 17 symmetry groups helps the design of symmetric patterns, it is still difficult to find *interesting tiles* with paper and pen. In other words, even with the knowledge of 17 symmetry groups when using only paper and pen to design symmetric patterns the artistic talent is still important. The idea of using interesting symmetric tiles has a great use in architecture, art, science and education. Therefore, it is important to find interactive computational approaches to simplify the design of interesting tiles.

With the development of computer graphics, many interactive systems to design symmetric patterns have been developed. Most of existing symmetric pattern design systems are based on painting paradigm. For designing tiles, these systems are not fundamentally different than paper and pen. In a painting system, even if the users want to make small changes, they must erase existing images and redraw new ones.

One alternative approach is to use drawing paradigm. Kali developed by N. Amenta at University of Minnesota Geometry Center is an example of a system that uses drawing paradigm (Kali). Since drawing is based on objects such as points, lines and polygons that can be translated, scaled or rotated interactively, it is easy to change the shapes of the times. At the first look, this approach seems to be the appropriate choice. Unfortunately, we observe that even drawing paradigm is not appropriate for symmetric tile design. Tiles are polygons that come together without gaps and overlaps, on the other hand, drawing paradigm supports gaps and overlaps. The user has to be extremely careful not to include any gap or overlap when designing symmetric tiles.

We observed that symmetric tiles are inherently graphs embedded on surfaces without edge crossings, where lines are edges and line junctions are vertices. In other words, for symmetric tiles the internal representation must support not only points, lines and polygons but also graphs. We, therefore, propose that graph drawing paradigm is the most appropriate approach to develop a graph based algorithmic approach to design symmetric tiles.

In this work we have developed a graph-based approach for designing symmetric tiles. In our approach, users construct the graphs that represent symmetric tiles by drawing line segments. Each line segment corresponds to an edge of the underlying graph and endpoints of the lines give the vertices of the graph. The graph representation is constructed by attaching endpoints. In other words, when two vertices come close, they will snap together and become one vertex. We also provide intersection prevention to ensure the graph edges never intersect. We also provide an option that removes this constraint to enhance flexibility and improve usability.

Based on this approach, we have developed a system. By using our system one can produce drawings composed of graphs. These graphs can be modified interactively by moving the vertices, by adding new edges, and by dividing edges. In order to create better drawings collisions need to be avoided. For implementation we have chosen the Java programming language. That allows us to make use of the object-oriented aspects and to make our work available on the Internet.

2 Seventeen Planar Symmetries

As we have mentioned in introduction, there exist seventeen distinct symmetries. In literature (Grunbaum and Shephard 1987), the periodic symmetry groups are called as *p1, p2, p4, pm, pmm, p4m, p4m, cm, cmm, pg, pmg, pgg, p4g, p3, p6, p3m1, p31m* and *p6m*. Each one of these symmetry groups is a collection of symmetry operations: translation, rotation, reflection and glide reflection. The rotations can be either period 2, 3, 4 or 6. These operations are known as isometries, which preserve the distance of any two points. A 3x3 matrix can uniformly represent these isometries.

The complete list of the 17 symmetry groups [2] in plane can be classified in two categories: rectangular and hexagonal symmetries (12 of these 17 groups have rectangular symmetries and 5 of them have hexagonal symmetries). The rectangular and hexagonal symmetries are shown in Figures 2 and 3.

3 Methodology

For some symmetry groups, the drawing operations require checking all the vertices and edges. Checking all vertices and edges is not possible since the graphs that represent symmetric tiles have infinitely many vertices and edges. Fortunately, for symmetric tiles, it is not necessary to check all vertices and edges. We observe that since repeating a unit block can generate symmetric tiles, the whole graph can be represented by a simple unit graph and all the operations can be done on this simple graph.

Based on this observation, we have developed a simple algorithm (and supporting data structure) for drawing rectangular symmetries. We show that the drawing algorithm for rectangular symmetries can also be applied to hexagonal symmetries with a minor modification. We also show that, based on this drawing algorithm, collisions can easily be detected.

3.1 Drawing Algorithm for Rectangular Symmetries

As known from topology (Firby and Gardiner 1982), rectangular symmetric tiling is a covering space of the rectangle with identified opposite sides, which is topologically equivalent to a torus. Because of this property, rectangular symmetries can easily be obtained by modulo operations. It is, therefore, especially easy to develop an algorithm for rectangular symmetries since for rectangular symmetries it is possible to simply repeat a rectangle with modulo operations. This rectangle is called the unit cell. With the unit cell we get all information on the drawing and are able to perform operations based on this information. So, instead of dealing with the whole drawing we only need to consider the objects in a single cell.

Based on this observation, the algorithm becomes extremely simple. We use two graph data structures. The first one represents the actual drawing and the other one (unit graph embedded over toroidal surface) represents rectangular unit blocks. We call these internal representations "drawing" and "unit graph" representations. Unit graph representation is obtained in two stages from drawing representation.

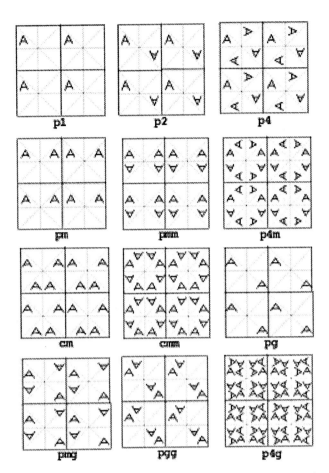

Figure 2. Rectangular symmetries.

For a given rectangular symmetry group, first related symmetry operations, i.e. a combination of translation, rotation, reflection and glide reflection operations are applied. As a result of these symmetry operations a set of new lines are computed. By using mod operations in x and y directions, these lines are cut into shorter pieces that exactly fit inside of unit cell. Figure 4.a shows a collection of lines drawn by the user and Figure 4.b shows the corresponding lines in the unit cell for symmetry group PG (Grunbaum and Shephard 1987). Once the unit graph is obtained, the final drawing is obtained by simply translating all the lines in unit graph as shown in Figure 4.c.

Note that both "drawing" and "unit graph" representations are internal representations and they are completely hidden from users. During the design process, users have only to deal with the symmetric tiles such as the one shown in Figure 4.c. As a result, they can focus mainly on the design of interesting tiles without the need to know the internal representations and the symmetry group they are currently using.

3.2 Drawing Algorithm for Hexagonal Symmetries

Hexagonal unit blocks do not simply provide convenient operations as given in rectangular unit blocks. (In fact, It is well known [3] that rectangles with identified opposite sides give a torus while hexagon does not correspond to any valid topological surface which is a closed compact 2-manifold.)

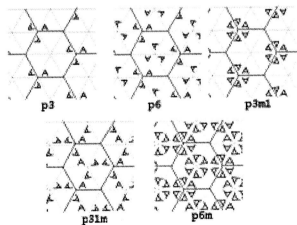

Figure 3. Hexagonal symmetries.

One of our contributions in this paper is the development of a unified approach to include hexagonal symmetries. In order to avoid hexagons, we look for simpler unit cells for hexagonal symmetries and show that hexagonal symmetries can also be represented by a repeating rectangular unit block, which is shown in Figure 5. We prove that regardless of the symmetry group, all symmetric tiles can be represented by a *simple unit graph*, which can be embedded over a toroidal surface, thus can be

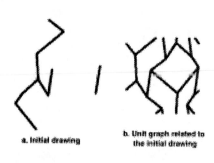

a. Initial drawing *b. Unit graph related to the initial drawing*

c. Symmetric tiles related to initial drawing

Figure 4. Illustration of our algorithm.

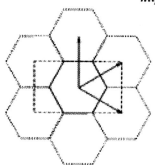

Figure 5. Hexagonal symmetry and related rectangular symmetry.

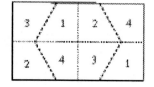

Figure 6. A hexagonally symmetric rectangle.

constructed by also using modulo operations. See Figure 6 for a intuitive illustration.

Based on this proof, in order to create the special rectangle unit cell for hexagonal symmetries we use the hexagon in the middle of the rectangle. To fill all the triangles in our rectangles we must translate the lines in the main hexagon. Thus, after performing the transformations in the hexagon the lines in the upper left region will be translated to lower right region and the lines in the upper right region will be translated to the lower left region.

3.3 Collision Prevention

An important issue in creating symmetric planar graphs is the collision avoidance. In our framework, the collisions can be avoided by checking only the lines in the unit cell, not on the whole drawing. As a result, by preventing intersections we can come up with planar graphs. Following is a high-level pseudo code of our system:

If any modification on the drawing is made

then if there is no collision in the unit cell *then*

translate the real line into the unit cell;

create the converted lines;

calculate symmetries;

update data;

generate the whole drawing by repeating the main unit cell.

4 Implementation

We have implemented two versions of the drawing algorithm explained in the previous section, one with C and OpenGL and another one with Java. The Java version is available to the public and it can be reached via Internet from the address

http://www/viz.tamu.edu/faculty/ergun/research/symmetric/.

Figure 7 shows the Java interface of symmetric tile designer. As shown in Figure 7 interface supports moving existing lines, adding new lines, breaking lines into two lines. The system also provides collision avoidance.

The Java applet provides only drawing borders of the tiles. In order to color the tiles, users need to copy the resulting image and color the tiles by using a painting program such as PhotoShop. Since the boundaries of each tile are clearly defined, it is easy to fill these tiles. Figure 8 show some colored examples of symmetric tiles we have designed using our software.

5 Conclusion

In this paper, we present a new approach for intuitive and effective design of periodic symmetric tiles. We observe that planar graphs can effectively represent symmetric tiles and graph drawing provides an intuitive paradigm for designing symmetric tiles. Based on the observation that rectangular symmetry groups can be represented as graphs embedded on a torus, we have developed a simple drawing algorithm based on modulo operations. Moreover, based on our theoretical work to represent hexagonal symmetry by rectangular symmetry, we are able to present all symmetric tiles as graphs embedded on a torus. This result enables us to develop a simple and efficient drawing algorithm for all periodic symmetric groups. We also extended the algorithm to handle collision detection.

We have implemented this algorithm both in Java and C. The Java version is available in Internet to all designers, architects and artists. By using this software, they can create interesting symmetric tiles directly on the web. We also have designed a few examples of symmetric tiles to show the effectiveness of the approach.

References

Firby, P. A., and C. F. Gardiner. (1982). *Surface Topology*. John Wiley and Sons Inc., New York.

Hargittai I., and M. Hargittai. (1994). *Symmetry, A Unifying Concept*. Shelter Publications, Inc. Bolinas, Ca.

Grunbaum, B., and G. C. Shephard. (1987). *Tilings and Patterns*. W. H. Freeman \& Co., New York.

Kali. *http://www.geom.umn.edu/java/Kali/*

Locher J. L. (1982). *M. C. Escher: His Life and Complete Graphic Work.* ed. Abrams, New York.

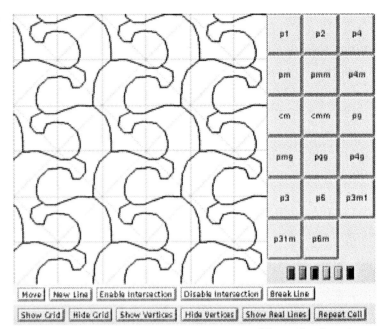

Figure 7. Java interface of Symmetric Tile Designer

Figure 8. Examples of symmetric tiles that are designed by using our system.

Introductory Computer Programming as a Means for Extending Spatial and Temporal Understanding

Mark Burry, School of Architecture and Building, Deakin University, Australia

Sambit Datta, School of Architecture and Building, Deakin University, Australia

Simon Anson, School of Architecture and Building, Deakin University, Australia

Abstract

Should computer programming be taught within schools of architecture?

Incorporating even low-level computer programming within architectural education curricula is a matter of debate but we have found it useful to do so for two reasons: as an introduction or at least a consolidation of the realm of descriptive geometry and in providing an environment for experimenting in morphological time-based change.

Mathematics and descriptive geometry formed a significant proportion of architectural education until the end of the 19th century. This proportion has declined in contemporary curricula, possibly at some cost for despite major advances in automated manufacture, Cartesian measurement is still the principal 'language' with which to describe building for construction purposes. When computer programming is used as a platform for instruction in logic and spatial representation, the waning interest in mathematics as a basis for spatial description can be readdressed using a left-field approach. Students gain insights into topology, Cartesian space and morphology through programmatic form finding, as opposed to through direct manipulation.

In this context, it matters to the architect-programmer how the program operates more than what it does. This paper describes an assignment where students are given a figurative conceptual space comprising the three Cartesian axes with a cube at its centre. Six Phileban solids mark the Cartesian axial limits to the space. Any point in this space represents a hybrid of one, two or three transformations from the central cube towards the various Phileban solids. Students are asked to predict the topological and morphological outcomes of the operations. Through programming, they become aware of morphogenesis and hybridisation. Here we articulate the hypothesis above and report on the outcome from a student group, whose work reveals wider learning opportunities for architecture students in computer programming than conventionally assumed.

1 Reasons for programming computers in architecture schools

The computer has been embraced early by practicing architects and therefore also within the education of architects. Schools still tend to be at the vanguard of experimental computer use, particularly in the area of design. Efficiency gains, especially in office management and streamlining construction documentation are still the usual focus of practices conducting research into computer use to enhance professional opportunities. The use of programming for structured problem solving in design, however, has a long tradition (Knuth, 1968; Weizenbaum, 1976; Winograd, 1986; Mitchell, 1987). Now that courses in CAD (computer-aided drafting, see note 1) are becoming less central to school curricula as successive waves of students enter more comfortable and familiar with the computer in general, there may be two main streams to CAD education. Typically there is one that continues to provide students with basic computer-aided drafting skills. This may be complemented by a possible second stream that looks at new opportunities to inform the design process through the use of the computer (CAAD - computer-aided architectural design). Going beyond the software designer's interface may not be included in either of these two streams, yet the outcome of an extended education in both CAD and CAAD can be significantly enhanced by doing so (Fox, 1989, Frew, 1989). Programming is a test of understanding with Weizenbaum making the landmark observation that

"One programs not because one understands, but in order to come to understand. Programming is an act of design. To write a program is to legislate the laws for a world one first has to create in imagination"(Weizenbaum, 1976 p 108).

The inclusion of low-level programming into the curriculum is one route to a more thorough understanding and exploitation of the computer's potential. Programmatically, a two-fold approach to finding form is necessary to explore design possibilities. First, one needs to frame the problem, and then one may explore the domain of possibilities that the frame establishes.

2 CAD programming, CAAD programming

Learning to customise software can enhance CAD use. Such useful adaptation aligned to an office management protocol or to an individual's particular preferences is encouraged by nearly all major architectural design and drafting software. Potential productivity gains are quite considerable. The work of specialist CAD managers in larger offices will generally include making the software conform more to the office's pre-CAD methodology in preference to directing the office towards adapting to new and quite different opportunities provided through CAD. Most customisation may involve the incorporation of some logic as a systemic response but it is less likely to involve any mathematics. Customisation of software at school level does not appear to be a major interest but even in schools where programming is taught at all, the majority of educators will probably feel that learning to customise software is a sufficiently risky incursion into this improbable domain for architects.

There are possibilities for programming in design. Streich presents a thorough discussion in favour of including programming knowledge in the design education of an architect (Streich, 1992). Maeda develops a pedagogy based on "design by numbers" and the understanding of visual design using computational processes and media (Maeda, 1999). Computation and design have not been linked significantly in most contemporary architectural education – the exceptions are notable. Opportunities arising from such an association are not especially obvious. There is, strangely, both more and less reason to consider computation in greater detail following the exit of Modernism as the core focus to design education. A liberating pluralism has replaced the didactic imperatives of the Modern Movement; pluralism sponsors a more liberal approach than the instructed method born of didacticism. But while pluralism might discredit the architectural program (computer or otherwise) as tending towards the 'progrom', equally, the program needs to be explored before being rejected for an imputed unhelpful linearity. This is to say, *it matters how the program operates more than what the program does.* The word 'program' is in fact unhelpful as it implies an attendant methodology, and a route to a known end. As a customising regime for CAD, such a view is both correct and logically defendable. Within the context of CAAD and the design process (see note 2), however, the challenge is for the computer programmer to devise some 'tools' that are complementary to the designer's particular route to a design without pigeon-holing the designer into a methodology that ends up being substantially controlling. Reviewing the software available for architects, usually marketed as CAD rather than CAAD, reveals some interesting traits. The use of software programs to explore constructed worlds and their relation to craft and abstraction is developed in McCullough (McCullough 1997). The intricate relationships between computers, software and design are well researched (Paul Adler 1992; Winograd 1996).

Office efficiency and productivity are the undisguised focus of volume market software for architects, especially in building representation. A few architects who are atypically able to access a medium that is considerably more costly than conventional architectural software are using software directed towards computer animators in the film industry. There is recognition of greater design potential here. In matters of form finding, such esoteric animation software offers opportunities that are inappropriate within typical CAD software use. The algorithms incorporated within the animation software to facilitate rapid production of sequential frames, each a subtle morphological variant on the previous, provide new opportunities for form finding. The work of Greg Lynn, for instance, clearly demonstrates the potential of animation film software to influence architectural spatial design experimentation (Lynn 1998). The software user in this instance does not need to be a mathematician.

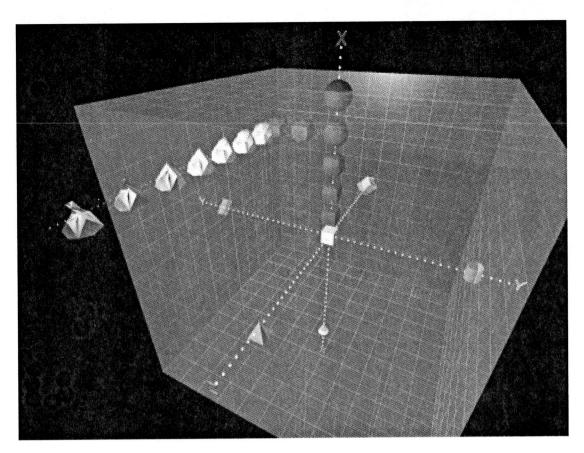

Figure 1. 'Our World'. The programming assignment required that a central form (in this case a cube) undergo a series of transformations. As an interactive program, the user can take the original form and steer it partly towards a sphere (in the example above), then partly towards a wedge, and finishing on a path beyond the condition of a pyramid.

It is unlikely that animation software engineers can anticipate all the needs for the designer working in a pluralist environment. *"If the designers themselves knew something of programming would they not be better equipped to commission software more closely aligned to their needs?"* This is the central question articulated in this paper as it reports on the outcome from a student group encountering low-level programming for the first time. The opportunities for learning through computer programming revealed by the work go beyond learning opportunities elsewhere in the curriculum. In the next section we sketch how Weizenbaum's "world" is developed along with the "legislation" of its functioning through a process of programmatic form-finding.

3 'Our World'

The universe of discourse, our world, is represented by a figurative spatial environment (figure 1). At the centre of 'our world' there is the form of a cube. The domain has been named in order to assist the conceptual understanding of a space used to marshal ideas rather than represent occupancy. A given number of morphological variants are located by the boundaries of this 3D space. They range between the initiating cube at the centre and six other Phileban forms that are located at each of the two ends of the three Cartesian axes, thus setting the limits of Our World (operation '1'). On the axial planes within this space at any other intermediate positions, there are hybrids of two transformations (operations '1' and '2'). Hybrids from three sequential transformations (operations '1', '2' and '3') are associated with the remaining Cartesian locations within the space. This construct exists simply to aid recognition of the possibilities to sponsor morphological change. The operation 1->2->3, is a statement of three sequential transformations on the original cube. Used as an interactive program, the user has taken the original form partly towards a sphere, then partly towards a wedge, and finished on a path beyond a pyramid.

Predictions of the topological and morphological outcome of the three operations are sought from the students. The purpose of the exercise is for participants to gain further insights into topology, Cartesian space, morphology, morphogenesis, and hybridisation. The participants also become very conscious of the power of this level of computer - user interaction through programming, as opposed to simple one-off and direct manipulation. They now experience a completely different relationship with the computer, as designers. It is a relationship redolent with opportunity for experimentation and innovative form seeking even at this rather trivial level (in terms of actual programming).

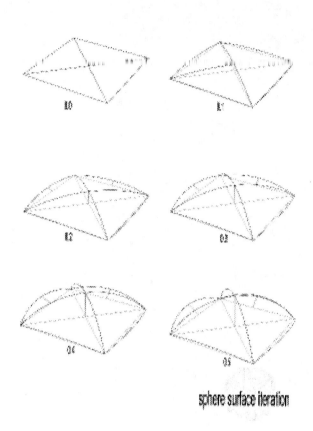
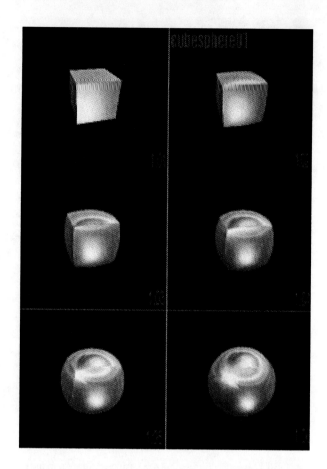

Figure 2. Sequence of changes to the twenty-four surfaces that describe both the original cube and the sphere showing the cube tending towards the sphere.

Figure 3. Sequence of changes to the twenty-four surfaces that describe both the original cube and the sphere showing the cube tending towards the sphere. The imperfections to the surface of the sphere are deficiencies in the surface algorithms in the chosen software.

4 Same topology, different morphology

Figure 2 shows the iterative route from cube to sphere. All the students undertake this first planning exercise. They have to devise a collective topological approach within given software in order to effect a smooth transformation from one to the other. All subsequent transformations are allocated as individual problem solving tasks (for example student 1 transforms a cube into a pyramid, student 2 works towards a cone, student 3...). So that the individual algorithms can be combined and the route 1->2->3 (->...) can be any of forty-eight unique combinations, all individual outputs must be compatible. Each transformation must occur iteratively, the number of iterations being at the discretion of the programme user. Each iteration or morphological change event outputs a file used finally as one of a series of frames in animation.

The highest common denominator in this process is the cube. It has the most parameters: six faces versus the single spherical surface etc. Conceptually a common understanding is required. Points and lines have names conforming to an agreed shared notation to ensure that each algorithm operates with common symbols and is therefore interoperative. The face of the cube is divided into four triangles (figure 2): these triangles are essentially the foundation class for the project. The program needs to convert the linear curves that bound the triangular cube face components into non-linear curves - in the case of the sphere these curves will be sector arcs. Also, in the case of the sphere, the points at the corners of the cube correspond with their equivalents for the sphere: they are coincident. Therefore a point that describes a mid-point for each curve moves taking the curve with it with the result that an associated surface transforms from a plane to a sector of a sphere. The result is shown in figure 3, and an equivalent transformation from cube to cylinder is shown in figures 4 and 5.

Regardless of the mathematical simplicity, there are many unfamiliar aspects for architects in this

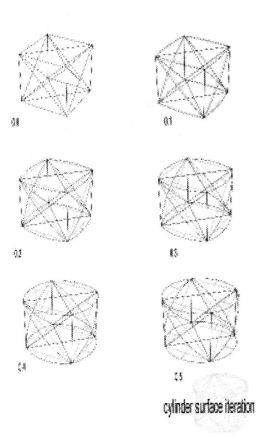

Figure 4 Sequence of changes to the twenty-four surfaces that describe both the original cube and the cylinder (see figure 1). This figure shows the cube tending towards the cylinder. The imperfections to the surface of the cylinder are deficiencies in the surface algorithms in the chosen software.

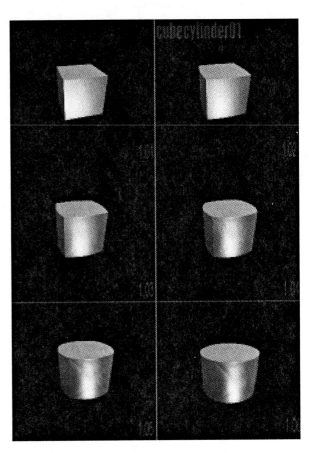

Figure 5 Sequence of changes to the twenty-four surfaces that describe both the original cube and the cylinder (see figure 1). This figure shows the cube tending towards the cylinder. The imperfections to the surface of the cylinder are deficiencies in the surface algorithms in the chosen software.

procedure. It serves to kindle interest and subsequently more complex problems can be approached with confidence. Reducing a cube to a pyramid, for instance, leaves the problem of what to do with the top face that reduces to nothing while the change from a cube to a cone has even more philosophical and practical difficulties. Here the algorithm reduces the top face of the cube to a point that is the apex to the cone (as for the pyramid). As its area diminishes, the base transforms from a square to a circle. The intermediate iterations show a rounding square at the base with a perfect reducing square at top until the apex of the cone is reached. This is an aesthetic problem, and the programmer is obliged to include a proportional system to compensate for an otherwise inconvenient visual effect

5 Stepping outside 'our world'

The students have thus learned the fundamentals of programming. If they had no real grasp of Cartesian space before the project (and it is surprising how many of our students do not) they do so after completing this project. They have also learnt about the complexities of formal problem solving using both logic and mathematics. In the realm of aesthetics, however, they are challenged with quite unfamiliar circumstances: semiautomatic design. Most students can predict the effects of 1->2 transformations, if not mentally they are at least able to derive the outcome through sketching. Predicting the results of the third transformation step seems to be especially demanding, and the outcome from a fourth transformation step impossible to visualise it seems (figure 6). This represents an unusual dilemma. The computer can often produce interesting and unpredictable forms through error, which are unrepeatable and probably unable to be used in making buildings. With this programming assignment students are able to act as agents for curious yet computationally (but not intellectually) predictable forms that are repeatable, and therefore of potential use in architectural design. Where matters move into fundamentally new territory is stepping outside the Phileban territory we have called 'our world'. Here the possibilities are quite extraordinary (figures 7 and 8). Through producing more iterations than proportional steps, forms of self-intersecting yet topologically

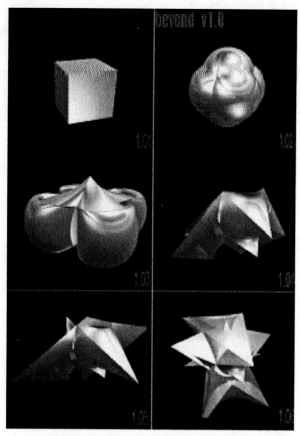

Figure 6. Sequence of changes to the twenty-four surfaces that describe both the original cube and a hybrid form (see figure 1 steps '1' '2' and '3'). This figure shows the cube tending towards first a sphere (partway) then partway towards a pyramid and finally a rhomboid.

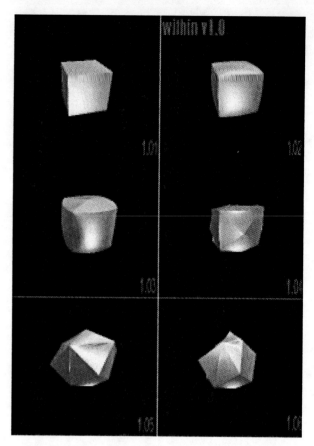

Figure 7. Too much hybrid vigour. The figure shows a sequence of changes that go beyond the boundaries to 'our world' (figure 1). The original cube has developed into a hybrid form (see figure 1 steps '1' '2' and '3') that distorts the original Phileban objects to guided but conceptually unpredictable outcomes.

equivalent descriptions challenge the designer to find a practical use for their new programming skills.

References

Fox, C. W. (1989). Integrating computing into an Architectural Undergraduate program. In *The Electronic Design Studio: Architectural Knowledge and Media in the Computer Era*. Malcolm McCullough, W.J. Mitchell and P. Purcell (eds).The MIT press. 377-386.

Frew, R. S. (1989). The organisation of CAD teaching in design schools. In *The Electronic Design Studio: Architectural Knowledge and Media in the Computer Era*. Malcolm McCullough, W.J. Mitchell and P. Purcell (eds).The MIT press. 387-392.

Knuth, D. E. (1968). *The art of computer programming*. Addison-Wesley Publishing Company. Reading, Mass.

Lynn, G. (1998). *Animate Form*. Princeton Architectural Press, New Jersey.

Maeda, J. (1999). *Design by Numbers*. MIT Press, Cambridge.

McCullough, M. (1997). *Abstracting Craft : The Practiced Digital Hand*. The MIT Press, Cambridge.

Mitchell, W. J. (1987). *The art of computer graphics programming: a structured introduction for architects and designers*. Van Nostrand Reinhold, New York

Streich, B. (1992). Should We Integrate Programming Knowledge into the Architect's CAAD-Education? In *CAAD Instruction : The New Teaching of an Architect* eCAADe Conference

Figure 8. Too much hybrid vigour. The designer can experiment with the algorithm and seek formal responses to given architectural problems. The debate centres on whether they have encapsulated a 'design process', or merely produced an effective 'tool' to aid compositional strategies.

Proceedings, Barcelona (Spain). 399-406.

Weizenbaum, J. (c1976). *Computer power and human reason: from judgment to calculation.* W. H. Freeman, San Francisco.

Winograd, T. (c1986). *Understanding computers and cognition: a new foundation for design.* Ablex Pub. Corp., Norwood, N.J.

Winograd, T. (1996). *Bringing design to software.* ACM Press, New York, N.Y.

Notes

1   The acronym CAD is often misinterpreted as 'Computer-aided design' where the 'D' stands more accurately for drafting, not design (representation, not synthesis).

2   The design process is presumed not to be a prescriptive situation but something unique to the designer. The semantic difficulty comes from the use of the word 'process', process implies something that can be defined, and automated.

The Intelligent Sketch: Developing a Conceptual Model for a Digital Design Assistant

Rohan Bailey   Victoria University of Wellington, New Zealand

Abstract

Keywords: CAAD, Sketching, Protocol Analysis, Design Thinking, Design Education

The computer is a relatively new tool in the practice of Architecture. Since its introduction, there has been a desire amongst designers to use this new tool quite early in the design process. However, contrary to this desire, most Architects today use pen and paper in the very early stages of design to sketch.

Architects solve problems by thinking visually. One of the most important tools that the Architect has at his disposal in the design process is the hand sketch. This iterative way of testing ideas and informing the design process with images fundamentally directs and aids the architect's decision making.

It has been said (Schön and Wiggins 1992) that sketching is about the reflective conversation designers have with images and ideas conveyed by the act of drawing. It is highly dependent on feedback. This "conversation" is an area worthy of investigation. Understanding this "conversation" is significant to understanding how we might apply the computer to enhance the designer's ability to capture, manipulate and reflect on ideas during conceptual design.

This paper discusses sketching and its relation to design thinking. It explores the conversations that designers engage in with the media they use. This is done through the explanation of a protocol analysis method. Protocol analysis used in the field of psychology, has been used extensively by Eastman et al (starting in the early 70s) as a method to elicit information about design thinking. In the pilot experiment described in this paper, two persons are used. One plays the role of the "hand" while the other is the "mind"- the two elements that are involved in the design "conversation". This variation on classical protocol analysis sets out to discover how "intelligent" the hand should be to enhance *design by reflection*. The paper describes the procedures entailed in the pilot experiment and the resulting data. The paper then concludes by discussing future intentions for research and the far reaching possibilities for use of the computer in architectural studio teaching (as teaching aids) as well as a digital design assistant in conceptual design.

1 Introduction

Architecture as a profession has always relied on tools to get the job done. The computer, the latest of such tools used in practice, is so recent that most senior practitioners have little or no experience using it. Today, its use has been mainly in the realm of drafting and production. Notwithstanding this, there has been a desire amongst designers to use this new tool quite early in the design process. Practical reasons such as the need to get information digital as early as possible and the computers potential to generate several options have added some credibility to this desire.

Despite this willingness, most Architects, even today, still use pen and paper in the very early stages of design to sketch. (Novitski 1991; Haapasalo 1997). Based on this observation, it would seem that computers are unsuitable for the early stages of conceptual design. At present, it is widely admitted that characteristics of the computer make it inept when used with "traditional" methods of design thinking, *especially* in the earlier stages of design. (Soufi and Edmonds 1996; Haapasalo 1997;

Novitski 1991). The fact is; Architects still prefer the simple interface and tactile feedback of sketching to using computers (Palmer 1998). This places an importance on comprehending the role the sketch plays in the activity of conceptual design.

This paper discusses sketching and its relation to design thinking by exploring the *conversations* that designers engage in with the media they use. It suggests two essential players (the mind and the hand) in these conversations. The paper introduces a pilot experiment derived from protocol analysis with a view to examining the activity of sketching. This unique analysis is designed to determine the nature of the interaction between hand and mind, specifically how intelligent the hand has to be in order to enhance the design process. Descriptions of the procedures entailed in the pilot experiment and the resulting data is given. It then concludes by discussing future intentions for research and the far reaching possibilities for use of the computer in architectural studio teaching (as teaching aids) as well as realising the computer as a digital design assistant in conceptual design.

2 Sketching and the Design Process

Design process is seen largely as the activity of organising ideas in order to produce a desired result. It involves synthesising or analysing various parts of the "problem" in order to understand or reveal the overall "essence" or solution.

Architects design by thinking visually. This visual activity makes extensive use of images. The designer understands an idea by putting it down on paper "to see if it works". The process by which images are used as fundamental objects for design decision making can be called graphical thinking (Laseau 1989), or design drawing (Lockard 1982), or simply sketching. This iterative way of testing ideas and informing the design process using images fundamentally directs and aids the architect's decision making. Therefore, one of the most important tools that the Architect has at his disposal in the design process is the hand sketch.

2.1 Conversations in Design

One school of thought sees the early stages of design as conversations being held with the materials of a design situation (Schon and Wiggins 1992). Sketching, therefore can be referred to as the reflective conversation with images and ideas conveyed by the act of drawing (Schon and Wiggins 1992). In his book "Graphic Thinking for Architects and Designers", Paul Laseau agrees with this premise by claiming that the process of graphic thinking can be seen as conversations with ourselves in which we communicate with the use of sketches (Laseau 1989).

Using Schon's argument we can infer that a reflective conversation is about the designer seeing what is there, drawing in relation to it, seeing what is drawn and so further informing the design. To put it simply, The Architect makes a mark, criticises it and makes a decision based on this criticism (with a desired result in mind). New ideas are really new ways at looking at and combining old ideas with the use of the eye, brain, hand and sketch (Laseau 1989). The activity of sketching is therefore interactive and highly dependent on feedback. This interactivity involves chiefly two thought processes - the coming up with ideas and the interpretations of those ideas in order to represent them in a physical sense and spatial sense. The brain through the eye reacts to the sketch the hand has drawn. This can be translated into two players – the mind and the hand. The question is - What is it the "hand" should know to better inform the "mind"?

2.2 Drawbacks with sketching

Despite being a premium tool for design there are some limitations in the activity of sketching. The sketch is a passive medium and relies on initiative from the designer. The designer has to be experienced in order to identify and react effectively to some of the multiple design issues embedded in a sketch. The fact that the sketch isn't digital (or compatible with CAD information) is another limitation. The reality that all information in the industry is digital puts the sketch at a disadvantage and poses the problem of transferring information into digital format that can be handled by the design team. The sketch is also labour intensive. Ideas usually require lots of reworking or redrawing resulting in information loss (Herbert 1993). Any attempt to bring the sketch into the digital realm would be welcomed by designers

3 Research

Research attempts to investigate and address the problem have ranged from examining emergent shapes (Soufi and Edmonds 1996) to applications that recognise sketch diagrams made on screen (Gross 1996). Most of the concentration in research however has been in making the *content* of sketching digital rather than considering its interactivity as an aid to thinking and taking advantage of that quality in the digital realm.

Understanding the *act* of sketching is crucial to understanding how we might apply the computer to enhance the designer's ability to capture, manipulate and reflect on ideas during conceptual design. This comprehension would enhance designing by making the computer a partner in the process. The interaction of the designer and the media (in this case the computer) would be through the provision of an environment for decisions to be made. Research energy would be directed towards a design environment where there is sufficient feedback for the designer to be informed. Emulating this "conversation" is an area worthy of pursuance.

One technique of understanding the conversation that characterises sketching is by using a derivative of protocol analysis. This variation on classical protocol analysis sets out to discover how "intelligent" the hand should be to enhance *design by reflection*.

3.1 Protocol Analysis

Protocol analysis used in the field of psychology to study human problem solving and information processing techniques, has been used extensively by Eastman et al (starting in the early 70s) as a method to elicit design thinking (Eastman 1970). A protocol is the recorded behaviour of the problem solver or (in this case) the designer. This usually takes the form of " sketches, notes, video or audio recordings" (Akin 1986).

This research method usually involves sole designers verbalising their thoughts while they sketch and tackle the design problem. Since the 1980s, however, single person study has crossed over into team design activity. Protocol analysis has recently also been used to investigate techniques in computer mediated collaboration (Gabriel and Maher 1999).

3.2 Criticisms of Classical Protocol Analysis

Despite its popularity in eliciting "design thinking" classical protocol analysis has been criticised by some researchers. Critics usually say that:

- The small sample does not produce enough data

That protocol analysis techniques lack sufficient subjects to get a large enough sampling in which to make generalisations. Arguments to the contrary suggest that the dozens of observations found in the protocols of subjects offset the small size of the sample (Akin 1986).

- Concurrent verbalisation alters subjects' behaviour

Critics argue that placed under a "microscope" in this way make designers conscious of their actions and so tend to engage in activity they think the researcher wants to see rather than action they normally engage in. This criticism isn't easily refuted and can only be minimised if special care is taken to avoid this and the observer is as unobtrusive as possible.

- Experiments are not reflective of real design episodes

Supporters of this view point to the fact that there is no negotiation with clients, no discussion of ideas with peers and no opportunity for reflection (away from the task) (Lloyd, Lawson and Scott 1995). This view while being valid doesn't take into consideration that only the period of specific activity is under investigation and not the factors that indirectly *influence* design process.

4 A different approach to protocol analysis

Considering these criticisms and the aim of getting a clearer picture of the designer's expectations of the tools, an unexampled variation of the protocol analysis method has been developed to determine the interaction between hand and mind in design activity. This variation integrates classical analysis with that of collaborative environments. In the pilot experiment described in this paper, two subjects are used. One plays the role of the "hand" while the other is the "mind"- two elements that are involved in the design "conversation". The designer or *mind* tells the *hand* what to do. The *hand* then has the responsibility of coming up with images that would greatly assist the mind to grasp the problem and progress towards the design solution. The goals of this modification is as follows:

1. To determine the importance of *hand* sketching to the designer.
2. To examine the role images/sketches play in design activity.
3. To validate the purpose of a "design partner/assistant" in the design process.
4. To find what it is a computer needs to know to help the designer "sketch".

The protocols are established with the subjects being given a design problem to solve.

Figure 1. Design session 2 – student/hand, practitioner/mind

4.1 Advantages of this method

Approaching the investigation in this manner has some advantages. By allowing a dialogue between the subjects and looking at the questions the subjects ask each other one can begin to speculate on what sort of dialogue occurs when the designer is alone. Easily identifying the nature of the images and information requested by the designer to inform the process (and enhance his strategy) was thought worthy to investigate rather than solely concentrating on the designer's strategy. In addition, by using this technique it allows one subject the benefit of sketching without the added distraction of verbalisation (except to ask for clarification which itself can indicate importance of elements to represent data). The other subject verbalises without worrying about sketching. The behaviour of the subject is less affected by this arrangement. Data collected would illustrate two different approaches to design instead of one hence providing more data for analysis.

5 A pilot experiment

Two subjects - one a practitioner with over 9 years experience and the other a third year architecture student - participated in the experiment (Figure 1). The decision to use a practitioner and a student stemmed from the desire to witness what effect experience has on the activity. The experiment consequently was done in two design sessions.

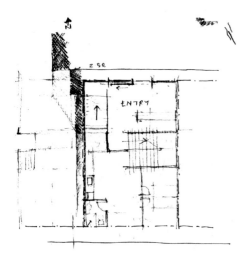

Figure 2. Design session 1 – sketch for an architect's studio.

In the first session the practitioner was given the role of "hand" and the student as the "mind" was given a design program for an architect/artists studio and gallery on an inner-city site (Figure 2). In the second design session the roles were changed and the practitioner as the "mind" was asked to design a 4-bedroom residence on a beach site.

During the experiment, the subjects had to adhere to the following "rules of engagement":

Hand:

1) Follow instructions of the *mind*; only asking questions as they relate to the image (except in 3)

2) Draw or illustrate concepts that you think would enhance the understanding of the *mind*. *The* hand *has a right to ask what projection/representation to illustrate (plan/elevation/section/3D) and what scale if any.*

3) Advise on the consequences to other design domains that are not being investigated. *The hand has a right to point out potential problems and discrepancies overlooked that has to do with the objective (practical) side of the design.*

Mind:

1) Design a solution relying on images and information presented by the *hand*

2) Ask specifically for the image/information needed to make decisions. *The* mind *has a right to tell the* hand *exactly what is necessary in the image and what is redundant.*

3) Set out and specify the kinds of questions you want the *hand* to ask

4) Request any "non-visual" information from the *hand* i.e. solar paths, distances, max. room widths, stair configurations etc.

The designer was instructed to go as far as the end of the schematic design stage i.e. when the *mind* considered the scheme was ready for "drawing up" (i.e. ready for technical drawing/entering on the computer). The following *minimum* however, was required:

Floor plans (to some scale)

Site section (to some scale)

Elevation and/or another section (to some scale)

3D sketch (optional)

On average, each session took one hour (this was the time specified by the researcher). On both occasions a video camera was used to record marks on paper (by the "hand") as well as any gestures by the "mind" in directing the sketching operations. The sessions were also recorded on audiotape while the observer took notes of the activity. Prior to and after the experiment the participants were given a short questionnaire and engaged in a discussion with the observer about the activity respectively.

5.1 Subject responses to the experiment

Both participants in the experiment expressed delight in the exercise and thought it was a novel way to look at design. They declared surprise at their ability to verbally communicate design ideas well enough to get the needed feedback for further development of the design.

Persons in the role of "mind" claimed full authorship of their respective schemes despite having no physical connection to it; meanwhile the "hands" felt no stake or connection to the design despite producing the images. Interestingly the persons who sketched asserted that there was no "thinking" involved in their activity.

Subjects saw the experiment as mainly an exercise in planning with no architectural concepts involved. It was mentioned that they usually spend more time doodling (sometimes not "building things") before starting to design at which point codes and ergonomic issues "take over". This was attributed to the time limit imposed on the sessions.

Participants felt their usual process (whether sketching or designing) had to be modified in order for the other person to understand intentions but not to the detriment of the design. The student as "mind" expressed appreciation and benefit from having the answers "spat at me" in that it "made it easier to get your mind around the problem". The claim was made that the design was more "purposeful" when questioned (by the practitioner) as to spatial and physical aspects of elements. On the other hand, the practitioner found it frustrating having to specify precisely what image was needed. Both subjects reported frustration at not using their hands to draw.

5.2 Analysing The Data

The protocols of the subjects were transcribed and examined in conjunction with the video evidence by the researcher.

In order for protocols to be properly scrutinised to determine a suitable model of the activity, it is usual for a coding scheme to be developed. The development of the code is usually dependent on the researcher's view on design methodology. This influences how information derived from the experiment is examined and described.

According to Dorst and Dijkhuis, there are two different paradigms for looking at design methodology (Dorst and Dijkhuis 1995). One paradigm sees design as a rational problem solving process and so is more interested describing the process and examining concepts like acts, goals, contexts etc. The other viewpoint takes a constructionist approach and is influenced by Donald Schön's theories of design as a process of reflection-in-action. This takes a more content oriented approach while maintaining some link to process.

Since we have aligned our theoretical stance with that of Schön our approach to analysing the data, while being interested with the process, was more interested in the interaction between the two subjects and how they interacted with the images and information traded between them.

The observations and results presented below are based on first impressions of the data (as well as other observations used in the design of the pilot). Unfortunately, since we are looking at a preliminary overview of a pilot experiment, we can only at this point speculate on a likely coding scheme. Whether or not this coding scheme will resemble previous schemes or is unique is based in part, on how the results relate to previous analysis (Akin 1986; Gabriel and Maher 1999; Suwa, Gero and Purcell 1998). This researcher acknowledges that further detailed analysis is required to confirm first impressions and elicit other relevant pieces of information from the investigation.

P	Transcription (speaking)	Action	Observations
M	Storage space is going to be under there so entrance is from this side so coming in there at the back of this space we are going to have another staircase which will lead upstairs.		
H	Is it going to be running this way or is it going to be that way.	Gestures	
M	Yeah running this way.	Gestures in direction	Spatial Gesture
H	That way.	Repeats gesture	Clarification
M	Towards us yeah.		
H	Okay so how high do you want your floor to ceiling in the ...	H draws stair and calculates treads	Info for stair representation based on height
M	In the reception area um lets call it 3 meters which is the height of the ...	Looks around room	Seeks relationship for dimensions
H	How wide do you want this staircase?		Info for stair representation
M	The staircase is going to be 3 meters wide. No... it has got to be in the middle of the....	Points to halfway line on drawing	Corrects hand
H	In the middle of here?		Clarification
M	Yep.		
H	Okay, 3 meters wide.	Starts to draw stair	
H	All in one direction? It's not wrapping around?		Expert Advice
M	How much space does that give us?		Request for information
H	Ahhhh, if you have got to go up 3 meters, that is, how many? 15... about 18 steps generally.		Expert Advice
M	Okay		Confirmation
H	175 so 1, 2, 3, 4, 5, 6, 7, 8, 9.	Measures and counts	
M	Oh... good God no		Responds to information & counting on image
H	You could wrap it		Expert Opinion
M	Yeah we are going to have to wrap it.		Confirmation
H	Okay		
M	Which way though? It is going to have to be in so maybe we should bring it around this way. Which way is this, that is the little building so, ... but that is not up there.	Indicates/gestures turning stair around	Spatial Gestures
	(silence)	H darkens stair, M thinking by looking at drawing.	Examining
M	See, I want the gallery space to be south lit so um.		

Figure 3. Transcript excerpt from design session 1. M = Mind and H = Hand

5.3 Observations from the transcripted protocols

The interaction and subsequent dialogue that occurred between the two protagonists can be categorised as follows: The Mind: Examining, Requests, Gesturing. The Hand: Clarification, Advice, Labelling, and Gesturing. Figure 3 displays an excerpt from the transcripts that illustrate some of these actions.

- Looking and examining

Looking and examining included looking at the hand's sketching activity, and the comparison of images. Information gathered from examining could be seen as cues that trigger decisions or further moves. Looking and examining usually resulted in requests.

- Requests

This action on the part of the mind included requests for information as well as requests to see particular drawings (or marks on a particular drawing). Requests usually entailed asking for distances and heights. This happened more frequently in session 1. Information gained from requests was used to make design decisions that related to "existing" elements.

- Gesturing, Pointing or touching image with hands

Pointing at the image and moving the hand over it to indicate spatial and directional movement (like movement through a door) usually occurred when participants referred to a physical element.

- Clarification

During the experiment, the hand would repeat pieces of information uttered by the mind. This usually occurred when placing elements for the first time.

- Advice

The hand, for the most part advised or questioned the mind as to aspects of the design (especially when the practitioner was hand) that might not work. This usually included information that could only be known when drawing and measuring.

- Labelling

The hand would use text labelling to identify elements e.g. stair, void, studio and drew furniture to provide context for the mind. Concrete decisions by the mind were "darkened in" i.e. made bolder to depict and emphasise that decision.

5.4 Discussion of results

The protocols confirmed similar observations from previous experiments (Suwa, Gero and Purcell 1998; Do 1997). These observations found that designers labelled spaces and used graphic symbols, illustrated design contexts by dimensional reasoning and furniture, sketches tended to be orthographic (two-dimensional), sketches served as external memory that were revisited and provided visuo-spatial cues for thinking about functional issues. The protocols also provided the following observations:

- Designers preferred seeing drawings side by side. This was important (especially between floor plans) although some tracing of information took place (this was more a shortcut than anything else).
- Designers wanted as much information as possible put on individual drawings. The information quality of the practitioners sketches tended to be a lot richer than that of the student.
- Designers looked around the room to determine relative sizes. They then related sizes and dimensions of immediate surroundings to existing elements in drawing.

In addition to these, other interesting events occurred. For instance, the student was a little intimidated by the practitioner and so in the case of being the mind did not totally control the situation. The student also hesitated to make many changes that required a lot of redrawing and erasing but when practitioner designed there was no hesitation to try ideas.

Little concurrent verbalisation took place by the mind while waiting on the other subject to draw. It was observed, though, that the subject was still thinking by looking at what the hand was doing whether or not this (drawing operations) helped the thinking is an area to be examined. Reciprocally, the hand had difficulty keeping track of spaces and elements despite interacting closely with drawings.

6 Discussion and Future Work

The information processed by the designer during the activity of sketching is both interesting and complex. We have suggested an important relation between sketching and the design process. Sketching is seen as a "conversation" that the designer engages in with the use of images (and related information). The designer makes a statement by making marks on paper, responds by examining and criticising this statement, makes further marks and so progresses in design. We have implied that there are two players in the activity of sketching – the hand and the mind. By literally employing two separate individuals in this conversation we are able to take a closer look at the communication between these two players in the design process.

Our empirical studies involving 2 subjects while confirming similar research (Do 1997; Suwa, Gero and Purcell 1998) have also shown that there is a certain give and take that is necessary when sketching. It also shows that designers spend time during the process questioning and interpreting the functional implications of their ideas in broad terms. It revealed that designers rely on dialogue and interaction with images to produce.

Besides providing a platform to understand the sketch further, this experiment can also point the way to the development of design aids for education and practice that constantly question the emerging design.

6.1 A design tutor

Research in this direction could lead to the development of teaching aids in which students (who have limited design vocabularies) allow the computer to deal with the practical issues leaving more time for the development of ideas. An application of this kind could alert students to the myriad of issues involved in design. Further investigations into this issue could take place in the design studio where a new kind of relationship between student and tutor is developed, analysed and compared to existing techniques.

6.2 A design partner

Further investigations could also look at the practitioner with an experienced partner (instead of the student) and examine the performance and response then. It may reveal the need for a design support application that is more interactive than present offerings.

6.3 Conclusion

To take a stronger position on this issue more substantial and analytical results would be needed. Other factors could be investigated separately. For instance examining the effect on subjects if the session wasn't face to face but instead behind two workstations (Gabriel and Maher 1999). The preliminary observations presented in this paper are not enough to make a concrete position. What we have seen however gives some value to advocating moving the sketch from being less passive in design to a position where it prompts and cues the designer. The computer should be able to answer your questions and supply the answers in such a way that aids critical thinking. Employing the computer in this way allows the designer the opportunity to communicate on one aspect of the problem while the computer examines other domains in relation to it. This *intelligent sketch* is important for designers (especially inexperienced ones) to grasp the issues being investigated better.

Sketches usually are about possibilities and should not be seen as final objects (Laseau 1989). Energy therefore should be directed towards providing tools that interpret, respond to and question therefore enhancing the designers understanding of the design situation rather than automate it or transform it (the drawing). The importance of the handsketch as a means of communication, inference of things, and aid to critical design thinking should be preserved when using the computer in design.

Reference

Akin, Ö. 1986. *Psychology of architectural design*. London:Pion Ltd.

Do E. Y.-L. 1997. Computability of design diagrams : an empirical study of diagram conventions in design. In *CAAD Futures 97*, ed. R. Jungs, 171-176. Munich:Kluwer.

Dorst, K and J. Dijkhuis. 1995. Comparing paradigms for describing design activity. In *Design Studies, Vol. 16 No. 2*, 261-274. Elsevier Science Ltd...

Eastman, C. M. 1970. On the analysis of intuitive design processes. In *Emerging methods in environmental design and planning*, ed. G. Moore, 21-37. Cambridge Mass.: MIT Press.

Gabriel, G and M. Maher. 1999. Coding and modelling communication in architectural collaborative design. In *Media and design process*, eds. O. Ataman and J. Bermúdez, 152-166. ACADIA '99.

Gross, M. D. 1996. The electronic cocktail napkin – working with diagrams. In *Design Studies, Vol. 17 No. 1*, 53-69. Elsevier Science Ltd..

Haapasalo, H. 1997. The role of CAD in creative architectural sketching. *Challenges of the Future (15th ECAADE conference proceedings)*.

Herbert, D. 1993. *Architectural study drawings*. New York: Van Nostrand Reinhold

Laseau, P. 1989. *Graphic thinking for architects and designers*. New York: Von Nostrand-Reinhold.

Lloyd, P., B Lawson and P. Scott. 1995. Can concurrent verbalisation reveal design cognition? In *Design Studies, Vol. 16 No. 2*, 237-259. Elsevier Science Ltd.

Lockard, W. K. 1982. *Design Drawing*. Tucson: Pepper Publishing

Novitski, B. J. 1991. CADD Holdouts. *Architecture*, August.

Palmer, B. B. 1998. Digital sketchbooks. *Architecture*, July.

Schon, D. and G. Wiggins. 1992. Kinds of seeing and their functions in designing. In *Design Studies, Vol. 13 No. 2*, 135-156. Butterworth-Heinemann Ltd.

Soufi, B. and E. Edmonds. 1996. The cognitive basis of emergence: implications for design support. In *Design Studies, Vol. 17 No. 4*, 451-463. Elsevier Science Ltd.

Suwa, M., J. Gero and T. A. Purcell. 1998. The roles of sketches in the early conceptual design processes. *Proceedings of twentieth annual meeting of the Cognition Science Society*. Ed. L. Erlbaum, 1043-1048. Hillsdale, New Jersey.

Off The Page: Object-Oriented Construction Drawings

Michael Kilkelly, Edificium, Inc., USA

Abstract

This paper discusses methods in which inefficiencies in the construction documentation process can be addressed through the application of digital technology. These inefficiencies are directly related to the time consuming nature of the construction documentation process, given that the majority of time is spent reformatting and redrawing previous details and specifications. The concepts of object-oriented programming are used as an organizational framework for construction documentation. Database structures are also used as a key component to information reuse in the documentation process. A prototype system is developed as an alternative to current Computer-Aided Drafting software. This prototype, the *Drawing Assembler*, functions as a graphic search engine for construction details. It links a building component database with a construction detail database through the intersection of dissimilar objects.

1 Introduction

Since the early beginnings of graphic software, the computer has been touted as a means to achieve efficiency and productivity in the architectural office. This has been largely through the use of Computer-Aided Drafting (CAD) software in the production of construction drawings. However, despite the widespread use of CAD in the majority of architectural offices, the computer has had little influence on the nature of construction documents. While the tools to produce the drawings have changed, from pencil and paper to mouse and monitor, the methodology has essentially remained the same. Until recently, CAD software has been used largely as a means to replicate known methods of work. As Malcolm McCullough indicates in *Abstracting Craft*, CAD is a process of task automation, where the computer is used to perform known processes more efficiently as opposed to changing the underlying working process (McCullough 1996). What is necessary is a rethinking of the architect's traditional methodology and an examination of how the inherent capabilities of the computer can be better utilized to achieve a more accurate and consistent transfer of information from designer to builder.

2 Object-Oriented Programming

One area that has received a great deal of attention regarding computer-aided design research is object-oriented programming. Object-oriented programming (OOP) is a set of concepts that have been used extensively in software design and engineering in order to effectively construct and manage large-scale computational systems. While computer programs are certainly not buildings, the concepts of OOP provide a means to organize information in an effective and meaningful manner.

The overriding concept of OOP is the division of complex tasks into small, easily managed pieces, called objects. These objects are computer abstractions that model the components of the system being simulated. In addition to greatly reducing the complexity of a given system, these objects can also be reused in other projects or combined to create more complex software modules. Object-oriented programming also allows for easy modification and extension of individual components without requiring the programmer to re-code the entire component from scratch. (Cox and Novobilski 1991)

2.1 Object-Oriented CAD

Within the last few years, several object-oriented CAD packages have been commercially introduced. Microstation Triforma by Bentley and the recently released Revit platform are two such examples. Typically referred to as "building modelers" these applications use objects to represent building components. The design is three-dimensionally modeled or "built" using these objects. In addition to geometric properties, attributes such as cost or performance criteria can be incorporated into the object. Drawings and other reports are automatically generated and linked to the 3D model, ensuring that all information is accurate and consistent with the model.

Building modelers seek to computationally simulate the constructed reality in its entirety. Plan, section, and elevation drawings are produced as a by-product of this process. These drawings generally indicate what components are to be used and where they are to be located. However, they do not directly indicate how a particular component is to be assembled to its neighboring components. This is largely the domain of the construction detail drawing. Despite the obvious advantage to using a building modeler, the architect is still required to manually locate the necessary details from the firm's detail library or create the detail from scratch. The intelligence of the software does not extend this far into the construction documentation process. What is needed is a system that recognizes the component nature of construction and provides an immediate means to access the depth of a firm's construction knowledge.

3 Implementation

In order to directly address the deficiencies related to the construction documentation process, a prototype system, the *Drawing Assembler,* was developed to facilitate information reuse in the documentation process. The *Drawing Assembler* provides access to the extents of a firm's accumulated detail library by making such information readily available to the user in a contextual manner. It is an approach to construction documentation that functions at the level of the component.

Other research has been conducted into the use of component based construction drawings, specifically that of Harfmann (Harfmann 1993) and Gross (Gross 1996). Both, however, focus primarily on early stages of design and on developing precise geometric representations. Their emphasis is on resolving the relationships between components as they are assembled in either two dimensions (Gross 1996) or three (Harfmann 1993). In contrast, the *Drawing Assembler* operates on the level of the detail. Rather than resolving the geometric relationship of the interfacing components, the *Drawing Assembler* searches and generates details that are specific to the components. It functions more as an interactive search engine for construction details than a drafting or modeling program.

Fundamentally, the *Drawing Assembler* (Fig. 1) is a graphic interface that links two databases. The first database contains a collection of building assemblies and components. The second database contains a series of parametrically defined construction details. A single classification system is used to structure both databases. Several classification systems, such as Masterformat, Uniformat, and CI/Sfb, are already widely used within the construction industry. These systems elementalize the building into assemblies and components and provide a logical hierarchy for organizing this information. Given its prevalence in the United States, the Masterformat system is used to structure the databases within the prototype system.

As will be discussed in the next section, objects are entered into the component database through use of the *Object Editor*. As the object is created, the user determines the definition of the object. Similar to the keynote numbering system used in the American Institute of Architects' *ConDoc* drawing system, the definition consists of two parts: the first part established by the Masterformat designation, followed by a suffix chosen by the architect. A 3'x7'x1-1/2" solid core wooden door, for example, would be defined as "08200_A1". Similarly, a 6'8" version of the same door would be "08200_A2". Detail drawings are organized within the detail database using the same system. Details are classified by the components assembled with that drawing. A detail illustrating the connection between 2x4 wood framing at 12" on center and a hollow metal door frame would be defined at "06062_A+08100_B2".

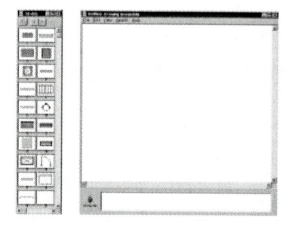

Figure 1. The Drawing Assembler *interface.*

3.1 Object Editor

Objects in the component database are created and modified using the *Object Editor* (Fig. 2). The *Object Editor* establishes the various graphic representations of an object (both plan and section) as well as its particular definition and parameters. Defining objects using the *Object Editor* requires three steps. In the first step, the object is defined according to the Masterformat system, as was described in the previous section. Next, the user enters values for the object's particular parameters. These parameters define the geometric dimensions of the object and are used to generate the resultant detail once a proper match has been made. In the final step, the user selects the graphic symbols that will be used to represent the object in the *Drawing Assembler*. These symbols are the primary means of manipulation in the *Drawing Assembler* but are not necessarily directly associated to the object's parameters. As in traditional drawing techniques, a simplified symbol can be used to abstractly represent a more complex geometric component. It is at the level of the detail that the particular geometric properties of a component will be illustrated in depth. Once a series of objects have been defined and made part of the component database, they can be organized into project specific libraries.

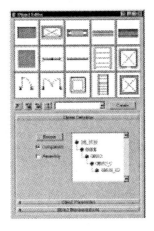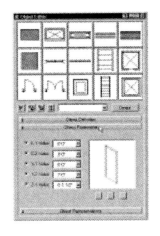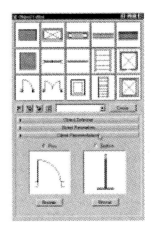

Figure 2. Object Editor *menus.*

3.2 Drawing Assembler

The main interface of the *Drawing Assembler* (Fig. 3) is used to assemble a set of components into the building representation. The *Drawing Assembler* uses a "drag and drop" input system. A plan or section is assembled by selecting a particular component from the library and dragging it to the work surface. This component can be positioned as needed. If the component happens to be a variable system, such as wall or floor type, the user is prompted to enter specific values to define this system.

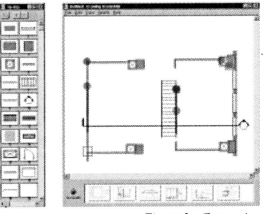

Figure 3. Generation Sequence - Details are generated based on the intersection of dissimilar objects.

When the building has been assembled to a reasonable level of completion, construction details can be determined by activating the "Generate" button. Once activated, the system isolates all of the intersections between dissimilar components. Each component's definition is identified and added to the intersecting component's definition, forming a compound definition for the particular assembly. The system then uses this compound definition to search the detail database. A double hung window, for example, intersects with a masonry wall component. The window is defined in the component database as "08XXX-D1". The masonry wall is defined as "04200-A". The system then searches the detail database for any details defined as "04200_A+08XXX_D1". Similar to Internet search engines, the *Drawing Assembler* will locate details that most closely match the compound definition. In instances where there is more than one matching detail, the user is presented with the selection from which to choose (Fig. 4). In this sense, the *Drawing Assembler* can act as either a strict documentation tool, searching for a specific detail, or as a more suggestive tool, providing the architect with a range of potential solutions.

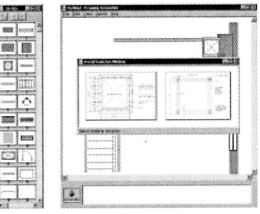

Once a detail has been selected, the system reads the parameters for each component and generates the detail based on these values. The finished detail is then placed in the detail window located along the lower edge of the interface and a marker is generated at the intersection of the components to indicate the existence of such a detail. Similarly, if no details match the compound definition, a marker is generated to indicate that there is no detail for this specific intersection (Fig. 5). At this point, the user can either change the definition of the objects and search again or create a specific detail to address that particular condition. Throughout the course of this search and generate process, the *Drawing Assembler* maintains a list of the details generated and checks if instances of a particular detail have already been created in order to

Figure 4. Generation Sequence – Detail selection window prompts user to select appropriate detail.

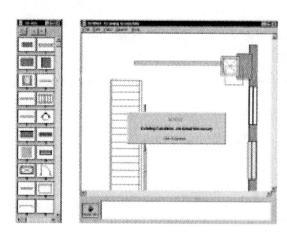

Figure 5. Generation Sequence – Alert window indicates that no matches were found in the detail database.

prevent redundant information. If a detail has previously been generated, the subsequent similar intersections are indicated with markers referencing the initial generation.

In addition to component objects, the *Drawing Assembler* also makes use of notational objects. The section object is used in the same manner as other component or assembly objects and is dragged and positioned on the work surface. Clicking the section object replaces the plan view with a section at that particular location. As was stated earlier, objects created in the *Object Editor* are defined with both plan and section views as well as parameters for each. The section object recognizes the objects it intersects and creates a view placing the section representations relative to their location in plan. However, when objects are entered into plan view, the *Drawing Assembler* does not request input regarding their position in the Z-axis. When the section object is first used, it is necessary to position the objects relative to the Z-axis. Again, the intention is to focus on the intersection of objects, rather than their precise location in three-dimensional space.

Understandably, a section often contains specific information that is not visible in plan. The section object works in a similar fashion to the plan view, allowing the user to drag and drop objects into place and then search and generate details. In order to relate the section to the plan, a plan object is created in the section, creating a linkage between the two representational views. In either case, it is possible to create multiple representations by creating either plan or section objects accordingly. This provides a consistent referencing structure among the various location drawings. Unlike the notion of a comprehensive three-dimensional building model, this approach makes use of the efficiency afforded by abstract two-dimensional representations while maintaining an integrated framework for building description and documentation.

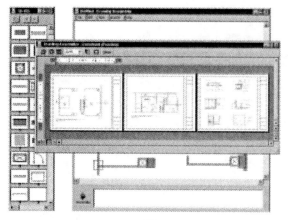

Figure 6. Print Sequence – Details and location drawings are generated and keyed appropriately.

Once a building has been assembled and the details generated, the *Drawing Assembler* organizes the information on drawing sheets. The user first specifies a particular organizational structure (by drawing type, element, or scale) and the system then places the details on the sheets according to this structure. At the same time, location drawings (plan, section, and elevation) are generated and appropriately keyed to the location of the details on the sheets, relieving the user of the tedious task of keying each detail's location. As a final step, the drawings are printed as a set (Fig. 6) and a file encapsulating the drawing information generated and saved.

4 Conclusion

While CAD software is often promoted as a means to achieve efficiency and productivity in the architectural office, it merely replicates known methods of work. Similarly, the current generation of building modelers, while certainly an improvement over traditional CAD applications, do not provide the depth of information required in a set of construction documents. The *Drawing Assembler* automates the process of construction documentation by providing the architect with instant access to an existing knowledge base of construction details. To further test the applicability of the concept, an AutoCAD version of the prototype is currently under development. Research into accessing remote databases through the Internet is also underway.

The intention of this project has been to develop a tool that supports the objectives of the architect through the strategic use of digital technology. Current methods of working do not fully exploit the potential of the technology. The *Drawing Assembler* challenges the traditional methodology of the architect through investigating alternative methods of working while rethinking the appropriate use of information technology in the practice of architecture.

5 References

Cox, Brad J. and Novobilski, Andrew J. (1991). *Object-Oriented Programming: An Evolutionary Approach*. Reading, MA: Addison-Wesley.

Gross, Mark D. (1996). Why Can't CAD be more like Lego? CKB, a program for building construction kits. *Automation in Construction 5,* 286 - 299.

Harfmann, Anton. (1993) Component-Based, Three-Dimensional "Working Drawings". In *ACADIA '93,* 141.

McCullough, Malcolm. (1996) *Abstracting Craft.* Cambridge, MA: The MIT Press.

Classroom

The classroom, particularly the architecture studio, is a laboratory for empirical research into design methods and cognition, as well as being a place for instruction and learning or established facts. The articles in this section continue a tradition of applying computer tools in classroom environments and then observing how students and teachers react and adapt. The article by Hotten and Diprose describes the opportunities introduced by software for creating digital panoramas. Students can use the software in expressive and exploratory ways to represent space beyond merely the pictorial and photo realistic. Ataman addresses a long ranging controversy regarding how computing affects learning of fundamental design principles. His paper is a truly ground breaking contribution to define both the good and the bad of substituting computer methods for time honored traditional methods of drawing and model-making. The article by Chase and Murty poses an interesting question but leaves the answer open to future study: can a student's performance be assessed based on raw statistics about the CAD models that the student produces?

As computer methods inexorably move toward ubiquity in architectural education, educators, researchers and architects can expect continued rigorous explorations that lead to inarguable conclusions regarding the impact of a changed educational system.

From Dreamtime to QuickTime: The Resurgence of the 360-Degree Panoramic View as a Form of Computer-Synthesised Architectural Representation.

Robert D. Hotten, University of Auckland, New Zealand

Peter R. Diprose, Unitec, Auckland, New Zealand

Abstract

The conference theme 'eternity, infinity and virtuality' may be considered in terms of *time, space and the other*. One form of representation that captures all three of these fundamental dimensions, at a glance, is the 360-degree panorama, a medium that is currently making a comeback in the architectural studio. This paper explores the use of the computer-synthesised panorama as a means of *representing* architectural space and landscape experience, and as a method of informing the design. The panoramic mural is differentiated from two subcategories of QTVR panorama, the *subjective* and the *objective*. The use of panoramic views enable landscape architecture students to design using a 2D image format which can be rendered to provide a 3D spatial effect. In summary, the paper contends that the process of design, in architectural practice and in architectural education, is significantly enhanced by the dynamic representations of time and/or space offered by the computer-synthesised panorama.

1 The panoramic view: Eternity, infinity and virtuality.

The conference theme 'eternity, infinity and virtuality' may be considered in terms of *time, space and the other*. One form of representation, which captures all three of these fundamental dimensions, at a glance, is the 360-degree panorama, which reached its height of popularity more than a century ago. As Comment states –

> *The panorama was one of the most popular and most typical phenomena of the nineteenth century, of which it is in a way the signature. A motley crowd in search of wanton, enigmatic and rarely denied pleasure would rush to see these spectacular paintings... A fundamental shift had taken place in the logic and focus of representation.* (Comment, 1999)

In general, the panoramic photograph or painting technique records and simulates comprehensive views of a portion of the earth's surface, landscape, or built environment (Oettermann, 1997). Between 1787 and 1900 panorama painting was a medium through which ordinary people could access and experience *the other*. Namely, for those living in the large established European cities, this 'other' was life beyond typical mundane existence, a reality experienced by others elsewhere at some other time. Through the panorama newly discovered exotic colonial landscapes and architecture were able to be 'captured' by teams of painters for homeland audiences. For example, "Panorama of the Congo" by Alfred Bastien and Paul Mathieu (painted in 1913, measuring 15m x 115m) was created for the National Exhibition of Ghent. Being sponsored by the government of the time, this panorama was as much a work of colonial propaganda as it was a work of art, with expressed intention to give young Belgians *"a taste for the colonies"* (Comment, 1999).

The viewer of this period was also able to gaze upon the totality of significant events *in time and space* through a single work. For example "Panorama for the struggle for Tyrolean independence in 1809", by Michel Zeno Diemer (painted in 1896, measuring 10m x 100m) depicts the third battle of Bergisel. The panorama tells the tale of the 15,000 valiant Tyrolean peasants led by Andreas Hofer and their defeat of Napoleon's 16,000 strong force commanded by Marshall Lefebvre. This was the nineteenth century equivalent of "Saving Private Ryan" with the viewer being transported to a hazardous time and location to experience a situation of spectacular interest in relative safety and comfort.

At the beginning of the twentieth century the still panorama was quickly displaced by film as the means of vicarious experience. Nonetheless the human desire for panoramic representation lingered. Consequently a moving variation of the panorama briefly emerged with the introduction of Cinerama in the 1950s – with its 160° horizontal angles and 75° vertical angles of vision, together with 360 degrees of sound (Oettermann, 1997). This form of cinema did not last given the substantial cost created by the technical requirements filming in the round. Notably, no feature films were ever produced in Cinerama format. Like Cinerama, the more recent IMAX movie format is also the domain of the travelogue/spectacular to the exclusion of any genuine narrative content.

With the introduction of television, and more particularly the proliferation of personal computers over the last decade, screen based media, which satisfy the human desire for vicarious experience have become pervasive. More recently, virtual reality computer simulations and cyberspace have become the objects of research (Anders, 1999; Heim, 1998). Given these most recent technological advances, initially, it seemed surprising that a renewed interest had been shown in the panorama as a means of creating 'virtual environments'. With further investigation, however, the return to the panorama was in fact forged by software developers' desire to facilitate virtual environment navigation on *personal computer hardware*, rather than the recreation of panoramic artwork from a century ago. As Chen describes,

> *Traditionally, virtual reality systems use 3D computer graphics to model and render virtual environments in real-time. This approach usually requires laborious modelling and expensive special purpose rendering hardware. The rendering quality and scene complexity are often limited because of the real-time constraint. ... a new approach which uses 360-degree cylindrical panoramic images to compose a virtual environment* [is feasible]. *The panoramic image is digitally warped on-the-fly to simulate camera panning and zooming. The panoramic images can be created with computer rendering, specialised panoramic cameras or by "stitching" together overlapping photographs taken with a regular camera. Walking in a space is currently accomplished by "hopping" to different panoramic points. The image-based approach has been used in the commercial product QuickTime VR, a virtual reality extension to Apple Computer's QuickTime digital multimedia framework.* (Chen, 1995)

QuickTime VR utilises an *image-based rendering system* which allows for (i) 'cheap' complexity, which uses texture maps; (ii) the ability to use 2D images to create a 3D scene, which is especially useful given the time required to build 3D models; (iii) rendering which is independent of scene complexity - a great bonus for complex 3D models which bring even the fastest personal computers to their knees if navigated on the fly (Harvey and Rangaswamy, 1997).

QuickTime VR panoramas, like the panorama paintings before them, have retained the capacity to produce vicarious experience, metaphorically transporting the viewer to another time and space.

2 The panorama in the context of architecture and landscape architecture
2.1 Design and the vicarious experience of architecture and landscape architecture
Computer aided design technologies have offered designers greater opportunity for the thorough investigation of space. The ability to easily visualise, create and present a multitude of images from different viewpoints is important for architectural design, and especially important for the design of landscape architecture because of its reliance on the visual to *produce landscape experiences* (Riley, 1997). Landscape experience is the realm in which visual stimulus goes beyond perception and cognition, into affect, evaluation and meaning, which are crucial components of a phenomenological design process. Because panoramic representations assist in the production of vicarious experiences they are a medium useful to the design process of architecture and landscape architecture.

Summerfield, for example, argues for the portrayal of architecture set within its actual visual context, including environment-project interactions. He identifies architectural experience as being incredibly sensitive to the relationship between the project-model and the context, a relationship, which must be represented accurately if evaluative judgments are to have validity. Summerfield has also proposed a process (bearing some similarity to that of the QTVR panorama), which recreates the environment that surrounds both building and observer, as the means of resolving this essential but problematic feature of realistic imagery on real sites (Summerfield and Hayman, 1999).

2.2 Panoramic representation

Emphasis as to the validity of the panorama in the design studio has stemmed, in part from Corner's call for architects to expand their repertoires beyond the relatively small number of techniques used in the landscape, architectural, and planning arts. Corner challenges the designer to augment and redevelop their palettes with respect to *"analyses of image construction" and examine great works of art - including maps, paintings, collage, performance arts, or cinematic and digital media"* (Corner, 1998).

Two main varieties of panorama have been encouraged in the design studio. The first of these is the *panoramic mural*, which is digitally collaged from still photographs or slides and then printed. The second variety of panorama is the *Panoramic VR*. In this case QuickTime Virtual Reality Panoramas (or QTVRs) are able to be constructed out of panoramic murals using QTVR Make Panorama, or produced directly from a 3D modelling package such as ArchiCAD 6.0. For clarity these are tabulated below.

2.3 Panoramic murals

The panoramic mural gives the viewer the capacity to see an entire space, albeit stretched out, at a glance. From experience, the panoramic mural tends towards the sublime, often transcending the subject being depicted. This may occur because in mural form the panorama is a 2D perspectival abstraction rather than a direct attempt to create virtual space in the round. This aspect of the panoramic mural finds parallel in what Comment calls the 'Rundblick', or *"circular gaze that embraces the whole horizon in one, or almost one go"*. He suggests that the status of the individual becomes paradoxical because the dominance she craves presupposes personal annihilation and the loss of real space in order to hold onto the fictional space of the representation (Comment, 1999). While 'real' spatial experience is reduced, the circular gaze heightens the visual impact of the architecture or landscape depicted. Through enhancing the visual impact of the image the panoramic mural is particularly effective at taking the viewer towards the realm of *landscape experience*.

The creation of seamless panoramic murals created from digital images shot with a digital camera has not been encouraged in studio (We have therefore chosen to omit this seamless form of panoramic collage from table 1). We considered that the seamless representation of architecture inherently denied the potential for serendipitous spatial conjunctions or formal intrigue through the removal of multiple/shifted viewpoints, which ultimately reduced the experience of architecture and landscape. Instead, a style of highly textured panoramic mural has developed which bears an affinity with David Hockney's photographic collages. 'Nude, London' (1984), commissioned for the film 'Insignificance', which starred Theresa Russell as Marilyn Munroe, has been described as follows

> *"the girl's body is fragmented so that one sees the front, back and side views at the same time. The contortions of her body are tantalising: she sprawls on a pink silk sheet, eyes firmly on the viewer and tongue between her lips. Unlike a typical calender girl, whom the eye can take in at one go, Hockney's pin-up requires the viewer to make slow and careful examination of every part of her body...*[Hockney himself then comments that] *my pin-up requires you to look very slowly, you are forced to move over every inch of her body which makes it look more interesting, more erotic."*(Webb, 1988)

By rendering architecture and landscape in the form of a *textured* panoramic mural the architect is required to analyse and evaluate the subject more closely, given the representation's higher level of 'cognitive' detail.

New architectural forms may also be undetermined by a design process which utilises increased information provided by multiple viewpoints. Vidler points out, "the perspective distortions and compositional freedom of Frank Gehry's assemblages rely on techniques already developed in the cinema, such as angled shots framed from below and rapid shifts of viewpoint" (Vidler, 1999). What will be the architectural, or urban design outcome of the textured panoramic collage? Some examples of textured panoramic murals are illustrated at the end of this paper.

Figure 1. Kata Tjuta, Central Australia Robert Hotten, 1999.

2.4 Panoramic VRs

There are two distinct sub-categories of panoramic VR: the *subjective panorama*, in which the viewpoint is centralised; and the *objective panorama* where the object/model is centralised. The subjective panorama places the individual at the centre, and thus in control of the virtual world, whereas the objective panorama places the individual above or beyond the modelled virtual world, detached yet godlike as if in an infinitely mobile tower. This idea requires further exploration given the fundamental importance of *viewpoint* in panoramic representation and social power structures. Here, Foucault's examination of circular architectural space seems relevant: Panorama painting had as its historical analog circular architecture. These designs were produced during a similar period to Barker's patented panoramic effect of 1787, for example, Boullée's Cenotaph to Newton c1784, and Bentham's Panopticon of 1791. Foucault notes that circular architecture at that time -

> *"was the expression of a particular political utopia"* ... *"from the logic of spectacle passed down to us from antiquity (temples, theatres, circuses where 'the inspection of a small number of objects is made available to a multitude of men') we arrive at modern logic, in which, at the other extreme, it is a question of 'procuring for a small number of people, or just one person, the simultaneous view of a great multitude'."* (Comment, 1999; Foucault, 1975)

Expanding Foucault's critique to encompass the recent development of the QTVR panorama (and particularly the subjective panorama) the status of the viewpoint within panoramic representation can be identified as expressing/increasing the power of the individual over that of the environment.

A contrasting interpretation of the subjective QTVR panorama can be given. Firstly, the viewer does not see the whole scene at glance but in a (slow) turning process within a *QTVR Scene*. The limited view angle denies the user the status of omniscience. This is reinforced by the zoom feature, which further narrows (or widens to a preset maximum) the gaze. Secondly, the cylindrical space of the QTVR Scene engulfs the individual, belittling them in the *big* environment/landscape. Thus rather than the individual dominating nature, nature can be identified as dominating the individual. (The exploration of VR nodes (hot points) may be undertaken in a later paper. Here we are principally interested in the panoramic effect as it relates to the representation of an individual scene).

2.5 The panorama applied

The panorama as a 'new' form of digital representation is unavoidably altering the way that we practice and teach architecture. Using automated rendering techniques (such as ArchiCAD 6.0) architectural ideas and landscapes can be realistically represented in a few minutes to a few hours in panoramic form using a desktop computer, rather than one year on average for a team of painters to create the same in the nineteenth century (Oettermann, 1997). The use of the computer-synthesised panorama has become invaluable as a means of representing architectural and landscape experience, and as a method of informing design:

- In the communication of architectural and landscape ideas on the Internet, where speed of data transfer remains an important factor. Notably the QTVR panorama is popularly used by the real estate industry, by travel agents and hoteliers alike as the means of conveying 3D images of remote interiors, exotic locations and events.

- To convey spatial architectural design ideas in practice. The QTVR is a very accessible means of presentation for practitioners and clients alike. Experience has shown that clients particularly enjoy the subjective panoramic viewpoint, which places them at the centre and (implicitly) in control of the virtual model's environment.

- In the presentation of 3D virtual simulacra (historical reconstructions). In the studio QTVR provides easy access to remote, exotic or lost architecture. Locally created examples include the Taj Mahal, Brazilia, and the Barcelona Pavilion.

2.6 The panorama and design pedagogy

The panorama offers the student architect a technique for the investigation of spatial and formal dynamics. It should be noted that until the designer has first developed an understanding of space the development of skills in 'planning' remains a diversion, *"the plan is the generator, but planning is not necessarily the first thing the student should learn. Spatial understanding and a sense of formal dynamics must be developed first. Otherwise planning is mere abstract pattern making. This is a process that cannot be rushed"* (Heath, 1993). The value of the panoramic mural in

Figure 2. Versailles, Outside Paris, Robert Hotten, 1999.

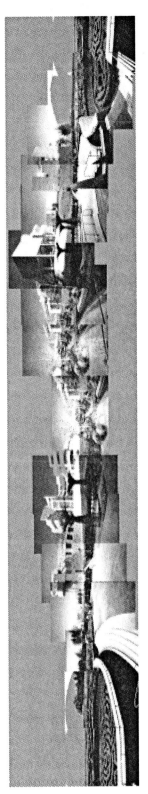

Figure 3. Irwin Garden at the Getty Centre, Los Angeles Robert Hotten, 1999.

Figure 4. The Tuileries Garden, Paris, Robert Hotten, 1999.

Figure 5. The Tuileries Garden, Paris, Robert Hotten, 1999.

architectural education is in the fact that it allows students to work in a relatively simple 2D format (photographically, through drawing, and digital imaging) and then render their design idea quickly and easily in the round (using QTVR Make Panorama). Consequently students are able to develop spatial understanding without having to first learn sophisticated 3D modelling packages.

A short design exercise for landscape architecture students has been developed which utilises the (above) process of panoramic collage combined with the architectural operations of insertion, intervention, materiality, reciprocity, and threshold developed by Berrizbeitia and Pollak (1999). The outcomes of this studio program will be presented at the conference.

3   Summary: Time, space and the sublime

"Today's instructional landscape must inevitably evolve or die, like biological species, since its environment is being radically altered by volatile visualisation technologies. This ongoing displacement of fixed, monochromatic type by interactive, multi-dimensional graphics is a tumultuous process. In the realm of the artificial, as in nature, extinction occurs when there is no accommodation." (Stafford,1997).

A panoramic vision of landscape and architecture has re-emerged, which in our estimation is as *affective* as it has ever been. While the panoramic mural has an ability to capture the inherent beauty of landscape, revealing views that are not perceivable by the eye ordinarily, the QTVR panorama has evolved to be a popular means of conveying 3D images of exotica and event. With the capacity to take the observer into the vicarious realm of landscape experience, of time, space and the *sublime,* the computer-synthesised panorama has a role within landscape architecture and design. May our architectural dreamtime be realised in QuickTime, for in the words of Walt Disney *"if you can dream it, you can do it."*

References

Anders, P. (1999) Extensions: Some implications of cyberspace for the practice of architecture, in *Acadia '99 Media and Design Process*, Ataman, O. and Bermudez, J. [Eds], The Association for Computer-Aided Design in Architecture.

Appleton, J. (1996) *The Experience of Landscape*, Chichester England: John Wiley and Sons

Berrizbeitia, A. and L. Pollak. (1999). *Inside Outside: Between Architecture and Landscape.* Gloucester: Rockport.

Chen, S. E. (1995) "QuickTime VR - An Image-Based Approach to Virtual Environment Navigation", *Proceedings of SIGGRAPH 95, Computer Graphics Proceedings, Annual Conference Series,* Robert Cook [Ed], Los Angeles, California, Addison Wesley.

Chen, S. E. and L. Williams. (1993) View Interpolation for Image Synthesis. *In Proceedings of SIGGRAPH 93*, pp. 279-288, ACM.

Comment, B. (1999) *The panorama*, London: Reaktion.

Corner, J. (1998) "Operational Eidetics: Forging New Landscapes", *Harvard design magazine,* Fall. Cambridge Ma: The MIT Press.

Foucault, M. (1975) "Le panoptisme", *Surveiller et punir*, Paris

Harvey, J. and S. Rangaswamy, (1997) "Image-Based Rendering", *presentation for paper 6.838, MIT*, at http://graphics.lcs.mit.edu/~sudafed/6.838/presentation/

Heath, T. (1993), "The architectural theory of Rudolph Arnheim and its implications for Teaching" in *The Journal of aesthetic education*, Vol 27, no4, Winter.

Heim, M. (1998) *Virtual Realism*. Oxford: Oxford University Press.

Hillier, B. (1996) *Space is the machine: A configurational theory of architecture*. Cambridge: Cambridge University Press.

Lynn, G. (1997), Animate form, New York: Princeton Architectural Press.

Oettermann, S, (1997) *The panorama: history of a mass medium,* translated by D. Schneider, New York: Zone Books.

Riley, R. B. (1997). "The visible, the visual, and the vicarious: Questions about vision, landscape, and experience", *Understanding ordinary landscapes*, Groth, P. and Bressi, T. W. [Eds] Ann Arbor: Edwards Brothers Inc.

Rowe, C. and F. Koetter, (1978) Collage city, Cambridge, Mass. : MIT Press.

Stafford, B. M. (1997). *Good Looking: Essays on the Virtue of Images*. Cambridge: The MIT Press.

Summerfield, A, S. Hayman. (1999), "On capturing context in architecture", in *proceedings of building simulation '99*, Volume 1, pp 233-240.

Design Media	Process of creation & Software	Presentation format
Panoramic Mural	Digitally collaged using PhotoShop 5.5 from scanned still photographs or slides.	Printed

Panoramic VR	(i) QTVRs constructed from panoramic murals using QTVR Make Panorama
	(ii) QTVRs produced directly from a 3D modelling package, for example, ArchiCAD 6.0
	   a. The Subjective Panorama (subjective viewpoint)
	   "VR Scene" (ArchiCAD 6.0)
	   b. The Objective Panorama (objective viewpoint)
	   "VR Object" (ArchiCAD 6.0)
		Screen, Projected or Internet

Table 1. A (non-exhaustive) typology of digital panoramic design media.

Figure 6. 3XL City. Project for the Third Millennium, Venice, Peter Diprose and Robert Hotten, 1999.

Figure 7. Guggenheim at Bilbao Robert Hotten, 1999

Some Experimental Results in the Assessment of Architectural Media

Osman Ataman, Temple University, USA

Abstract

The relationship between the media and architectural design can be an important factor and can influence the design outcome. However, the nature, direction and magnitude of this relationship are unknown. Consequently, there have been many speculative claims about this relationship and almost none of them are supported with empirical research studies. In order to investigate these claims and to provide a testable framework for their potential contributions to architectural education, this study aims to explore the effects of media on architectural design. During 1995-1997, a total of 90 students enrolling in First Year Design Studio and Introduction to Computing classes at Georgia Tech participated in the study. A set of quantitative measures was developed to assess the differences between the two media and the effects on the architectural design. The results suggested that media influenced certain aspects of students' designs. It is concluded that there is a strong relationship between the media and architectural design. The type of media not only changes some quantifiable design parameters but also affects the quality of design.

1 Introduction

The task of creating and manipulating representations for the purpose of design requires media. Media as a word has been defined in many different ways. Its most popular definition in today's culture refers to the mass carrier of communications; radio, television, newspapers, and magazines. Some see media as new audiovisual aids; some as information technology. A general definition that has gained popularity recently is "a tool." When we consider the literal meaning of the word itself, we see that media is the plural form of the word medium, a term broadly understood as being "the middle." This understanding is the foundation for defining medium as a tool between the user and information to be created, received, stored, manipulated, or disseminated. A tool is the middle between the user and the task being addressed.

In architecture, media is defined as apparatus for selecting, gathering, organizing, storing, and conveying knowledge in representational forms. More specifically, media is a tool or a combination of tools that are used to create graphic representations such as drawings, images and models. From a theoretical viewpoint, media can be regarded as an important and influential factor in the design process. Consequently, the potential for a relationship between media and architectural design can be seen when the interaction between cognitive processes and characteristics of the environment is considered (Kozma 1993; Salomon 1993; Salomon, Perkins, and Globerson 1991). Given this, it would be appropriate to assert that the nature and power of the available media facilitates what is conceived and accomplished. In the generation of new ideas, the media can be regarded as a tool of primary importance. Conversely, limitations in the design can result from the limitations of the media. In this respect, media can be thought of as cognitive tools that serve constructive thinking, transcend cognitive limitations, and engage in cognitive operations not capable otherwise (Pea 1985).

The general agreement among architects, architectural educators, and researchers is that new technologies, –digital media in particular– will play a critical role in the future of the profession. But, a debate rages about how architects should be trained to interact with these media. We do not have a clear answer to this issue. The problem is that there is not even an established relationship between media and architectural design. The primary reason is not the lack of this relationship but the lack of empirical studies. As a result, our understanding of media is fuzzy and unclear. Perhaps, this is partly due to the lack of adequate systematic research, and partly due to difficulties in formulating essential questions. Moreover, existing arguments are often based on implicit conjectures, and these may block the formulation of productive research questions. Consequently, there have been many speculative claims that the capabilities and limitations of the media have a direct effect on the outcome of the design.

In order to test these claims and to provide a framework for their potential contributions to architectural education, this study aims to study media and its' effects on architectural design, particularly architectonics. It focuses on a specific level of architectural education, two types of media and the ways they relate to major aspects of design, such as space-making and form-building. It provides an opportunity to compare the effects of different media and consequently to establish a link between media and design.

2 Background and Related Studies

In architecture, there are scattered studies that attempt to address the issue that media influence design process. Even though, these studies are valuable and contribute to the accumulation of knowledge in this field, they are not able to establish a relationship between digital media and design. There are several reasons for this failure. Most of these studies were performed without comparing their results with traditional media, such as Akin (Akin 1990), Eastman and Lang (Eastman and Lang 1991). The results they concluded are only reinforcements of their claims, especially in the studies of Danahy (Danahy 1991; Danahy 1990) and Saggio (Saggio 1992). The second reason is that the sample size of existing studies was too small to be considered as valid systematic research, such as Walters (Walters 1985), and Smulevich (Smulevich 1993). Another reason is the reliability of these studies. Most of them did not use explicit methods that would have allowed the repetition of the study by other researchers. Still another reason is that these studies are more impressionistic than empirical, personal observation is used as the main method, such as Cigolle and Coleman (Cigolle and Coleman 1990; Cigolle, Mark, and Coleman 1990), Parsons (Parsons 1994). Finally, some of them remain only at a theoretical level, such as Herbert (Herbert 1992; Herbert 1994) and (Mitchell and McCullough 1991).

Each one of these studies seems to support the main hypothesis presented in this study, that media has a particular effect on architectural design in general, to the design process in particular. Unfortunately, however, they are mostly narrative and descriptive: they provide individual case histories and detailed portraiture of one particular media. Many strong claims are made but almost none of them have been empirically substantiated or clearly tested in experiment conditions. Therefore, these studies can be termed as synthetic reports, because they do not depict the big picture, but rather relations among selected components such as a particular studio and computer media. A major criticism of the previous work in media effect is methodological. The method of introspection is questionable since the authors relied on their observations, interpretations, and the subject's self-reports but not on rigorously evaluated findings.

3 Research Design

During 1996-97, a total of 90 students who were enrolled in a first year design studio at Georgia Institute of Technology participated this study. Some of these same students were also enrolled in an introduction to computing class during the same time. The experimental group consisted of the students who took the design studio and computer course together (Group 1). The control group consisted of design studio students not enrolled in the computer class (Group 2). Both groups worked on the same design project, Group 1 used digital media while Group 2 used manual media. Digital media included computers with hardware and software (drafting, modeling, rendering, animation). Manual media included traditional drafting tools such drafting board, T-square, parallel bar, scale, pencil, paper, etc. and physical model making tools such as cutting boards, x-acto, foam core, chipboard, wood, etc. Any students registered only to the computer course were excluded from the sample, as were students who had taken the studio previously. Through an informal preliminary survey, two groups appeared to be equivalent in terms of education and knowledge level except that the experimental group was exposed to the independent variable "Digital media" and the control group was not.

Because of factors influencing the sample and other experimental conditions, a quasi-experimental research design was used. The independent variable and the dependent variable of this study were "media" (both digital and manual) and "design" respectively. Since architectural design is still considered partially as an art and is generally evaluated on subjective grounds with few quantitative measures, the following procedures were developed in order to assess the differences between the two media and the effects on the dependent variable (design).

First, relevant conceptual and operational definitions of the first year architectonic design issues related to this study were identified. Second, a set of quantitative measures were developed in order to provide criteria for the evaluation of students' projects and to allow for a quantitative assessment of the differences between the two groups to be made. The evaluation criteria were based on the architectonic design issues related to the design problem both groups worked on. All of these issues were defined and exercised in earlier studio assignments. After reviewing the design course's notes, evaluation criteria and numerous other design literature, several factors related to the design projects were identified, sorted and reformulated for quantitative measurements. Third, all students' designs were merged into one media presentation (digital media) and assessed independently from their method of generation. All quantitative evaluation criteria were applied and measured.

Although these evaluations measured the quantitative effects and differences of designs developed in different media, they did not provide valid verifications of these quantitative assessments, nor did they necessarily suggest solid indicators of "design quality." Therefore, qualitative measures were taken in order to address these issues. The primary objectives of the qualitative evaluations were: (1) to identify the qualitative differences between the groups; (2) to understand the relationship between media and design quality; and (3) to verify the validity of the quantitative assessment for the two groups.

3.1   Procedure

All students were given the same instructions and treatment. Overall, all students had to meet certain procedural requirements for the course and follow the same schedule. The same instructors (both main instructors and teaching assistants) taught all studio sessions. Likewise, the same instructors taught the computer classes. All studio students were given the same lectures and they all had to go through group pin-up and discussion of alternate schemes, revisions, and partial design evaluations. Even the crit groups were distributed randomly by including both digital and manual media users. The final requirements were exactly the same. The only differences were the media they employed and some presentation requirements were optional for the digital group.

4   Measurements

Relevant conceptual and operational definitions of the first year architectonic design issues related to this study are identified. Since the assessment of architectural design is difficult (because there are few quantitative measures), a set of quantitative measures is developed in order to lay out the procedures that provide criteria for the evaluation of students' projects and allow for a quantitative assessment of the differences between the two samples to be made.

Two levels of measurements were taken in this study: Quantitative and Qualitative. Quantitative measures intended to measure aspects such as categories, numbers, degrees, proportions, size, location, etc., and qualitative measures intended to measure as designers' subjective evaluations of a project based on several survey questions. In terms of statistical data types, both categorical and continuous data types were used for quantifiable aspects of design, and numerical types for the qualitative aspects of design.

Quantitative measures were taken based on the research questions and hypotheses of this study. In order to measure students' design projects, three major design issues were described and operationalized (Design Conceptualization, Space Making, Form Building). Later, the components of these properties were identified and quantified for measurements. These components were standard issues used for formal or informal evaluations of regular Design Studio projects at this level without any (digital/manual) media intervention. Throughout the experiment, the definitions, operationalizations, and evaluation criteria of these components were discussed and exercised in the design studio.

Two different levels of qualitative measurements were taken. In the first level, a blind review method was used. For that purpose, a survey questionnaire was designed and given to ten designers and design educators as a base to evaluate the students' projects. A total of nineteen questions were asked in the same six categories that were used in quantitative measurements. The Likert scale was used as a scale construction method. All projects were presented together in a random order and their presentation format was identical (see Figure 1).

Figure 1. Project Presentation Format

5 Results and Discussion

5.1 Concept Development

In all analyzed conceptual categories (parti, spatial organizations, and ordering systems), it was found that unclear conceptualizations were more likely to appear in the manual media group regardless of the sequence of the concepts they employed. During the assessment, a new "Unclear" category needed to be added to classify unidentified concepts. This new category accounted for a large share of the manual media groups' design conceptualization analyses. Over one fifth of the manual media group projects were evaluated as inappropriate for one of the predefined concept categories. For example, in "Spatial Organizations" 34%, likewise in "Ordering Systems" 24% and in "Parti" 18% of the manual media group's projects were labeled as "unclear." Meanwhile, the "unclear" category in the digital media group was 2% on average. For reliability, these findings were compared with the average results of three judges, including the author of this paper. According to the results, with the exception of the unclear category in parti and spatial organizations, the total numbers of other types were fairly close. However, those similarities did not occur necessarily in the same projects. As seen in the table below (Table 1), overall, digital media project categorizations were agreed on more often than the manual group in all categories. These results further support the argument that the digital media projects were clearer in their concept definitions.

Another important finding of the concept development analysis that would appear to be effected by the media was the variation of the samples. The manual media group seemed to produce some easy-to-build concepts and created fewer categories. For example, in developing "parti", the manual media users distributed their designs among two major categories (Tri-Zone with 40% and Bi-Zone with 16%). In "spatial organizations" and "ordering systems" the manual media group used three major categories whereas the digital media users distributed their designs more homogeneously over various categories. Furthermore, the resulting conceptual implementations by this group tended to be less complex and more ambiguous and displayed fewer features than the digital media group. The digital media group appeared to overcome this problem. These results indicated that from the manual media users' point of view, there was simply not enough flexibility and/or sufficient time to develop and explore a wide range of alternatives and refinements. This kind of exploration and efficient conceptual representation of content is essential for effective concept development. Moreover, it seemed that certain conceptual issues were related to some specific capabilities of a particular media. For example, the extensive use of grid organizations in the digital group projects can be explained with the constraint and snapping capabilities of digital media. Manual media can handle only a restricted formal movement with limited efficiency to allow conceptual design exploration.

These results suggest that the employment and utilization of digital media gave students enough flexibility to study, to execute and to maintain desired or expected concepts. The relatively more homogeneous distribution of design concepts in all concept categories and the clarity and readability

	All Judges -Parti	All Judges- SO	All Judges -OS
Match Results - Digital	66.7%	80.0%	73.3%
Match Results – Manual	51.1%	60.0%	62.2%

Table 1: Comparative matching results between the two groups by three judges

of these concepts in the digital media group's projects were supported with the consistency of the sequential concept developments. The main problem with the manual media group's projects appeared to be the difficulty in manipulating these issues. One explanation is the cross-examination of these conceptual principles after their development. For example, once manual media students decided their parti types and started using organizational principles, their initial partis either collapsed or lost their specificity. Therefore, a large number of unclassifiable, unclear concepts were seen mainly in the manual media group's projects. This problem was also related to the lack of consistency among conceptual stages. According to the cross-comparative analysis results, the digital media group exhibited more sequentially consistent concept developments than the manual group. The measured relationships were mostly consistent in the digital media group projects whereas there were several inconsistencies in the manual group projects. For example, in the digital group projects certain sequential relationships were established in various combinations (i.e. Bi-Zone [parti] – Grid [Spa. Org] – Hierarchy or Repetition [Ord. Sys]) (see Figure 2).

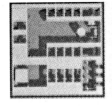  

Figure 2. Sequential conceptual developments in digital media projects

Moreover, the results indicated that certain conceptual issues were related to some specific capabilities of a particular media. Some of the findings showed, however, that at least some conceptual ideas such as axis, linear organizations, symmetrical order and nine-square parti were universal and, thus, that the development of these concepts was not necessarily limited to particular media. One explanation is the ease of constructing those concepts within the given design problem and constraints. Another explanation is the popularity of these concepts among the students. Certainly, this issue needs further exploration.

5.2 Space Making

Overall, the digital media group appeared to be more actively involved in space making activities than the manual media group. In comparison, the digital media group produced significantly different results on most measures related to architectonic space making and these differences suggested a relationship between media and measured architectonic design issues.

The first, and one of the most significant differences between the two groups was the definition of the spaces. According to the results, students who used digital media developed designs that suggested more understanding of architectonic space and clear distinctions between the conceptual and perceptual spaces. The proportional differences between the groups (well-defined vs. perceived) implied that certain attributes of media made a notable difference in space definitions. In comparison to the other group, the digital media group created significantly more well-defined spaces and qualitative analysis later suggested a strong correlation between the well-defined spaces and better design quality.

In all, students were encouraged to explore the design at each stage using study models, so that the three-dimensional implications of design decisions were more fully understood. With movement and sequence as important characteristics of the spatial composition, interior views and the general architectonic quality of the design as seen from the inside took on greater importance.

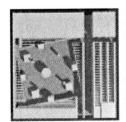  

Figure 3. Spatial deformations in manual media group projects

In the manual media group, students utilizing traditional cardboard study models seemed to not carefully examine the spatial relationships and organization of spaces. Therefore, many opportunities to enrich the design from this point of view were lost. For example, the diagonal or oblique views that existed within a design structure that was primarily orthogonal were easily overlooked if the visual representation was limited to the two-dimensional plan view. Manual media students naturally attempted to overcome the presumed monotony of the grid by inventing skewed, shifted, or warped planes, which immediately displayed their nonconformity in plan (see Figure 3 below).

When the physical model was eventually created it simply confirmed the earlier assumption of contrast provided by the skewed elements without really testing the corollary that a composition predominantly of right angles and orthogonal planes produced a varied perspective including many oblique views. To be convinced, students needed to view this concept directly in their design as decisions of form were being made. However, because of the labor-intensive nature of physical model building (or of changing a pre-existing model), the discovery was delayed and the effort to revise the project accordingly was often not made.

In contrast, digital media students were able to quickly model their design from the outset. This was certainly aided by the abstract, architectonic quality of the design problem, which minimized the complexity of modeling. Using drafting, modeling and rendering programs, the digital media students were able for the first time to really get their eyes inside the project and experienced the changing perspective of the spatial sequence from a non-stationary view point. As a result, the character of a student's approach to design seemed to change in subtle ways. Several discoveries were made. First, digital media students developed projects that embodied a clear sense of spatial definition. Second, there appeared to be more appreciation of the complexity that was created when just a few simple spatial relationships interacted with each other. Forming and orienting the spaces, for example, in relation to the given constraints and to the field, took on greater architectonic meaning. Third, the circulation and spatial sequence were studied as a dynamic problem taking into account the oblique views mentioned earlier. Finally, there was the ability to manipulate various characteristics such as entrance and size without compromising the attention to basic spatial quality.

These issues were further supported with additional findings. Space construction results indicated that the digital media group relied more heavily on the primary wall planes to create their spaces whereas the manual media group used mostly horizontal and secondary planes for space creation (in total numbers). This was an important finding to support the argument that with the help of digital media, students in that group were able to see the spatial value of primary planes and utilize them in space making. Although secondary wall planes were easier to use to create spaces because of the flexibility of orientation and horizontal planes were practical to cover unsolved organization, the digital media group saw primary planes as major space definers. The main reason was the control of this group over the spatial organization, various spatial relationships and the entire design composition. The manual media group's reliance on other planes, especially on horizontal planes indicated that their efforts were not focused on considering the spatial composition. Simply, they could not solve the spaces, their organization, and their relationship as successfully as the digital media group. Almost all of the other space-related findings, especially roof/space ratio support this explanation.

5.3   Form Building

The results indicated that media influenced the typology of design by affecting certain elements of form that contributed to the development of form building. Overall, digital media group articulated their planes, emphasized the penetration and continuity of its surfaces, handled the openings to visually organize the volumes, utilized their object elements and formed more balanced compositions than the other group.

These results suggested that the digital media influenced the exploratory phase, where the search for possibilities occurred in a deliberate and controlled manner. For example, as seen in the figure below (Figure 4), upon arriving at an initial *parti*, digital media users built digital models on the computer. At this point variation and transformation was easily accomplished and a number of alternative studies were created for comparison. Each new model was completed in terms of graphic representation, as this task was instantaneous on the computer. Various views, both external and internal to the model, were examined. The experience of sequence as a progression was studied in a series of perspective views. Subtle changes affecting interior lighting conditions (natural light) were tested by trial and error. Although these kinds of comparative studies have always been encouraged by critics and are common practice in some design offices, the amount of time involved in creating precise drawings or models by traditional means is a frequent dissuasion to the single student working alone.

Another important finding was the compositional differences between the two groups. The results indicated that media made a significant difference on formal compositions in student designs. The digital media group created more balanced compositions than the other group (see Table 2). Therefore, in comparison, their designs were clearer, more consistent and were assessed of having better design quality than the manual media group.

An unexpected finding was that contrary to my expectations, the results showed almost no difference in spatial density for both groups. It was found that both groups had similar densities regardless their involvement of different media. It was unclear why spatial density was not effected by media choice. Further studies are needed to investigate some possible explanations such as the limitations, constraints and scale of the project.

Overall, these findings indicated that digital media help to enable the study, exploration and formation of visual and spatial continuity between different architectural formal elements and therefore effected the basic principles of form in design. This suggests that digital media allow students to see their designs as a formal organization and to develop balanced compositions.

5.4 Design Quality

Overall, the results showed considerable differences between the two groups. In a randomly selected sample, all design issues and projects (with one exception) were evaluated favorably for the digital media projects. Since this measurement was taken based on categorical survey questions, it was possible to identify certain aspects. Accordingly, in digital media projects, "Spaces" and "Design Concepts" received significantly higher quality scores whereas manual media projects scored below average.

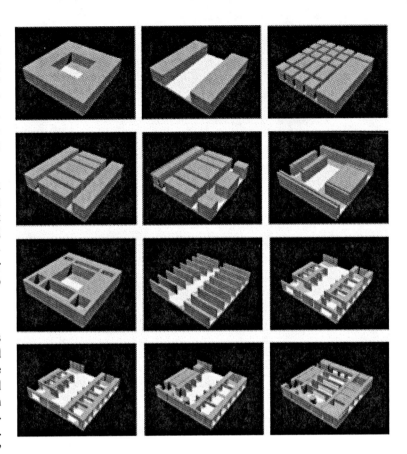

Figure 4. Sequential exploration of form in a digital media group project

These results were later verified with a second round of evaluations of all samples and the results of the second evaluation correlated with the previous one by favoring the digital media projects. On average, the digital media group scored above average (0.56) and the manual media group below average (-0.16) on a Likert scale. Furthermore, comparative analyses showed significant correlations between the quantitative and qualitative results and suggested a relationship between media and design. According to the results, certain design issues were correlated more than others. For example, "donut" and "nine-square" partis, "grid" organizations, "datum" and "repetition" ordering systems in design concepts category seemed to be related to better design quality. All of these conceptual types were found overwhelmingly more often in the digital media group's projects. Other design issues, such as planes' porosity, spatial definitions, orthogonality, balanced compositions were significantly different in the digital media group's projects and these differences were correlated with better design quality. For example, The more porous the primary walls, the higher the design quality became ($r = 0.65$, $p=<0.0001$) (see Figure 5).

Descriptive Statistics

	Mean	Std. Dev.	Std. Error	Count	Minimum	Maximum	# Missing	Range
Digital – Spatial Design/Composition/Balance	-1.000	1.552	.231	45	-5.000	0.000	0	5.000
Manual – Spatial Design/Composition/Balance	-2.511	2.149	.320	45	-5.000	3.000	0	8.000

Table 2: Descriptive statistics of balance in both groups.

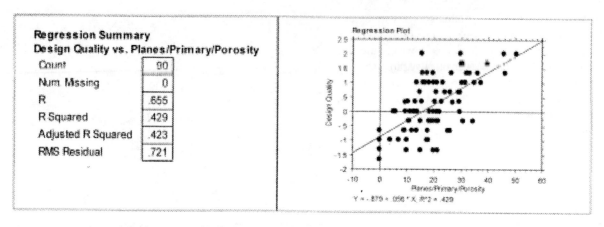

Figure 5. The results indicated a strong correlation between the porosity level of primary planes and the overall design quality

One interesting finding was the combined effect of these issues on design quality. The multiple regression results showed that these issues made individual impacts on the overall design quality in varying degrees but this impact was increased when they were used all together. Another interesting finding was the one-sided, independent effects of some issues. For example, the accessibility of the openings correlated significantly with higher design quality scores, whereas non-accessibility did not seem to make any qualitative difference. In other words, when a design included both accessible and non-accessible openings, the number of accessible ones made a positive difference even though there was no effect for non-accessible openings. The same effect was seen in some other design issues, such as space definitions, space entrance, and object element usage. Moreover, certain important design issues seemed to be missed by the evaluators. These issues were related to the previous one and could even provide an explanation. For example, the surface coverage of horizontal planes was correlated with better design qualities whereas the ratio of space to horizontal plane showed almost a zero correlation. One explanation would be that the evaluators either missed or ignored or were not interested in this kind of ratio while assessing the quality of the project. Regardless of their spatial relationships, using horizontal planes seemed to contribute to the density of the form and that influenced the evaluators. Other explanations would be the identification of the design issues, operationalization, evaluation method or a combination of these. In either case, this issue needs further testing.

Overall, these findings suggested that media not only created quantitative differences in design projects but also affected the quality of the projects. The effects of digital media on basic design properties seemed to have a direct and essential impact in the way architectural design was produced. Students appeared to develop a better understanding on the nature of the design project and made better design decisions.

Furthermore, the results suggested a substantial correlation between the quantitative and qualitative aspects of design. According to these findings, it is fair to conclude that there is a considerable relationship between the media and architectural design. The type of media not only changes some quantifiable design parameters but also affects the quality of design.

6 Bibliography

Akin, O. 1990. Computational Design Instruction: Towards a Pedagogy. In *The Electronic Design Studio*, edited by M. McCullough, W. J. Mitchell and P. Purcell. Cambridge, MA: MIT Press.

Cigolle, M., and K. Coleman. 1990. Computer Integrated Design Studio: Transformation as Process. In *The Electronic Design Studio*, edited by M. McCullough, W. J. Mitchell and P. Purcell. Cambridge, MA: MIT Press.

Cigolle, M., D. Mark, and K. Coleman. 1990. Computer Design Studio: Work in Progress. *Journal of Architectural Education* 43 (3 Spring):26-33.

Danahy, J. 1991. The Computer-Aided Studio Critic: Gaining Control of What We Look At. In *CAAD Futures '91*, edited by G. N. Schmitt. Zurich, Switzerland: Vieweg & Sohn Verlagsgesellschaft.

Danahy, J. W. 1990. Irises in a Landscape: An Experiment in Dynmaic Interaction and Teaching Design Studio. In *The Electronic Design Studio*, edited by M. McCullough, W. J. Mitchell and P. Purcell. Cambridge, MA: MIT Press.

Eastman, C., and J. Lang. 1991. Experiments in Architectural Design Development Using CAD. In *CAAD Futures '91*, edited by G. N. Schmitt. Zurich, Switzerland: Vieweg & Sohn Verlagsgesellschaft.

Herbert, D. M. 1992. A media course in architectural study drawings: American Institute of Architects Education Programs Monograph, 1991 Education Honors.

Herbert, D. M. 1994. A Critical Analysis of Design Processes and Media: Applications for Computer-Aided Design. *ACADIA '94: Reconnecting*:133-146.

Kozma, R. B. 1993. Will Media Influence Learning? Reframing the Debate. *Educational Technology Research and Development* (1):1-31.

Mitchell, W. J., and M. McCullough. 1991. *Digital Design Media*. New York, NY: Van Nostrand Reinhold.

Parsons, P. 1994. Craft and Geometry in Architecture: An Experimental Design Studio Using the Computer. *ACADIA '94: Reconnecting*:171-176.

Pea, R. 1985. Beyond Amplification: Using the Computer to Reorganize Mental Functioning. *Educational Psychologist* (20):167-182.

Saggio, A. 1992. Object-based Modeling and Concept Testing: A Framework for Studio Teaching. Paper read at ACADIA '92 Proceedings: Mission, Method, Madness, at University of Southern California.

Salomon, G. 1993. No Distribution Without Individuals' Cognition. In *Distributed Cognitions*, edited by G. Salomon. New York, NY: Cambridge University Press.

Salomon, G., D. Perkins, and T. Globerson. 1991. Partners in Cognition: Extending Human Intelligence with Intelligent Technologies. *Educational Researcher* 20 (3):2-9.

Smulevich, G. 1993. CAD In The Design Studio: The Discovery of Inhabitation. *ACADIA '93: Education and Practice*:69-75.

Walters, R. 1985. CAAD: Shorter-term gains; longer-term costs? Paper read at Computer-Aided Design Futures, at Netherlands.

Evaluating the Complexity of CAD Models as a Measure for Student Assessment

Scott Chase and Paul Murty, University of Sydney, Australia

Abstract

The feasibility of a proposed CAD project is often judged in terms of two conceptions of complexity: design complexity, based on visible features of the object to be modeled; and CAD complexity, based on the actual CAD embodiment of the design. The latter is suggested as a more useful guide. Clearer articulation of this underutilized concept is proposed for use in both educational and industrial settings. A formal model of CAD complexity is introduced, and initial experiments to determine the complexity of CAD models are described.

1 Introduction

A frequent culmination of computer aided design (CAD) teaching is the self-directed project, for which a student produces a CAD drawing or model. Each student selects a suitable design and develops and implements strategies to produce and display their model. During discussions with students on choice of project and general approach, matters of complexity inevitably arise. For any individual there is an optimal range of complexity. A too modest project may fail to challenge and extend, if the potential to extend the individual's technical knowledge is not exploited. An overly complex undertaking, if not recognized and corrected early, may consume many fruitless hours of effort, leaving the individual frustrated, demoralized and mistrustful of CAD technology.

Two interpretations of complexity are often discussed at the outset. One is based on the appearance of the object to be modeled; we call this *design complexity*. The second, *CAD complexity*, is based on the actual CAD embodiment of the design.

Design complexity is the more popular indicator of manual drafting task magnitude, because it is visible before work commences. Appearances can be misleading, however, especially in CAD production, where the magnitude of a task is highly dependent upon the designer's interpretation, what is modeled, and methods of representation. Superficial aspects of drawings and photographic images can mislead and short-circuit a designer's detailed analysis and planning at the commencement of their CAD task unless they are balanced by equally clear notions of the intended model.

CAD complexity is associated with the actual CAD embodiment of the design. It derives from the strategic use of CAD functions applied to both organization and production of the completed model. It is potentially a more useful notion than design complexity, because it directly concerns task outcomes, but it appears to have been underutilized. There are several reasons why this may be so. First, the concept of complexity is not entirely clear (Corning 1998). Although there is an abundance of published literature on complexity (e.g., Garey and Johnson 1979; Shannon and Weaver 1963; Simon 1996), much is about complexity in nature and relatively little is relevant to CAD. There is a need to clarify the sense of the term as it applies to CAD.

Another difficulty is that CAD complexity is not evident from the appearance of drawings generated from a completed model. Other indicators, such as the number of files or file sizes are no more revealing, unless some account is taken of the file contents. There is a need to identify the essential components of complexity.

Informal observations of students undertaking CAD courses in the Faculty of Architecture at the

University of Sydney indicate that many find it difficult to appreciate broader organizational aspects of CAD until their work is well advanced. A likely reason for this is a need to experience the consequences of different strategies in order to understand their significance. The possession of a tangible model-in-progress to see and discuss is obviously helpful as well. To bring tangibility to the start of projects there is a need to develop a consistent and coherent nomenclature of CAD complexity in a form that can be presented and understood before modeling commences.

Greater understanding of CAD complexity may also be useful to performance of a range of management activities in educational and other settings. Educational tasks could include

- matching project complexity to student knowledge and skill levels more accurately at the onset of a project;
- developing bases for modulating complexity during the course of a project; and
- developing objective criteria of use in comparison and assessment of completed CAD models.

Other strategic uses could include support for the development of

- bases for evaluating and coordinating the integration of CAD and related software;
- improvements to specific CAD techniques; and
- a general CAD methodology.

The remainder of the paper is structured as follows. Section 2 identifies concepts of complexity we consider in our study. Section 3 describes the subsystems of CAD organization that form the basis for our model of CAD complexity. Sections 4-6 describe ongoing experiments in testing the formal model of CAD, and future work. Section 7 offers some conclusions.

2 Concepts of Complexity

We begin by defining concepts considered important in understanding CAD complexity. In this paper the term "CAD model" refers to one or more computer files that are intended to describe or represent visual or other properties of a design.

2.1 Properties of Complexity

Corning (1998) identifies properties commonly associated with the term 'complexity'. He states that complexity often implies the following attributes:

- A complex phenomenon consists of many parts;
- There are many relationships/interactions among the parts;
- The parts produce combined effects that are not easily predicted and may often be novel.

2.2 Interpretations of Complexity

Although complexity has been described above in a broad sense, we offer some common interpretations of the term and select those that are relevant. These are described below.

Degree of Difficulty. It is recognized that complexity of a CAD task can influence its difficulty. Since many other factors also influence task difficulty, we do not explore this relationship.

Real Complexity. There is a difference between 'real' complexity, objectively measurable and substantially irreducible, and 'apparent' complexity, a matter of perception and interpretation, varying from one person to another. Our interest here is in measuring real complexity.

Necessary Complexity. Human artifacts typically contain both necessary and unnecessary elements, both intended and unintended. The CAD complexity of this study is that which may be regarded as intended and necessary. We do not consider here the area of CAD intentions, but acknowledge that CAD models produced for one purpose are frequently put to other uses.

Organized Complexity. Weaver (1948) distinguishes between disorganized and organized complexity. Since CAD models can be considered ordered systems, we focus here on organized complexity.

2.3 Complex Systems

CAD models are systems, in that they combine any of the above attributes of complexity within some integrated form. Complex CAD models are complex systems, based on the Simon's description that complex systems are "made up of a large number of parts that have many interactions." (1996, p. 183)

Research into complex systems has been stimulated in recent years by studies of chaos. One outcome of this research has been a greater interest in the study of complexity in its own right (Simon

1996, p.181; Salingaros 2000), including the study of ordered complex systems.

CAD models, at least as we currently understand them, can be considered ordered complex systems, in both: a) design complexity, since order can be considered an objective of design; and b) CAD complexity, since the CAD model is an embodiment of some form of order. This need not always be true; some aspects of design complexity, and some functions of CAD modeling, such as surface representation, may involve the intentional use of chaos, e.g., for artistic purposes.

Simon (1996) makes the following observations about complex systems:

- Complexity of a system depends critically upon how it is described.
- Most complex systems contain a lot of redundancy.
- Simplicity of description can be achieved by finding the right representation.
- Hierarchies of complex systems can often be described in economical terms.

In applying these observations to CAD models we conclude that a first step towards achieving an economical description of CAD complexity is the identification of CAD hierarchies.

2.4 Complexity Criteria for Graphic Systems

A number of different criteria have been identified and used as measures of complexity for graphic objects. One of the earliest measures was developed by Birkhoff (1933), who based shape complexity on the number of sides of a polygon, leading to a formula for measuring aesthetic values. Attneave (1957) used matrix grain, curvedness, symmetry, number of turns, degree of compactness and angular variability as parameters in his experiments. Stiny and Gips (1978) suggested that the lengths of shape descriptions and generative specifications define shape complexity, following similar work in information theory (Chaitin 1975). Salingaros (1997) has used an analogy with thermodynamic complexity to describe the complexity of drawings of buildings by measuring thermodynamic temperature and architectural harmony. A recent Ph.D. thesis (Cha 1998) develops measures for shape complexity using pattern representations.

2.5 CAD vs. Design Complexity

The complexity of a CAD model is influenced by design complexity to the extent that properties of the design or modeled object are represented in its CAD embodiment. It may be inferred that the distinguishing elements of CAD complexity derive from something other than these properties. An object may be interpreted and represented in different ways by designers for a number of reasons, and in different ways by CAD systems due to variations in system functionality. One could also observe that distinctions between a CAD embodiment and the designed object arise from the fact of representation. We therefore believe that distinguishing elements of CAD complexity can arise from characteristics of CAD interpretation and representation.

2.6 Sources of CAD Complexity

Three possible sources of CAD complexity can be distinguished: CAD data, or the information content of the CAD model; CAD structure, associated with the model's file organization; and properties associated with application software functionality.

CAD data. Here we consider element type and differentiation (variety) within a model. Items in this category include the actual components of the CAD model, i.e. shapes and annotations:

- Shapes or figural information includes vectors and inserted raster images. Graphic symbols, such as North points and hatch blocks may also be considered as belonging to this category.
- Annotation includes dimensions, other numeric data, and drawing notations, such as headings, notes or title blocks. Also included is documentation to facilitate communication, but not necessarily part of the model.

Measures of CAD data include quantities such as numbers and variation of objects, shape complexity and non-geometric properties. In measuring the complexity of notation, fonts, scales and other properties that fulfill specific presentation requirements become relevant. Further distinction can be made between data that is part of the design and data that is part of its presentation. It should be noted that raw CAD data may appear to be repetitious, difficult to analyze and reflect design complexity more than CAD complexity.

CAD structure. Here we consider the organization of the CAD data in a model. Items in this category include file variables and inter-file variables:

- File variables include functions that support differentiation and organization of data within individual files, such as colors, line types, layers and complex objects. Complexity measures may be similar in principle to those used for measuring CAD data.

- Inter-file variables include functions that support organization and inter-file referencing of data. Typically files are of the same type: use of different file types may require data translation.

CAD model structural elements are highly capable of analysis and decomposition by reference to CAD functions. Many support hierarchical organization, making them suitable for use in describing CAD complexity based on organizational subsystems (described in Section 3).

Application software. CAD software varies significantly in the extent and manner of its support of CAD production, editing and display functions. This influences not only how models are created, but also what is created. Given the large number of different CAD products, this is beyond the scope of our project.

We do offer some indication of the manner and extent of software variations by using as reference two different CAD applications, AutoCAD and ArchiCAD. Significant differences of approach and function are highlighted where appropriate in the description of each of the organizational subsystems.

3 Subsystems of CAD Organisation

At this point we identify and describe various CAD model hierarchies, categorizing five subsystems of CAD organization, on the basis of organizational processes. There are four categories described, in order from low to high level of organization. This order coincides with the least to most technically advanced, with the least to greatest potential to provide high levels of efficient model realization. We include a fifth category (pre-sets) that incorporates peripheral factors, which are integral to the communication of a model, but are not part of it.

3.1 Object Differentiation

Differentiation is a simple, non-hierarchical structuring that implies grouping within a model file. It may be achieved by varying one or more appearance characteristics, enabling one to visually identify different classes of element, or particular parts of a model. Its main characteristics include:

Shape. Different shapes can represent different objects. Proximity and orientation of shapes to each other or to some ordered form, such as a grid, may also be employed to assist recognition.

Color. Variation in hue, saturation and other object color properties enable different classes or conditions of objects to be visually distinguished regardless of shape. Typical CAD software allows association of colors with pens, thus enabling plotted line thickness to be modulated by means of color.

Line type. Particular repeating patterns of shorter lines, dots, symbols and spaces facilitate the visual distinction of linear objects, such as centerlines, particularly when they overlay other objects.

3.2 Object Grouping

Grouping is a method of relating objects within a model file, to act as one, by means of one or more of the following functions:

Figure 1. Object differentiation: varying shape, colour, line type

Informal or unnamed grouping. CAD software supports informal, one level groupings in different ways, e.g.:

- AutoCAD 'polylines' may be drawn as a continuous string of lines or formed by converting a series of end-to-end objects into a complex polyline.
- The ArchiCAD 'Drafting Modifier' option allows a designer to draw a continuous string of lines. These may be converted into one continuous object, through use of one of the ArchiCAD building tools, e.g. the Slab tool.

Formal object-class grouping. CAD applications support open ended class groupings by allowing designers to assign elements to named layers. The use of layers enables designers to control display properties, such as color and line type, and selection properties of different classes of design elements. Layer hierarchies, of two or more levels, may be a feature of the system, or can be created implicitly by the use of layer naming conventions.

Formal or named-object grouping. The ability to group objects and build complex hierarchies of nested objects has long been associated with drawing applications. Use of named 'blocks' in AutoCAD to 'modularize' a design enables designers to achieve significant economies of file size and simplify the production of a CAD model.

Patterns. An additional grouping is the pattern, generally not supported in commercial CAD systems currently available. A pattern can describe such relationships between objects as translation and rotational symmetry; these may be intentionally created by the user, but are not explicitly stored in the CAD model. Sophisticated pattern recognition routines are typically utilized to identify such relationships in a design (Cha 1998); however, the complexity of most CAD models would likely prohibit effective utilization.

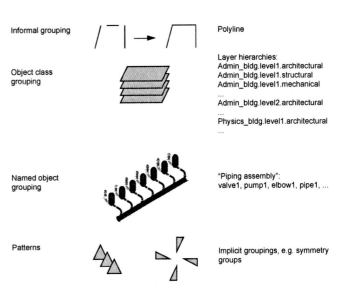

Figure 2. Different types of object grouping

3.3 File Grouping

Complex CAD models that require a significant amount of production time, or more than one author, generally warrant the organization of design objects into multiple files. AutoCAD External Referencing allows a drawing file to be 'attached' to another. ArchiCAD supports file grouping by means of Library files, an alternative to AutoCAD blocks. On large projects external references may be used instead of blocks as a means of reducing inconsistencies among files. Both systems allow hierarchies of attachments to be developed and include validation procedures to prevent circular referencing.

3.4 Application Grouping

A trend in the evolution of computer applications is toward increasing functionality and complexity. This is indicated by the number of additional functions, increasing memory and disk space requirements with each new version of software. Associated with the general growth is the growing mobility of data among applications.

Linking CAD software to external database or spreadsheet applications is now commonplace. Recent trends toward the development of sophisticated dynamic models, capable of simulating complex facilities, will further stimulate multiple file and application structuring, making this a fertile source of new hierarchies.

3.5 Pre-sets

Predefined settings (pre-sets) that control object display can facilitate communication of a model of substantial complexity. While not part of the model, pre-sets can be considered agents for the expression of the model's organizational hierarchy. We therefore consider them as part of an overall strategy to manage complexity. Examples of pre-sets include

- *Filter lists.* Filter options in AutoCAD permit designers to limit the display of different classes of object, based on color, line type and other properties, such as location, current in-use status, or their association with externally referenced files.
- *Layer Sets.* Combinations of layers in ArchiCAD files may be defined, named and saved, as named layer sets in the Layer Menu.
- *Named Views.* The View command in AutoCAD permits designers to store combinations of viewpoint coordinates, orientation and zoom in the form of named views.
- *Other Display settings.* There are many other useful pre-sets, e.g. page layout functions, which include ArchiCAD Plotmaker and AutoCAD Paperspace/Layout.

4 CAD Model Construction

Here we describe a number of experiments in constructing of CAD models, to be later evaluated according to the complexity criteria. There are a number of ways that model construction can be varied in order to test our model of complexity. We describe them below, noting which ones are examined in our pilot project and which could be explored in further research.

4.1 Modelling techniques

A building can be modeled using 2D representations such as plan, section and elevation, or by 3D representations such as wireframe, surface or solid representations. Model organization can also be varied by the use of devices such as layers, blocks, external references, and single vs. multiple file organization. We focus here on the organizing devices.

4.2 CAD systems

This can have profound effects upon the representation of the model. For example, AutoCAD is a generic CAD system, requiring the user to model with geometric primitives such as lines, surfaces and solids. ArchiCAD uses a very different modeling paradigm, oriented toward the architectural user, who primarily models higher level architectural elements such as walls, doors and roofs. We therefore expect that a model constructed with one system will have different measures of complexity to one constructed with another system.

4.3 Design complexity

How does one compare the two designs in Figures 3a and 3b? 3a depicts the design of a student residence that has many components, with heavy use of repetitive elements. Does this produce a more complex model than that in 3b (Rietveld-Schröder house), a smaller building with fewer components but little repetition?

Measures of design complexity could stem from the measures of shape complexity described in Section 2.4. Stiny and Gips *(1978)* define aesthetic value of a design as the ratio length of its description: length of its generative specification.

The length of a description is analogous to the size of a CAD model file, as information such as color tables, block descriptions and instances are often stored internal to the file. The generative specification is analogous to the sequence of commands used to construct the model. A generative specification is precise, while a designer's CAD construction methods will vary from person to person, and even session to session. Protocol studies could, however, be useful in generating specifications for CAD model development (Flemming, Bhavnani, and John 1997).

We note that design complexity may also influence the choice of CAD system and modeling technique. Experience has shown that, for a design consisting of curved surfaces and 'freeform' shapes, students are more likely to choose a CAD system such as FormZ, which allows easier modeling of such objects than AutoCAD.

4.4 Individuals

Each individual develops her or his own style and modeling technique. Part of our study consists of comparing models of the same design, but constructed by different individuals.

As an example, compare two AutoCAD models of the same building (Figures 3d and 3e), developed by different students. The modeling techniques varied, with a significant difference in CAD file size (file D is more than twice the size of file E). Analysis of these models and similar ones are described in the Appendix.

While we use multiple subjects to construct the models, measuring the variability of the results by user requires a larger number of subjects and models constructed than possible for our initial study. We therefore give our subjects specific guidelines for model construction in order to control the variability of technique. Our goal is to develop data extraction and analysis techniques that can be applied to any CAD model, thereby enabling recognition of particular patterns or inclinations in student modeling.

5 Measurement of Complexity

At this point, data is extracted from the CAD models and analyzed. The results give us measures of the complexity of the models. Among the criteria used in comparison are:

- counts of element types;
- use of blocks, external references and layers;
- other types of repetition and differentiation.

As an illustration of the some of the analysis issues, results from a group of student produced AutoCAD files are described below, with a small number illustrated in the Appendix.

Our initial studies have involved examination of models produced by students using AutoCAD in introductory courses. The work of the architects Glenn Murcutt and Tadao Ando are popular modeling choices for students in our Faculty. The designs often contain a large number of repeated elements, thus serving as a good basis for design and model analysis. We have a small but useful sample of models that can be used as a basis for comparison.

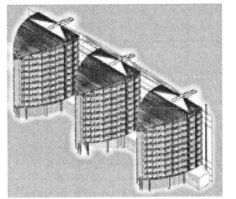

Figure 3a. Clingancourt student residence

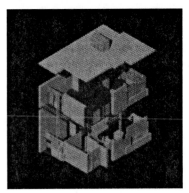

Figure 3b. Rietveld-Schröder house.

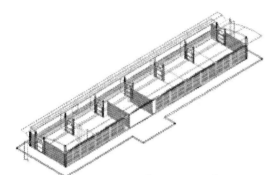

Figure 3c. Magney house (Glenn Murcutt).

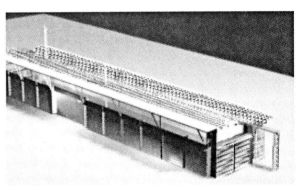

Figure 3d. Magney house (Glenn Murcutt).

Figure 3e. Magney house (Glenn Murcutt).

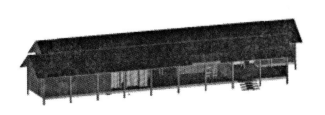

Figure 3f. Marie Short house (Glenn Murcutt).

Figure 3g. Marie Short house (Glenn Murcutt).

As expected from novice modelers, the files vary substantially in their respective quantities of objects, suggesting different modeling approaches among files, and even inconsistencies within files. Files produced by more experienced individuals are likely to show more consistency.

The main observation from this small sample is that measured quantities of various file elements are not especially revealing on their own, but may be useful indicators of where one should look to determine particular file characteristics. These include inconsistencies of technique, or extensive use (or lack) of various organizational or production methods.

In the current study students create designated CAD models according to specific criteria. Comparisons are made of the utilization of certain modeling techniques, including:

- Blocks vs. non-grouped objects vs. xrefs
- Layers
- Multiple file usage, including xrefs
- Color styles

We have focused initially on block descriptions and layer usage, the two most common organizational tools of the novice user. Measurements are taken of:

- Model file size;
- Number of objects (this includes graphical objects such as arcs and polylines, nongraphical objects such as layers and linetypes, and block definitions);
- Numbers of block definitions and block instances (user defined only);
- Model file size and number of objects after one iteration of block/element explosion; these values give a measure of the extent to which blocks and other complex elements are utilized.

The ratios of these values provide a crude metric of relative complexity, particularly as a means of indicating where a student may have used these organizational tools to a great or lesser extent (Table 1). Future work will involve refinement of these metrics.

	Clingan-court	Rietveld-Schröder	Magney house			Marie Short house	
Student	A Fig. 3a	B Fig. 3b	C Fig. 3c	D Fig. 3d	E Fig. 3e	F Fig. 3f	G Fig. 3g
file size (KB)	5087	3715	1161	2113	994	332	2876
no. objs	1967	3071	874	695	1164	5808	2797
no. layers	26	42	18	7	23	55	108
no. block defs	43	0	13	1	9	23	20
no. block instances	290	0	120	7	29	1367	272
objs/block instance	6.78	N/A	7.28	99.29	40.14	4.25	10.28
instances/block def	6.74	N/A	9.23	7.00	3.22	59.43	13.60
objs/layer	75.65	73.12	48.56	99.29	50.61	105.60	25.90
size/obj	2.59	1.21	1.33	3.04	0.85	0.06	1.03
EXPLODED							
file size (KB)	26346	5569	7547	3199	1801	6151	7462
no. objs	4662	9812	1999	2294	2301	129298	9556
objs/block instance	16.08	N/A	16.66	327.71	79.34	94.59	35.13
objs/layer	179.31	233.62	111.06	327.71	100.04	2350.87	88.48
size/obj	5.65	0.57	3.78	1.39	0.78	0.05	0.78
COMPARISONS							
exploded size/orig objs	13.39	1.81	8.64	4.60	1.55	1.06	2.67
orig size/explode size	0.19	0.67	0.15	0.66	0.55	0.05	0.39
orig size/exploded objs	0.42	0.31	0.44	0.30	0.51	0.04	0.29

Table 1. CAD model data.

How can one combine these various measures to give an accurate assessment of CAD complexity? Is this even necessary? In terms of student assessment, a simple weighting of the criteria could suffice. This may, however, reflect the student's usage of a particular feature rather than the actual complexity of the model.

6 Formal Model Evaluation and Future Work

We are currently in the process of automating the extraction process in order to produce statistical summaries of model file data and organization. These can then be utilized in formal assessment of student models.

In a future stage of work we will evaluate the formal model to determine whether it provides a useful measure of CAD complexity. By examining the CAD model analysis, we will determine whether any normalization of the data is possible, whether there are any trends or anomalies to be found, and whether the results coincide with our expectations drawn from experience. The evaluation of this experiment also allows us to determine the feasibility of continuing the project on a larger scale by utilizing a larger sample set of CAD models and testing more of the complexity criteria from our formal model.

The results should provide insights regarding the use of formal measures of complexity to improve the usage of CAD technology in the selection and assessment of student projects, as well as in practice.

7 Conclusions

The CAD subsystems described above provide a basis for measurement of five different aspects of complexity. Within each there are more variables to measure.

Complexity, like intelligence, or the weather, includes both interdependent components and others that act independently. Unlike intelligence, CAD complexity itself is not an objective; the goals are to optimize and manage complexity. Unlike the weather, complexity can be controlled. Measurement of CAD complexity is fundamental to both optimization and control.

The implications of these observations extend beyond the educational context. Ultimately, CAD is about communication, and that changes everywhere technology progresses. CAD usage is evolving beyond single task "throw away" functions of project-based design and construction, towards interoperability and longer-term applications, such as large-scale system simulations and facility management. Interoperability requires greater consistency in the use of CAD as well as the design of CAD software. Long-term applications demand both consistency and durability of CAD models. As these factors grow in importance, so does the need to further develop and refine principles and concepts of CAD organization, based on objective measurement.

Acknowledgements

The models shown in this paper were constructed by students in introductory CAD classes in the Faculty of Architecture, University of Sydney, during the period 1998-2000. This research is partially funded under the Small Grant Scheme of the Australian Research Council.

References

Attneave, Fred. 1957. Physical Determinants of the Judged Complexity of Shapes. *Journal of Experimental Psychology* 53 (4):221-227.

Birkhoff, George David. 1933. *Aesthetic Measure*. Cambridge, Mass.: Harvard University Press.

Cha, Myung Yeol. 1998. Architectural Shape Pattern Representation and Its Implications for Design Computation. Ph.D. thesis, University of Sydney.

Chaitin, G. 1975. Randomness and Mathematical Proof. *Scientific American* 232:47-52.

Corning, Peter A. 1998. Complexity Is Just a Word! *Technological Forecasting and Social Change* 59:197-200.

Flemming, Ulrich, Suresh K. Bhavnani, and Bonnie E. John. 1997. Mismatched metaphor: user vs system model in computer-aided drafting. *Design Studies* 18:349-368.

Garey, Michael R., and David S. Johnson. 1979. *Computers and Intractability: A Guide to the Theory of NP-completeness*. San Francisco: W. H. Freeman.

Salingaros, Nikos A. 1997. Life and Complexity in Architecture From a Thermodynamic Analogy. *Physics Essays* 10.163-173.

Salingaros, Nikos. A. 2000. Hierarchical Cooperation of Architectural Scales, and the Mathematical Necessity for Ornament. *Journal of Architectural and Planning Research* 17, forthcoming.

Shannon, Claude Elwood, and Warren Weaver. 1963. *The Mathematical Theory of Communication*. Urbana, Ill.: University of Illinois Press.

Simon, Herbert A. 1996. *The Sciences of the Artificial*. 3rd ed. Cambridge, Mass.: MIT Press.

Stiny, George, and James Gips. 1978. *Algorithmic Aesthetics: Computer Models for Criticism and Design in the Arts*. Berkeley: University of California Press.

Weaver, W. 1948. Science and Complexity. *American Scientist* 36:536-544.

Appendix

We provide here a more detailed analysis of the models described in Section 5. Some analysis of the data and images of the models follow the table.

A comparison of files A and B illustrates the issue of design complexity vs. CAD complexity. Both models were created by students who appear relatively capable with CAD technology, as evidenced by their final presentations. The file sizes are of the same order, with a ratio of about 1.4:1. However, Model A (Clingancourt student residence) represents a design with a considerable amount of repetition, while Model B represents one (Rietveld-Schröder house) with relatively little. This is borne out by the relative use of blocks in the two files (none at all in file B[*]). A one iteration explosion of file elements increases file A fivefold, but file B only 50%.

Variations in students' modeling techniques can be seen in files C, D and E, which represent the same building. File C makes significant use of blocks, the others, less so.

There may not be a direct correspondence between file size and number of objects, as evidenced in files D and F:

- File D is very large for the number of objects it contains. The object/file size ratio is approximately 1:3. The author has created only one effective block definition, this being the triangular element repeated along the high edge of the roof. The high file size is largely due to the louvers, each of which is an individual 3D solid.
- File F, in contrast, contains a large number of objects given its size, with a size/object ratio of approximately 17:1. An examination of the file indicates that extensive use is made of blocks in the drawing of the roof structure, skylights and louvers, explaining the relatively small file size. However, some block definitions are comparatively small and specialized and there are a number of them, e.g. the roof panels. The large number of objects can be explained by the combination of simple blocks and line work. This file can be considered a good example of tectonic modeling, i.e. an assembly of the actual construction components of the design.

File G is a large file with an object to file size ratio of approximately 1:1 despite having a large number of block instances. A possible explanation is the author's extensive use of individual 3D solids in addition to blocks.

---

[*] The omission of blocks could reflect upon the student's CAD modeling skills or his understanding of the design itself as lacking repetitive elements.

Web

Since the popularization of the Internet and the protocols known as the World Wide Web, computing has token on a dramatically altered character. Computing is merging with communications, personal, print and broadcast, in what is becoming known as ICT (Information and Communications Technology). As research within ACADIA in networked collaboration and hypermedia predates the Web, it is fitting that ACADIA 2000 should include new experiments that explore how the latest incarnation of ICT can aid the design process.

In the first article in this section, by Jung and Do, the authors report the invention, implementation and trial of a new tool supporting architectural collaboration by annotating VRML models. Users can post notes and commentary onto the VRML model, which they have successfully done in a real world design project. The paper by Jabi also describes new software for collaborating using the Web, this time focused on the programming or pre-design stage of an architectural project.

The final paper, by Chan, reports on a practical effort to assist in attaining conformance to building code restrictions using 3D visualization of an urban environment. Although it makes use of high end modeling environments such as immersive virtual reality systems, the work is also intended to be distributed to the profession and the public using the Web.

The range of computer-aided communication and collaboration applications for architects is very broad and remains little explored. These articles suggest that researchers are working hard to apply the technology in imaginative ways to real-world problems.

Immersive Redliner: Collaborative Design in Cyberspace

Thomas Jung, Design Machine Group, University of Washington, USA

Ellen Yi-Luen Do, Design Machine Group, University of Washington, USA

Abstract

The Immersive Redliner supports annotation of three-dimensional artifacts in collaborative design. It enables team members to drop annotation markers in a VRML world that are linked to comment text stored on a server. Visitors to the world later can review the design annotations in the locations where they were made. We report on two phases of the Redliner project: the first involves a hypothetical design scenario, the second a real application on a rehabilitation in a residence building in Strasbourg.

Keywords: annotation, collaboration, design, virtual worlds, redlining.

1 Introduction and Motivation

Comments and critique are essential components of a successful design process. In physical domains such as architectural design, critique and comments usually refer directly to design components or are otherwise bound to a particular location. Traditionally, designers record and exchange review comments and critiques through annotation of design drawings, or 'redlining'.

Design collaboration can occur in a synchronous or asynchronous way. With the rapid development and information accessibility of the Internet and the World Wide Web, we explore the idea of putting a three-dimensional design representation on-line for asynchronous virtual visits, commentary, or redlining.

Our Immersive Redliner provides a framework for Web based critiquing of three-dimensional designs. The current system employs a VRML browser, Java applets, and server-side CGI scripts to mediate the actions of multiple viewers who visit a virtual model and leave behind annotation markers (like PostIt notes) with comments on the design.

2 Communication and Collaboration in Cyberspace

Collaboration among architects, their colleagues, and clients by commenting on design documents is a well-accepted practice. The traditional method of communication and collaboration among designers at different locations is sending the information via paper media. For example, when designing the Carpenter Center for the Visual Arts, Le Corbusier collaborated with the site architects in Boston by mailing documents, drawings, and photographs of the physical models from France (Sekler 1978).

Currently, architecture firms use communication modes such as express mail, telephone, and fax machine to communicate with colleagues around the world. Some use electronic media such as email and file transfer to send drawing files or specification spreadsheets to their collaborators at different locations. This is a straightforward way of communication. However, sending files across the Internet creates new management problems. Architects must consider time differences between remote locations and provide version control mechanisms for shared documents. It is therefore desirable to have a virtual space for all concerned parties to visit, review and make changes to the design at their convenience. Our Redliner project explores the idea that the space should take a three-dimensional form that allows reviewers to leave their comments for others to consider later.

3 Related Work

The Redliner project was developed with three major concerns in mind: collaboration, annotation and 3D representation. It supports indexed annotation of 3D artifacts in a virtual world for workgroup collaboration. Below, we briefly review some related research projects and commercial software.

Annotation has been studied in various domains of collaboration. Marshall (Marshall 1998) studied annotation of physical texts to understand the implications for hypertext authoring in a shared commentary practice. Many papers at Human Computer Interface (HCI) conferences emphasize the need for and focus on the means to enhance awareness of collaboration from remote locations (Greenberg, 1992). In design, many systems have been built to support three-dimensional representation (Schweikardt, 1998), on-line critiques (Wojtowicz, 1995), synchronous collaboration through drawing (Qian, 1999), and using gestures to create virtual worlds (Donath 1996).

With similar goals to ours, McCall et al (McCall 1998) added to his PHIDIAS system a 3-dimensional representation module called "Web PHIDIAS". Based on VRML, it allowed users to click on certain objects and leave comments about these pre-selected objects on a system server. Craig and Zimring at Georgia Tech developed a system that allows people to drop arrows and other objects in a VRML scene (Craig, 1999). Campbell tried communicating construction documents with a contractor through 3D VRML models to fabricate a flight of stairs (Cambell 1998). Although similar to our Immersive Redliner, these systems are less versatile, because the design objects must be specially prepared to accept annotation. In the Immersive Redliner, any VRML model can be imported and serve as the basis for annotation.

Some commercial applications also allow users to annotate while viewing 3D objects. For example, eZ (http://www.ezmeeting.com/) viewer, like Microsoft's NetMeeting, provides viewing of operations and mark-up on documents stored at the server site from all client sites. It supports synchronous communication but the viewer does not capture or record the process or results of the collaboration for future reference. The SolidView program from Solid Concepts (http://www.solidview.com/) provides utilities to make presentations such as a slide show or cross section measurements of a prepared three-dimensional model. Users can send the proprietary viewer or slide player to collaborators to show design concepts or assembly procedures. Collaboration by sending explanations with model slide shows is useful, but it is limited to one-way communication.

In the Redliner system design we focus on the need for different stakeholders to choose their own time and pace to explore the design and to post questions and proposals for other participants to review, and thereby to engage in communication and collaboration. We built the Redliner project to facilitate communication among all parties involved in the design development process: architects, engineers, contractors, and clients can review and comment about design issues directly on the design artifacts. We used VRML and Java to build Redliner so it is accessible and easy to use for anyone with a Web browser.

In the following, we describe our efforts building a system that supports critiquing of designs in a virtual environment, and the lessons we learned from our experience with real use testing of this system.

4 First Study: Pavilion House

This section explains the first test of the Immersive Redlining system. We report here a collaboration process and interaction between different design team members in a shared virtual world. A detailed explanation of the functions and features of this scenario is reported elsewhere (Jung, Do, Gross 1999). Here we summarize the procedures of using the basic Redliner system. The second study described in the next section (5) is an extension of this system with more versatile functionality with layer control.

The first step in using the Immersive Redliner is to post a VRML model, constructed using a standard 3-D modeler (we used autodessys's form•Z), on the Redliner Web site. Once it is posted, all design team members can visit the model using a VRML browser. Each visitor can browse the initial model, or the model augmented with annotation markers left by other team members.

Figure 1 below shows an initial login screen. One enters the system by registering name, email address and choosing a color for annotation marks.

Figure 2 shows the layout of the Redliner site. User identification and comments are displayed on the left with a white background; the VRML model of the design is displayed on the right with a black background.

Architects also provide a set of viewpoints (Figure 3) to guide reviewers through the design space. This provides an easy means of navigation, a guided path to experience the design. Of course, reviewers can also wander off at any time and explore the design independently of the path. Any annotation markers dropped later on will also generate a new viewpoint into the list.

4.1 Posting Annotation Markers

To add an annotation to the model, the visitor clicks on a surface or an object, leaving an 'annotation marker' (a color-coded sphere: each visitor selects a color for their markers). The Redliner pops up a comment window for the visitor to enter a title and text for the annotation. The Redliner numbers each visitor's markers sequentially. Figure 4 left shows the interior of an architectural model ("the Pavilion House") and Figure 4 right shows a numbered annotation marker with its associated type-in comment window.

Figure 1. Login screen (left), user inputs email address and chooses an annotation color (right).

Visitors can view comments left by others by clicking on an annotation marker in the model. Each annotation marker records the visitor information and viewing position and links to a time stamped comment stored in a text file on the server. Visitors can also view comments made by each of the other visitors individually, or the entire comment collection sorted by authors and time sequence. Each comment links back to its marker in the model, so a visitor browsing the comment logs can easily examine the part of the model under discussion. In the same way, all annotated models can be displayed on the "list of projects" for easy retrieval of the last annotated project. Figure 5 shows the comment log left by one of the Redliner visitors.

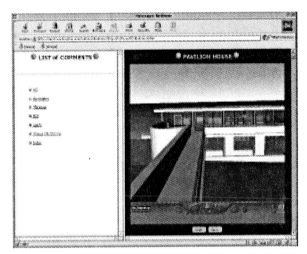

4.2 Design History

The Redliner framework allows posting of any design in a VRML format to facilitate "on site" design communication and collaboration. The three-dimensional space functions not only as repository for comments in the space (on location) but also as a design history, because all comments are time coded and can be retrieved by author index as well.

Figure 2. The Redliner basic layout (text on the left, white – model on the right, black)

4.3 Design Alternatives

In addition to annotating the 3-D virtual world and viewing annotations left by other users, makers of Redliner models can offer visitors design alternatives. Figure 6 shows how, using a menu at the bottom of the browser window, visitors can select among several wall arrangement alternatives for defining the lower floor corner area in the Pavilion house. Alternatives are stored as partial VRML models, and the Redliner adds them to the base model in response to the visitor's requests.

5 Second Study: Housing Rehabilitation

With the initial success of using Redliner for a simple, single residence design, the Pavilion House, we decided to put the system to test in a real design situation involving renovation of an apartment building in Strasbourg, France. We next describe extensions of the original Redliner to accommodate this usability test.

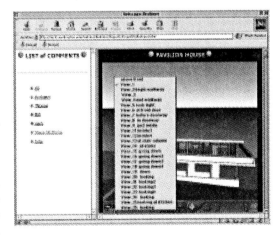

5.1 Building site and program

The site is adjacent to the center of Strasbourg, located at about equal distance from the train station and the universities. It is situated at the edge of the historic area with a view of the well-known cathedral. Although the neighborhood is currently in decay, the city has recently been encouraging construction to revitalize the district. For example, the new Modern Art Museum of Strasbourg has just been built in front of our building, and the new tramway will run through the street right next to the site. The building is a densely occupied four-story apartment complex. The owner wanted to create two new apartments in that space at the top of the building to make maximum use of the space under the eaves of the roof.

Figure 3. Pre-set viewpoints guide visitors through the design.

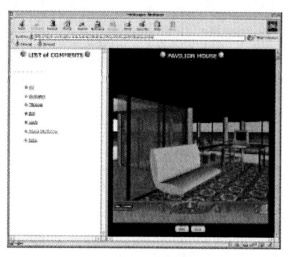 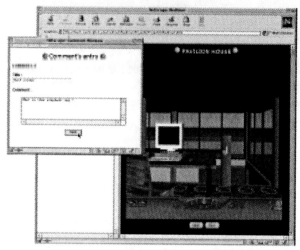

Figure 4. Pavilion house interior (left). Annotation marker in the scene (on the railings) with a comment window (right).

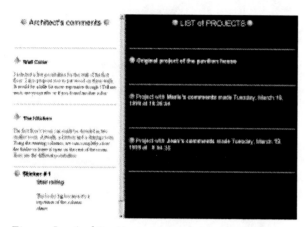

Figure 5. Architect's comments (left) and list of projects with different visitor's annotations (right).

The owner contacted the ARIM, (Association for Building Rehabilitation) to identify an architect. Then we assigned roles to the participants in the experiment: Two architects (including one of us) were part of the architectural team that renovated the whole building, the client also the owner of the building, and a contractor, a technical person from the CRAI (Center for Research in Architecture and Engineering). We used this opportunity to test how the Redliner could work to facilitate communication among members of this team and the client.

During the course of design, participants were informed via postings on the Internet. The information included presentation of the design proposals as text files, plans, sections and pictures of the spaces at the existing stage as pdf or jpg files. Most importantly, the actual design project was presented in Redliner as a three-dimensional model for the design team to explore and comment on.

The project took place over a period of three months with three design phases. The first phase was a "coded" representation of the upper two floors - a hybrid representation combining a traditional 2-

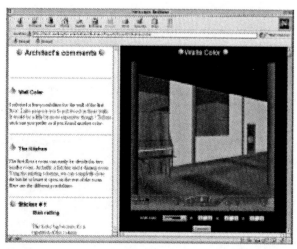 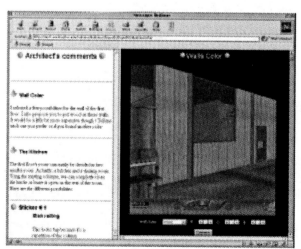

Figure 6. Design alternatives: painted wall (left), wood panel wall (right). Bottom menu allows visitors to mix paint by changing RGB value and selecting wall texture options.

D floor plan with some 3-D model elements. These were represented in an explanatory form. A module was added to Redliner to allow users to view or filter selected layers of the model. For example, figure 7 shows the possibility to view either one or two floors of the same model and figure 8, below, displays either the existing structural constraints such as columns, beams or the existing plumbing configuration, or/and the first design intentions concerning the design of the new apartments.

During the second design phase the architects incorporated comments and suggestions made during the initial 3-D/VRML representation of the site and posted to Redliner a remodeling design proposal (figure 9).

Finally, the third phase involved a proposal of several design alternatives in response to the user comments. We posted on the Redliner several design options concerning issues that were raised

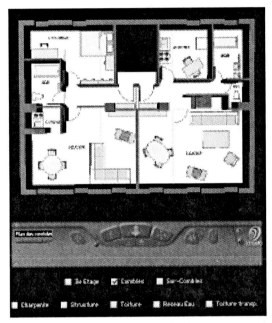 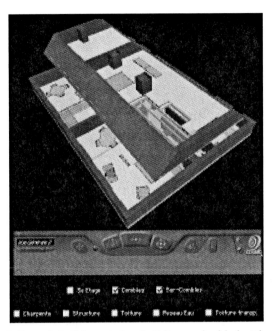

Figure 7. Design Phase I (Hybrid representation). The 3-D model of the existing building embedded with several layers (checkboxes at the bottom of the browser) for participants to explore different design issues. Left. floor plan with furniture layout. Right. the relationships between two floors.

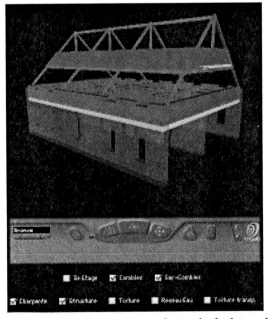 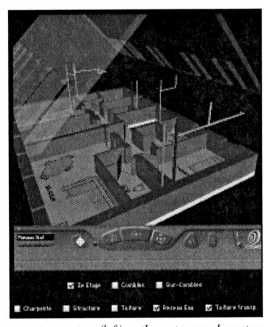

Figure 8. Participants can select only the layer showing structure system (left) or the water supply system (right).

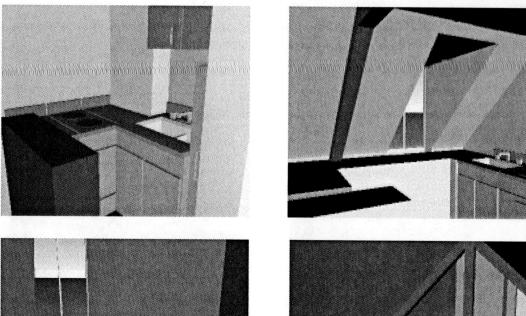

Figure 9. Design Phase II (3-D Model). The design proposal in 3D VRML form for Redliner showing different views (kitchen alternatives, bathroom, corridor).

during the first and second phases of this project. For example, the building owner had asked the architects whether the beams above the living area could be removed. The contractor commented that it would increase the remodeling expenses. The architects then responded with two design alternatives. Figure 10 below shows two views of the same space with and without the beams.

5.2 Design development through comments

Each table presents some comments and responses made by different participants and the design modifications that were proposed. We show below, examples of conversations that occurred in Redliner concerning different design decisions.

This first example shows the basic interaction between the two architects. They used the markers

Figure 10. Design Phase III (Alternatives). The client questioned whether perhaps the space would be better without the beams.

> STAGE ONE (Hybrid representation)

• 04/29/99 at 7:12 pm - **Architect 2**: Issue: **Door**
" I looked at the regulation, it seems that we must put a second door in between the living room and the restrooms. What are your suggestions about that?"

• 05/02/99 at 3:08 pm- **Architect 1**: Issue: **Door**
"As I see it there's only two possibilities, either in the corridor, we could keep the existing bathroom door, or in between the entrance and the living room, some kind of big double door (more expensive). In that case we'll also have to extend the partition wall some more".

> STAGE THREE (Alternatives):

The two propositions were visualized in 3D. (Figure 11)
(Later the decision was made: the cheapest version was adopted).

Table 1. Code regulation discussion between two architects.

posted on the Redliner model to discuss design alternatives on a building code problem. The 3D see-through view of the floor plans provided visual tests for how the proposed modification would impact the rest of the building. The alternatives are shown in Figure 11.

Table 2 shows a typical owner-architect discussion over a question of organizing the space. The owner observed that the space in front of the stairs appeared to be too small when he browsed the 3D model. He left an annotation marker to identify which space he was referring to. Later the architects responded to his concerns with several design alternatives.

The following transcript shows a longer conversation that took place between the architects and the contractor about replacing windows in different places. The Redliner annotation markers helped identify which windows were under discussion and the approximate locations for the new additions. Seeing markers on the scene and "on the spot" directed attention to the right place.

6 Implementation
6.1 System Architecture

The current version of the Immersive Redliner uses the Java External Authoring Interface to connect and communicate with a VRML scene. A touch and proximity sensor for the entire scene is the only VRML interactive command in the system; Java handles everything else. When the system event handler detects a click, the touch sensor code identifies the object the user designated and

> STAGE ONE (Hybrid representation)

• 04/29/99 at 10:44 am - **Owner**: Issue: **Daylighting**
"This corridor looks very narrow, it won't be too dark there? Can we widen it a bit?"

• 04/30/99 at 9:28 am - **Architect 1**: Issue: **Daylighting**
"It's 90 cm wide. We'll see if we can do something to bring natural light in there"

05/05/99 at 10:25 am - **Architect 2**: Issue: **Daylighting**
"We could think of piercing the stairs' wall... We'll show you what's possible"

> STAGE THREE (Alternatives):

Three alternatives were proposed: Two design options involved creating a hole in the wall and a third one proposed a glass door for the living room. (Figure 12)

Table 2. Daylighting discussion between the building owner and the two architects.

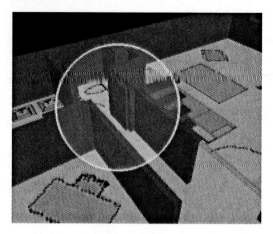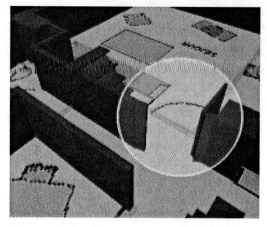

Figure 11. Another architect remarked on the need for two doors between the living room and restrooms. Two design proposals responded to this comment. Panels showing wall additions, portions to be retained and existing walls to be demolished.

Figure 12. Architect's alternatives to answer the owner's question about daylighting in the corridor. Original design proposal (left), with a hole (middle), with a glass door (right).

sends the coordinates of that click to the main Java class. Java then pops up a type-in window for the visitor's comment and sends back VRML code to implement the new 3-D sphere with its associated number. Once this is done and the user decides to save the comment, the text and its references are sent to a CGI Perl script running on the Redliner server to log the files containing the annotation markers (with links to text files) for each user. When the visitor exits the world, another part of the Java code writes the VRML code for the 3-D spheres, and with the help of a CGI script creates a new VRML file on the server. When later a visitor wishes to see the current visitor's comments, the Redliner loads the base model and the new annotations VRML file. Each annotation marker links to its respective user comment file and selected color.

6.2 Event Handling

The annotation events are handled by a Java applet named Sticker. The Sticker applet runs whenever the selected VRML model is open. A Java "callback" method waits for VRML events. When the user clicks in the model the callback method collects the click coordinates and the normal vector of the selected surface, and writes a VRML string to place a sphere on the surface. Another "action" method waits for events to happen inside the Java applet. When the user hits the save button, the action method takes all the accumulated VRML strings corresponding to the annotation spheres and sends these to a Perl script running on the server. That script then organizes the information it receives and creates or appends to HTML and VRML files on the Redliner server.

Displaying different layers of design concerns (e.g., structure, roof, pipes, etc) is handled through a DisplayLayer Java applet. It collects user input of a single or a multiple-view selection and uses the getEventIn method to load VRML files as requested.

7 Discussion and Future Work

Participants from our Redliner design experiment provided interesting and useful feedback for the future development of the system. For example, the architects found that interacting with three-

> STAGE ONE (Hybrid representation)

• 05/06/99 at 9:03 am - **Contractor**: Issue: **Windows**
"Will we have to replace all the windows?"

> STAGE TWO (3-D model)

• 05/06/99 at 7:14 pm - **Architect** (note 1):
"Yes, we want to change all the windows for PVC ones. We're keeping the shutters though"

• 05/06/99 at 7:20 pm - **Architect** (note 2):
"We're also going to add two roof windows. Here to bring some light in the living room"

• 05/06/99 at 7:23 pm - **Architect** (note 3):
"And here for the bedroom"

• 05/13/99 at 1:13 pm - **Contractor**:
"How may are they, total?"

• 05/15/99 at 11:55 am - **Architect**:
"All of them: 10.
So we have 10: 160x80 PVC windows
And 2: 78X128 PVC roof windows"

Table 3: Window discussion between an architect and the contractor.

dimensional design models is a good way to explore design alternatives. The contractor appreciated seeing comments and discussions positioned at the right locations and this reduced confusion and miscommunication. Some participants at first questioned how realistic the models are (color, texture, space) and whether the view angle in VRML might misrepresent the real space (too wide, too narrow). However, later they commented that they were able to connect the projected reality of the design space to the on-screen VRML model. They agreed that seeing the design in 3D helped them to visualize the space and to communicate with each other. The architects, contractor and the client all wanted more functionality in the Redliner so that they could explore making or modifying designs in the virtual space.

In sum, the communication system in Redliner was used to efficiently communicate ideas and exchange points of view without scheduling a face-to-face meeting. Everyone could view the latest design proposition and react, annotate, question or respond at any time from anywhere. Retaining a trail of what happened and how certain decisions were taken along the design process is also useful for the architects as well as for the clients.

We are currently porting the system to a Java3D platform and extending the annotation capabilities to allow both written text display and sketching modifications onto the VRML objects. We are also structuring user comments in a hierarchy to organize the threaded history of modification decisions.

8 Acknowledgements

This research was supported in part by the National Science Foundation under Grants No. IIS-96-19856 and IIS-00-96138. The views contained in this material are those of the authors and do not necessarily reflects the views of the National Science Foundation. The authors want to thank Olivier Malcurat and Jean-Claude Bignon (from the CRAI, Center for research in Architecture and Engineering, in Nancy), Marc Peter and the ARIM for their help and comments and feedback during the experimentation phase. The first pavilion model has been built in VRML by Jimmy Davidson. Dongqiu Qian, Peter Kappus and Mike Weller helped with some Java and Perl debugging. Mark D. Gross provided valuable suggestions and assisted with preparing the paper.

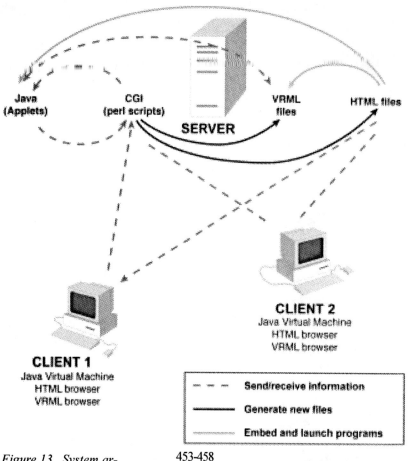

Figure 13. System architecture of the Redliner.

References

Campbell, D. (1998) Architectural Construction Documents on the Web: VRML as a Case Study, Digital Design Studios: Do Computers Make a Difference? [ACADIA Conference Proceedings] Quebec City (Canada) October 22-25, 1998, pp. 266-275

Craig, D. L. and Zimring, C. (1999) Practical Support for Collaborative Design Involving Divided Interests, Media and Design Process [ACADIA '99] Salt Lake City 29-31 October 1999, pp.126-137

Davidson, J. N. and Campbell, D. A. (1996) Collaborative Design in Virtual Space - GreenSpace II: A Shared Environment for Architectural Design Review, Design Computation: Collaboration, Reasoning, Pedagogy [ACADIA Conference Proceedings] Tucson (Arizona / USA) October 31 - November 2, 1996, pp. 165-179

Donath, D., Kruijff, E., Regenbrecht, H., Hirschberg, U., Johnson, B., Kolarevic, B. and Wojtowicz, J. (1999) Virtual Design Studio 1998 - A Place2Wait, Architectural Computing from Turing to 2000 [eCAADe Conference Proceedings] Liverpool (UK)15-17 September 1999, pp. 453-458

Donath, Dirk and Regenbrecht, Holger, 1996 Using Virtual Reality Aided Design Techniques for Three Dimensional Architectural Sketching, ACADIA 96, (eds) P. McIntosh and F Ozel, Tucson, AZ

Dorta, T. and LaLande, P. (1998) The Impact of Virtual Reality on the Design Process, Digital Design Studios: Do Computers Make a Difference? [ACADIA Conference Proceedings] Quebec City (Canada) October 22-25, 1998, pp. 138-163

Greenberg S., Roseman M., Webster D., 1992 "Issues and Experiences Designing and Implementing Two Group Drawing Tools, Readings in Groupware, 609-620

Jung, T., Do, E.Y. and Gross, M.D. (1999) Immersive Redlining and Annotation of 3D Design Models on the Web, Proceedings of the Eighth International Conference on Computer Aided Architectural Design Futures] Atlanta, 7-8 June 1999, pp. 81-98

Marshall, C. 1998. "Toward an ecology of hypertext annotation", ACM Hypertext 98, 40-49.

McCall, R. (1998) World Wide Presentation and Critique of Design Proposals with the Web-PHIDIAS System, Digital Design Studios: Do Computers Make a Difference? [ACADIA Conference Proceedings] Quebec City (Canada) October 22-25, 1998, pp. 254-265

Qian, D. and Gross, M. D. (1999) Collaborative Design with NetDraw, Proceedings of the Eighth International Conference on Computer Aided Architectural Design Futures, Atlanta, 7-8 June 1999, pp. 213-226

Sekler E. F. and W. Curtis, Le Corbusier at Work, Harvard University Press, Cambridge, MA

Wojtowicz, J. (ed.), "Virtual Design Studio", Hong Kong University Press, 1995, pp.41-51.

http://www.tenlinks.com/CAD/cad_viewers.htm

WebOutliner: A Web-Based Tool for Collaborative Space Programming and Design

Wassim Jabi, University at Buffalo, The State University of New York, USA

Abstract

This paper discusses a web-based tool that allows members of a design team to collaboratively specify a hierarchical spatial program for an architectural project. Given its object orientation, the represented artifacts have built-in data and methods that allow them to respond to user actions and manage their own sub-artifacts. Given that these components are hierarchical allows users to filter information, analyze and compare design parameters and aggregate hierarchical amounts in real-time. Furthermore, the software goes beyond outlining functions to support synchronous collaborative design by linking each item in the spatial program to a detail page that allows file uploading, real-time group marking of images, and textual chat. Thus, the software offers a seamless transition from the largely asynchronous definition of an architectural program to synchronous collaboration. In addition, and in contrast to commercially available groupware, the software allows multiple collaboration sessions to run at the same time. These sessions are artifact-based in the sense that they get automatically initiated once participants visit the same architectural space in the program hierarchy. The software employs a three-tier object-oriented, web-based scheme for a richer representation of hierarchical artifacts coupled with a relational database for server-side storage. The prototype integrates this technology with Java-based tools for synchronous web-based collaboration.

1 Introduction

Software that supports collaborative work (groupware) usually belongs to one of two categories: synchronous and asynchronous. Synchronous groupware supports the real-time aspects of collaborative work such as group meetings. Examples of synchronous groupware include chat programs, video-conferencing, application sharing, and shared whiteboards. Asynchronous groupware supports the longer-term aspects of collaboration such as workflow and project management, issue discussions, and review processes. Examples of asynchronous groupware include e-mail, newsgroups, shared workspaces, and task management software. Some aspects of collaborative work, such as voting, can happen either synchronously or asynchronously. Those types of activities need software support that is flexible enough to operate in either mode. While current applications may support one or more of these functions, many have failed to fully integrate the synchronous and asynchronous requirements of collaborative work. Furthermore, the majority of groupware applications supports general-purpose collaboration and, thus, is not equipped to support domain-specific functionality. Architectural design requires specialized vertical knowledge that goes beyond the sharing of marks on paper or the multi-casting of video images. This paper briefly surveys current groupware applications and outlines the need for vertical and integrated support of synchronous and asynchronous design collaboration. The paper also describes a software prototype under development that uses a three-tier persistent object-oriented, web-based technology for a richer representation of hierarchical architectural artifacts. The prototype contributes to earlier work that defined a framework for a shared workspace consisting of Participants, Tasks, Proposals, and Artifacts. These four elements have been found through observation and analysis to be adequate representations of the essential components of collaborative architectural design. These components are also hierarchical which allows users to filter information, analyze and compare design parameters and aggregate hierarchical amounts. Given its object orientation, the represented artifacts have built-in data and methods that allow them to respond to user actions and manage their own sub-artifacts. In addition,

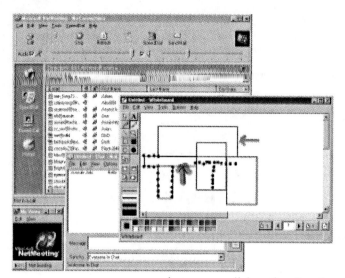

the prototype integrates this technology with Java tools for ubiquitous synchronous web-based access. The prototype uses architectural programming (defining the spatial program of a building) and early conceptual design as examples of seamlessly integrated groupware applications.

2   Examples of current groupware applications

Given the lack of bandwidth, real-time videoconferencing has met limited success and is only available to large corporations and to a relatively small number of distance-learning centers within academic institutions. Instead, many users of the Internet rely on desktop conferencing applications such as CU-SeeMe and Microsoft's NetMeeting for near real-time audio and video communication (Figure 1). NetMeeting also has whiteboard capabilities, the exchange of files and the sharing of applications. Aside from reliability problems and network congestion, NetMeeting on its own provides only general-purpose collaboration functionality. The sharing of single-user applications is not the most effective way to multi-author a document. NetMeeting shines in its one-on-one videoconferencing capability. However, CU-SEEME has the advantage of its ability to multi-cast several video images such that a group meeting can take place.

Figure 1. Microsoft NetMeeting Screen Shot.

A second breed of web-based collaboration technologies is based on the idea of a shared virtual workspace (Takemura and Kishino 1992). In some cases, the application may use a synthetic three-dimensional space that multiple users can inhabit and meet through a representational avatar. In other cases, these applications, such as the one webex.com offers for free, allow you to have a non-dimensional virtual office. Using your web browser, you can upload documents and guests can leave you messages, request meetings, check your shared calendar and conduct real-time meetings using chat software, a whiteboard, and multi-casting of PowerPoint presentations.

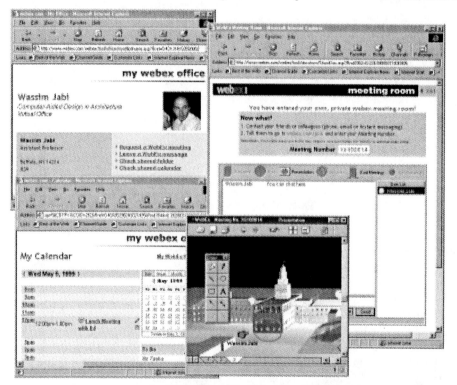

With the advent of the Java programming language, several smaller shareware applications (applets) are available that allow whiteboard functionality, document annotation, and real-time textual chat. An example of that class of software is Groupboard from www.groupboard.com (Figure 3). Again, we find that this type of application is suited for casual meetings that need only to sketch and chat without the need to carry out organized tasks that need any specialized software.

Figure 2. Webex.com Virtual Office Screen Shot.

3   The Case for Domain-Specific Groupware

General-purpose groupware applications such as those described in the previous section are very well suited for their intended purpose. They allow geographically dispersed users to meet, communicate, point at, annotate and share synthetic artifacts in near-real time. Some also allow the remote control of a computer or application. Yet, there is a whole class of needs that is not addressed in these applications (Nardi 1994). For example, if a musician would like to collaboratively create a piece of music, then someone must write a collaborative music authoring application from the ground up or convert a single user application into a multi-user one. In most cases, the latter has proved to be inadequate due to differences in user interaction modes. The same can be applied to the field of architecture. Architects sometimes need to carry out domain-specific tasks that general-purpose collaborative tools simply cannot handle. In this paper, I use the example of co-creating a building program (the specification of the spatial requirements for a building) to illustrate the need for domain-specific groupware. It is important to note here that I am not arguing for a replacement of current collaboration software, but simply the need to augment them.

4 WebObjects

Apple's WebObjects software is a high performance application server (Figure 4). It provides an object-oriented application framework for developing three-tier client-server applications as well as dynamic publishing. The three tiers are (1) Storage, (2) Application-Layer, and (3) Web Interface. By using components in templates that are linked to actions and data in the WebObjects application, the server can act on user actions dynamically, configure a response HTML page and return that to the user for further action. WebObjects provides mechanisms for maintaining information, called state, during a session or even after a session has terminated. Because of that functionality, multiple participants (clients) can view and edit the same information while being logged on to the same WebObjects application.

5 WebOutliner

Fundamentally, WebOutliner is a web-based application that represents and manipulates hierarchical elements using Apple's WebObjects technology (Wilson and Ostrem 1998). WebOutliner is built using specifications and earlier research found in (Jabi and Hall 1995a; Jabi and Hall 1995b; Jabi 1996a; Jabi 1996b; Jabi 1998; and Jabi 1999). WebOutliner is composed of reusable components that can be adapted for several needs. In its current implementation, WebOutliner manages the components of a simple building program. Following an object-oriented approach, WebOutliner's components belong to one of three categories: (1) Model, (2) View, and (3) Controller (Krasner and Pope 1988). The Model is mainly composed of a tree-like object that stores data and methods that represent an architectural space. A space can contain within it other sub-spaces and so on. The total area of a space is computed as the sum of the areas of its descendant spaces plus an additional area that is unassigned to any of its descendants. A space manages its own sub-spaces. For example, if a space is copied and pasted as a sub-space of another space, it will copy and paste with it all its descendant sub-spaces. In practical terms, a user can copy a whole department with multiple sub-rooms from one level and paste it on a second level. All the sub-rooms will be copied with it. If a space is edited, added, or deleted, the area of its parent space will be re-computed to reflect that change.

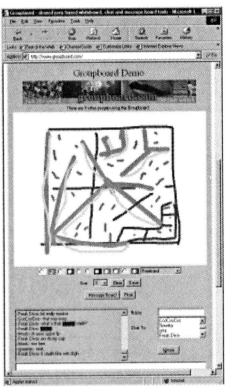

Figure 3. Groupboard.com Whiteboard Screen Shot.

5.1 Asynchronous collaboration

When a user connects to WebOutliner's web site, he/she is presented with the current status of a building program. The user is asked to enter his/her name for identification purposes. A magnifier button is provided that enables the user to search for a particular item in the hierarchy (Figure 5).

By clicking on the underlined item name, that item is selected and a toolbar of options is displayed that allow the editing and manipulation of that item (Figure 6). Next, a hierarchical list is presented. By clicking on the triangle next to an item, a user can collapse or expand an item to reveal or hide its sub-items (Figure 7). The user is able to copy/cut/paste/delete items to edit the hierarchy. He/she can also re-order the items that have a common parent item. The user can also zoom-in on an item temporarily making it the root item. Using this mechanism, a user can filter the overall building program and concentrate only on part of it (Figure 8). By clicking on the Edit Item button, a user can change the name of an item and enter a numeric value. In this example, we are using the numeric value to represent area (Figure 9). Obviously, it is a simple matter to extend the application to include other parameters such as cost and volume. Once the area is entered, the overall area is aggregated using a recursive algorithm (Figure 10).

5.2 Seamless transition to synchronous collaboration

By clicking on the upper left button, a user can go to that item's particular page to examine it in more detail (Figure 11). It is in this simple move that a user transitions to synchronous collaboration. If another user happens to visit the same item at the same time (or they have scheduled a meeting in that space ahead of time), the users will be presented with a page that contains real-time Java applets for chat, and a shared whiteboard. They are immediately aware of who else is working on this item and they can communicate with them in near real-time (Figure 12).

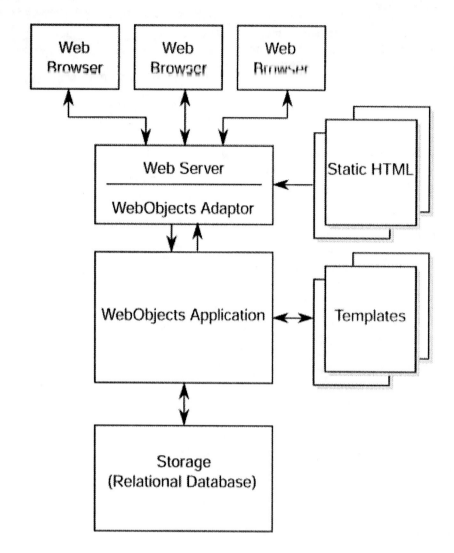

Figure 4. Apple WebObjects Framework.

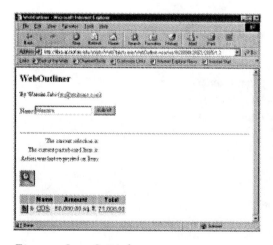

Figure 5. Initial WebOutliner Screen.

The power of WebObjects is evident here in that the design of the application only has one template for the item's page. However, by assigning the item's unique ID to that template, multiple users can synchronously collaborate on multiple items at the same item. For example, John and Mary can be collaborating synchronously on the design of the lecture hall while Ed and Jane can be discussing the design of the conference room. At the same time, Bob is adding more spaces to Level 1.

It is important to note that while currently the represented artifact is a simple GIF image, theoretically any synthetic artifact can be uploaded, embedded in this page, and displayed using the proper plug-in (e.g. VRML, DWF, or AVI files).

6 Conclusion

This paper illustrates the need for domain-specific collaborative software. Integrating a database, an object-oriented application server, and a web-based interface can prove to be a powerful and flexible solution for customizing behavior and adding intelligence to shared artifacts. Obviously, user testing is needed to verify these claims. Future research will concentrate on such testing and will be reported. The specification of a building program is used here only as a simplified example of a domain-specific functionality that cannot be found in any of the commercial collaborative applications available today. This new class of tools should be regarded as complimentary to current general-purpose tools.

As mentioned earlier, WebOutliner is a component within a larger framework, currently under development, that will provide a dynamic shared workspace for collaboration in architectural design. The workspace will manage design workflow by allowing users to synchronously and asynchronously create tasks, proposals, and artifacts. Mechanisms will be embedded that allow evaluation and selection of design alternatives as well as the capture of design rationale.

Acknowledgements

I wish to thank Professors Harold Borkin, James Turner, Judy Olson and Edmund Durfee for supervising the doctoral research project of which WebOutliner is a part. I also wish to thank Theodore Hall who provided valuable feedback on earlier experiments with collaborative software and co-authored with me two papers on the subject. Apple and WebObjects are trademarks of Apple Computer, Inc. Microsoft and NetMeeting are trademarks of Microsoft Corporation. CU-SeeMe is a trademark of CUseeMe Networks, Inc. Webex.com is a trademark of Webex Communications, Inc. Groupboard is a trademark of Groupboard.com.

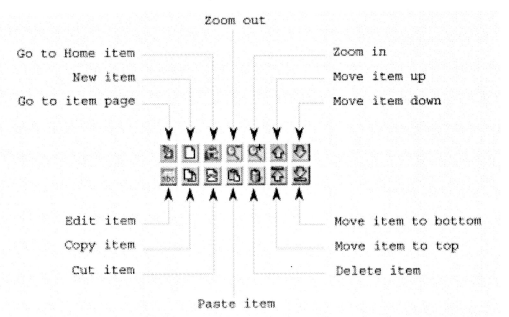

Figure 6. Toolbar and Commands.

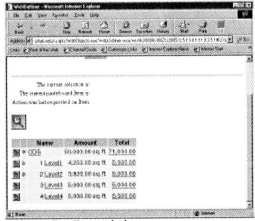

Figure 7. Expanded Building Program

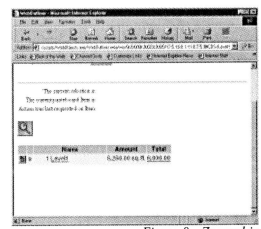

Figure 8. Zoomed-in on a Sub-item to Filter Out Information.

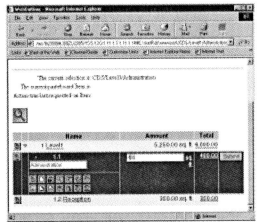

Figure 9. Editing Name and Area of an Element.

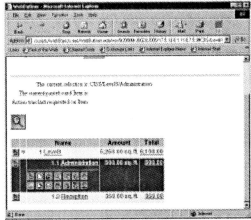

Figure 10. The Building Program Computes and Maintains an Aggregate Area.

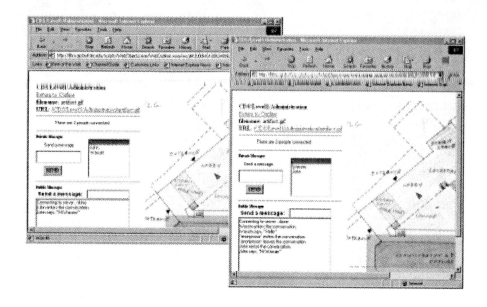

Figure 11. Synchronous Collaboration (one participant).

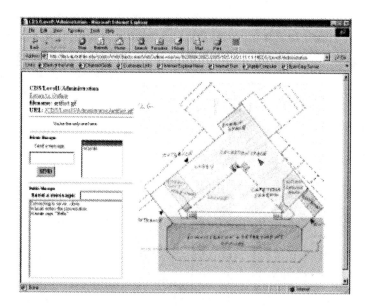

Figure 12. Synchronous Collaboration (two participants).

References

Jabi, W. and T. Hall (1995a). The role of computers in synchronous collaborative design. *Proceedings of the 14th International Congress on Cybernetics*: 71-76. Belgium: International Association for Cybernetics.

Jabi, W. and T. Hall (1995b). Beyond the shared whiteboard: issues in computer-supported collaborative design. *Proceedings of the Sixth International Conference on Computer-Aided Architectural Design Futures*: 719-725. Singapore: National University of Singapore.

Jabi, W. (1996a). An outline of the requirements for a computer-supported collaborative design system. In *Open House International*, vol. 21, no 1, 22-30.

Jabi, W. (1996b). Domain-specific tools for collaboration in architectural design. *Proceedings of the 3rd International Conference on Design and Decision Support Systems in Architecture and*

Urban Planning: 248-259. Eindhoven, Netherlands: Technical University of Eindhoven.

Jabi, W. (1998). The role of artifacts in collaborative design. *Proceedings of the Third Conference on Computer-Aided Architectural Design Research in Asia*: 271-280. Osaka, Japan: CAADRIA, Department of Architecture and Civil Engineering, Kumamoto University.

Jabi, W. (1999). Integrating databases, objects and the world-wide web for collaboration in architectural design. *Proceedings of the focus symposium: World Wide Web as Framework for Collaboration in conjunction with the 11th International Conference on Systems Research, Informatics and Cybernetics*. Baden-Baden, Germany: The International Institute for Advanced Studies in Systems Research and Cybernetics.

Krasner G. and S. Ppop (1988). A cookbook for using the model view controller user interface paradigm in Smalltalk-80. In *Journal of Object-Orientated Programming*, vol. 1, no 3, 26-49.

Nardi, B. (1994). Collaborative multimedia: getting beyond the obvious. *Proceedings of The Second ACM Conference on Multimedia*: 119-120. New York: The Association for Computing Machinery.

Takemura, H. and F. Kishino (1992). Cooperative work environment using virtual workspace. *Proceedings of the Conference on Computer-Supported Cooperative Work*: 226-232. New York: The Association for Computing Machinery.

Wilson, G. and J. Ostrem (1998). *WebObjects developer's guide*. Cupertino, CA: Apple Computer, Inc.

A Virtual Reality Tool to Implement City Building Codes on Capitol View Preservation

Chiu-Shui Chan, Iowa State University, USA

Abstract

In urban planning, the urban environment is a very complicated system with many layers of building codes cross-referenced and interacting together to guide urban growth. Especially, if a new urban design is located in a historical area, additional restrictions will be imposed upon regular zoning regulations to maintain the area's historical characteristics. Often, urban regulations read as text are difficult to understand. A tool that generates adequate urban information and a quick visualization of the design will ease decision-making and enhance urban design processes. The goal of this research project is to develop a virtual reality (VR) tool with high resolution, speedy computation, and a user-friendly environment.

This project initiates an interactive visualization tool to enforce city-planning regulations on viewing access to the state capitol building in Des Moines, Iowa. The capitol building houses the Iowa Legislature and is a symbol of state power. Maintaining the view from surrounding areas will preserve the building's monumental and symbolic meaning. To accomplish this, the City Community Development Department and the Capitol Planning Committee developed a Capitol View Corridor Project, which sets up seven visual corridors to prevent the view toward the capitol from being blocked by any future designs. Because city regulations are not easy for the public and designers to interpret and comprehend, this project intends to develop a VR tool to create a transparent environment for visualizing the city ordinances.

1 Background

An urban environment is a very complex system that has many layers of building codes interacting together to guide urban development. Particularly, if a design project sits in a zone with a unique historical context, additional regulations will be enforced over regular zoning restrictions to preserve and emphasize the area's historical characteristics. Codes also vary between city zones. Thus, urban designers and planners expend much effort to find the right codes to meet regulations, especially considering the complexity of high-rise building designs at different geographical locations.

When planners conceive concepts to solve urban issues in the planning and design process, they draw diagrams or build urban models to explore possible solutions and evaluate outcomes. Deficiencies exist in the drawings as well as physical models. For instance, it is difficult to sense the three-dimensional volume through a two-dimensional drawing, and it is impossible to accurately comprehend the proportions of urban spaces, because the scale used in physical models is too small. Thus, drawings and physical models lose details that usually embody meaning and express intentions. Less detail increases ambiguity. Therefore, these conventional presentation tools are not powerful enough to offer opportunities for perceiving interactions that may occur among inhabitants and their surroundings.

A tool that automatically generates urban zoning information and provides an immediate visualization of the design will ease decision-making, enhance urban design processes, and indirectly improve the urban environment. Particularly, the three-dimensional expression of urban codes will turn the legal and technical aspects of planning regulations into transparent visual guidance. A virtual reality (VR) system can serve these purposes. Virtual reality, a highly advanced human-computer interaction tool (Durlach & Mavor, 1995; Mine, 1995), provides diversified media for an interactive, multimedia experience of activities and behaviors conducted in cyberspace. VR is an excellent tool to visualize objects that do not yet exist. By applying VR, planners and designers will be able to understand spatial qualities of their own designs intermediately. They can comprehend their work by walking through a virtual space to visualize the volumetric impact of the design to the existing space, and the proportions of the spatial layout. Designers can use such an environment as a visualization tool to aid the design process and urban planners can apply it to improve the urban fabric. This project intends to develop a VR tool to make these goals possible.

Advanced virtual reality facilities have been installed in the Virtual Reality Applications Center at Iowa State University. The center uses its state-of-the-art resources to apply virtual reality to engineering and scientific problems. These resources include a variety of computer systems used with wall display systems, head-mounted displays, and interaction devices including stereo glasses, trackers, instrumented wands and gloves, vehicle and aircraft bucks, and a motion base. A number of successful VR applications have been generated in the center, such as architectural design tool (Chan, Hill and Cruz-Neira 1999a, 1999b), architectural reconstruction (Chan, Maves and Cruz-Neira 1999c), virtual prototyping, multidimensional data analysis, and engineering simulations.

2 Concept development

This project is to develop a VR tool for designers, planners, students, and state officials to perceive and manage future urban growth. The process of tool development will rely heavily on technical support from state officials. The relations established between the academy and the public will enhance the outreach aspect of the university. The generated tool from this project will serve as the planning tool for the state government and professional practitioners.

Applying this tool, the public can comprehend the impact of the environment from viewing it through the VR model; designers can input new designs into the tools and plug the design into the model to see through the cityscape how the design meets urban regulations. Planners can examine whether the design violates city codes for issuing building permits. The purpose is to evaluate quickly, easily, and accurately whether a new design located within a particular area meets the urban regulations. This planning tool will be a promising means for controlling the city environment and an efficient instrument for the general public to learn and supervise how public policies shape urban forms.

"The Iowa Capitol is widely acknowledged to be one of the finest state capitol structures in the United States and one of the nation's great treasures. Its exquisite detail and craftsmanship have been heralded by nationally recognized experts as an incomparable example of period architecture. ... Majestic views of the capitol building from several vantage points in the Capitol City deserve preservation as well. These views not only celebrate the structure's beauty, but also contribute to the unique character of the city, especially as an important symbol for the East Des Moines downtown (Dikis, 1999)."

The state capitol building sits on a hill on the east bank of the Des Moines River. The geographic location and the contours of the site make the building visible from far away (see Figure 1). This visibility enhances the building's roles as symbol and monument. Because the building houses the state government of Iowa, it acts as a symbol of the power of the state in the urban context. Also,

Figure 1. The state capitol building of Iowa.

since it was built, the form has served as a monument and embodies historical significance. Such a building should continue to stand fully visible in the capital city of the state of Iowa to fulfill its purpose of symbol and monument.

With increased urban growth, such a role of visibility has been challenged. On the west bank of the Des Moines River, high-rise buildings were erected to meet the downtown area's economic development needs. In consequence, the view toward the capitol building has been blocked, which is a critical issue in city planning. To maintain the view accessibility in a particular region (see Figure 2), state officials have been working with the city toward developing a plan that would guide future downtown development in a way that would preserve and enhance the visual prominence of the state Capitol and the character and scale of Capitol Park. Since June of 1990, the city of Des Moines has developed seven capitol view corridors (see Figure 3).

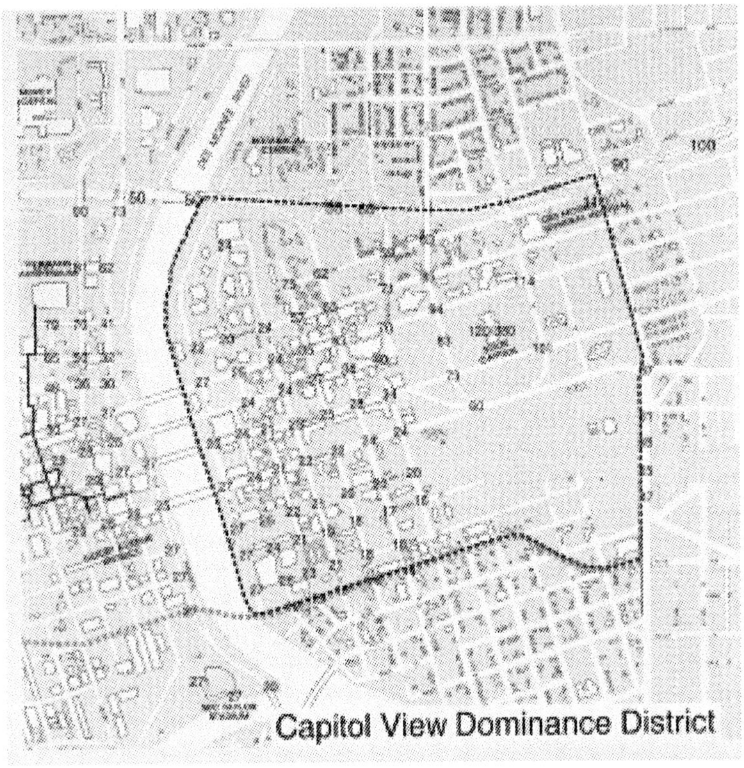

The view corridor is a three-dimensional corridor bounded by prominent public viewing points in several places with a building height restriction imposed to define the sight line to the dome of the state capitol building. A calculation formula for evaluating the height has been established by the city. Special functional purposes are associated with each corridor. In July 1999, the state Legislature authorized the city to enact zoning regulations to preserve the dominance of the capitol building dome and the view from prominent public viewing points.

According to the building codes, any new designs located within these corridors will have a specific building height limitation and setback requirements. For instance, the limitation on the Second Avenue/Freeway corridor #4 is restricted to 225 feet (see Figure 4) toward the base of the capitol's beautiful golden dome, and differs from the 194-foot limitation on the East 15th Street/Freeway corridor #2 (Figure 5). The seven corridors have different sets of height limitations ranging from 80 feet to 450 feet.

The height of the building is determined by the formula of $H = (\tan\theta \times B') - E$, where H is the building height on site, θ is the view angle from the viewpoint at a child's-eye level of 33", B' is the distance from viewpoint to the site, and E is the result of subtracting viewpoint elevation from site elevation (see diagram shown in Figure 6).

Currently, the conventional way to test whether a design meets the view regulation is to examine drawings, physical models, or digital models constructed by the designers. Economically, it is an expensive and very time-consuming process. Regarding perception, viewers cannot share a mutually inclusive view of the results. Therefore, the tools and methods for presentation need to be improved to provide an accurate, efficient, and easily understood result. This project will build a digital model of the east bank of the Des Moines River to represent the buildings three-dimensionally in a virtual reality environment. Then, the building height formula and associated city regulations together will be converted into

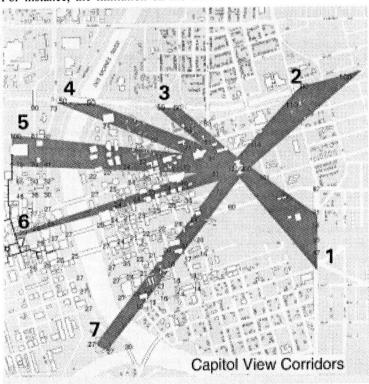

Figure 2. Capitol view dominance district.

Figure 3. Seven capitol view corridors.

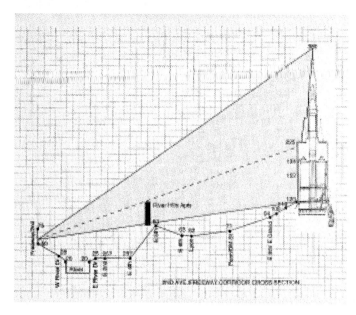

Figure 4. E. 15th/Freeway corridor #4.

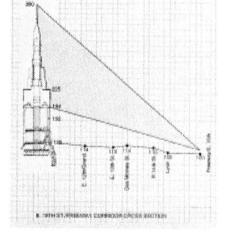

Figure 5. Second Ave./ Freeway corridor #2.

computer source codes implemented in a digital city model. The digital model is constructed by a CAD system. The center of the model is the capitol, which is surrounded by seven conceptual corridors with various height regulations. Thus, different functions and algorithms are installed to establish the basic structure of the tool.

Methods of evaluating the building height restrictions of each corridor will be executed by animation, navigating from the beginning of the corridor to the dome of the capitol building. Animation is utilized by installing navigation paths along a child's-eye level to test the view accessibility. If the dome of the capitol cannot be seen at a child's-eye level, then a height violation exists and the design must be revised. The entire tool, after completion, will be converted into Virtual Reality Modeling Language (VRML) models and displayed on the Web for public access. It is hoped that designers can submit and plug their design projects into this VR environment and through animation, evaluate whether the design meets city codes.

3 Methods of tool generation

Tool-generation methods include digital modeling of the city in the VR environment, converting urban codes to computer codes, embedding these codes within the VR model components, and creating a user interface between the model and codes. The digital city model will be generated by AutoCAD on PCs and MultiGen Program on SGI platform. Modeling information is based on drawings provided by the city (see Figure 7) and photos taken on the site.

The model will have schematic representation of the body of buildings locate within the corridor. The roof shape of each building will be constructed in more detail than the body part. Inside the MultiGen model, animation paths for each view corridor will be defined by a series of algorithms implemented by VEGA — a MultiGen Application (API) package executed in the MultiGen environment and displayed through the Performer. A number of paths would be assigned in each corridor, starting from certain prominent viewpoints toward the dome.

4 Current progress

The project is in the starting stage and the work is on constructing wireframe representation of the state capitol, the capitol park, and the surrounding blocks. After the skeleton of buildings on blocks is completed, a first animation will be encoded, installed, and tested. This article is a working paper. Some high resolution of the image will be completed for presentation in the fall of 2000.

At this stage, corridor #2 is the focus. Corridor #2 can be called the I-235 corridor, which is tightly connected to a highway reconstruction project supervised by the Iowa Department of Transportation. The IDOT developed an I-235 Master Aesthetic Plan for evolving planning and design ideas for the transportation corridor. Conceptual ideas for the aesthetic elements of Interstate 235 have been addressed, which include roadway landscape development, vehicular and pedestrian bridges, and functional structures related to roadway development, e.g., retaining walls, roadway lights, etc. One of the suggested goals is to showcase Iowa's capital city and its resources. Therefore, the view corridor #2 is responsible for preserving the capitol view from the highway.

Figure 8 shows the topography of the corridor area. Figure 9 displays photo animation of the highway westbound. Figure 10 demonstrates AutoCAD wireframe animation viewed from the highway to the capitol building.

5 Expected final results

Four products of the tool will be generated. The period of time needed to complete each product varies, and each product is a continuous effort.

- A VR tool equipped with the digital city model, and a set of databases containing urban codes implemented by C++ and interacted with users through head-mounted display (HMD). To view a VR model through a HMD, a MultiGen digital model should be converted into the Performer environment. This is the primary version of the tool that runs on Silicon Graphic machines. The time frame for each corridor is scheduled as two months of modeling and two months of setting up the corridor boundaries, codes for height, and defining paths for animation.

- A PC version of the tool will be converted from the MultiGen model into an AutoCAD/MAX model. Its urban codes and user interface will also be executed by animation in MAX. This low-end version is developed for design practitioners and small firms using PCs. The generation of this product is feasible, because there are import and export functions shared by AutoCAD, MAX, and MultiGen software to make a digital model mutually compatible. Each corridor will require a two-month effort to (1) convert models from MultiGen into ACAD/MAX, (2) polish the model in MAX after transforming the file, and (3) develop MAX key frame animation.

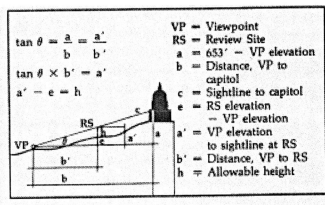

Figure 6. Capitol view preservation height calculation formula.

- A VRML model of the tool will be converted directly in MultiGen and displayed on the Web for public viewing. This VRML model will have default animation to simulate the view corridors. The expected time frame for each corridor is one month for converting plus setting up the pages on the Internet.

- The MultiGen model will be converted into a new version of a CAVE model (advanced version of the Cave Automatic Virtual Environment, or CAVE facility) to create an immersive VR projection for full-scale perception. The newer CAVE facility, C6, available at the Virtual Reality Applications Center (VRAC), is a synthetic (Cruz-Neira, Sandin and Defanti, 1993) environment providing a full-scale setting for image projection and perception. C6 is one of only four six-sided rear-projection VR display facilities in the world at this time.

Figure 7. Digital map of the capitol park.

Ultimately, a virtual city is created. Users can tour the city, select a building in a particular corridor to study its regulations, or replace a building with a different one on a particular site to evaluate the related city codes in PC version or SGI version. Designers also can view the city and obtain planning information through the Web. Thus, this is a generative and/or evaluation tool.

6 Methods and procedures of tool generation

Unlike any other development of a virtual reality city or historic building in cyberspace, this is a VR tool for planners and designers to interact with the urban form. Bill Jepson and his urban simulation team at the UCLA Urban Simulation Laboratory are constructing the city of Los Angeles. Within the virtual city, users can walk, drive, or fly through (Jepson and Friedman 1998). Similar projects on modeling historic buildings can be found in Chan, Maves and Cruz-Neira (1999), whose work produced models representing seven historic architectural styles. Applying the knowledge and similar techniques from precedents, this project intends to show the feasibility of developing a tool to help city planners manage the future environment of a city.

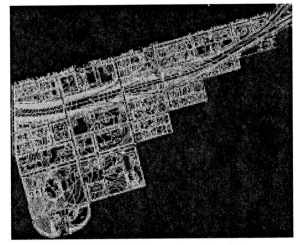

Figure 8. Topography of corridor #2.

There are future advantages and possibilities resulting from this project. Converting urban codes into

Figure 9. Photo animation.

computer codes has rarely been done in the field of urban planning. The algorithms and subroutines developed in this tool can create a new area of research. The digital city model and its associated planning data can assist efforts at simulating public transport, evaluating the traffic environment, designing for modality, developing strategies for urban management, controlling environmental pollution, increasing tourism, studying cultural heritage, and conducting urban renewal case studies, among others.

7 Future directions

The city model will be expanded to also cover the opposite bank of the Des Moines River to complete the entire capital city of Des Moines. Using this as a starting point, the model can be further developed to simulate the entire city planning ordinances. It has several future potential benefits to a number of user groups as described in the following:

- Designers, contractors, and city planners can use this tool to guide urban form. Many interrelated aspects of the urban environment, from transportation and mobility to social elements, can be tested in the database and allow users to visualize the result immediately.
- For city planners and administrators, it can be used to guide urban growth.
- For students in academic institutions, it is a tool to study the relationship between codes and forms.
- For citizens, it is a way to visualize, understand, and supervise public policies — it can be used as a complementary public-hearing tool.

Results collected from this project will extend our understanding from urban planning to information technology and from modeling to systematic encoding of urban regulations. The efforts will set up a new initiative for the application of VR information science to the planning and design professions, a new tool that hasn't been created or implemented before. Methodologies gained from this project will be simultaneously applied to develop a planning tool for the capital city. This project is significant to help visually implement the city ordinances starting from view protection. Applying the same city model, other city ordinances can be further installed to serve as a planning tool for the public, a learning tool for students, and a guarding tool for the state planning officials.

Acknowledgements

The author is grateful to the Des Moines Community Development Department for technical support, the Renaissance Design Group of RDG Bussard Dikis Inc. for advice and for valuable drawings of the old state capitol building, and the Graphics Division, Engineering Department, City of Des Moines for all city maps. Without their generous assistance, this project could not begin.

References

Chan, C. S., L. Hills, and C. Cruz-Neira. (1999a). Can Design be Done in Full-scale Representation? Proceedings of the 4th Design Thinking Research Symposium

- Design Representation. II:139-148. Boston: Department of Architecture, MIT.

Chan, C. S., L. Hill, and C. Cruz-Neira. (1999b). Is It Possible to Design in Full Scale? A CAD Tool in Synthetic Environment. In Proceedings of the 4th Conference on Computer Aided Architectural Design Research in Asia (CAADRIA'99), eds. J. Gu and Z. Wei, 43-52. Shanghai: Scientific and Technological Literature Publishing House.

Chan, C. S., J. Maves, and C. Cruz-Neira. (1999c). An Electronic Library for Teaching Architectural History. In Proceedings of the 4th Conference on Computer Aided Architectural Design Research in Asia (CAADRIA'99) eds. J. Gu and Z. Wei, 335-344. Shanghai: Scientific and Technological Literature Publishing House.

Cruz-Neira, C., D. Sandin, and T. DeFanti. (1993). Surround-Screen Projection-Based Virtual Reality: The Design and Implementation of the CAVE. Proceedings of the ACM SIGGRAPH 93, 135-142.

Dikis, W. M. (1999). Capitol View Protection. Presentation to Planning and Zoning Commission, Des Moines.

Durlach N. I., and A. S. Mavor. (1995). Virtual Reality: Scientific and Technological Challenges. National Research Council Report. Washington, DC: National Academic Press.

Jepson, W., and S. Friedman. (1998). It's a Bird, It's a Plane, It's a SuperSystem. Planning, 64(7): 4-7. Chicago: American Planning Association.

Mine, M. (1995). ISAAC: A virtual environment tool for the interactive construction of virtual worlds. UNC Chapel Hill Computer Science Technical Report. TR95-020.

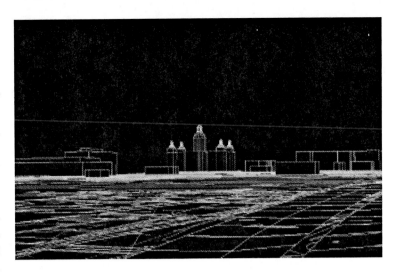

Figure 10. Wireframe animation.

Work in Progress

Short papers that present explorations that have not yet reached a point of conclusions have frequently had much influence and garnered much interest at ACADIA conferences. The working papers presented in this section show a breadth of concerns among architectural computing researchers. They may also provide a glimpse of future contributions and help us to retain roles as early adopters of the best and most imaginative new technologies.

Research that applies computing to technical areas has long been a topic for ACADIA presentations. Historical studies by Martens, Uhl, Tschuppik and Voigt and also Zhou share how digital models can be used to preserve or reconstruct important parts of our global cultural heritage. Kensek, Leuppi and Noble present an algorithm for solving long span structural problems with a particular construction method. Miller, Wang and Jenkins describe the use of 3D modeling and kinematic animation to derive more accurate anthropometrical models for use by designers.

Genetic programming appears in three papers to establish itself as an emerging area of study for design generation. Testa, O'Reilly and Greenwold describe a search for improved office designs by breeding alternatives to invent unanticipated designs. Urban form is particularly susceptible to modeling by genetic programming methods, as demonstrated in the article by Streich, Oxman and Fritz. At the opposite end of the scale of architectural concerns, Ceccato, Simondetti and Burry present an application of genetic programming to the design of door handles and other hardware.

Other papers attest to an expanding role for computing in architectural education. The old arguments about computing in design have faded, perhaps due to overwhelming evidence from practice as architects embrace computer use and even depend upon it. Kolarevic's article is a valuable overview of how computer methods have extended the expressive and formal possibilities for architects and achieved acceptance in some of the most prominent members of the avant garde.

Education in architectural computing may also have moved toward a routine and accepted component of most schools of architecture. A new trend is apparent in the use of computing pervasively across the architecture curriculum. Articles by Harfmann and Akins and also Liapi introduce novel and apparently very effective ways of teaching construction and structures that take advantage of 3D modeling and animation. Dokonal, Martens and Plosch describe how students can produce a comprehensive digital model of a city by careful designation of standards and use of databases to manage the operation. Computer methods for auditing and analyzing student performance in virtual design studios are presented in the article by Fischer, Herr and Ceccato, ushering in a new approach to computing as part of the fundamental infrastructure for teaching and assessment of students.

Observed as a group, the working papers suggest a field of exploration that remains vibrant, diversifying and tantalizing.

Synagogue Neudeggergasse: A Virtual Reconstruction in Vienna

Bob Martens, Vienna University of Technology, Austria

Matthias Uhl, Mediatecture, Austria

Wolf-Michael Tschuppik, Vienna University of Technology, Austria

Andreas Voigt, Vienna University of Technology, Austria

Abstract
Issues associated with virtual reconstruction are first dealt within this paper. Visualizing of no longer existent (architecture-) objects and their surroundings practically amounts to a "virtual comeback". Furthermore, special attention is given to the description of the working procedure for a case study of reconstruction sounding out the potentials of QuickTime VR. The paper ends up with a set of conclusions, taking a close look at the "pros" and "cons" of this type of re-construction.

1 Introduction
Irreversible destruction having removed identity-establishing buildings from the urban surface for all times is the principal cause for the attempt of renewed "imagining." When dealing with such reconstruction first the problem of reliability concerning the existing basic material has to be tackled. Due to their two-dimensional recording photographs only supply us with restricted information content of the object under consideration. Thus the missing part has to be supplemented or substituted by additional sources. Within the process of assembling and overlaying of differing data sets the way of dealing with such fragmentations becomes of major importance. Priority is given to the choice of information. One of the most elementary items of information regarding perception of three-dimensional objects surely is the effect that color and material furnishes. It seems to suggest itself that black-and-white shots hardly will prove valid in this respect. The three-dimensional object doubtlessly provides us with a by far greater variety of possibilities in the following working process than the "cardboard model with pasted-on facade photography". Only the completely designed model structure makes for visualizing the plastic representation form of architecture in a sustainable manner. Furthermore, a virtual model can be dismantled into part models without amounting to a destruction process thereof. Apart therefrom the virtual model permits the generation of differing reconstruction variants regarding color and material. Moreover, architecture models of a physical nature are inherently connected to locality as such.

2 Fundamental Principles
Simulation or the faking of reality aims at approaching the impact of a constructional state no longer existing or to be constructed. What precision this produces depends both on the specific possibilities of implementation of the simulation technique used and on the input time (degree of detail) invested. In this context the phenomenon of virtual reality has great expectations having become very fashionable recently, however. As far as accuracy of terminology is concerned please note that the virtual reality refers to the reality we know despite all technological advancements. Reality is that where mankind finds himself and what results for him due to planning and developing of a environment to be built in future. The other way round it also includes the look back with regard to reconstruction of no longer existing building substance.

2.1 QTVR-Technique

QuickTime® is a spatial simulation technique first developed by Apple™ Computers and meanwhile having been adopted as animation standard by several hardware platforms. The basic approach of this technique is to develop virtual worlds by means of pure software-expansion based on the conventional or commonly available PC-technology. The generation of virtual space relies on the principle of ramified picture sequences, i.e. various picture segments corresponding to spatial navigation paths are united at predetermined junctions, the so-called "hot spots". Thus the user can select the sequence of predetermined scene by means of the junctions available. This approach uses photographic and/or computer-generated images for the production of spatial sceneries. The utilization possibilities of QuickTime VR (QTVR) within architecture are manifold as an efficient structure for (re-) construction of spatial sceneries. Additionally the degree of detailing to be reproduced by means of QTVR-technique can hardly be achieved by other 3D-formats such as QuickDraw3D (QD3D) or Virtual Reality Modeling Language (VRML) also necessitating disproportionably great requirements concerning the hardware of the playing system. The viewing possibilities of QuickTime VR-scenes make for actively driven experiencing of spatial situations according to the user's liking. The attractiveness of QTVR is considerably enhanced due to its close connection with Internet, as www-pages may contain QTVR-scenes as components or may be integrated in QuickTime VR-scenes likewise..

2.2 Navigation

Navigating through reality with all the pertaining tools usually is reserved to the human eye. Navigation in virtual space calls for a translation, an abstraction into forwards, backwards, sideways, quick and slow. The angle of view at our disposal compares to the restricted field of vision through the windscreen of a vehicle. The relation between space and space viewer remains a distant one. The reception matches that of a recording of a TV-picture. Maneuvering in this context is to be regarded as a shifting of picture frames, an impression increased by the QTVR-technique. Moving via "mouse" makes for continuous simple handling of drive by means of the picture cylinder compiled in advance. The VRML-viewing environment compares to a virtual cockpit. The steering and maneuvering equipment features well-known devices, proves pretty awkward in use, as operating the VRML-joystick reminds you of turning a steering wheel by means of a pair of pliers.

2.3 Modeling/Visualizing

Two processes can be differentiated during (re-) construction of a spatial object structure: modeling and subsequent visualizing. The available software packages try to satisfy both intentions, however, having specific shortcomings and strongholds. In the course of modeling, considerations regarding available geometrical tools and the software to be implemented are to be made, a procedure reminding us somewhat of building with (digital) Lego-bricks. Some programs attempt to reproduce the working behavior of creators of architecture using terms for digital building elements such as "ceiling", "wall", "roof", etc. Building parts already generated can be repeated over and over again and stored in a building part-library. Parametrics is the major goal; questions as to accuracy while input - in other words as to detail variety - still have to be solved. Moreover, the issue of scale is a matter of definition. Furthermore, sections of a project can be assembled at a later stage.

Visualizing, i.e. a viewable representation, is based on geometrical information modeling. The wire mesh model featuring all edges outlining the structure is produced in a matter of no time. Some users prefer this kind of representation and take it for granted that the viewer will be able to make head or tail of this jungle of lines. The so-called "Hidden-Lines-Representation" reduces the number of depicted lines, this leading to frequent errors. Shading procedures represent the next step in representation means, also making for color and material differentiations. Scanned or textures produced by a paint program are projected on a surface by means of "texture mapping" and various light sources can be positioned additionally within the space. The parameters to be determined usually are direction of light, radiation angle and intensity.

With the (complete) 3D-model any desired sections through this model can be generated and subsequently processed as 2D-drawing document. The point of viewing can be varied as required, making for a quick and simple perspective check of the input-objects.

2.4 Chronological Overlapping

The computer-assisted representation evidently has an orientation "to the future" substantially having the future development in mind. Using catchwords such as efficiency and productivity the virtual "heaven on earth" is promised. These techniques dedicated to advancement simultaneously also furnish us with the "learning look" at the past. Construction serving reconstruction or reconstruction in terms of construction may lend itself as motto.

Regarding computer-assisted reconstruction the question arises to which extent such visualizing of already destroyed building substance rather provides us with a construction method based on abstract, i.e. fragmented data. These data sets are bound to contain some fuzziness; the required supplementations and their resulting "falsification" of the historical picture are to be studied carefully. Reconstruction of a substance also amounts to delaying the chronology of decay or of changes in some way or the other. What was lost is somehow regained. A specific historical moment is detached from its chronological context, to be considered as an "absolute value" in various respects obtaining the status of autonomy and resistance as far as chronological sequences are concerned. "Moves" are achieved by means of the QTVR-technique, which integrates the object structures reconstructed into the photographically recorded reality. The virtual and the real meet and overlap in the picture window, the joint between physical and virtual reality: a dynamic approach regarding dialogue between viewer and reconstruction.

3 Context

Vienna, one of the historically most interesting capitals of the world, is constantly accompanied by its ever-present past with every step forwards. Wherever one goes traces of the past are witnessed, amidst the urban scenery as well as in the maze of underground development. Cultivation of this past has already become a specific program. The past and its "animation" serve as a major attraction for many tourists to Vienna. Several oppositional spots, however, have remained unnoticed, as "blind spots" hidden in the urban scenario full of places of historical interest.

3.1 Surroundings

The Neudeggergasse 12 inhabits one of those barren, weather-beaten municipal housing projects, the dating of which is pretty evident. Put up haphazardly in the fifties, the so-called post-war period, it is located where an impressive, historical interesting building had been up to November 1938. The Synagogue in Neudeggergasse erected according to Max Fleischer's plans was a sublime Neo-Gothic exposed brick building dominating the surrounding street space adding to the "characteristics" of the vicinity. With a height practically double as high as the surrounding buildings its towers rose into the sky and gave the tranquil street a dominant vertical line. Other works of the architect Max Fleischer include the synagogues in Schmalzhofgasse and Müllnergasse in Vienna and other buildings in Budweis, Pilgram and Lundenburg.

3.2 Collection of Source Material

Research work on the Synagogue in Neudeggergasse in the Jewish Museum Vienna, the Historical Museum of the City of Vienna and the Picture Archives of the Austrian National Library only produced meager findings, such as individual pictures of varying quality mainly of the main facade and the interior. The complete plans submitted (horizontal projections, axial and cross sections) in the 1:100 scale with all modifications from the period of 1897 to 1903 as well as a "demolishing plan" stemming from 1938 were discovered (fig. 1).

4 Reconstruction Work

4.1 In-situ pictures

Panorama views from various viewpoints in the Neudeggergasse were made. Seven shots per viewing point were produced using a miniature reflex camera and 15mm-wide angle objective, the two adjacent pictures partly overlapping. In addition, the complete facade of the residential house Neudeggergasse 12 was photographed from the other side of the street.

4.2 Panorama View Points

First the pictures taken are digitized. The photographs are transmitted to a PhotoCD directly after developing in differing resolutions. The now digital material is imported picture for picture in the QTVR Authoring Studio Software™ (processing surface "Panorama Stitcher"). After entering the specific values of focus (15 mm) and the desired compression (Cinepak 75) and the

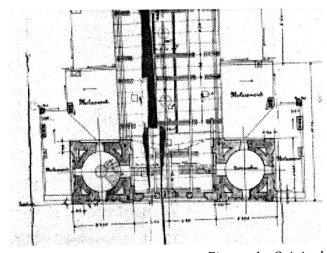

Figure 1. Original ground floor plan

Figure 2. Main facade and tower section.

picture size (512x384 Pixel /3:4) three files are available:

a.) a plane cylinder view (development of the panorama ("pict");

b.) a "tile-file", an automatic re-entering Quicktime file containing all information of the compression of the QTVR panorama view point ("mov");

c.) a QTVR-panorama file ("pano")

This procedure is repeated for the other views, thus producing a "vicinity model" with a great degree of details.

4.3 Three-dimensional Modeling

The synagogue is modeled by means of the available set of plans using the program ArchiCAD. The complete project is broken down into easily comprehensible sections, such as the facades, towers, furnishings, etc.. In the course of modeling processing procedures such as multiplication, reflection and changes in dimension are modified using varying parameters. Upon completion of the individual sections they are put together to make up a total.

4.4 Texturing

The next step towards the virtual model is the texturing of the individual building parts according to their original appearance, i.e. the visual appearance of the surface is simulated. Adequate surface patterns are scanned in or produced in picture-processing programs. These patterns are matched to the respective building parts by means of ArchiCAD and materials, i.e. the building parts obtaining the same texture, are grouped together. No reliable findings as to colors and materials of interior decoration of the synagogue in Neudeggergasse were available. Thus texturing of the interior were subjected to an abstraction leaving all building parts in gray, only for the Holy Shrine in the very center ("Aron Hakodesch") being gold-plated.

4.5 Model and Surroundings

ArchiCAD also makes a VR-Panorama for integration of the generated 3D-model of the synagogue into the also available QTVR panorama of the surroundings of Neudeggergasse. Therefore those locations are to be chosen corresponding to the real- picture camera position in situ. Focus and angle of view are to be adjusted accordingly. By means of picture-processing the superpositioning is accomplished. The result can finally be put together in the QTVR Authoring Studio under the processing surface "Panorama Maker" to make up a QTVR panorama file.

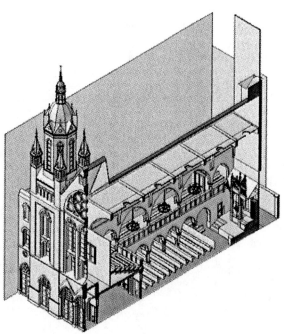

Figure 3. View into the dismantled model

Synagogue Neudeggergasse: A Virtual Reconstruction in Vienna

4.6 QTVR Scenery

Linkage of the produced QTVR elements by re-importing the already available panorama files in the QTVR Authoring Studio (processing surface "Scene Maker") result in a "walk-through" scenery. The individual viewing points are entered by so-called "Hotspots."

5 Conclusions

The present project is sounding out the potential of QuickTime VR throughout the framework of a computer-generated reconstruction of the synagogue "Neudeggergasse 12" in Vienna. Adapted from the complex perceptive procedures within the daily vicinity also the virtual reconstruction attempts to consider the coherent viewing of scenery. The inevitably necessary falling back upon the everyday world we are accustomed to requires transmittal of such experience into the experiences throughout the virtual world. Thus the entirely free moving in space is impaired, is forced into the rigid structure of perception we know. The world we then are moving in naturally only exists in fragments and collections thereof, major parts of which are added automatically anyway in our thoughts. On the screen we once again find ourselves in a collection of virtual objects, a patchwork of different sections of the picture reminding us over and over again that we are dealing with a completely artificial motional space, a world in which we can only move in leaps from room to room. The "hotspots" to be regarded as the keyholes partially evoke the impression of representations merging in parts into each other. What is to be pointed out anyhow, is that the entry into each following scenery amounts to an actual peeking into the neighboring room. But when does this ever happen in our everyday world? The areas of transition, i.e. the normally leading-up thresholds, are missing. Critically seen, there is somewhat of a flavor of artificialness, a characteristic rather clinging to the computer-generated with regard to its visual form of appearance. On the other hand possibilities are developed hardly to be physically experienced in the real world. The practically simultaneous leap into the past and back makes for the basis gaining ground for establishing new interrelations. Past and future are merely a mouse-click apart.

Figure 4. Existing versus reconstructed situation

The experience gained throughout the reconstruction of a synagogue in the Neudeggergasse (Vienna) demonstrated that the effective reconstruction has been accomplished and thus a sustainable confrontation with history initiated. The implementation of computer-generated building structures in an assembled real-picture surroundings furnished us with a reality level approaching the complex procedures within human perception.

Figure 5. Panorama Neudeggergasse

References

Genée, P. (1987). *Wiener Synagogen 1825 - 1938*. Wien: Löcker Verlag.

Genée, P. (1992). *Synagogen in Österreich*. Wien: Löcker Verlag.

Reconstruction work on synagogues in Austria:

http://info.tuwien.ac.at/raumsim/IRIS-ISIS

http://www.mediatecture.at/synagogue.html

Reconstruction work on synagogues in Germany:

http://www.cad.architektur.tu-darmstadt.de

http://www.cad.architektur.tu-darmstadt.de/synagogen/inter/menu.html

Following www-addresses provide more information on QuicktimeVR and VRML:

http://www.apple.com/quicktime/qtvr/

http://www.qtvr.com/

http://www.iqtvra.org/

http://www.vrml.org/

http://www.web3d.org/vrml/

Architectural Education: Students Creating a City Model

Wolfgang Dokonal, Graz University of Technology, Austria

Bob Martens, Vienna University of Technology, Austria

Reinhard Plösch, Graz University of Technology, Austria

Abstract

This paper describes experiences with the creation of a 3-D City Model at our University of Technology. It presents an innovative approach in establishing a city model with the support of the students in the study fields of Architecture and Surveying. The main goal of this work is directed at the implementation within the framework of architectural education. This contribution presents the concept in detail. It also discusses matters concerning the level of detail for different uses of such a 3-D model.

Keywords: Urban Modeling, 3-D Modeling, Architectural Education, Collaboration

1 Introduction

The idea for the creation of a 3-D city model resulted from the situation that innumerable design and urban projects were modeled individually at the Faculty of Architecture in the past, focusing on various parts of the City. All these computer-based models were created for several purposes and accidentally in different ways. Unfortunately, re-using these models for other projects was not possible and in the course of the time several parts of the city were modeled again and again. However, this work improved the skills of the students basically in computer modeling, but did not deliver any further benefits or any added values for the faculty or the city.

2 Objectives

The starting point of the procedure for the creation of a 3-D city model is the potential contribution by a large number of students. By means of bundling and coordinating all efforts in city modeling a perspective for collecting and assembling all the entire parts of the city modeled in the framework of different study courses is developed. Moreover, a sharing and re-using within the framework of the curriculum is intended. The main data source for this model is the photogrammetrical evaluation of aerial pictures supplied by the Department of Survey. This is a reliable source for larger areas in the city, as the digital cadastral map proved to be not sufficiently accurate. For small parts of the city also data from the terrestrial survey are available. The efforts behind this project are generally coordinated with the Faculty of Geometry. The photogrammetrical evaluation of aerial pictures provides data about the configuration of building roofs (eaves and ridges), but not about the exterior walls. For this reason a site analysis is necessary to check e.g. the distance between eaves and the exterior walls and also important detailing elements concerning the façade. However, there remains a certain difference towards the accuracy of the terrestrial survey and estimation. The 3-D city model is based on models of individual buildings within the city. For every building an AutoCAD-drawing is produced by using 3-D polylines. After conversion into 3-D faces, there is still a possibility of changing the model of every individual building.

3 Working Principles and Ideas regarding Realization

Comprehensive data on the existing buildings are to be compiled, to be processed for further analyses and to be made available for simulations of constructional approaches and planning by digital systems. The required data are recorded gradually and furnished to the data base management system. The governing data principles are to be defined unambiguously and are to allow for tracing back in order to grant usefulness. The data once recorded thus can be supplemented and analyzed and lend themselves to numerous uses. As data gathering is patchwork delivered by different individuals, the pertaining defined guidelines are to be carefully observed. Therefore, any information to be added to the 3-D city model is for this reason recorded on a data sheet. This makes for tracing back and controlling the input of the data afterwards; concerning more accuracy this information can be reviewed. Building data are entered into the database at varying "LoDs" (level of detail), depending on availability of basic data. The first LoD contains photogrammetrically evaluated aerial views as AutoCAD file *.dwg- and/or *.dxf-format. Thus the roofscape is determined to a large degree by the horizontal projection and the altitude development. An in-situ picture, however, will prove indispensable in order to correct any possible mistakes of aerial evaluations and moreover, to determine the location of facade surfaces with respect to the roof outline (estimation). Based on these data the girding surfaces for every individual building are constructed in AutoCAD and stored as *.dwg- and/or as *.dxf file.

The second LoD deals with the additional information derived from evaluation of aerial pictures (e.g. dormers of roofs, chimneys, etc.) in an individual file. So required it is linked to the basic model. Links to the next, the third LoD make for information on space-defining elements recorded in in-situ pictures of the facades (e.g. balconies, bays, etc.). Insofar as detailed models are available due to terrestrial surveying and detail planning, resp., these are added to the database as the fourth LoD. If required these are used instead of the basic model and the other LoDs.

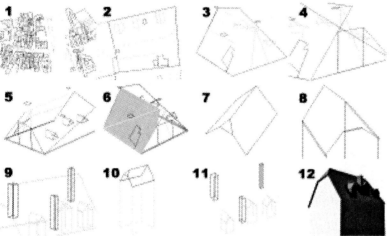

Figure 1. Characteristic steps within the working procedure [1] Basic data of the area evaluated; 2) Basic data of the building to be covered; 3) 3D-view of the basic data - shows obvious mistakes at the gable end and dormers of roof; 4) 5) subsidiary line constructions; 6) construction of a roof area; 7) main roof areas; 8) facade areas; 9) main roof and detail elements; 10) exported basic model; 11) exported detail level-1 model; 12) shadowed 3D-model.

4 Preparation of Data Records and Management System Thereof

A detailed documentation sheet on every individual building, as pointed out above, is kept up-to-date stating clearly data source, any mistakes regarding basic data, data corrections, etc. This documentation represents an essential component of the data records, as any missing description would make the data obtained useless for the database, as the data source (and thus its correctness) could not be definitely traced back at a later stage. Thus the word-document template "digcity.dot" was developed, making for storage of each individual building according to name of street house number. The geometry data are stored in the various file formats (*.obj., *dxf and *.3ds). Presently, data management puts a file-system with hierarchic directory-structure to use, access via various levels: street name, house number and type of file. A Perl-script is used to this end. In future a GIS-system is to be implemented for this purpose.

5 Findings and Outlook

Most of the existing city models are built as a 3-D city information system for public consultation or planners. The main goal of the creation of this 3-D model is to establish improved resources for architectural education - both on level of urban design as well as (architectural) project design - by using the potential of a "mass university" on a low budget. Other schools of architecture might benefit from this experience. As an educational approach, the experience can be the starting point for future studies.

The actual state is as follows: approx. 300 buildings have been covered according to above guidelines. Time consumption per premise amounts to approx. 10 buildings per student within roughly 2 days. Due to his experience the same person would cover further 10 buildings within only one working day. Subsequent treatment follows thereafter, mainly consisting of checking for completeness and correctness of the data records furnished. Based on the total building stock in the city area approx. 26.000 will have to be covered. Determining preferential treatment will prove wise, particularly concentrating on the downtown area. Quadruplicating the existing building inventory, a representative basic stock of approx. 1.000 buildings could be registered. Intended building activities would require innumerous documents by the authorities, thus submitting a specific (corresponding) 3-D data model would also be handy.

Though commissioning an outside provider with the production thereof would seem meaningful, this paper focuses on production delivered by students. The expansion of the city model presently is linked to several study courses thus granting different degrees of motivation on behalf of the students due to the different "usefulness" of the model products within the framework of the specific study course.

Motivation of the students proves sometimes difficult and "drop-outs" leave us with "white spots" (unfinished geometries) in our city model. In order to minimize this rate the study course for this project is be turned into a studio workshop making for more efficient continuous control of the process and immediate troubleshooting. The creation of the required basic geometry (sometimes a bit tedious for the students) is to result quicker by supplying a basic 3D Geometry for the buildings they are working on. The aim is to produce a "rough" model automatically by the photogrammetrical evaluation of aerial pictures. This project is being performed by one of our students - who is also a professional programmer - as a joint project with the Department of Survey of the Graz municipality and first results should be available by the beginning of the next semester. All these adjustments to our project will positively increase the speed of the "growth" and the quality of the city model by allowing the students to concentrate on the main aspects. The main goal of this project remains the process of creation of the model itself, as utilization of the city model can be a very helpful and important tool in architectural education.

Figure 2. The "rough" model and an example of the application in the framework of a project (a) sectional inventory photograph/ (b.-c) 3D-model with facade mapping / (d) computer-assisted simulation of renovation.

References

http://www.digcity.tu-graz.ac.at contains a more detailed description concerning the guidelines resp. working procedure. A careful explanation of techniques is furthermore presented there.

http://xarch.tu-graz.ac.at, is the experimental web server of our students which contains a big autocad supply page by Reinhard Urban

http://vrglasgow.co.uk, which contains a City model of Glasgow, which was modeled by a group of students at the University of Strathclyde under the direction of Tom Maver.

Dokonal, W., Martens, B. and Plösch, R. Graz: The creation of a 3D City Model for Architectural Education. In: ECAADE 18 [Proceedings of The 18th Conference on Education in Computer Aided Architectural Design Research in Europe], Weimar (Germany) 22.-24. June 2000, pp.171-175.

Day, Alan K. and Radford, Anthony D. Imaging Change: The Computer City Model as a Laboratory for Urban Design Research. In: Sixth International Conference on Computer-Aided Architectural Design Futures, Singapore, 24-26 September 1995, pp. 495-506.

Kaga, A., Shimazu, Y., Yamauchi, T., Ishihara, H. and Sasada, T. City Information Visualizer Using 3-D Model and Computer Graphics. In: CAADRIA '98 [Proceedings of The Third Conference on Computer Aided Architectural Design Research in Asia], Osaka (Japan) 22-24 April 1998, pp. 193-202.

Radford, A., Woodbury, R., Braithwaite, G., Kirkby, S., Sweeting, R. and Huang, E. Issues of Abstraction, Accuracy and Realism in Large Scale Computer Urban Models. In: CAAD Futures 1997 [Conference Proceedings], München (Germany), August 1997, pp. 679-690.

Use of Computers in Reconstruction of Ancient Buildings

Ming Zhou, Wenzhou Institute of Architectural Design and Research, China

Abstract

Many cities in China today are in the midst of a profound architectural transformation. Among these rapidly developing cities, most of them are many centuries old, possessing rich historical architecture of distinct local traditions. However, the ancient buildings and the neighborhood are disappearing quickly, because of the wholesale demolition for urban development or many years of neglect. In this paper, the use of computers in reconstruction of ancient buildings is briefly discussed with some case studies. The advanced computer technology provides a powerful tool for the ancient architecture preservation and reproduction. It makes the reconstruction engineering more efficient, true to the original, and low cost.

1 Introduction

Ancient architecture is of social, cultural, scientific and nostalgic importance. Its unique design and decorative techniques are valuable and can be used in modern architecture. How to preserve these vernacular buildings of many centuries old is nowadays a major task faced by many historic Chinese cities that are undergoing rapid changes. The use of computers in preservation and reconstruction of ancient architecture has been shown to be a very powerful and effective way.

2 Preservation and Reconstruction

Many ancient buildings, which survived the vicissitudes of history, need a number of repairs because of the damage caused by the elements. This preservation process may involve the replacement of some ruined components. However, sometimes, we even have to disassemble a building into parts first and put it back at a new location. When this happens, the reconstruction process is probably the only way to save such a building from being permanently destroyed.

Computers find a lot of important applications in the preservation and reconstruction process of ancient architecture. The applications can be divided in the following aspects:

2.1   Digital Representation of an Ancient Building

Before an ancient building is disassembled and moved to a new location, it is important to digitize the whole structure of the ancient building, including survey and drawing, the present appearance and status quo ante.

2.2   Selection of New Location

Where the ancient building will be relocated is one of the key issues of the process. It should fit in well with the surrounding buildings and neighborhood at the new location. Its building style and space structure should be in harmony with others. In particularly, these factors have to be considered: building heights, colors, materials, roof structures, orientation, and the distance to other buildings. With the help of a computer, we can visualize the fitting effect of the ancient building into a possible location. The location selection has never been easier by using the computer technology.

2.3   Disassembly and Inventory

Based on the computer drawings and the digital representation of the building, the best way to disassemble the building can be determined with a minimum damage. An inventory of all parts with detailed dimensions and drawings is generated with a computer. The computer drawing can be

Figure 1. White Horse Taoist Temple (after reconstruction).

used for the duplication of the part, if the replacement is necessary. Hence the repairs and assembly can be combined during the reconstruction stage.

2.4 Reconstruction

The digitized information about the building from the computer is used for the accurate and precise restoration of the building during the reconstruction stage. The attention has been paid to that the reconstructed building should remain the same style and appearance as the old one. In order to achieve this, the steps listed below have been followed.

- The reconstruction is done precisely according to the working drawing from the computer.
- The original parts have been put back into the right positions as they were.
- The duplicated part used to replace the damaged one should be made of the same material, shape and size as the original.

3 Case Studies

Here are a few examples of the ancient buildings which have been recently repaired or to be reconstructed in Wenzhou, China.

Figure 2. Detailed wood structure of the White Horse Taoist Temple.

3.1 Bai Ma Dao Guan (White Horse Taoist Temple, Wenzhou, Zhejiang, China)

This Taoist Temple was originally built in 618 AD, during the transition of the Sui Dynasty to the Tang Dynasty. The building has the unique and prominent feature of the classical Chinese architecture – the timber framework composed of columns, beams, purlins and a multitude of corbel brackets. The wood structure of the building was reconstructed in 1997 at the original location. Figure 1 shows the interior structure of the building after reconstruction. As a Taoist Temple, although it is different from other kinds of structures, the building follows the basic principle for a Chinese structure - balance and symmetry. Figure 2 shows one of the details of the wood building structure.

3.2 Miao Guo Si (Magic Fruit Buddhist Temple, Wenzhou, Zhejiang, China)

Shown in Figure 3 is the building layout of Miao Guo Si. This Buddhist Temple was initially built in the Tang Dynasty (714 AD). Its flying eaves, pointed roofs and layers of rookeries reflect the flourishing Tang Dynasty which was a period of great prosperity. It differs from the Taoist Temple as shown in Figure 1 in the layout of buildings, ways of groupings, system of colored paintings and themes of engravings. Portraits of Buddhas, murals, engraved tables, calligraphy, Buddhist utensils, furnishings, and Buddhist scriptures are carefully kept in the construction. As a cultural relic, all the wood structure was reconstructed at the original location in 1984. Figure 4 shows the interior structure after reconstruction.

3.3 Zheng's Stele Pavilion (Wenzhou, Zhejiang, China)

The Pavilion to be reconstructed was originally built in the Ming Dynasty (1608 AD). Figure 5 shows one possible location for this Pavilion. As shown in Figure 5, the pavilion consists of a main gate at the center, two wings extended from either side of the main gate to form other two rooms, and surrounding winding corridor. The main purpose of this pavilion is to keep three big stone steles which are precious with engraved calligraphy.

4 Conclusions

The protection of ancient constructions as cultural relics has been an urgent issue in China. A lot of efforts have been spent for the preservation and reconstruction of these buildings. In this specific area, the computer technology has found its unique role in the survey and drawing, urban planning, and reconstruction. With its help, not only is the restoration more accurate and efficient, but the construction time and cost are dramatically reduced too.

Figure 3. Building layout.

Figure 4. Interior structure after reconstruction.

AGENCY GP: Genetic Programming for Architectural Design

Peter Testa, School of Architecture and Planning, Massachusetts Institute of Technology, USA

Una-May O'Reilly, Artificial Intelligence Laboratory, Massachusetts Institute of Technology, USA

Simon Greenwold, Emergent Design Group, Massachusetts Institute of Technology, USA

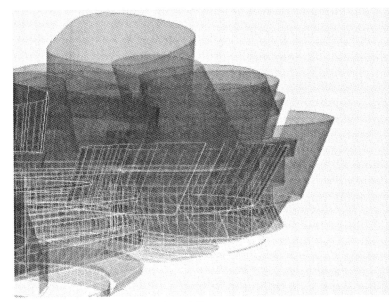

Abstract

AGENCY GP is a prototype for a system using genetic programming (GP) for architectural design exploration. Its software structure is noteworthy for its integration into a high-end three-dimensional modeling environment, its allowance for direct user interruption of evolution and reintegration of phenotypically modified individuals, and its agent-based evaluation of fitness.

1 Overview

AGENCY GP is a software framework we are developing to explore the possibilities for architectural design of offices and workspaces that arise from new concepts for organization and management theory that include non-hierarchical and emergent organizations.

1.1   Maya Integration

Through the Alias|Wavefront Maya platform's API, we are building a genetic programming system operating over a language capable of expressing three dimensional designs and the free-form deformation of space to create morphologies that a designer may not have otherwise imagined possible. The Maya platform allows us to abstract the representation of three-dimensional forms so that we can operate freely on them without concern for the complexity of the underlying geometry. The language we have developed manipulates spatial constructs at a high enough level that its individual operations are meaningful to a designer. This language, in its representational power combined with its simplicity of expression, is the first major innovation of AGENCY GP.

1.2   User Control

Typically interruption, intervention, and resumption (IIR) of the evolutionary process is difficult to achieve in genetic programming environments because in most systems it is impossible to map changes of the external (phenotypic) individual back onto the internal genotype. However, because of the high level of transparency of our GP language, we have been able to design a system that will allow for IIR. A designer will be able to employ statements of the language himself to manually alter the forms of members of the population and reintegrate them for continued evolution. IIR, the second software innovation of AGENCY GP is a primary objective of research, and a major area for our continued investigation.

1.3   Agents

The third innovation AGENCY GP will employ is the determination of fitness from the point of view of various agents that inhabit the space. Agents are not necessarily single users; they may also represent emergent organizational elements such as a group of users who express a coherent need, a resource that has allocation demands, or a group of resources that provide a service. An agent may represent the pattern of a group, its needs for privacy, meeting space and collaborative surfaces, or it may undertake the concern of management structure or productivity. What agent-based fitness allows for is a modular structure for the integration of multiple criteria for fitness. We intend to abstract the agent structure so that new agents may be developed and employed for new applications without rewriting the entire system. This agent-based evaluation of fitness is well suited to expressing the conflicting, non-linear, multi-level spatial requirements of emergent organizational structures.

2 Background and Motivation

AGENCY GP is the software arm of a larger project called AGENCY. The project seeks architectural responses to the radical transformation that business organizations are currently undergoing. The pace of organizational change is being driven by the rapid development of commercial technology, global markets and reengineered, quality oriented organizations. This constant need to change gives rise to organizations that are no longer stable, but continuously adapting to their shifting environments. Such organizations can be said to be "emergent" and include many of today's commercial and governmental organizations.

Vertically structured office buildings no longer provide the model for most business organizations. With the advent of widespread use of telecommunications, information technology, and corporate reorganization in the 1990's, new forces are actively reshaping the architecture of office buildings. There is a shift in the United States toward research and development, management and finance, consultancy, and the culture industry, productive activities less prone to standardization and bureaucratization. Driven by the demand to improve office productivity, businesses and organizations have begun to experiment with a variety of alternative officing methods. However, there exist no working models of an intelligent adaptive architecture. The AGENCY project focuses on application oriented basic research to develop new design software that generatively models the complex interaction of physical space and information technology within emergent organizations. Using the research software this project will also generatively design and test spatial systems and work environments for emergent organizations.

We have chosen genetic programming to address these challenges because the strengths of the model are well matched to our system's desired characteristics. First, we are aware of the impossibility of modeling emergent organizations deterministically. To try to design a top-down algorithm for the creation of workspaces would certainly fall victim to our inability to name every constraint the problem entails. Therefore we look to the bottom-up solutions, Artificial Life (ALife), and in particular, GP affords, to construct solutions that are consistently sensitive to complicated interactions that a user need not explicitly codify. Second, we are interested in the genetic model's ability to offer a user an entire population of solutions to peruse and potentially to reevaluate. We are aware the process we are involved in is not a simple optimization with a single goal, but has many potential fruitful avenues of exploration. The multi-tracked exploratory process of population evolution provides a designer multiple alternatives with which to interact at any point. Our goal is to develop GP as a design partner, offering options that would otherwise not come to light.

3 Methodology

3.1 Tool Design and Implementation

We are implementing our software as a plug-in extension of Alias|Wavefront's Maya package, a leading tool for the creation and visualization of complex virtual environments. Maya is of widespread use in the fields of three-dimensional animation for film and broadcast, but has only recently begun to see broad application to explorations of morphology such as AGENCY GP. Maya's open architecture allows for software developed using all modern high-level languages features to exploit the power of its inbuilt library of three-dimensional operations. Any imaginable three-dimensional form is expressible in terms of Maya's available spatial transformations and Boolean operations.

3.2 System Overview

Our implementations of the GP's main generational loop, selection, mutation, and crossover are conventional. The individuals in the population, described below, are fairly complicated structures. Some of the data they contain is of fixed length and type, and is therefore evolved in place, while some of it is in the form of a variable-length sequence of language operations. Therefore we use a hybrid GA/GP to manipulate both types of values.

3.3 Representation and Language

We use a combination of Maya and C++ objects for the internal representation of individuals in our population. A user begins the process with a Maya scene containing one or more closed NURBS (non-uniform rational b-spline) curves selected. These curves should be coplanar but may be of any closed form and may intersect. In the interpreted phenotypic representation, these curves will be extruded into space. (Fig. 1-2)

When the AGENCY GP is invoked from within Maya, a C++ object is permanently attached to each NURBS curve. This C++ construct contains evolvable values pertaining to the shape and architectural function of the region the curve encloses. The object also contains an evolvable sequence of operations in our GP language to be applied to this curve. Each curve is given a height of extrusion and treated as a NURBS surface extending from the base plane into space.

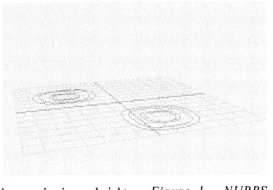

Figure 1. NURBS Curves in Maya.

The operations in our language are simple but powerful transformations of these NURBS surfaces. The images below demonstrate the operations of our language applied to the left-hand NURBS surface from the scene. (Fig. 3-8)

These operations form the core commands of our language. Mutation may consist of addition or deletion of an operation, or the change of a parameter. Execution is strictly linear; there is no facility for conditionals or branching. This simple program structure contributes to our ability to implement IIR.

We are counting on these surfaces to intersect with each other in ways we cannot predict. Each Boolean operation we apply—intersection, union, or subtraction—forms a new enclosed surface that may be assigned its own architectural function based on values in the GA section of the curve.

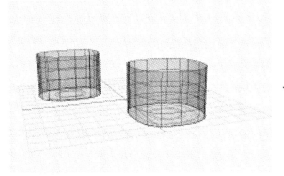

Figure 2. NURBS Curves Extruded.

Each individual in a population, therefore, is comprised of several separate Maya/C++ objects each of which carries a NURBS surface, certain evolvable values, and a list of operations. That we never directly query or modify the low-level geometry of the Maya objects, but allow Maya to perform all needed transformations and Boolean operations is what makes the language high enough level to be useful for the direct intervention of a designer.

3.4 Agent-Based Fitness

Integration of GP with a high-end three-dimensional modeling tool allows us to apply extremely abstract and computationally expensive heuristics as measures of fitness. We are developing a framework into which individually developed software modules can be placed that evaluate our designs from various perspectives. These modules are called agents because each has a specific agenda for determining fitness. Some agents may represent actual users of the space, while others will be interested in issues such as fire-code compliance, or energy efficiency. Virtually any criterion for evaluation can be coded and dropped in as an agent to our framework. We can specify that workspaces require a certain quotient of natural light or that circulation spaces desire width enough to allow for conversation. Using agent-based evaluation, we will be able to model management structures and determine their influence on potential designs.

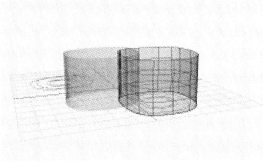

Figure 3. TRANSLATE (X, Y).

The fitness of a design will be determined by combining the various satisfactions of the agents deployed into the space. We will be able to integrate any calculable metric to our system through this architecture, so that AGENCY GP's richness and power can grow incrementally as we continue to develop agents.

3.5 Interruption, Intervention, and Resumption

Once a population has been ranked by fitness, the AGENCY GP becomes open to IIR. The entire population of interpreted designs is available for viewing by the user, who has several options. The user may simply re-rank individuals and allow evolution to continue, or he may take a candidate and apply one or more operations from our language to as many of the NURBS surfaces that com-

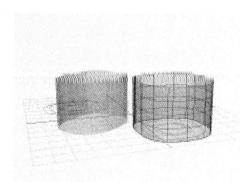

Figure 4. ROTATE (DEGREES).

prise it as he wishes. The transformations the user applies will be added to the list of operations in the internal representation of the individual. By providing the basic operations of three-dimensional modeling through our language we enable designers to make targeted modifications of designs before allowing evolution to continue.

4 Conclusions

We have demonstrated that it is possible to outline a methodology for the integration of artificial life into architectural design exploration that empowers both the programmer and user of the system to influence the process.

5 Future Software Research

Our first order of business is to continue the implementation of the proposed system. When complete we will be able to devote our attention to the creation of a variety of agents suited to different tasks. The issue of user-intervention opens up research possibilities into how subjective selection interacts with computed fitness. Which agents, for instance, are the ones that a designer tends to favor? Are there agents who are difficult to satisfy simultaneously? Observational and statistical analysis of agent-based fitness and user selection will certainly lead to interesting insights into our software and our preferences as designers.

References

Bonabeau, E.W. (1997). From Classical Models of Morphogenesis to Agent-Based Models of Pattern Formation. In *Artificial Life,* vol. 3, 199-211.

Goldberg, D.E. (1989). *Genetic Algorithms in Search, Optimization, and Machine Learning.* Reading, MA: Addison-Wesley Publishing Company Inc.

Resnick, M. (1994). Learning About Life. In *Artificial Life,* vol. 1, 229-241.

Testa, P., and O'Reilly, U.M. (1999). Emergent Design Studio. In *Media and Design Process, ACADIA Annual Meeting Proceedings,* 338-339.

Testa, P., et al., (2000). MoSS: Morphogenetic Surface Structure - A Software Tool for Design Exploration. In *Proceedings of Greenwich 2000: Digital Creativity Symposium,* 71-80.

Wilensky, U. and Resnick, M. (1999). Thinking in Levels: A Dynamic Systems Perspective to Making Sense of the World. In *Journal of Science Education and Technology,* vol. 8, no. 2, 3-19.

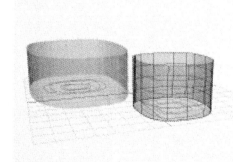

Figure 5. SCALE (X, Y).

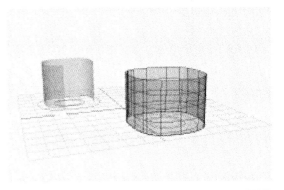

Figure 6. CUT (START, STOP).

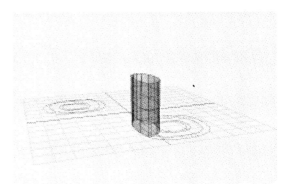

Figure 7. Boolean Intersection.

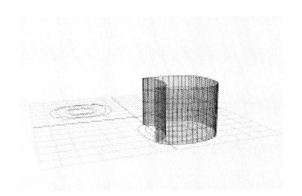

Figure 8. Boolean Subtraction.

Computer-Simulated Growth Processes in Urban Planning and Architecture

Bernd Streich, University of Kaiserslautern/University of Bonn, Germany

Rivka Oxman, Technion, Haifa, Israel

Oliver Fritz, University of Kaiserslautern, Germany

Abstract

Urban structures, developed and grown over a period of time, are created by processes that, due to the number of influential factors, are not longer comprehensible as a whole. Their development is very complex and depends on a big number of reciprocal factors that even architects or planners sometimes cannot recognize the formal, functional and rational processes of thinking behind it. The involved mechanisms however are particularly obvious in historical urban structures that came to exist over a period of centuries. The planned relationships within these conglomerates are governed by nearly indiscernible rules and show similarities in form and shape to living and non-living forms in nature. They are clearly analogous to fractals or systems with chaotic behavior. In the course of the research project "media experimental design", financed by the German Research Foundation, algorithms are sought that are able to simulate urban analogous structures digitally. To this effect the main rules of growth processes are researched and extracted. Then, by following these rules, virtual structures are developed and shown by using powerful three-dimensional techniques. The developed mechanisms allow urban planning to be process-oriented, interactive and flexible for permanently changing parameters. With an implemented set of rules the computer is able to create a design and to react to changing situations.

In several experimental studies structures were successfully generated which have different forms and qualities depending on their set of rules. For example, structures were programmed which are similar to a big city while other look like a village in hilly landscape. Diverse rules and strategies have been used in order to reduce them to shape specific factors. The rules for growth are administered by a specifically developed databank with sophisticated search mechanisms using the Issue-Concept-Form tool as case-based-reasoning method.

Keywords: Simulation; urban growth-processes; virtual reality

1 Simulation of alterations in urban development

The making of architecture is a process affected by numerous different influences. Architectural and urban planning's are cutouts of a large-scale structure and refer to a certain scale. Depending on the chosen or given precision the abstractions of the desired or planned reality are drawn. With this well-established and necessary procedure indistinctnesses are generated. It results in an urban situation with a certain detail. External influences as for example topography, existing green and buildings, direction as well as building relevant data like program, structural density or proportion make the overall design. Sometimes there is just a hierarchic road system the integral part of a design, on other times it is a whole village with all the single houses thought out down to the last detail. The levels of detail, which are not captured in the respective scale develop individually and are not controllable. They are beyond the architects control and his formal, functional and rational considerations. These principles can be seen particularly well with historic urban structures, which have grown over centuries. The planned coherence within these conglomerates is complex and it is difficult to detect discernible rules. Interestingly these settlements are similar in form and shape to

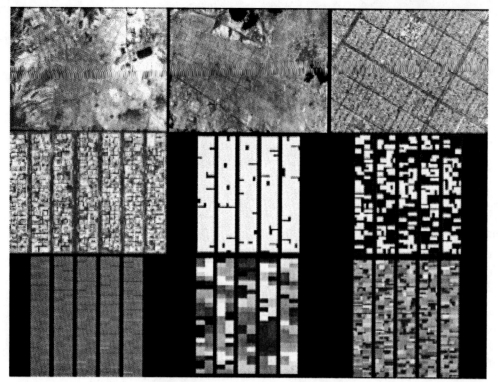

Figure 1.

the animate and inanimate nature. Aerial photographs and satellite pictures of these structures remind of the expansion of plant populations and cell formations.

The research project 'Media-Experimental Designing in Architecture and Urban Planning' sponsored by the DFG is dealing with a creative use of computers in the field of architecture. Under the leadership of Prof. Dr.-Ing. Bernd Streich (University of Kaiserslautern) and Mrs. Dr. Rivka Oxman at the TECHNION in Haifa / Israel, growth processes of urban structures are explored and programmed. The aim is to make out the apparently unplannable courses of urban growth and to convert them into algorithms.

These growth rules implemented into a Virtual Reality environment via computer allow simulating artificial city growth. By programming the rules, standards and laws of a virtual world this technique and philosophy makes it possible to let urban structures grow and to observe their individual behavior. Several experiments on different levels of abstraction led to promising results. As in a test-tube, cities can be bred. One part of the current research actually is to 'interbreed' urban development modules and their algorithms evolutionary and genetically. These thoughts are derived from the field of 'Artificial Life', where from information technological view artificial organisms are created and bred in a computer. Because of the similarity of organic behavior and urban growth this thought seems to be natural.

2 Village Generator: Urban Structures as Organisms

In this virtual environment just a few different elements were implemented. Direction and topography are to be absolutely important for the growth of the building. The virtual buildings are produced by generators moving independently in space. On their way they check the prevailing attractivity of a position, which results from the given 'natural' environmental factors. The generators were programmed to perform a kind of 'social' behavior among themselves, so that they are able to change direction depending on the proximity to a neighbor. This so called 'flocking behavior' is known from nature and adapted from birds or insects. When the given conditions are met the generator produces a building. Because of interactions among the generators this relatively simple programming results in very harmonic and even motion paths, which wouldn't have been predictable like in this case. The emerging forms of life are organic in the sense of a term in architectural theory, meaning that they developed from the inside. Essential in this experiment was to see, that the adjusted behaviors were not directly derived from the experiences in urban development but are very similar to existing village structures in mountainous regions. This kind of using analogies for developing complex architectures were explored for instance at the Institute for Lightweight Structures at the University of Stuttgart under Prof. Frei Otto, the designer of the roofing for the Olympic Stadium in Munich. There architectonic form was adapted from examples found in nature.

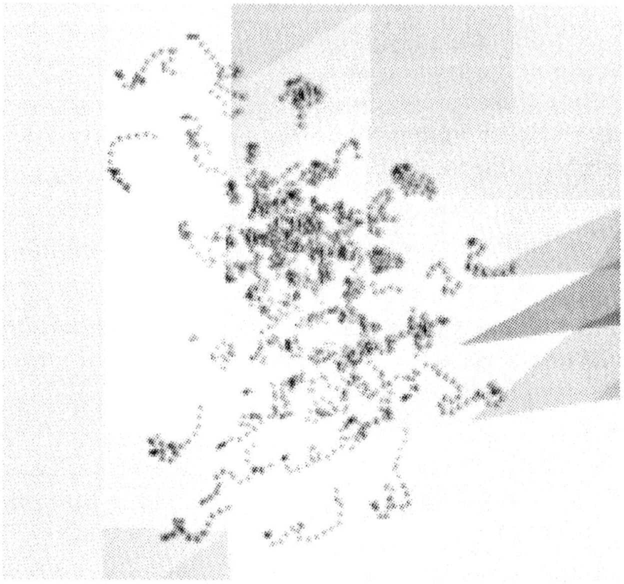

Figure 2

3 City Generator: Simulation of Formation Processes in Cityscapes

In their use of form structures of villages seem organic, incomprehensible and complex. They are also less subject to formal rules than the 'grown' city. The cityscape is characterized by axes, squares and spatial density. For a simulation of a cityscape other rules and behaviors for the urban development modules had to be determined. Whereas simple and clear rules ensure the necessary lighting and circulation of the virtual houses, wide regulations of behavior patterns are needed to control position and alignment of the neighbor modules. This happens discreetly within the whole virtual city, which means, that every single house refers formally to his environment. Every building is telling his environment where from his point of view the follow-up buildings can be positioned. As a base for communication a grid of attractions was introduced in which the single factors are added. The more powerful the influence of a neighbor on a city module is, the more it will align orthogonal to it and turn the open side if possible towards the imaginary roadside. Building line and squares result from an extra high attractivity given to the sides or the firewalls. Structures and building blocks can be imported into the city generator, so that he has to react to the existing. Especially with these experiments astonishing similarities to real urban situations were achieved. Older building formations become surrounded by the growing city with distinct axes and squares and integrated into the designed center.

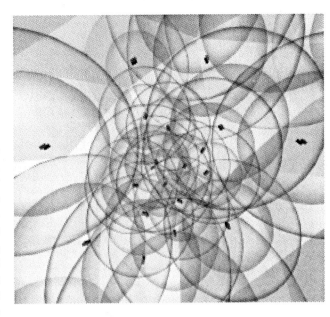

Figure 3.

4 Compression Machine: Three-Dimensional Quantitative Analysis of Urban Situations

One of the most important and most difficult tasks in the field of architecture and town planning is building in an existing environment and the compression of urban situations. A proper classification of the numerous influence factors, which regulate the attractivity of the single building sites, is essential. With a concrete example a guided re-compression process was produced in a computer simulation. By means of CAD a building block was drawn and given properties in a virtual world. These are quantitative values like structural density, land price and population density, which are filed in data fields, as well as formal factors like size, use, topology and semantics, which are assigned directly to the objects. The process data can be given values depending on how the designer thinks this is relevant for the situation. The following attractivity is visualized real-time as a three-dimensional object in the virtual environment.

Figure 4.

It is possible to view the single factors separately or as the total amount. The result is an abstract building of which its shape already can be used for inspiration. The designer determines, which conditions the new building structure has to meet within his design, e.g. the desired population density or the rough distribution of the single building types within the area. Furthermore he defines the limits of the building types (max. height, optimal orientation, depth of the building etc.). The software now proposes compression measures and computes the respective effects. In this way programmed loops and recursive functions produce an optimal result under the given conditions allowing the designer to intervene at any time.

5 Design Machine: Work in Progress

Besides the clearly defined rules there are especially in the field of designing a multitude of factors, which can't be expressed numerically or logically. In the appearance of architectures non-programmable design mechanisms turn up as for example zeitgeist, local materials and the individual taste of the architect or client.

The current work is concentrating on developing software, where different urban development modules learn to design themselves. Using neural nets, a kind of programming and genetic algorithms adapted from the human brain, allows training the elements of the virtual world, an intuitive

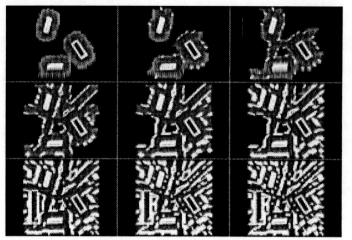

Figure 5.

behavior. With support of Prof. Michael M. Richter of the department 'Expert Systems and A.I.' at the University of Kaiserslautern it is supposed to succeed in teaching these intelligent elements a specific perception of their environment and to increase their knowledge in training sessions. The modules get confronted with an urban situation transferred from reality. According to their reactions the designer can support or forbid certain behaviors depending on his opinion and design knowledge. The modules trained in this 'arena' can be released into the virtual world, where they have to maintain themselves with regard to other modules. Particularly successful modules can 'interbreed' with others and pass on their genetic knowledge, less successful will die. The roots of growth and resulting, their structural development, can be fixed within the WebPAD (a specific database, developed at the Technion in Haifa, Israel). This process happens over a continuous period of time. These evolutionary principles raise the hopes to achieve further knowledge about the characteristics of natural urban growth and to find new ways of planning for a sensible dealing with the built environment.

The German Research council (DFG) is sponsoring the research project 'Media-Experimental Designing' since 1997.

References

Alexander, C. (1984). Pattern Language (Arch+ 93). Aachen: Arch+ Verlag.

Flusser, V. (1992). Virtuelle Räume – Simultane Welten (Arch+ 111). Aachen: Arch+ Verlag.

Gery/Eisenman. (1995). Entwerfen am Computer (Arch+ 128). Aachen: Arch+ Verlag.

Koolhaas, Rem (1995). S,M,L,XL. New York: Monacelli Press.

Lynn, G. (1995). Spezialeffekte in der Architektur (Arch+ 124/125). Aachen: Arch+ Verlag.

Mitchell, William J. (1977). Computer-Aided Architectural Design. New York: Van Nostrand Reinhold Company.

Negroponte, Nicholas (1970). The Architecture Machine. Massachusetts: MIT Press.

Otto, Frei (1975). Adaptable Architecture. Stuttgart: Karl Krämer Verlag.

Otto, Frei (1991). Non-Planned Settlements. Stuttgart: Karl Krämer Verlag.

Otto, Frei (1995). Pneu and Bone. Stuttgart: Karl Krämer Verlag.

Figure 6.

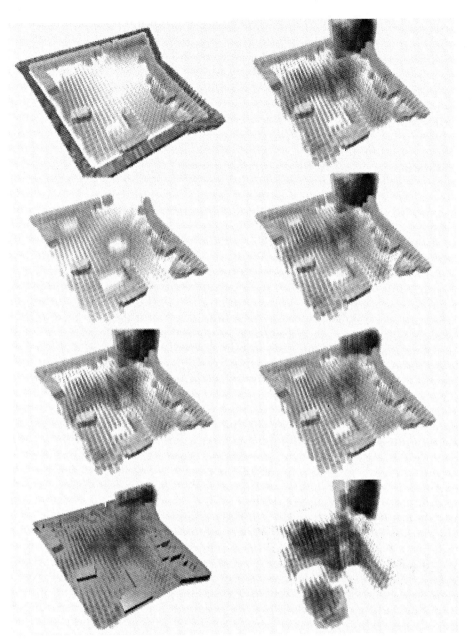

Figure 7.

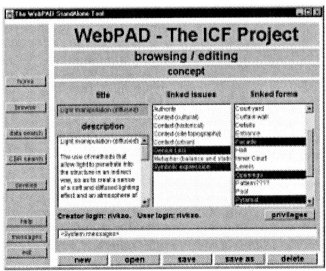

Figure 8.

Mass-Customization in Design Using Evolutionary and Parametric Methods

Cristiano Ceccato, The Hong Kong Polytechnic University, China

Alvise Simondetti, The Hong Kong Polytechnic University, China

Mark C. Burry, Deakin University, Australia

Abstract

This paper describes a project within the authors' ongoing research in the field of Generative Design. The work is based on the premise that computer-aided design (CAD) should evolve beyond its current limitation of one-way interaction, and become a dynamic, intelligent, multi-user environment that encourages creativity and actively supports the evolution of individual, mass-customized designs which exhibit common features.

The authors describe this idea by illustrating the implementation of a research project, which explores the notions of mass-customization in design by using evolutionary and parametric methods to generate families of simple objects, in our case a door handle. The project examines related approaches using both complex CAD/CAM packages (CADDS, CATIA) and a proprietary software tool for evolutionary design. The paper first gives a short historical and philosophical background to the work, then describes the technical and algorithmic requirements, and concludes with the implementations of the project.

1 Introduction

The idea of Mass-Customisation is not a new one. Shipbuilding is a good example of individual designs being borne out of common lore of common, effective design elements. This lore would manifest itself in 'ship classes', or families of related designs, in which the basic root scheme reflected the general function of the ship. Brigantine, Cruiser, Battleship, etc. each define a 'class' of discernible designs, but the fascination lies in the way how the different designs find different functional advantages, while remaining within their respective classes. In fact, each battleship design, even within a closely related class, was unique, reflecting the newest military knowledge or specific functional modifications. However, to integrate each of these unique features meant altering, or *customizing*, the root design. It is of particular interest, then, to observe the dissipation of acquired knowledge in time through the *evolution* of successive designs.

The idea of being able to manufacture a family of objects or products which have a common foundation in their design, structure and functionality, but are each unique in their individual manifestation, has long fascinated architects, designers and engineers. The basic understanding of a design family has always been tied to the notion that within a family variation is possible, indeed desirable and often necessary. This understanding is always inextricably linked to some form of implicit or explicit collection of 'rules' or 'guidelines' that decree the nature of the produced object. It is the flexibility of operation within the constraints, or 'parameters', of these rules that produces a 'family' of objects, and the voluntary or involuntary breaking of these boundaries which either broadens the range of a family or gives rise to a new one.

Elements of flexible manufacturing at both the design level and the assembly level have been increasingly evident in the last thirty years. These are driven by economic considerations. A good example is the aircraft industry. After the Second World War, manufacturers could no longer afford to offer a different aircraft for a different requirement. The speed at which markets developed meant that it was faster and cheaper to derive *variants* of an existing design, *modified* to fulfill new needs (e.g.: Boeing 367-80 ® Boeing 707 passenger jet, KC-135 tanker, E-3A AWACS sentry). This has become even more evident in the latest designs, in which not individual models, but whole *families* of aircraft are launched. These consist of an array of *related* models, which share parts, manufacturing, and flight-training *commonality* while containing enough 'room' for growth within the *root* design (e.g. Boeing 777 family) (Sabbagh 1996). This is also evident in the automotive industry, where individual users (customers) are able to specify a wide range of components. In the end, each *instantiation* of, for example, the Volkswagen Golf, is unique in its combination of chosen components, from basic inexpensive model to muscled sports car, while remaining a true Golf.

The emergence of new manufacturing methods, from CNC machining and CAM to flexible molding and robotic production lines, means that the rapid diffusion and development of Information Technology has much more to offer to the process of design and manufacturing than just computerized control of factories and assembly lines. The ability to combine an understanding of creative rule-based design systems with flexible methods of production will enable a new form of manufacturing which is freed from predefined geometric constraints and which efficiently translates rules which govern a design into tangible form. By varying these rules, we are able to achieve a broad family of interrelated, industrially manufactured, individually unique products.

In our research, we have concentrated on a simple design object – a door handle – through which to explore the ideas set out in this paper.

2 Mass-Customization Through Parametric Design

Basic Mass-Customization is achieved by modifying the definition parameters within a design framework. A basic design is established in its morphology, which does not change during the customization process. In this sense, there is no one 'root design', but rather many variations of it, each of which is instantiated by its individual, unique parametric values. In the case of our door handle, a basic design can consist of length, thickness, width and so on, as many as are required to define a handle. Obviously, the design can be more *fine grain* in its definition by employing a larger set of parameters. Once established, the parameter set that defines the design is not changed.

2.1 Parametric Design Systems

The employment of a powerful CAD/CAM software package can provide a strong foundation to the project. In our research we have been employing CADDS, an extremely sophisticated parametric solid modeler, and more recently CATIA, which has its origin in the aviation industry where Dassault Systèmes originally developed it for the design of jet fighters. Both systems have crossed over from engineering to within the areas of industrial design and architecture. CADDS has been successfully used on various design projects (Burry 1996; Goulthorpe and Burry 2000) while CATIA has famously proven its mettle on Frank Gehry's Guggenheim Museum in Bilbao.

2.2 Parametric Mass-Customisation using CADDS

Like many powerful CAD packages, CADDS can interact with external databases and generate geometry from numeric data. In this case, a definition of a door handle was built up within CADDS, and driven by parameters (variables) in Microsoft's Excel spreadsheet software. The Excel document contains the data necessary to describe curvature, size, etc. of a set of complex 3D surface geometries, which are connected to form a single solid volume of the handle. The data is transferred to CADDS which generates the solid.

The solid's structure is defined in CADDS in terms of the curves which describe it and how these are interconnected. Parametric control, however, also implies value constraints of minima and maxima within which a particular parameter must lie in order to define a *valid* shape – in our case, 'valid' means a viable door handle which has correct proportions in terms of leverage of the handle to the spindle, etc. Thus, a user can 'design' his or her door handle by manipulating the individual parameters within Excel to produce various *topologically identical* yet *morphologically diverse* objects. The handle was then manufactured using Rapid Prototyping machines such as Actua.

In short, both the morphological structure of the design and the definition-space of all permissible parametric values within the design describe a "design family"; the role of the designer undergoes a paradigm shift from *master craftsman* of an individual design to *master programmer* of a design system.

3 Mass-Customisation Through Evolutionary Design

Evolutionary Design describes methods that use rule-based evolutionary algorithms to generate a common family of individual designs. These can be optimized according to particular criteria, or can form a wide variety of hierarchically related design solutions, while supporting our design intuition. Detailed explanation of this innovative form of design computing is beyond the scope of this paper and can be found elsewhere (Frazer 1995).

In the case of our door handle project, we were keen to transcend the limitations of a purely parametric system such as the one described above, and broaden our solution range within the design's scope.

3.1 Encoding Methods

In order to operate on the design numerically through evolutionary tools, our door-handle must be able to be 'digitized' as a three-dimensional object. There are different understandings of how a design should be encoded in terms of the description of its form and geometry. This can be described as **Step 1** in the overall process. Methods include:

(1) Parameters are assigned to definition curves that define spline-surface, which make up the handle object;
(2) The handle object is treated as a topological surface, which is defined by a cloud of surface points.

Method (1) can be explored through the CADDS or CATIA systems, while method (2) makes use of a proprietary software tool developed by the author.

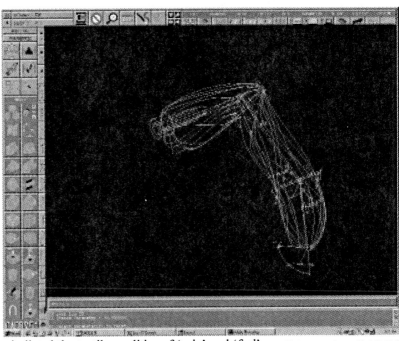

Figure 1. CADDS Modeling System.

3.2 Design Criteria

Door handle manufacturers such as FSB have assimilated the tactile qualities of 'grip' and 'feel' have been assimilated into a '*lore*' of door-handle design. Concentration on the tactile rather than visual aspect challenged us to transcend our architect's intuition and engage the design in a more critical way. In order to evaluate these qualities within an evolutionary mechanism, the participation of a body of users is necessary to determine in which design they are emerging in a desirable way.

3.3 Generation Parameters

A generative design tool uses a Genetic Algorithm to extract information which makes up a successful design by breeding families of related forms and testing them against a selective environment. In our project, the parameters driving the generative process are described as follows:

- Establish evaluation criteria: Grip
- Establish scoring (value) system: Feel
- Determine data type: Handle Geometry
- Encode data: Geometric Description

3.4 Generative Cycle

The cyclical process of encoding, generating and evaluating outputted forms through a generative system is described below. The steps are:

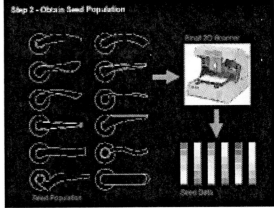

Figure 2. Scanning a seed population.

Step 2 – Obtain Seed Population: The root of any generative process requires a seed – an initial set of data which is then modified. Given FSB's acquired knowledge of door-handle design and fabrication, a selection of their best-known pieces in production was used as a starting population. The designs are codified by using a 3D scanning system (3D digitizer) or by configuring existing CAD data obtained from FSB.

Step 3 – GA Sequence: The core step of the generative process. The GA generates a new population of

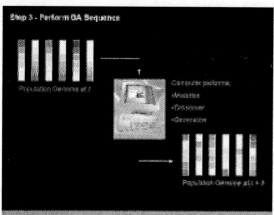

Figure 3. Genetic Algorithm generative sequence.

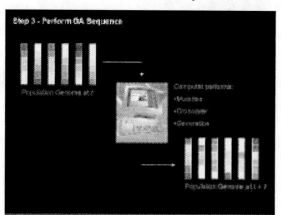

Figure 4. Evaluation of population.

form data by generating a child population using breeding, crossing over and mutation of the initial data (Figure 3).

Step 4 – Evaluate Population: The generated data is translated into tangible form through the use of CNC/CM or rapid prototyping machinery. The manufactured door-handles are tested in a real environment – in this case, a collection of 'demo' users consisting of students, colleagues and outsiders. Each of these users is required to give a verdict on various tactile and possibly visual aspects of each handle, on a scale of 1 – 10. These values are compounded to a 'score value'. These values are used as *fitness* value for the GA in the next generation. A repetition of this sequence soon generates a collection of door handles, which reflects the user group's preferences within the design (Figure 4).

3.5 Evolutionary Parametric Design Using CATIA

CATIA is a modeling and construction tool that combines a suite of "workbenches" for lines and surfaces to create complex solid models. Like many solid modelers, CATIA employs a tree-based nested representation for the models being created, in which the design is broken down into subtree components, and each leaf describes a design component, such as an individual shape, and outline 'sketch', a Boolean operation, and so on. In this sense, CATIA enforces a clear, hierarchical *grammar* of the design, in which certain components may only be placed in certain sequence of the design-tree, in order to produce a coherent, logical design. Figure 5 shows a screenshot of CATIA V.5; the tree-structure is visible on the left of the image.

Thus, CATIA defines designs by two criteria:

(1) The design-tree grammar which establishes the morphology of the design;
(2) The actual parametric definition data within the design-tree elements.

For parametric control, we establish a basic design within CATIA with a set of user-definable parameters. Through the Knowledge workbenches, we are able to program a set of parametric constraints that govern the range values of the parameters. These values may be explicit dimensions, but can also be implicit functions such as ratios, volume, or, through the integration of analytical tools within CATIA, structural performance values of a design instance, based on the application of a certain material.

Figure 5. CATIA Modeling System.

The parametric design capabilities of CATIA described above are strongly complemented by a set of analytical tools, which include options for controlling parametric designs through rules and checking, plus the ability to elaborate design solutions by using rule-based control capabilities. The latter form a workbench known as Knowledge AI / Generative Design, which can be controlled through Visual Basic scripts (and in future, C++ plug-ins), and data processing by means of external databases or spreadsheets such as Excel in similar ways to CADDS. In particular, these features made CATIA a more versatile platform on which to develop the project further.

As described above, the system's objective is to generate a family of related door handles, which can be evolved into increasingly 'tacitly desirable' designs based on the population of test-users' feedback. Given CATIA's *grammar* tree-structure approach, this can be driven in two ways ('grammar' here does not refer to the work of George Stiny et al., although an association or application thereof would be of interest):

(1) Using a basic root-design framework, evolve parameter sets which define the door handles;
(2) Evolve new versions of the design-tree itself, to produce new *grammar* configurations for defining the designs.

The latter, in particular, poses a great challenge as the logic behind the modeling system's description of designs must be catered for. In a sense, only grammatically correct designs are permissible, thus making grammatical correctness a further factor in evolution.

3.6 Origine – A Generative Design Tool for Form Exploration

While CATIA is extremely powerful, its dependence on system-defined entities (objects) and tree-structure definition limits the design's ability to transcend limitations of structure in dramatic or geometrically unforeseen ways. Therefore, a radically different approach to the storage, representation and construction of design data had to be taken.

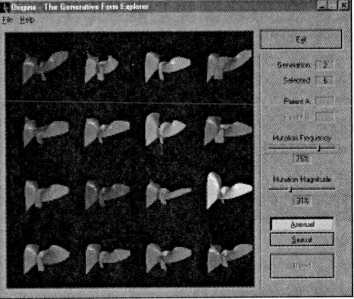

Figure 6. Origine – The Generative Form Explorer.

In our case, it consisted in understanding the design as a single complex volume, which was determined by a given set of points in space. Thus, the door handle object is treated as a *topological* surface, which is defined by a *point-cloud* of surface points. The system evolves the spatial location of individual points, and then places a *skin* over the point-cloud to create a volume. Figure 6 shows the tool we developed, named Origine, showing a family of related shapes during an evolution sequence.

Geometrically, the system employs a Convex Hull algorithm (O'Rourke 1998) to create a surface volume from the given set of points (Figures 7, 8). This presents obvious limitations given that this algorithm does not generate complex non-convex volumes. We hope to improve on this in future by implementing more advantageous algorithms based on spatial proximity and the spatial relations of points, such as the Hoppe or Crust algorithms.

4 Conclusions

The task of integrating Parametric and Evolutionary Design with Mass-Customization efficiently requires considerable computing expertise, time as well as a commitment to determining feasible form generation and production methods. The discourse on how to best encode a tactile, three-dimensional form and manipulate the resulting data is equally if not more of philosophical nature than technical. Furthermore, geometric and parametric manipulation methods have a fundamental influence on the nature of the resulting forms. Maintaining full flexibility becomes a technically demanding issue, and increases computational development time greatly. In our case, we determined a simple, if effective, generation method in order to achieve tangible results within the project's time frame.

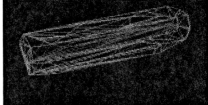

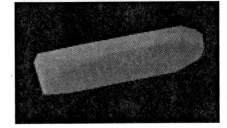

At the time of writing of this paper, the project is still ongoing, and it is hoped that the final results of the work described will be published at a later date. Additional work is required both to the parametric user interfaces and the geometric description of complex 3D forms within Origine. However, feedback from colleagues and students is very promising, in particular with regards to the fundamental idea of using sophisticated computational methods to support a simple goal: to sustain intuition in creating individual, customized objects using automated manufacturing technologies.

Figures 7,8. Convex Hull for generating closed volumes.

References

Burry, M., Gomez, J., Coll, J. and Juan, M., (1996). *La Sagrada Familia: de Gaudi al CAD* (Barcelona, Spain: Ediciones UPC (University Press) 1996)

Ceccato, C. (1999). The Architect as Toolmaker, in Gu, J., and Wei, Z, eds., *Proceedings of the Fourth Conference on Computer Aided Design Research in Asia* (Shanghai: Scientific and Technological Literature Publishing 1999)

Ceccato, C. (1999). Mendel, in Bentley, P., ed., *Evolutionary Design by Computers*, accompanying CD-ROM (London: Morgan Kaufmann 1999)

Duarte, J. and A. Simondetti (1997). Shape Grammars and Rapid Prototyping: Computer Generation and Fabrication of Designs, in Heinisuo, M., ed., *Proceedings of the 4th Workshop of the European Group for Structural Applications of Artificial Intelligence (EG-SEA-AI)* (Lahti, Finland: 1997)

Goulthorpe, M. and M.C. Burry (2000). Paramorph: a Gateway to the South Bank, London. In *Domus* No. 822 (Milan, Italy: Editoriale Domus 2000)

Frazer, J. H. (1995). *An Evolutionary Architecture* (London: Architectural Association 1995)

Lee, K. (1999). *Principles of CAD/CAM/CAE Systems* (New York: Addison-Wesley 1999)

O'Rourke, J. (1998). *Computational Geometry in C*, Second Edition (Cambridge: Cambridge University Press 1998)

Sabbagh, K. (1996). *Twenty-First Century Jet: The Making of the Boeing 777* (New York: Macmillan Publishers 1996)

Simondetti, A. (1998). Rapid Prototyping Based Design: Creation of a Prototype Environment to Explore Three Dimensional Conceptual Design, in *Conference Proceedings, Cyber-Real Design, 5th International Conference on Computer In Architectural Design* (Bialystok, Poland: 1998)

Thompson, D. W. (1961). *On Growth and Form* (Cambridge: Cambridge University Press 1961)

Responsive Architecture: An Integrated Approach for the Future

Stylianos C. Zerefos, Aristotle University of Thessaloniki, Greece

Anastasios M. Kotsiopoulos, Aristotle University of Thessaloniki, Greece

Andreas Pombortsis, Aristotle University of Thessaloniki, Greece

Abstract

An integrated approach towards a responsive architecture is presented. This new direction in architecture is based on recent scientific advances and on available technology in materials, telecommunications, electronics and sustainability principles. The integrated responsive architecture is not confined to offices or housing, but may well extend to intelligent neighborhoods and to intelligent cities. The dynamics of these future systems focus on security, comfort and health for the inhabitants.

1 Introduction

Traditionally, the intelligent building has been defined by the latest innovations in heating, ventilation and air conditioning (HVAC) systems, telecommunication technologies, electronics, security, automation and generally building control and management systems. According to Atkin (1988) the Intelligent Building (IB) is a building that "knows" what is happening inside it and immediately outside, a building that "decides" the most efficient way to provide an appropriate environment for its occupants and responds quickly to their requests. There is little doubt that in the future we will be moving towards advanced technology buildings and complexes of buildings in interactive environments that protect the occupants from several hazards (security, environmental pollution), as well as providing them with optimal individualized comfort, thus enhancing the quality of life and productivity and at the same time these buildings will be environmentally friendly.

In the last few years we are witnessing the emergence of "Responsive Architecture", a result of the scientific and technological evolution in electronics, automation, artificial intelligence and their applications to the intelligent building. This new direction in architecture is based on the design process of the "Interactive Intelligent Building" a building that apart from the "intelligence" of the evolutionary technologies coexists with the inhabitant and is fully customizable and interactive. The present work is part of research done towards a Ph.D. thesis that, apart from the design process, includes algorithms that can be used with control systems and suitable algorithms in an integrated approach towards an intelligent, responsive dwelling.

2 Existing and Evolving New Technologies

The evolution of telecommunications and electronics today has expanded the capabilities of intelligent building systems. The range of services mostly applied in existing buildings have been summarized by Flax (1991) as follows:

- Energy Management
- Temperature Monitoring
- Lighting Control and Reduction
- Access and area locate
- Security
- Fire Safety

- Telecommunication
- Local Area Networks
- Management Information
- Maintenance
- Heating, Ventilation and Air-Conditioning (HVAC)

Although most of the existing intelligent buildings tend to be office complexes, the responsive architecture scheme includes all types of built environments, such as housing, offices, laboratories, hospitals, etc. Moreover, the before mentioned list is not exhaustive and does not include major dynamic interactions pertaining to an intelligent building. This is because of the ever-increasing speed at which science and technology are currently evolving. Current developments offer more services that can be added to the list such as pollution control, environmental comfort, noise suppression and advanced telecommunications utilizing the vast amount of information provided by the Internet and Local Intra-building Wide Area Networks.

If we explore further, we can distinguish some even more advanced concepts, such as dynamic modifications of the external envelope of the building and of the interior spaces, according to the needs of the occupants, as well as the extended use of new "intelligent" materials that extend the effectiveness of existing control systems. Architectural design has always depended on the materials and the technology available at each time period. Therefore, according to Kroner (1997), the invention of new materials such as concrete and glass, as well as the popularity of the automobile have had a major impact on the architecture of their time. The advanced technology of today could also have the potential of transforming a dynamic built environment with interactive buildings instead of static ones.

3 The Proposed Integrated Scheme

3.1 Integration

Kroner (1997) states that intelligent architecture refers to built forms whose integrated systems are capable of anticipating and responding to phenomena, whether internal or external, that affect the performance of the building and its occupants. Therefore, all the services and systems mentioned should be integrated to one building control system (BCS). This system is handled by a dedicated central workstation that collects data from various sources, processes and in turn outputs the resulting data to the BCS.

As described by Derek (1997), a centralized intelligent building may use sophisticated technology, but cannot respond effectively to the many changes the occupants need during the course of a working day. Decentralized control allows the environment to be managed in zones, but the ultimate refinement is the user intelligent building, where local centers are linked to the central information processes and give the individual some choice.

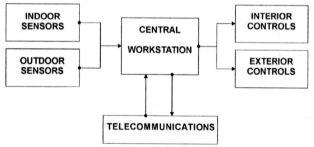

Figure 1: Input and Output of the Central Workstation.

As shown in Figure 1, the collected data come basically from sensors, which are placed indoor and outdoor of the building, as well as a Wide Area Network (WAN). The sensors communicate their measurements to a data processing application, which includes algorithms that can process each type of data and provide an integrated result that in turn is sent to the BCS for application and transfer it to other building control systems for processing. Finally, the BCS processes the resulting data and distributes it to the interior and exterior control systems for operation. The occupants can also modify the control settings. In this case, the central workstation sets priorities so that the occupants may also have individual control of the whole system.

3.2 Sensors

The data to be processed is mainly collected by sensors. These sensors, shown in Figure 2, are divided into two categories: indoor and outdoor. Each one of the categories collects different types of data, which are distributed, to the central workstation. The processing application contains algorithms to be able to process each and every type. The type of data collected is described in the following paragraphs.

3.3 Indoor Sensors

The indoor sensors are subdivided into two categories providing information, the environmental information and the human presence information sensors. In turn the environmental information sensors collect data for lighting intensity in a space, monitor the indoor temperature, humidity and fire detection and with air quality monitors give detailed information about the pollution that penetrates the buildings' envelope. On the other hand the human presence information sensors indicate the presence of humans in the different interior spaces of the building.

3.4 Outdoor Sensors

The outdoor sensors are also subdivided into the before-mentioned categories. However, the environmental information sensors, apart from temperature, humidity, fire detection and pollution information, also collect solar radiation and noise pollution data. The human presence sensors serve the same purpose: to provide human presence information outside the building.

3.5 Telecommunications

Telecommunications play a vital role in modern life and since we live in the information age, the intelligent building should be up-to-date with the current technological trends. Therefore, the central workstation collects data from the Internet and from a Local or even Wide Area Network (LAN or WAN) and outputs the information to the processing application. This information combined with the sensor data, described above, produces the final results that are, in turn, sent to other intelligent buildings, (or part of the building if there is a complex of buildings) in the immediate area for evaluation and processing. This is the concept of the "intelligent neighborhood", a neighborhood where the buildings exchange information about hazards and comfort issues in their immediate area. Details about the types of data being collected and sent are described below.

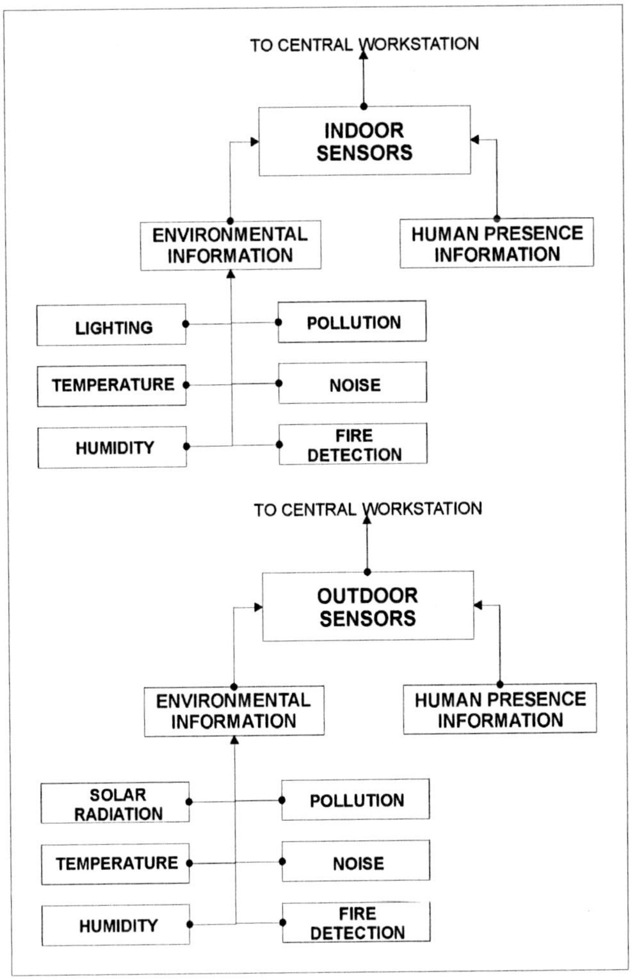

Figure 2: Flow-chart Diagram of the Indoor and Outdoor sensors providing input to the system.

3.6 Collected Data

Data can also be collected through the Internet and LANs or even WANs. The Internet can provide the central workstation with information concerning weather forecasts and pollution data, to help evaluation and prediction of hazards for the occupants and the building itself. The above networks provide local types of information to the system such as security, noise and immediate pollution data, which is evaluated and processed by the processing application.

3.7 Sent Data

After the final results for each type of data are produced, they can be sent to other intelligent buildings as stated above for evaluation and processing.

3.8 3Control

In the final stage, the BCS collects the resulting data from the processing application and distributes orders to the controllers (Figure 3). There are two types of controllers: Interior and Exterior, which are described below.

3.9 Interior Controllers

Interior controllers control security, energy efficiency and indoor comfort issues. Security controls the data received by the human presence and fire detection information sensors. Energy efficiency is subdivided in: lighting, heating, ventilation, air-conditioning and power prioritization issues. Finally, indoor comfort controls indoor air quality, lighting, temperature and humidity, as well as any other customizable comfort control issues (such as music control).

3.10 Exterior Controllers

Exterior controllers consist of external envelope and security controllers. As before security controls the data received by the human presence and fire detection information sensors, while the external envelope controllers modify the façade dynamics and optics to control solar radiation and noise pollution. In the façade dynamics, the form of the external envelope dynamically changes for

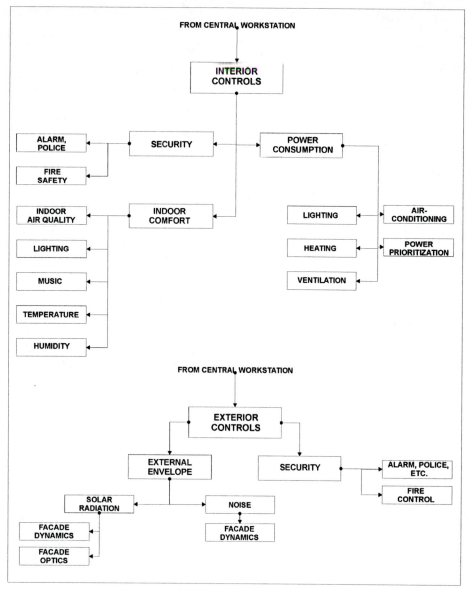

Figure 3: Flow-chart Diagram of the Interior and Exterior controls.

optimal control, while in the façade optics, the colors of the external envelope, whether glass or wall, change. All these controllers are based on existing technology and are available in the international market.

4 Conclusions

This work proposed an integrated approach towards an Intelligent Building of the future. This approach, termed Responsive Architecture by earlier scholars, is based on the need to live and work in a healthier, safer and more sustainable shelter. The integrated approach consists of complex algorithms incorporated in central workstation connected with a variety of Networks including the Internet and WANs. State of the art outdoor and indoor sensors output their measurements, and complex algorithms collect them and control dynamic changes in the interior spaces and the external envelope of the building. The proposed WANs can remit to intelligent neighborhoods and why not, intelligent cities.

References

Atkin, B. (1988). Intelligent Buildings – Applications of IT and Building Automation to High Technology Construction Projects. New York: Halsted Press.

Derek, T. (1997). What do we mean by Intelligent Buildings? In Automation in Construction, vol. 6, 395-400. Amsterdam: Elsevier Science B.V.

Flax, B., M. (1991). Intelligent Buildings. In IEEE Communications Magazine, April 1991, 24-27. New York: The Institute of Electrical and Electronic Engineers.

Kroner, W., M. (1997). An Intelligent and Responsive Architecture. In Automation in Construction, vol. 6, 381-393. Amsterdam: Elsevier Science B.V.

Digital Architectures

Branko Kolarevic, University of Pennsylvania, USA

Abstract

This paper surveys different approaches in contemporary architectural design in which digital media is used not as a representational tool for visualization but as a generative tool for the derivation of form and its transformation. Such approaches are referred to as digital architectures – the computationally based processes of form origination and transformations. The paper examines the digital generative processes based on concepts such as topological space, motion dynamics, parametric design and genetic algorithms. It emphasizes the possibilities for the "finding of form," which the emergence of various digitally based generative techniques seem to bring about.

1 Introduction

The Information Age, like the Industrial Age before it, is not only challenging what we are designing but also how we design. Technological architectures are being replaced by computational, digital architectures of topological, non-Euclidean geometric space, kinetic and dynamic systems, and genetic algorithms. "Architecture is recasting itself, becoming in part an experimental investigation of topological geometries, partly a computational orchestration of robotic material production and partly a generative, kinematic sculpting of space," argues Peter Zellner in "Hybrid Space" (1999).

As digital infrastructures are being inscribed into cities and buildings, new forms and methods of spatial organizations are emerging (Mitchell 1995). The generative and creative potential of digital media is opening up new emergent dimensions in architecture. As seen by Bart Lootsma (Zellner 1999), "instead of trying to validate conventional architectural thinking in a different realm, our strategy today should be to infiltrate architecture with other media and disciplines to produce a new crossbreed."

2 Digital Architectures

Digital architectures refer to the computationally based processes of form origination and transformations. Several digital architectures are identified based on the underlying computational concepts such as topological space (topological architectures), isomorphic surfaces (isomorphic architectures), motion kinematics and dynamics (animate architectures), keyshape animation (metamorphic architectures), parametric design (parametric architectures), and genetic algorithms (evolutionary architectures), as discussed in the following sections.

2.1 Topological architectures

In his essay on "architectural curvilinearity" Greg Lynn (1993) offers examples of new approaches to design that move away from the deconstructivism's "logic of conflict and contradiction" to develop a "more fluid logic of connectivity." This new fluidity of connectivity is manifested through folding, a design strategy that departs from Euclidean geometry of discrete volumes represented in Cartesian space, and employs topological, "rubber-sheet" geometry of continuous curves and surfaces.

In topological space, geometry is represented not by implicit equations, but by parametric functions, which describe a range of possibilities. The continuous, highly curvilinear surfaces that feature prominently in contemporary architecture (figure 1) are mathematically described as NURBS – Non-Uniform Rational B-Splines. What makes NURBS curves and surfaces particularly appealing is the ability to easily control their shape by manipulating the control points, weights, and knots

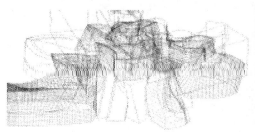

Figure 1. Topological architecture: Gehry's Guggenheim Museum in Bilbao.

(Piegl and Tiller 1997). NURBS make the heterogeneous, yet coherent forms of the topological space computationally possible

2.2 Isomorphic architectures

Isomorphic surfaces represent another point of departure from Platonic solids and Cartesian space. Blobs or metaballs, as isomorphic surfaces are sometimes called, are amorphous objects constructed as composite assemblages of mutually inflecting parametric objects with internal forces of mass and attraction. They exercise fields or regions of influence (figure 2), which could be additive (positive) or subtractive (negative). The geometry is constructed by computing a surface at which the composite field has the same intensity – hence the name – isomorphic surfaces.

Isomorphic surfaces open up yet another formal universe where forms may undergo variations giving rise to new possibilities (figure 3). Objects interact with each other instead of just occupying space; they become connected through a logic where the whole is always open to variation as new blobs (fields of influence) are added or new relations made, creating new possibilities. The surface boundary of the whole (the isomorphic surface) shifts or moves as fields of influence vary in their location and intensity. In that way, objects begin to operate in a dynamic rather than a static geography (Lynn 1999).

2.3 Animate architectures

Greg Lynn (1999) was one of the first architects to utilize animation software not as a medium of representation, but of form generation. He asserts that the prevalent "cinematic model" of motion in architecture eliminates the force and motion from the articulation of form and reintroduces them later, after the fact of design, through concepts and techniques of optical procession. In contrast, as defined by Lynn, "animate design is defined by the co-presence of motion and force at the moment of formal conception." Force, as an initial condition, becomes "the cause of both motion and particular inflections of a form." According to Lynn, "while motion implies movement and action, animation implies evolution of a form and its shaping forces."

In his projects, Lynn utilizes an entire repertoire of motion-based modeling techniques, such as keyframe animation, forward and inverse kinematics, dynamics (force fields) and particle emission. Kinematics is used in their true mechanical meaning to study the motion of an object or a hierarchical system of objects without consideration given to its mass or the forces acting on it. As motion is applied, transformation are propagated downward the hierarchy in forward kinematics, and upward through hierarchy in inverse kinematics. In some of Lynn's projects, such as the House Prototype in Long Island (figure 4), skeletons with a global envelope are deformed using inverse kinematics under the influence of various site-induced forces.

Figure 2. Isomorphic surfaces.

In contrast to kinematics, the dynamic simulation takes into consideration the effects of forces on the motion of an object or a system of objects, especially of forces that do not originate within the system itself. Physical properties of objects, such as mass (density), elasticity, static and kinetic friction (or roughness), are defined. Forces of gravity, wind, or vortex are applied, collision detection and obstacles (deflectors) are specified, and dynamic simulation computed. Greg Lynn's design of a protective roof and a lighting scheme for the bus terminal in New York (figure 5) offers a very effective example of using particle systems to visualize the gradient fields of "attraction" present on the site, created by the forces associated with the movement and flow of pedestrians, cars, and buses on the site.

2.4 Metamorphic architectures

Metamorphic generation of form includes several techniques such as keyshape animation, deformations of the modeling space around the model using a bounding box (lattice deformation), a spline curve, or one of the coordinate system axis or planes, and path animation, which deforms an object as it moves along a selected path.

In keyshape animation, changes in the geometry are recorded as keyframes (keyshapes) and the software then computes the in-between states (figure 6). In deformations of the modeling space, object shapes conform to the changes in geometry of the modeling space.

2.5 Parametric architectures

In parametric design, it is the parameters of a particular design that are declared, not its shape. By assigning different values to the parameters, different objects or configurations can be created. Equations can be used to describe the relationships between objects, thus defining an associative geometry—the "constituent geometry that is mutually linked" (Burry 1999). That way, interdependencies between objects can be established, and objects' behavior under transformations defined. As observed by Burry, "the ability to define, determine and reconfigure geometrical relationships is of particular value."

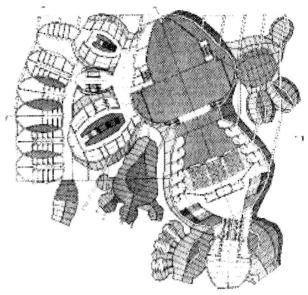

Parametric design often entails a procedural, algorithmic description of geometry. In his "algorithmic spectaculars" (Figure 7), i.e., algorithmic explorations of "tectonic production" using Mathematica software, Marcos Novak (1996) constructs "mathematical models and generative procedures that are constrained by numerous variables initially unrelated to any pragmatic concerns ... Each variable or process is a 'slot' into which an external influence can be mapped, either statically or dynamically." In his explorations, Novak is "concerned less with the manipulation of objects and more with the manipulation of relations, fields, higher dimensions,

Figure 3. Isomorphic architecture: Greg Lynn's proposal for the Cardiff Opera.

and eventually the curvature of space itself." The implication is that the parametric design doesn't necessarily predicate stable forms. As demonstrated by Burry (1999), one can devise a paramorph – an unstable spatial and topological description of form with stable characteristics.

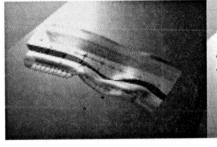 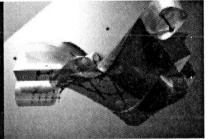

2.6 Evolutionary architectures

Evolutionary architecture proposes the evolutionary model of nature as the generating process for architectural form (Frazer 1995). In this approach to design, according to Frazer, "architectural concepts are expressed as generative rules so that their evolution and development can be accelerated and tested by the use of computer models. Concepts are described in a genetic language that produces a code script of instructions for form-generation. Computer models are used to simulate the development of prototypical forms that are then evaluated on the basis of their performance in a simulated environment. Very large numbers of evolutionary steps can be generated in a short space of time and the emergent forms are often unexpected."

Figure 4. Animate architecture: Lynn's House Prototype in Long Island.

The key concept behind evolutionary architecture is that of the genetic algorithm, "a class of highly parallel evolutionary, adaptive search procedures," as defined by Frazer. Their key characteristic is "a string-like structure equivalent to the chromosomes of nature," to which the rules of reproduction, gene crossover, and mutation are applied. Various parameters are encoded into the "a string-like structure" and their values changed during the generative process. A number of similar forms, "pseudo-organisms," are generated (figure 8), which are then selected from the generated populations based on predefined "fitness" criteria. The selected "organisms," and the corresponding parameter values, are then crossbred, with the accompanying "gene crossovers" and "mutations", thus passing beneficial and survival-enhancing traits to new generations. Optimum solutions are obtained by small incremental changes over several generations.

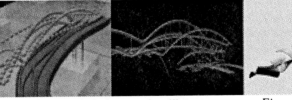

Figure 5. Animate architecture: Lynn's Port Authority Bus Terminal in New York.

In the process of genetic coding, the central issue is the modeling of the inner logic rather than

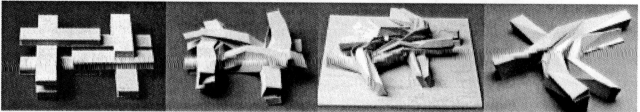

Figure 6. Metamorphic architecture: Eisenman's Offices of BFL Software.

Figure 7. Parametric architecture: Marcos Novak's "algorithmic spectaculars."

external form. Other equally important issues are the definition of often ill-defined and conflicting criteria and how the defined criteria operate for the selection of the "fittest". Equally challenging is the issue of how the interaction of built form and its environment are transcribed into the morphological and metabolic processes.

3 Implications

3.1 Dynamics and the fields of forces

Greg Lynn's work on "animate form" was very much inspired by D'Arcy Thompson "On Growth and Form" (1917), in which Thompson argues that the form in nature and the changes of form are due to the "action of force." With his work on using motion dynamics to generate architectural form, Lynn has convincingly demonstrated what Nicholas Negroponte (1970) had only hinted at in his seminal work from some thirty years ago, "The Architecture Machine," also acknowledged in Lynn's writing:

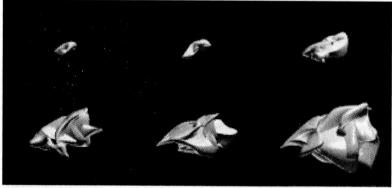

Figure 8. Evolutionary architecture: Frazer's "pseudo-organisms."

"Physical form, according to D'Arcy Thompson, is the resolution at one instant of time of many forces that are governed by rates of change. In the urban context the complexity of these forces often surpasses human comprehension. A machine, meanwhile, could procreate forms that respond to many hereto un-manageable dynamics. Such a colleague would not be an omen of professional retirement but rather a tickler of the architect's imagination, presenting alternatives of form possibly not visualized or not visualizable by the human designer."

Lynn argues that "traditionally, in architecture, the abstract space of design is conceived as an ideal neutral space of Cartesian coordinates," but that in other design fields, "design space is conceived as an environment of force and motion rather than as a neutral vacuum." He makes an argument that "while physical form can be defined in terms of static coordinates, the virtual force of the environment in which it is designed contributes to its shape," thus making the forces present in the given context fundamental to the form making in architecture. Lynn attributes to this position the significance of a paradigm shift "from a passive space of static coordinates to an active space of interactions," which he describes as "a move from autonomous purity to contextual specificity." Instrumental to this conceptual shift is the use of digital media, such as animation and special-effects software, which he uses as "tools for design rather than as devices for rendering, visualization, and imaging."

3.2 Emergence and the fields of indetermination

Topological space opens up a universe where essentially curvilinear forms are not stable but may undergo variations, giving rise to new possibilities, i.e., the emergent form. Designers can see forms as a result of reactions to a context of "forces" or actions, as demonstrated by Lynn's work.

Figure 9. Bernard's Cache "objectiles."

There is, however, nothing automatic or deterministic in the definition of actions and reactions; they implicitly create "fields of indetermination" from which unexpected and genuinely new forms might emerge. The capacity of computational architectures to generate "new" designs is therefore highly dependent on designer's perceptual and cognitive abilities. Their generative role is accomplished through the designer's simultaneous interpretation and manipulation of a computational construct (topological surface, isomorphic field, kinetic skeleton, field of forces, parametric model, genetic algorithm, etc.) in a complex discourse that is continuously reconstituting itself - a 'self-reflexive' discourse in which graphics actively shape the designer's thinking process.

3.3 Mass customization

The numerically controlled production processes of the past decade, which afforded the fabrication of non-standardized repetitive components directly from digital data, introduced into architectural discourse the "mass-customization" (Mitchell 1999) and the new logics of "seriality," i.e., the local variation and differentiation in series. In process, building construction is being transformed into production of the differentiated components and their assembly on site, instead of the conventional manual techniques. This transformation of building design and construction into digitally driven production processes was famously manifested in Frank Gehry's buildings, with his Guggenheim Museum in Bilbao being the most dramatic recent example.

For Bernard Cache (1995), in parametric design "objects are no longer designed but calculated," allowing the design of complex forms with surfaces of variable curvature that would be difficult to represent using traditional drawing methods, and laying "the foundation for a nonstandard mode of production." His objectiles (figure 9) are non-standard objects, mainly furniture and paneling, which are procedurally calculated in Microstation and industrially produced with numerically controlled machines.

For Cache, it is the modification of parameters of design, often random, that allows the manufacture of different shapes in the same series, thus making the mass-customization, i.e., the industrial production of unique objects possible. In other words, it is now possible to produce "series-manufactured, mathematically coherent but differentiated objects, as well as elaborate, precise and relatively cheap one-off components," according to Peter Zellner (1999), who argues that in the process the "architecture is becoming like 'firmware,' the digital building of software space inscribed in the hardwares of construction."

4 Conclusion

Digital architectures are profoundly changing the processes of design (and construction), but for many architects, trained in the certainties of the Euclidean geometry, the emergence of curvilinear forms poses considerable difficulties. In the absence of an appropriate aesthetic theory, the "hypersurface" forms (Perrella 1996) often seem to be utterly esoteric and spatially difficult to comprehend, and are often dismissed with as just another architectural "fad."

It is worth reminding that it was Le Corbusier's "free plan" and "free façade" that allowed for elements of variable curvature to emerge in the modernist projects of the mid-century. Eero Saarinen (1968) attributed the reemergence of the plastic form to the advances in building technology, while acknowledging "it is the aesthetic reasons which are driving forces behind its use." Saarinen is rather cautious in his use of plastic form, implying that it has a rather limited applicability and warning that the "plastic form for its own sake, even when very virile, does not seem to come off."

Saarinen's cautious approach to plastic form is exemplary of the apparent ambivalence of the modernists towards the curvilinear, an attitude that is still widely present. While it enabled them to break the monotony of the orthogonal and the linear, it also heralded the emergence of a new unknown geometry, about which they were still not sure (Cache 1995); the modernists "knew that they had, above all, to avoid two opposite pitfalls: a dissolution into the indefinite and a return to the representation of natural form," the former manifested in "the loss of form," and the latter in "the organicist maze into which art nouveau had fallen."

The skeptical, or at least ambivalent, attitudes towards the curvilinear are often compounded by a rather blasé attitude in contemporary critical discourse towards the ways ("methods") and means ("devices") of digital form generation, which intentionally seek indeterminacy in design processes. The accidental plays a rather prominent role in establishing the "fields of indetermination" from which genuinely new forms may emerge. Perez Gomez and Pelletier (1997) argue that tendency for accidental should be accepted as a legitimate design outcome, because the computer graphics systems impose a "homogenous space" that is "inherently unable to combine different structures of reference." As Mark Burry (1999) acutely points out, "emerging critical theory ... has no embarrassment in accepting, or benignly accommodating or even celebrating the accident or the error," with the implication that the "intellectual value of a perverse giving-up of authorship ('design') is neither judged with quizzicality, nor seen as a potential artistic impropriety."

In summary, the digital architectures described in this paper necessitate certain design strategies that provide for a dynamic manipulation of the designs with a high degree of indeterminacy. The existence of such strategies is not seen as a limiting factor in design –unpredictability, uncertainty, and indeterminacy are still present, as are the possibilities for the "finding of form," which the emergence of these digitally based generative techniques seem to engender intentionally.

References

Burry, Mark. (1999). Paramorph. In *AD Profile 139: Hypersurface Architecture II*. London: Academy Editions.

Cache Bernard. (1995). *Earth Moves*. Cambridge: MIT Press.

Frazer, John. (1995). *Evolutionary Architecture*. London: Architectural Association.

Lynn, Greg. (1993). Architectural Curvilinearity: The Folded, the Pliant and the Supple. In *AD Profile 102: Folding in Architecture*. London: Academy Editions.

Lynn, Greg. (1998). *Animate Form*. Princeton: Princeton Architectural Press.

Mitchell, William. (1995). *City of Bits: Space, Place, and the Infobahn*. Cambridge: MIT Press.

Mitchell, William. (1999). *E-topia*. Cambridge, MIT Press.

Negroponte, Nicholas. (1970). *Architecture Machine*. Cambridge: MIT Press.

Novak, Marcos. (1998). Transarchitectures and Hypersurfaces. In *AD Profile 133: Hypersurface Architecture*. London: Academy Editions.

Perez-Gomez, A. and L. Pelletier. (1997). *Architectural Representation and the Perspective Hinge*. Cambridge: MIT Press.

Perrella, Stephen (ed.). (1998). *AD Profile 133: Hypersurface Architecture*. London: Academy Editions.

Piegl, Les, and Wayne Tiller. (1997). *The NURBS Book*, 2nd ed. New York: Springer.

Saarinen, Aline (ed.). (1968). *Eero Saarinen on His Work*. New Haven: Yale University Press.

Thompson, D'Arcy Wentworth. (1917). *On Growth and Form*. Cambridge (UK): Cambridge University Press.

Zellner, Peter. (1999). *Hybrid Space: New Forms in Digital Architecture*. New York: Rizzoli International Publications.

Towards Real Time Interaction Visualization in NED

Thomas Fischer, Hong Kong Polytechnic University, China

Christiane M. Herr, University of Kassel, Germany

Cristiano Ceccato, Hong Kong Polytechnic University, China

Abstract
Where design education moves from the studio to computer networks, interaction information easily becomes unavailable for pedagogic analysis. In this paper we propose automated learning interaction visualization to solve this problem and show our progress in developing technical tools for this purpose.

1 Introduction
The concept of studio interaction and its traditional classroom predecessor has developed for decades and centuries. One of its advantages is the immediate physical presence of learners and teachers in the teaching scenario. It allows the direct observation and analysis of interaction. This instrument of direct observation will suffer as computer- and network based education will spread in the future: Where educational interaction is not visualized implicitly, as for example with avatars in virtual environments, information gets lost. This information has the potential to enrich learning situations in various ways and – even more importantly – it is the key to student assessment. Therefore we must find ways to adapt traditional studio interaction observation to NED (Networked Education in Design (see Falk et al. 2000)).

2 The Requirement for Ad-Hoc Interaction Analysis in Online Teaching
We regard teaching, as well as design, as a wicked problem. As a consequence, its strategies require constant monitoring and adaptation to dynamically changing problem variables. One central set of learning situation variables arises from interaction, as it is observable in the studio but hidden online. Logging interaction data provides us with a method to review what learners do and how they do it. But log file analysis is a time consuming and error-intensive activity for humans and not practical in the intervals in which teaching strategies should be reviewed. We propose visual representations as a means to solve these problems.

In order to record data on online learning software usage it is easily possible to enhance the software itself in a way that it generates protocols of its own execution. This is actually a common basis for example on the WWW server level of NED applications: log files of document requests and protocol errors are generated by default and can be reviewed if necessary. However, these technically oriented log files provide no means to track educational interaction on the individual and group levels teachers are interested in.

A major advantage of electronic protocols is their automatically persistent storage, which allows retrospective analysis whereas moments in traditional learning setups are fugitive and can only be prevented from getting lost by techniques such as video surveillance. Advantages like this have to be paid for with shortcomings in other regards: Machine-generated protocols typically only collect events which are initially expected to occur, describing them in a plain, non-interpreted sequence of log entries. Individual or group behavior, complex interaction patterns and correlation between them can hardly be identified intuitively in large protocols describing several weeks of course interaction in hundreds of kilobytes of rather cryptic data. In this context, entire or partial two-dimensional or three-dimensional data visualization has already proven to us to be an effective method to visually analyze learning interaction as well as an essential source of information for its assessment.

3 Early Field and Lab Tests

The 'Virtual Design Company' online learning application was the first manifestation of the networked approach to design education. Simulating a groupware platform of a design company, coordinating its globally distributed agencies, the application allows project based design education in the studio as well as over the Internet.

Data collected by this system during its first application in late 1999 was the material of our early visualization experimentation. The results included real time generated HTML bar diagrams, separately showing 'active' and 'passive' system usage (see figure 1) and post-produced graphics generated with MS Excel® processing comma-separated lists of interaction data. These two-dimensional visualizations could not communicate the timeline-oriented quality of our data. The simple HTML bars were used as a basis for assessment but in terms of the data's obvious potential this output design was as little satisfying as images manually post-produced using Excel.

Our investigation in visual data interpretation tools for didactic contexts was reinforced by several ad-hoc findings we made reviewing the first bar diagram shown in figure 1. This group shows a typical characteristic, which practically all learner groups of this course share in a more or less obvious way: One student of each group shows a significantly stronger performance than her or his group partners. Interestingly, these individuals are not necessarily those we know as particularly strong students. But in all cases these are the students who have initiated the respective group and therefore share a higher level of group awareness. This correlation is only one example of how visual activity representation allows didactic conclusions of a quality, which previously was available to physical classroom observation only.

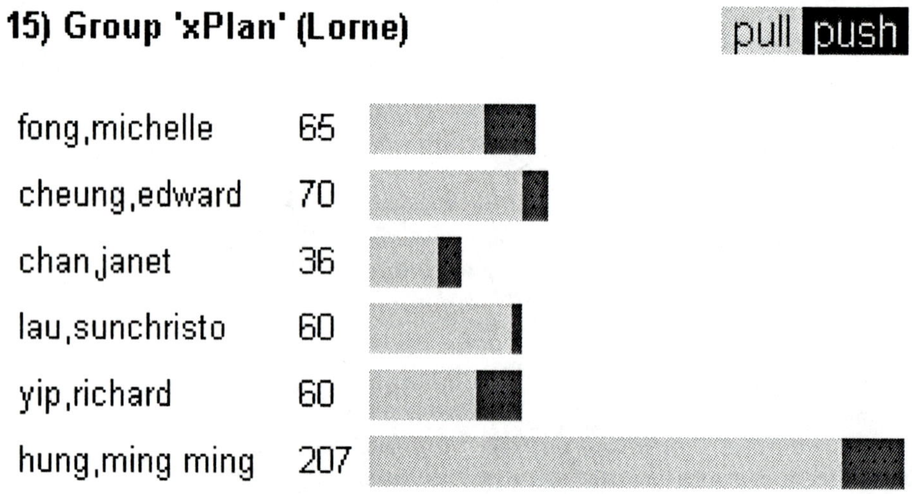

Figure 1. HTML bar diagram.

In later experimentation, the CGI-based strategy of HTML generation was adapted to dynamic VRML generation in order to exploit the third dimension to communicate the 'depth' of logged information. The amount of VRML data generated even from small data segments easily grew up to several megabytes which is too much to be handled by VRML browsers on current desktop PCs. While making these experiences we also understood that teaching contexts require highly extendable learning systems which is why we need a generic geometric solution for interaction visualization which itself is extendable to initially unforeseen requirements. To develop this generic geometry and generation procedures we chose 3DStudio MAX® as our (interim) prototyping platform.

4 Extendable Geometry for Extendable Applications

Teaching means dealing with unforeseen events, methods, content and media because throughout courses, teachers keep on monitoring learners, their activity and maintain assumptions on their individual levels of skills and knowledge. When new information results in changes of these assumptions, changes of initial didactic planning are likely to occur. For this purpose, learning software is best prepared if it is developed by its users themselves and full source code control is given. But once new forms of interaction are supported, the log protocol specification has to be extended accordingly to handle new aspects of interaction. Therefore, it has to be specified in an extendable fashion in the first place. One integer number associated with every entry identifies the individual interacting with the system. The second entry to be specified for a log protocol specification is the encoding for the actual interaction aspects. These aspects are directly selected by didactic analysis from interaction options supported by the application. In case of the *Virtual Design Company* application these options contained login procedures, the usage of supported TCP-IP-like services such as email, FTP, chat and news board postings as well as individual statements of student self-reflection. In log protocols we express these aspects with unique integer numbers. A third entry is optionally used where attributes for the respective interaction aspect are required.

As we implemented the interface between the protocol database and 3DStudio MAX® as a text parser written in Max Script, we produced a flat file version from the original log protocol database. A sample entry in this plain text version looks like the following:

1072869,13,¤ý£1

The first integer number in this like is the project second since the beginning of the course. The second one is the interaction aspect, which in this case (13) is the code for an email sent to a group. The third field is an ASCII-interpretation of a bitwise encoding of a subset of the course participants. This flat file database carries activities of individuals in dedicated files: It is person-oriented whereas the initial log protocol was timeline-oriented. We found person-oriented databases to be evaluated much easier and faster, especially when subsets of the entire course interaction have to be visualized. On the log specification level, the specification described above guarantees extendibility in all contained dimensions: The number of persons involved in a didactic situation, the number of interaction aspects supported by a learning software, the course timeline and the attribute encoding.

The same flexibility has to be supported by a generic geometry based on this data specification. To fulfill this requirement we have developed the architecture shown in the visualization of the Virtual Design Company data shown in figure 2.

This geometry exploits space for free visual extendibility in three dimensions: On the x-axis it handles an arbitrary number of individuals, on the y-axis it shows the course timeline and on the z-axis it handles the interaction aspects. The six large T-shaped forms are representations of course milestones such as course start, interim presentations and final presentations. This arrangement allows direct quantitative comparison between the performances of individuals because through iterative upwards moving, individual activity representations appear as a bar-diagram in the front view. Figure 3 shows a front view of the above visualization with representations of quantitatively comparable representations of chat room, news board and FTP server usage.

In future applications, when visualizations like this are generated in real time either as VRML using PERL or as static jpeg images using 3DStudio Max, an HTML GUI can allow teachers to select certain time frames, subsets of learners and subsets of interaction aspects to get isolated visualizations of interaction details. Therefore it is possible to selectively emphasize course interac-

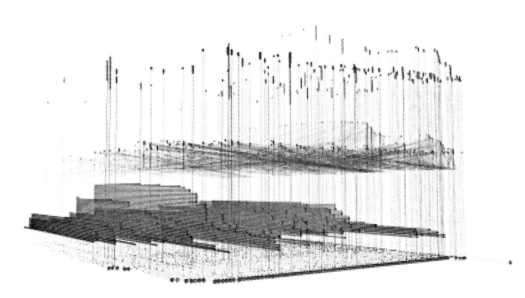

Figure 2. Overall Course Visualization.

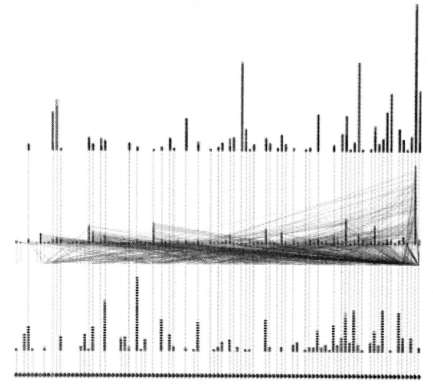

tion elements while maintaining graphic linearity whereas other non-linear strategies like fish-eye views cause difficulties in terms of visual performance comparison.

As figure 4 shows, interaction aspects are 'piled up' along the z-axis as separate modules (chat contributions, modification of the 'message of the day', email, posting and reading news board messages, FTP up- and download). While course participants and time in x-axis and y-axis can be easily displayed as linear and homogenous data, even when only small segments are visualized, the interaction modules on the z-axis are highly variable in size and order depending on subset selections. To handle this problem of potential inconsistency, we have implemented the 'activity modules' as separate *functions*: The main program is called with one argument that is the path to the flat file database. Then the module functions are called successively, generating geometry and then returning the used, dynamic z distances as their function values. These values are added by the main program in order to call each further function with a z coordinate from which to start.

Figure 3. Front view (interaction modules).

5 Conclusions

Though interaction visualization superficially appears to be a last additional step in learning software development, it plays a very central role from a pedagogical point of view as well as from a technical perspective. In this context, the log database specification appears to be a critical link between a learning system with its extendible user interface and real time visualization. This fact has to be considered in the early stages of a learning system's design.

As in our experimentation the presented geometry shows no problems to handle any didactic interaction data we assume it has a reliable generic quality and can be applied to various contexts in the future. Furthermore, its level of abstraction suggests the development of application-independent interactivity visualization tools such as authoring system add-ons that are the long-term aim of this work in progress.

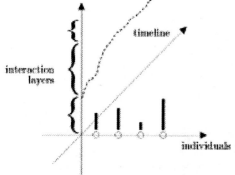

Figure 4. Proposed geometry.

References

Card, S.K., J.D. MacKinlay and Sneiderman, B. (1999). *Readings in Information Visualization. Using Vision to Think.* Morgan Kaufmann Publishers, San Francisco California

Falk, L., C. Ceccato, C. Hu, P. Wong, and T. Fischer. (2000). Towards a Networked Education in Design. A First Manifestation through the "Virtual Design Company" Studio In *CAADRIA 2000 Conference Proceedings*, ed. T. Beng-Kiang, 157 - 167. National University of Singapore

Rittel, H. and M. Webber (1973). Dilemmas in a General Theory of Planning. *DMG-DRS Journal* 8(1):31-39. University of California: Institute of Urban & Regional Development.

Plank Lines of Ribbed Timber Shell Structures

Karen Kensek, *3DCLIPPER LAB,* University of Southern California, USA

Judith Leuppi, *3DCLIPPER LAB,* University of Southern California, USA

Douglas Noble, *3DCLIPPER LAB,* University of Southern California, USA

Abstract

This paper discusses a method for determining the plank lines of ribbed timber shell structures. The information is necessary for the construction of the roof, but the information is usually not depicted accurately in three-dimensional modeling programs.

Keywords: geodesic line, finite element algorithm, ribbed shell structure, lightweight structure, timber construction.

1 Introduction

It is often a problem with digital modeling systems that the method of depiction of architecture does not correspond to the information needed to actually build the structure. This is decidedly the case with ribbed timber shell structures. The most common methods of portrayal consist of fairly arbitrary meshes that give a good indication of spatial characteristics, but fail to provide necessary information for the structural engineer (figure 1).

The typical construction of ribbed timber shell structures consist of wooden planks to form the ribs. These planks are approximately 3 x 16 cm, and several interlocked layers are used to form each rib (figure 2). These planks are screwed together; usually no glue is used. Each layer of planks is continuous in one direction. Filler boards are installed between these planks. The critical feature is

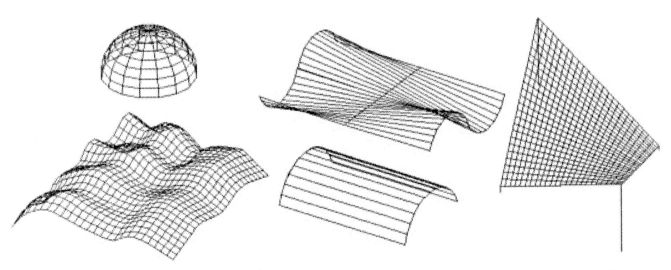

Figure 1. Images of AutoCAD meshes.

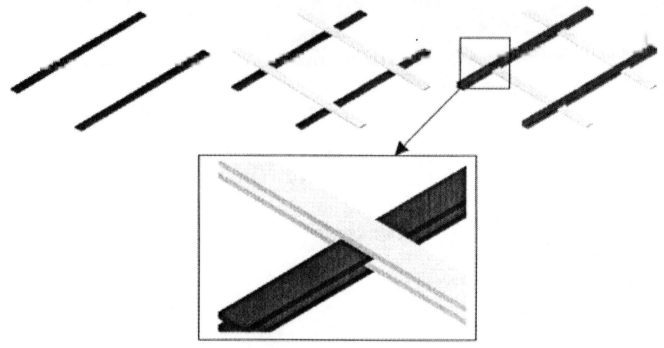

Figure 2. Interlocked construction method for wooden ribs (shown without filler blocks).

that the wooden planks can only be bent, within reason, in their weak axis of inertia, the long direction. If they are bent in the other direction, they break easily.

2 Example and Current Practice

An example of this type of construction is the exposition pavilion, the Polydôme, in Lausanne, Switzerland (1991) (figures 3 and 4). The roof is a partial sphere, approximately 25 x 25 meter square in plan, with a height of 7 meters. The radius of the sphere is 27.5 meters. The wooden planks follow the geodesic lines of the sphere.

Note that ribs in this spherical example follow the great circle lines, lines that pass over a surface and do not curve in the tangential plane. As mentioned earlier, this is crucial when using wooden planks. In the case of real structures, "great circle" or "geodesic line" may not be the correct terms to use because the wooden ribs have a real thickness. The term "plank line" can be defined as a line with an assumed width (such as a plank of wood) that passes over a surface and does not curve in the tangential plane and whose width is always tangential to the surface (figure 5).

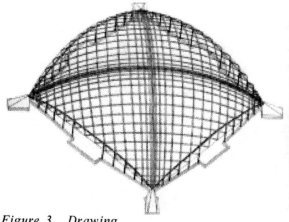

Figure 3. Drawing and photograph of the Polydôme (BCN Natterer; IBOIS).

Currently these plank lines are found in two major ways. If the roof has a simple geometric form like a sphere, then they can be found graphically with a three-dimensional drawing program. Sometimes this leads to roofs that are not structurally ideal, for example, they might be too flat, which causes buckling problems. For more complex shapes, a mathematician might be hired as a subcontractor. These shapes were often limited to those that could be described with geometrical equations. Each time the structure was changed during the design process, the mathematician would have to recalculate the lines. This could become very costly.

Figure 4. Construction photograph and detail of the Polydôme (IBOIS).

3 Proposed Solution

The solution proposed would take a three-dimensional design drawing of a ribbed shell structure, parse a dxf file to determine the necessary geometric entities, and run the calculations to discover

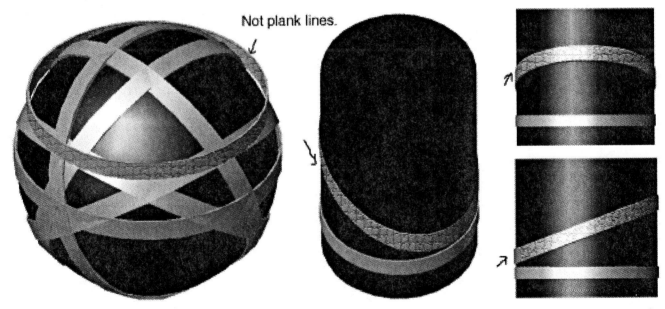

Figure 5. On the sphere, due to the width of the line, the red band is not a plank line; a cylinder cut with a 2D plane does not make a plank line.

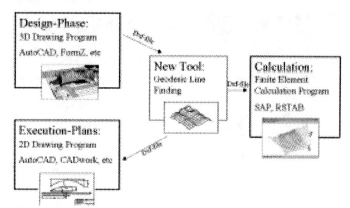

Figure 6. Relationship of proposed tool to design, CAD, and analytical programs

the positions of the plank lines (figure 6). It is important that the original design drawing follows a few guidelines; these include that the shape is defined by four edges, it has been meshed, and the mesh has been exploded into its component faces. C++ is being used for the development of this program. After the program's calculations are completed, the data is translated into a new dxf file and sent to drafting programs for inclusion into working drawings or sent to structural analysis programs.

The shapes can be divided into three classes: spherical and cylindrical, anticlastic, and free form. For each, the input will be the dxf file of a dense mesh (that will be used as the finite element grid mesh in the program), the number of planks or distance between planks, and the starting angle. The output will be the locations of the plank lines as a dxf file. For the free form shapes, in some cases there may not be a solution.

4 Finite Element Approach

Although it is possible to use geometric equations to solve for these intersection points in some cases, an approach using finite element algorithms was chosen for four reasons. In theory, it is simpler because one algorithm could be used for every kind of shape. Second, the grid of the structure is already similar to the finite element grid, so finding the solution is comparable to what the initial design problem is. Third, the initial shape is not constrained to being defined by geometrically definable forms; this gives the designer more freedom in the initial architectural design. Fourth, by using a finite element approach, the problem is broken down in many small, easier to solve problems; recursively the larger problem is solved.

4.1 Principle

The principle of using the finite element approach is straightforward. The program receives the dxf file with the shape's geometric information and finite element mesh, and the user defines the starting points of the planks. The program will choose one of the planks x,y,z location (on the edge) as the initial condition. It then needs to calculate the end point of the sub-line within the small finite element grid. This end point becomes the starting point for the next, neighboring element (figure 7). Step by step the line finds its way (through calculation) over the shape to the other edge thus defining the plank line (figure 8). This process is repeated for the starting point of each plank along the edge of the shape. It is necessary to set up local coordinate systems to aid in this process's calculations and provide the rules that govern the calculation of the end point of the sub-line.

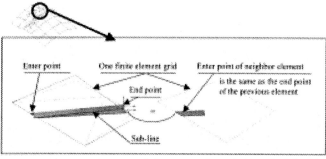

Figure 7. One finite element grid showing a sub-line, the part of the plank line within one finite element grid

4.2 Local Coordinate System

A local coordinate system is defined at the point where the line "enters'" a finite element grid. The X-axis is the longitudinal axis of the plank at the enter point. The Y-axis is perpendicular to the X-axis and lays in the plane of the finite element. The Z-axis is determined by the right-hand-rule and is perpendicular to the plane of the finite element. Each finite element's plane is determined by two corner points and the middle point of the other two corners (figure 9). Once the end point of the sub-line in the current finite element is calculated, the new orientation of the local coordinate system is established. This new orientation of the local coordinate system is also the start point of the new finite element, and the calculations are repeated until the other edge of the shape is reached. This occurs for each plank line.

4.3 4.3 Properties of Plank Line

Following a set of rules governed by the properties of the plank line, the program can determine the end point of the sub-line in a specific finite element. Rotation around the local X-axis is allowed for a small degree (twist of the plank). Rotation around the local Y-axis is allowed within limits (curvature of the plank over the shape). Rotation around the local Z-axis is forbidden (rotation in tangential plane; the plank would break!)

4.4 Intersection of Plank Lines

Once the plank lines are calculated, their intersections need to be found. It is improbable that the lines will hit exactly. The program must determine the closest that the lines come together at an implied intersection and then make allowances for the offsets. The x,y,z coordinates of the intersections are the information that the structural engineer needs. Currently the program does not calculate the intersection points, but instead generates the plank lines and outputs them as a dxf file.

5 Program Validation

The program has been tested on different surfaces, from relatively free form shapes to hyperbolic-paraboloid, anticlastic, barrel vaults, and spherical shapes (figure 10). Visually checking the results against existing projects (such as the Polydôme, see figure 3), indicates that the program is working correctly. Further testing must be done by comparison of mathematically calculated plank system lines with the program's output for the same surface. The student author plans to meet with the planners of one such project to compare the results.

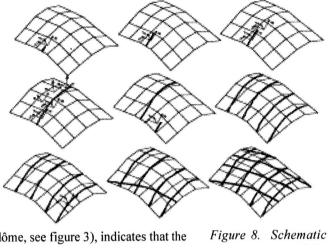

Figure 8. Schematic representation of the entire finite element sequence showing the incremental progress of sub-lines across the grid producing a plank line and then the repetition of the process for multiple plank lines

6 Program Optimization

Although this program will solve for the plank lines, its usefulness as a fully-developed tool is very limited. Future work still needs to address problems with the use of AutoCAD, problems in the program coding itself, and difficulties with the program's logical design and the user input. Briefly, AutoCAD has a few limitations that make the use of the program less than perfect. These include limitations on the length of text strings, minor problems in using the "option" feature in the output as dxf command, and conversion of files from AutoCAD 2000 to AutoCAD 14. Within the plank line program itself, dynamic arrays or linked lists should replace the static arrays that are currently used, and the user interface needs considerable reworking. This also applies to the user input section, and for added utility the program should check for maximum bending of the timber planks, locate the exact intersection points of the plank lines, propose meaningful solutions, and most importantly allow the designer more freedom in specifying starting and ending locations of plank lines.

The current version of the program can only be used by a designer who is experienced with ribbed shell structures. The necessary distance, the best orientation of the ribs, and the ideal form of the surface are based on the judgment of the person using the program. If bad input is given, the plank lines are calculated anyway. The program could be expanded with features for narrowing down the scope of the possible solutions to a handful of meaningful solutions and not allowing insignificant solutions. In addition, the program could be integrated with a structural analysis tools for calculations regarding structural performance (stability, stress distribution, and deflection).

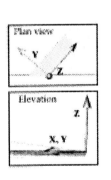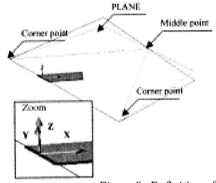

Figure 9. Definition of local coordinate system for sub-line.

7 Conclusion

This program will solve for a set of plank lines for ribbed timber shell structures. Although narrow in scope and work should be done to improve its overall usefulness, it does provide a real-life solution for architects and structural engineers who are struggling with this problem. Applied at different scales and for different materials, the program could also be used in other fields than for rib shell structures, for example, figure form work for double curved concrete structures; designing molds for glass, plastic, and lightweight cement; and for designing haute gammed furniture. Wherever a one directional element has to be curved and has a width larger than the height, the essential problem is the same.

Special thanks to Professors Schierle, Schiler, and Wagner, and Professor Natterer and his coworkers in the department of IBOIS, and offices BCN and IEZ, for using their pictures and tapping their knowledge.

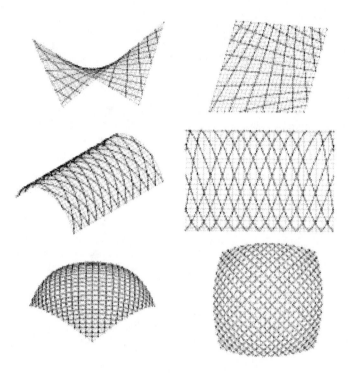

Figure 10. Sample output from the program for hyperbolic-paraboloid, barrel vault, and spherical shapes.

Computer Simulation and Visualization of Geometrically Changing Structures

Katherine A. Liapi, University of Texas at Austin, USA

Abstract

The design of building structures that change shape and form to adapt to different functions or weather conditions requires the application of innovative building technologies, as well as the invention of a new architectural morphology. This morphology is directly related to the kinematic conception of the structure. A computer simulation of the motion of the structure and the display of the structure as an animation of moving parts can identify problems in its initial geometric and kinematic conception. It can also assess the effect of the changing geometry of the structure on space definition, building morphology, and functionality.

1 Introduction

In the last 20 years there has been an increased interest in building structures that change shape and form to adapt to different functional or weather conditions. These are usually structures that include moving parts, consisting of "rigid" members connected by movable joints, which allow for the geometric expansion of the structure in space. Deployable structures that can be transformed from a "closed compact configuration to a predetermined expanded form in which they are stable and can carry loads" and which find applications in temporary structures and aerospace industries, also belong to the same group of structures (Gantes 91).

Structures that change shape and form to adapt to different functions and weather conditions have an obvious positive impact on the economy of environmental resources. Deployable structures, that can be moved from a place to another, can also offer an environmental alternative to massive building structures since they usually do not require heavy foundations, minimize the overall workforce and the total erection energy needed, and are re-usable and adaptable.

Despite the advantages and promising applications of such structures, they have not yet been addressed as a distinct building class, mainly because of the lack of standardized procedures in their engineering design and analysis. From the standpoint of architectural morphology and typology however, they certainly define a distinct category of structures that offers unlimited possibilities for formal expression and functionality.

An early phase in the design process of any structure consists of the development of a geometric concept, based on requirements set by programmatic needs and specific site conditions. In this particular case of structures kinematic and geometric conceptions are directly and uniquely related, and should therefore be addressed together at the very beginning of the design process. Furthermore, since this concept of structure may allude to an architectural expression we have no prior experience of, its kinetic conception may as well play a significant role in setting standards for a new morphology and a new building typology. It is therefore imperative that an initial study of such structures addresses form and space development as a function of motion.

In addition, a characteristic feature in the morphology of these structures is that they involve a complex 3D geometry that is sometimes hard to visualize and represent. A computer simulation and visualization procedure is thus recommended as the most appropriate tool for the early exploration of their kinematic performance and morphology.

In the following sections a brief description of the methods that allow structures to move is presented first. Next, the stages in the computer visualization of geometrically changing structures are identified and issues of critical importance in this process are presented. Software requirements and student projects that display the application of the suggested procedure are also presented.

2 Kinematic Conception of a Structure and Architectural Design Features

The method that allows a structure to move plays a crucial role in the conception, architectural expression and overall performance of the structure. Folding of building parts, or bringing the entire structure into a compact configuration is usually the result of the application of mechanism-design principles in building construction. Scissor units, sliding building parts including telescopic parts, and folding umbrella principles are just some examples of mechanisms that can be utilized in the conception and design of geometrically changing buildings.

Figure 1. Arched scissor structure (student design).

In most cases of geometrically changing structures the deployment method is based on the design of movable units that can be attached to each other to form 2D or 3D moving assemblies. A typical example is the scissor unit, which can be described as an assembly of straight rods of equal length connected by pivots in the middle, or at a lower position, and at the ends. The geometry of the scissor unit, and the way scissor units are linked to each other to build an assembly determine whether the structure will expand in one direction only or in two directions. Linear frames and flat or curved movable space frames can be developed in this manner (Pinero 62; Hoberman 90). Examples of curved movable space frames are shown in Figures 1 and 2.

Assemblies of basic movable units can be applied to various types of geometrically changing structures. They can be used for the spatial expansion of retractable structures that have one free end and one end permanently attached to another building part or the ground. An example is the design for the cover of a swimming pool in Seville by F. Escrig (Escrig et al 1996).

Figure 2. Spherical scissor structure (C. Hoberman design).

Assemblies of movable units usually form 2D trusses or 3D meshes which define the space of the structure in its various configurations but very often provide minimal enclosure and require additional covering for rainwater protection and controlled solar exposure and heat gains.

Combinations of fully functional deployable units, such as umbrellas, can be used to cover large open spaces. The pattern of the motion of individual units is related to the desired level of enclosure and solar exposure at each configuration (Figure 3). In some applications of the concept, such as in the Gartenrestaurant in Bauschanzi, Zurich, designed by S. Calatrava, all units open simultaneously, in others as in a student project illustrated below, that is based on the umbrella unit designed by Otto, each unit needs to follow a different pattern of deployment to avoid collision of parts with those of adjacent units (Figure 4). A potential advantage of the unit method is that by changing the geometry of the unit, a structure of a different morphology may be achieved.

A different method that allows for the redefinition of the enclosure of a building and which does not require the addition of any covering consists of sliding, or rotating entire building surfaces against each other. This is the main method employed in the design and construction of retractable domes and roofs in general.

Figure 3. Umbrella unit designed by F. Otto.

A similar method that addresses permanent structures and does not require the addition of covering is particularly related to the kinematic conception of space-defining elements, which can be relocated and which acquire a different spatial geometrical and functional definition in their new position. The vertical wall in Calatrava's design of the aluminum doors on the Erenstings warehouse, which lift to become an undulating shading canopy in its new position is a typical example (Tischhauser 1992).

Apparently, the kinematic and overall geometric conception of the structure is directly related to space definition and the level of space enclosure in each functional configuration. Space enclosure in particular determines the relationship between the exterior and the interior of the structure, the amount of solar exposure, the depth of shadows, rainwater protection and air movement through the structure, all of which have an impact on design quality and performance.

New methods or mechanisms, for changing the geometric configuration of surfaces or structures are

possible in the near future, due to innovations in structural materials. Eventually these methods will affect the kinematic conception, space definition and morphology of geometrically changing structures.

Figure 4. Multi-unit structure: Pattern of closing and opening umbrella units to avoid collision of parts.

3 Computer Simulations and Visualization

Since the kinematic conception of a structure imposes constraints on what can be realized and determines the form of the structure, a computer visualization procedure is recommended for a preliminary investigation of its kinematic performance and geometry in its functional configurations. The following stages may be involved:

3.1 Motion simulation and animation of the basic movable unit

This process applies to structures whose motion depends on the action of movable units. The same process can be applied to structures that behave entirely as one single mechanism.

Figure 5. Motion simulation of the umbrella movable unit.

The objective of this stage is to verify and evaluate the path of the moving parts, and detect interferences between members.

A basic understanding of mechanism design is required, as well as the use of a software that (a) allows for an accurate and precise graphic representation of the geometry of all members in a 3D environment, (b) provides a physically accurate simulation of mechanisms, and (c) displays the results of the motion simulation as an animation showing the motion of the system (Figure 5).

More specifically, the first task in this process is to develop the 3D geometry of the parts and their joints, and to define the movable parts, the way they are attached to each other and the way they move relative to each other. The development of additional kinematic diagrams for the analysis of the motion of the members of the structure may be necessary. Respectively, the software should allow for advanced 3D modeling, including complex surface developments and Boolean operations, and the application of motion constraints to the members using graphical joint definitions for motion types such as: hinge, slider, screw, etc.

Viewing the results as an animation showing the motion of the system will help in detecting member collisions and overall errors in the conception.

3.2 Visual simulation of the motion of the structure

This stage involves the display of the model of the entire building structure as an animation of moving parts. The objective is to study the effect of the changing geometry of the structure on space definition, building morphology, and functionality.

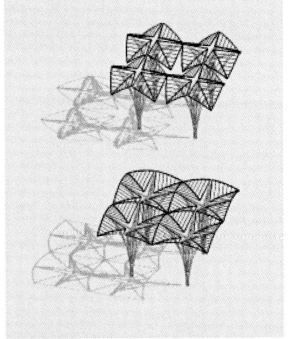

Figure 6. Animation of a multi-unit structure designed by S. Calatrava.

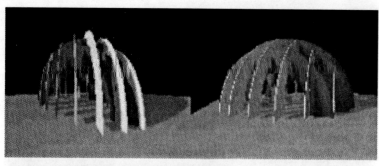

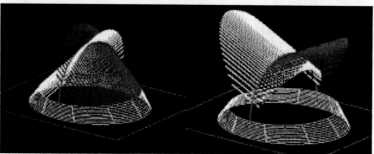

Figure 7. Examples of animation projects inspired by Origami art and a S. Calatrava design. Different animation techniques have been applied.

The motion simulation of all the components of the structure, following the procedures described in the previous stage, and their simultaneous animation may be cumbersome or impossible. A visual simulation of the motion of the entire structure is more feasible, especially if the structure is an assembly of movable units, and if the efficiency of the unit has already been verified. This part of the study also requires that motion paths or equations for the motion of individual parts or units have already been derived.

In general this stage requires an understanding of the motion of all components of the structure and software with advanced 3D modeling and rendering capabilities that allows for the simultaneous visual simulation and animation of the motion of design elements that perform identical or different types of motion. The animation of a camera view along a predetermined path, which will display the view of an observer while the structure is moving, is also a requirement. The 3D models of movable unit(s), which have been developed in the first stage of this study, should be used for the geometric description of the entire structure.

For the visual simulation of the motion of the entire structure the software should offer various techniques for animation, and the possibility of combining different techniques. Sometimes one single technique is not adequate, but if combined with other techniques may allow for the visual simulation of very complex structures. For example, frame animation requires that the designer knows already the position in space of basic components after motion has been applied. This implies that the motion of parts has already been studied in the first stage with a physically accurate motion simulation, or with the help of kinematic diagrams and physical models. The simultaneous display of animations of all components in a structure can detect interferences and collisions between the members and individual components.

In building structures with complex assemblies of moving parts where each part performs a different type of motion, the application of a technique that allows for the attachment of members in a hierarchical manner, (that is by stimulating the motion of one part of the assembly, any parts below it in the hierarchy will be also moved), may provide a solution for structures that include components that consist of parts attached one to the other (Figures 6, 7). In addition, parametric animation techniques allow the user to specify the geometric position and orientation of parts after the motion as a function of time. This requires that the equations of motion have already been derived. Giving values to variables of the equation will allow for the study of variations in the motion of the structure. An example is the visual simulation of the motion of the Kuwait Pavilion by Calatrava in which the use of parametric equations allows for different rhythmic patterns in the motion of the finger looking members.

An initial assessment of the response of the form and kinematic conception of the structure to different functions and climatic conditions can be conducted at this stage. Studies that can assess the functionality and architectural expression of the structure may include (a) the light/shadow pattern in the interior or exterior of the structure at different times throughout the year (b) the rainwater protection at different geometric configurations, and (c) the overall morphology of the structure. In the case of deployable structures the efficiency of the deployment procedure can also be studied at this stage.

Finally, the animation of a camera view along the path of a moving observer can provide some input on what the observer sees as he approaches, moves through and out of the structure in its functional configurations, or while the structure moves (Figure 8).

Computer visualization procedures, such as the ones described previously for a preliminary investigation of the form and kinematics behavior of geometrically changing structures, have been included in the content of an advanced CAD course taught by the author. All illustrations in this paper are produced by students in the class and attest to the effectiveness of the recommended visualization procedures.

4 Conclusions

Geometrically changing structures open unprecedented worlds of possibilities for architects and engineers, and respond to the continuously increasing demand for structures that reduce the environmental impact. Computer simulation and visualization offer tools for the exploration of their kinematic performance and the study of their space and form. Software requirements have been set in order to obtain highly accurate geometrically and kinematically animations that have been used in the study and visualization of existing and new structures.

References

Escrig, F., Valcarcel, J. P., Sanchez, J. (1996). "Deployable Cover on a Swimming Pool in Seville," IASS, Vol. 37, N 120, 39-46.

Gantes, C., Connor, J.J., Logher, R. D. (1991). "Geometric and Structural Design Considerations for Deployable Space Frames," MARAS '91, Southampton, U.K., April 9-11.

Hoberman, C. (1990). "Radial Expansion/retraction truss structures," USA Patent 50203.

Pellegrino S. (1999). "Deployable Structures," Summer Course notes, CISM, Udine, Italy.

Pinero, E.P. (1962)."Expandable Space Framing," Progressive Architecture, 43(6), 154-155.

Tischhauser, A. (1992). "Aspects of Movement in the Work of Santiago Calatrava," Architectural Monograph, No 46, Edited by Dennis Sharp, Academy Editions, p 215-21.

Figure 8. Animation.

The Composite Building Sketch

Anton C. Harfmann, University of Cincinnati, USA

Peter E. Akins, University of Cincinnati, USA

Abstract

This works in progress paper describes the development of an alternative method for teaching building technology using the composite sketch concept borrowed from police forensics. The composite sketch utilizes individual components and assemblies of construction in various combinations to explore the design implications of materials and connections on form and surface. To enhance the usefulness of the composite sketch, in-depth case studies of specific buildings are linked to the digital assemblies of the composite sketch so that students can see the basic concepts in actual buildings. The project currently models more than 500 combinations of components and includes approximately 200 catalogued images of buildings under construction.

1 Introduction

Having taught construction technology to large groups of students over the past years I have experimented with several methods for presenting what is often considered the most mundane topic in an architecture curriculum. Reviewing the student course evaluations (and perhaps taking them a bit too seriously) has resulted in an annual ritual of reformulating the course syllabus, exercises and teaching methods to address the negative comments lodged by the students. Consequently, virtually every technique has been explored to present the material in a meaningful and memorable way so that when confronted with a similar situation in their studio the student would actually consult their notes as a reference without being asked. A summary of the frustrations I've had with the necessary but evil lecture format of the large class can be categorized into three distinct topics.

1.1 Inadequacies of Traditional Media

The traditional media for teaching construction relies heavily on two-dimensional drawings done on the blackboard or overhead projections complimented by slide images of "in situ" examples of systems or assemblies. Sketching assemblies and principles on the board is dynamic but time consuming. Images prepared ahead of time for projection on the screen are often criticized by the students as going by too fast and impossible to take notes from. Furthermore, the static nature of prepared sketches or drawings makes it difficult to dissect them further when confronted with a question that probes beyond the image offered and our administration frowns upon using a marker to draw over an image of a slide on the screen.

While a great deal of product literature is readily available on the web and in the library much of it is myopic in its focus and offers either too much technical information for the sophomore mind to absorb or is too general and simplistic to be of any real help in the design studio. Product samples and full scale partial construction assemblies are also often integrated into the course but the cost of obtaining, constructing and storing these materials coupled with space limitations for their permanent display makes this method impossible to accomplish in our school and I would assume equally difficult to achieve at many other schools.

1.2 Class size vs. field trips

Due to the large class size at the undergraduate level of our curriculum, field trips to buildings under construction are nearly impossible to organize and orchestrate. The 50 minute Monday, Wednesday, Friday class time is less than ideal for including travel time not to mention trying to get the attention of 120 students in hard hats to point out a connection detail while balancing on a plank that spans over the excavation next to a foundation wall. For obvious reasons, visits by a class this large are discouraged by contractors fearing litigation should one of the 120+ students get injured on the site. While the site visit represents one of the best opportunities for students to develop a three-dimensional understanding of the complexity of construction, the technique simply fails for a class size of more than 20 to 25 students.

1.3 Internalizing and Integrating First Principles into Design

Regardless of how succinctly material is presented, most sophomore students seem to have difficulty in developing a diagrammatic understanding of complex assemblies. Despite the introduction of "first principles" the mindset of the typical second year student seems to be focused more on what it takes to get an "A" in the course rather than trying to internalize the choreographic nature of design and construction. While the studio setting is ideally suited for this type of integrative exercise it is not guaranteed that the departmental teaching assignments allow for the construction teacher to simultaneously teach the parallel sophomore studio. This makes it difficult to have input on the course development and to assess the integrative aspects of the design projects. Furthermore, the lecture course by definition covers more construction methods and assemblies than a single studio exercise could ever hope to integrate in one academic term. Consequently, students are forced to develop a basic understanding about a full range of principles presented in the construction class and may only have an opportunity to deploy a few of them in the parallel studio offering.

2 The Composite Sketch and Case Study

This work in progress describes my latest attempt to address the difficulties outlined above. The current reformulation of the sophomore construction course integrates computer modeling into the construction classroom in a dynamic and interactive way and incorporates two techniques for organizing and presenting design situations based on construction realities. The two techniques are the Composite Sketch and the Case Study and are discussed in the following sections.

2.1 The Composite Sketch Concept

Using a "standard" building size, various systems and their components are modeled in form-Z and dynamically interchanged to explore the design implications of combining various structural, envelope, and mechanical systems. These interchangeable components and assemblies form the basis of the Composite Sketch Concept, borrowed from forensic police work. For example, a pair of concrete frames can be shown to support simple wood joists or precast concrete "Ts" or even a series of cables. Alternatively, bearing walls could support these spanning elements with modifications to accommodate the thrust. (Figures 1a to f).

Two distinct types of composite sketches are being developed using this simple technique of substitution. The first concentrates on the overall effects of structure and site on the building form with an emphasis on overall design principles. For example, the outward thrust of an arch structure may be resolved by tension members, mass or repeating the form of the arch. Each has a different impact on the exterior form, site as well as the interior volume of the design. Issues of site, stability, etc. are also modeled and mined in class for design opportunities and implications on form and function. (Figures 2a to g).

The other type of composite sketch considers a more detailed integration of various elements and develops insight into the design of the joints between materials. These composite sketches focus on more specific design implications and uses the construction of a partial corner of a building as the site for investigation. The sketch begins with variations of "wall" and moves up and down from there. The wall is chosen as the point of departure since the body has the most direct relationship visually and physically with this element of architecture. From the wall, floor and foundation structures are explored followed by upper floors and roof assemblies. Variations in spanning members and the implications on the foundation walls are systematically explored. Additionally, the relationship between envelope/structure and site are explored and mined for design implications and opportunities. Several examples of the detailed assemblies are shown in Figures 3a to n.

Unlike the police forensic equivalent, the anomalies in the composite sketch are mined for inconsistencies and used to present basic concepts and general solutions to problems. For example, the addition of a masonry veneer to a steel frame results in an odd situation at the foundation that was modeled to hold up only the simple steel frame. The floating masonry opens to the exploration of a variety of envelope/frame design opportunities. (Figures 4a and b)

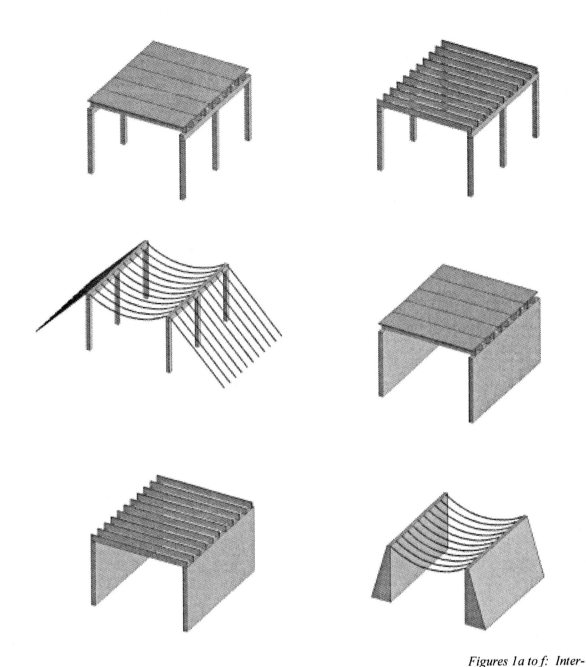

Figures 1a to f: Interchangeable components of construction used to develop a composite sketch of a building.

While the images presented in this paper are static, the model presented in class is dynamic. The 3-D assembly is rotated, rendered, exploded and otherwise manipulated to respond to questions from the students in the front row of the lecture class. To serve as a reminder of the lecture and as a study guide, labeled images of in-class explorations are mounted on a class web site. These images list many of the terms students are expected to know and illustrate the three-dimensional relationships between the elements as shown in Figure 5. Many students download these images and add them to their class notes as well.

2.2 The Case Study

Linked to the Composite Sketch are a series of case studies of specific buildings. Currently, images of buildings under construction are stored in a database and retrieved by topic. The focus of development is now turning to dynamically linking the various images to the topics and presenting them simultaneously to the specific composite sketch assembled. For example, the composite sketch assembly of a concrete frame with precast, double T spanning members will have specific example(s) of this assembly shown at the same time as shown in Figures 6a and b.

An additional intent is to link these specific images of the buildings back to the broader overall

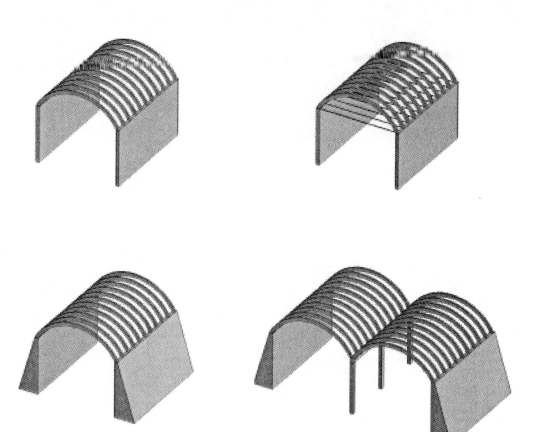

Figures 2a to d: The composite sketch used to explore overall building form and first principles.

Figures 2e to g: The composite sketch used to explore site and form relationships.

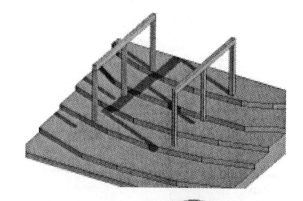

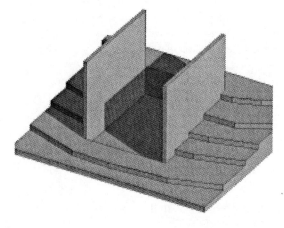
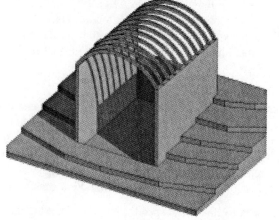

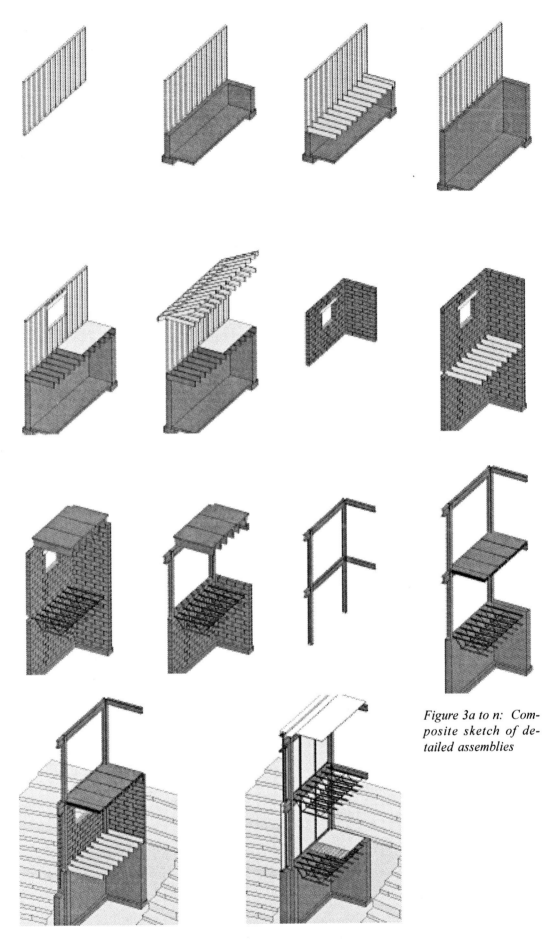

Figure 3a to n: Composite sketch of detailed assemblies

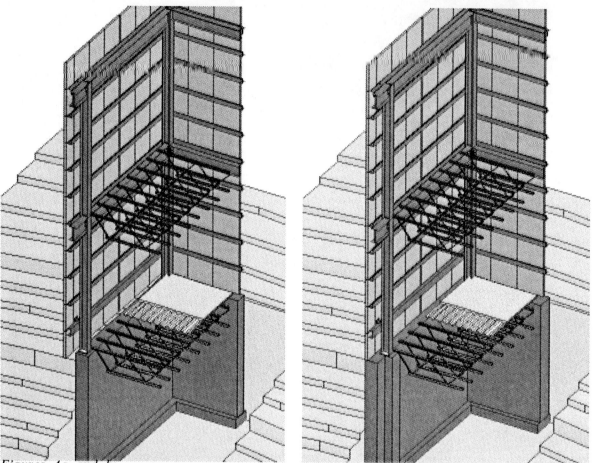

Figures 4a and b: Anomalies resulting from various combinations as the site for design intervention. Notice the floating stone panel wall that results from simply applying an envelope to the frame without any other consideration. The image on the right illustrates one of several solutions modeled in which the foundation wall is extended to support the first row of panels. Notice also that rather than making the entire foundation thicker, pilasters are left behind where the steel columns are as the wall moves out to greet and support the concrete panels.

building case study that explores all the systems in that building. From the holistic case study students can examine design decisions and building technology more carefully. Currently, the case studies are being constructed by upper level students in seminar courses and continue to be developed and expanded on from term to term. In some cases, the specific building case studies include digital models diagrammatically showing complex assemblies as well as actual construction photos (Figures 7a and b).

3 Summary and Future Goals

At present, the composite sketch portion of the project includes approximately 80 variations of simple foundation, structure, envelope and roof assemblies. There are more than 500 combinations currently possible with plans to expand this significantly to include more unique types of construction. There are also approximately 200 images that relate to the assemblies modeled with the goal of expanding this to 1000 images within the next year. Another goal for the composite sketch project is to include definitions and diagrams of first principles linked to the building elements modeled. This will serve as a reference and a Lexicon of construction with possible links to product literature and manufacturers.

The case study portion of the project currently has 11 specific buildings with more than 250 images of construction collected and entered into an evolving searchable database. With the framework in place, the goal for this portion of the project is to expand the image database and analysis significantly over the next two years. Anticipating a healthy response to the project I hope to include more faculty over the next year to extend the case studies to include investigations/analysis under their areas of expertise. This will allow the building case study to include other than construction related information such as interviews with designers, post-occupancy evaluations, structural analysis etc. so students may access the full range of issues regarding design.

An initial, non-structured version of the composite sketch and case study was incorporated in the sophomore building class with good results. Students reported that they enjoyed the interactive nature of the class and that they learned how the joint in construction is the site for design. Some solutions to problems could be solved and modeled in class while those requiring more thought and time were modeled after class and presented in the following session for discussion. By the next time the course is offered the rapidly expanding database of construction images from the case studies will be linked with the more formalized structure of the composite sketch. The open ended, modular nature of both the composite sketch and the case study allows for expansion and improvement annually rather than reformulating and reinventing.

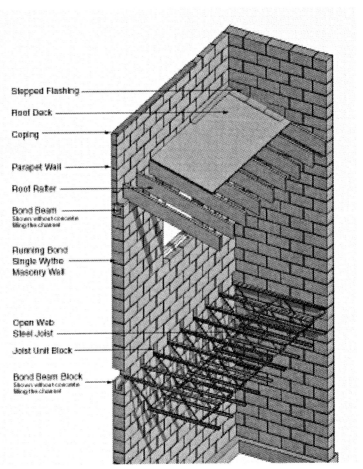

Figure 5: Image captured during lecture, labeled and mounted on the class web site.

Figures 6a and b: Parallel presentation of composite sketch assembly with site photo showing the actual installation of the element.

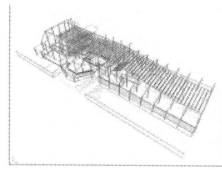

Figures 7a and b: Example images from the Cincinnati Country Day School case study.

The Anthropometric Measurement and Modeling Project

John Jay Miller, Mississippi State University, USA

Weidong Wang, Mississippi State University, USA

Gavin R. Jenkins, Mississippi State University, USA

Abstract

Disability is a product of the interactions between individuals and the environment they inhabit and the products they utilize. Disability is located on a continuum from enablement to disablement. Human physical characteristics as well as environmental factors will locate an individual on that continuum. The degree of disability or enablement will fluctuate, depending upon the attributes of the environment and the artifacts located there.

The ability of designers and architects to create environments and products that enable all people is directly tied to their ability to:

1. understand the abilities and constraints of the human body and,
2. model the physics of the body's interactions with artifacts and spaces.

This project is developing an anthropometric measurement protocol and computer-based design tools focusing on people with disabilities and the aging. The areas of interest for measurement are guided by real-world design needs. The measurements generated are translated into three-dimensional datasets compatible with commercial off the shelf software extended by the programming of additional scripts, functions, plug-ins, behaviors, etc.

1 Introduction

Disability is a common condition. There are currently approximately 43 million people within the USA with disabling conditions that interfere with their life activities (McNeil, 1993). In the past four decades the prevailing wisdom about the cause of disability has undergone profound change. Previous models of disability that viewed disability as a pathological process are being replaced by models in which disability is seen as an interaction between the characteristics of the individual with disabling conditions and the characteristics of their environment. The level of disability is not determined merely by levels of pathologies, impairments or functional limitations. Instead, it is a function of the extent to which the social and physical environment is accommodating to their particular needs.

Inadequately or poorly designed environments and tools of daily living impose barriers to the individual with a disability, which need to be addressed in order for people with disabilities to lead full and purposeful lives. These can be addressed by:

- Defining the physical characteristics and attributes of the people for whom they are being designed
- Provide these data in a form that is compatible with modern design tools and is relevant to the individual who wishes to use it.

Defining disability as an interaction between the person and their environment has played a key role in influencing the political system, through its role in designing public policy, to develop and implement legislation to address the barriers that the physical environment presents to persons with disabilities: barriers which discriminated against persons with disabilities and prevent them from leading a full and inclusive life. Perhaps the most encompassing of all this legislation is the Americans with Disabilities Act of 1990 designed to improve the prospects of people with disabilities to achieve a fuller participation in every domain of human activity.

The Americans with Disabilities Act (ADA) is a federal civil rights act enacted in 1990 prohibiting discrimination against people with disabilities. Discrimination in employment, access to places of public accommodation, services, programs, public transportation and telecommunications is prohibited by this law. Physical barriers that impede access must be removed whenever they exist.

One component to the removal of these barriers is through the construction and use of well-designed environments and artifacts. To achieve good design, in terms of both architectural and product design requires a solid understanding of the physical abilities of the population of people for whom the design is directed, i.e. a user-centered approach. One way that this can be achieved through the collection of anthropometric data and the application of those measurements to the design of consumer products, work places and equipment. Anthropometry describes the physical characteristics of humans in terms of attributes such as body size, reach and functional reach measurements, arm and hand strength measurements and field of vision measurements.

In order for the use of anthropometric data to be effective it must be appropriate to the design/use context and, more importantly it must be descriptive of the target user population. The first condition deals with the issue of static versus dynamic anthropometric measurements. Static dimensions - those "taken on the human body with the subjects in rigid, standardized positions, are easily obtained and readily applied to equipment design" (Damon 1966) are readily available in numerous reference works and texts, such as (Dreyfuss 1967; Panero 1979; Pulat 1992 and Pheasant 1986). However, these data sets, because of the way in which they were obtained, are not relevant to any specific design problem. Functional arm reach, for example, will change with each new placement and motion of the body or any of its segments, such as arms or fingers. The data required to specify specific design problems - dynamic dimensions, those "taken on the human body at work or in motion" are needed for a fully functional design environment (Damon 1966).

Another factor, with regard to appropriate data representation, are the liberties taken in characterizing some measurements. A widely used illustration of normal and maximal arm reach areas was constructed by showing two intersecting semicircles in which elbows, shoulder and hand joints are assumed to be fixed and rotating through one plane during motion. The widely used Farley's data sets are similar to this kind of data (Farley 1955). An illustration of such traditional data (Tilley 1993]) superimposed with data generated via a computer generated inverse kinematic model is shown in Figure 1.

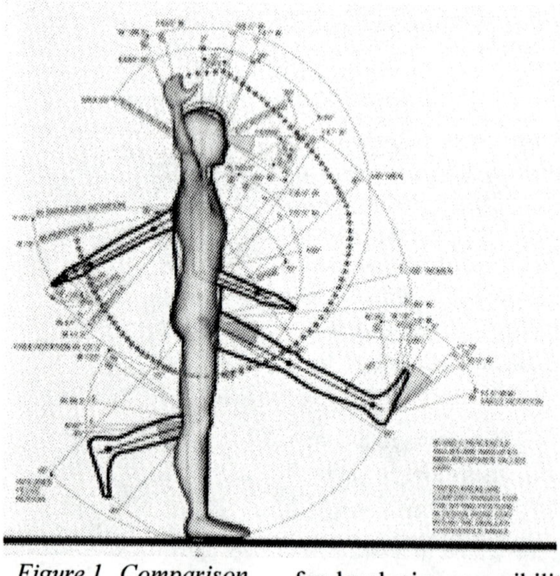

For anthropometric data to be useful to design for the disabled it must be collected from the target population to be descriptive of that population. Presently, the Army ANSUR data is the primary default human anthropometric database, representing typically young, fit people, which is not representative of the general US population let alone the population of persons with disabilities. This limitation in the data available to designers, architects, healthcare professional and policy makers presents a fundamental hurdle to the appropriate design of any products and environments or the creation of legislation to remove the barriers faced by people.

To illustrate this, the ADA has a uniform nationwide mandate that ensures accessibility regardless of local attitudes. The Architectural and Transportation Barriers Compliance Board (Access Board), whose responsibilities were significantly broadened as a result of the implementation of the ADA, is an independent Federal agency responsible for developing accessibility guidelines for buildings, facilities and transit vehicles.

Figure 1. Comparison of traditional ergonomic data and computer generated modeling (shown with dots).

The Access Board established minimum technical requirements for the design and construction of buildings and facilities when it published its Accessibility Guidelines (ADAAG) in 1991. These guidelines were written with a clear intent to increase the level of accessibility in the built environment in new construction, alterations and existing facilities. The guidelines, intended to provide the basis of design standards for living and working spaces that would accommodate people with disabilities, were largely based on the results of anthropometric research in human body size and reach obtained in the 1960s and 1970s.

Advances in medicine and rehabilitation techniques and the rapid proliferation of technology, has increased the numbers of persons with a wide variety of disabilities entering the mainstream of American life. It is also important to note that the traditional concept of the disabled population is on the doorstep of a dramatic shift in its make-up as the population ages.

Many of the original design standards were based on seated measurements of adults without disabilities. This model does not define the population of persons with disabilities.

Bradtmiller (1997) prepared an extensive bibliography of "Anthropometry for people with disabilities" for the U.S. Architectural and Transportation Barriers Compliance Board. In it he described that there existed a large body of anthropometric data on more than 11,000 persons of every age and a wide variety of disabilities. However most of the studies were conducted on specialized populations, many of them foreign, and therefore has very limited application to the general U.S. population of persons with disabilities. Dimension definitions and measurement techniques varied from study to study and, in many cases, samples were very small. He concluded that while there was a great deal of existing anthropometric data, any attempt to combine them into a useful database would be futile.

This project is developing the basic protocols to address this need for greater information and knowledge on issues of the functional abilities of people with disabilities, to improve access and the design and re-design of objects of daily living through the use of computer based modeling techniques, developed to be compatible with existing computer based design tools and environments.

2 Objectives

In general terms, the objectives of this project are to collect anthropometric body dimensions for a sample population of people with disabilities, distributed amongst the selected categories of pathologies. This data will then be used to create three-dimensional computer datasets, which will be used in an interactive computer design environment. These 3D datasets, when used in this way will enable an iterative design process that factors in relevant aspects of a particular disability, for example, strength capabilities, to allow the design of environments and artifacts with the least demanding of physical exertion.

In a CAD environment, datasets used to create an articulating figure, modeled with range of joint motion constraints as well as key strength characteristics, can interact with a device such as a door handle to determine if the chosen design is effective and efficient in its use. This information can then help guide the design or re-design of objects of daily living to maximize functional ability while minimizing unnecessary physical exertion.

3 Dynamic Environmental Modeling

One aspect of this project involves the determination of the three-dimensional boundary envelopes that will characterize the spaces in which a person can reach and manipulate objects. Animated visualizations can be made in near-real time using wire-frame mode and sparse data or fully rendered visualizations can be made for playback. Data can be queried for exact location and volumetric attributes.

The following sequence of still images illustrates the creation of visualizations concerned with the reach characteristics of a person in a wheelchair as they interact with a simple counter and cabinet environment. First, inverse kinematics is used to trace an outline of the reach envelope, which is indicated with white dots as shown in Figure 2.

Figure 2. Linear reach outline - indicated by white dots.

Next, a 3D envelope is developed as indicated by the gray shaded area bounded by white dots in Figure 3. The points of this volume are defined in three-space (xyz) and can be used for measurement and placement of surrounding objects. This shape can also be queried for volumetric information.

Finally, the reach envelope can be intersected with objects in the environment to determine the precise areas of interaction and utility. The union of the reach envelope and cabinet exterior is shown in Figure

Figure 3. Three-dimensional reach envelope shown in gray shaded area surrounded by white dots.

4. Other options will include the other standard Boolean operations so that objects and spaces can be inspected and measured in a number of different ways.

This paper and visual support materials may be found at:

www.sarc.msstate.edu/~wwang/ergo/acadia/

4 Future Work

The project will include a number of other longitudinal components which will utilize the data and information developed to educate and provide guidance to people with disabilities, insurance companies, policy making bodies and clinicians. As a more realistic assessment of people with disabilities emerges, better planning can be made regarding future physical needs and therapy decisions as well as public policy initiatives.

Acknowledgements

This work was partially funded by the Hearin Foundation.

References

Bradtmiller (1997) *Anthropometry for Persons with Disabilities: Needs for the Twenty-First Century.* (Contract # QA96001001) US Architectural and Transportation Barriers Compliance Board.

Damon, Albert, et al. (1966) *The Human Body in Equipment Design.* Harvard University Press.

Dreyfuss, Henry (1967) *The Measure of Man; Human Factors in Design*, New York: Whitney Library of Design.

Farley, R. R. (1955) Some Principles of Methods and Motion Study As Used in Development Work. *General Motors Engineering Journal*, 2(6).

McNeil, J.M. (1993) *Americans with Disabilities: 1991 - 1992 Current Population Reports*, Household Economic Studies. P70-33. Washington D.C.: US Bureau of the Census.

Panero, Julius and M. Zelnik (1979) *Human Dimensions & Interior Space*, New York: Whitney Library of Design.

Pheasant, Stephen, (1986). *Bodyspace: Anthropometry, Ergonomics and Design*, London: Taylor & Francis.

Pulat, Babur Mustafa. (1992). *Fundamentals of Industrial Ergonomics.* Prentice Hall, Inc.

Tilley, Alvin R. (1993) *The Measure of Man and Woman: Human Factors in Design.* New York: Whitney Design Library.

Figure 4. Union of reach capabilities and cabinetry exterior.

Printed in the United States
953700001B